ROUTLEDGE LIBRARY EDITIONS:
THE INDUSTRIAL REVOLUTION

Volume 1

BANKRUPTCY AND INSOLVENCY IN LONDON DURING THE INDUSTRIAL REVOLUTION

BANKRUPTCY AND INSOLVENCY IN LONDON DURING THE INDUSTRIAL REVOLUTION

IAN P. H. DUFFY

Routledge
Taylor & Francis Group
LONDON AND NEW YORK

First published in 1985 by Garland Publishing, Inc.

This edition first published in 2017
by Routledge
2 Park Square, Milton Park, Abingdon, Oxon OX14 4RN

and by Routledge
711 Third Avenue, New York, NY 10017

Routledge is an imprint of the Taylor & Francis Group, an informa business

British Library Cataloguing in Publication Data
A catalogue record for this book is available from the British Library

ISBN: 978-1-138-63291-2 (Set)
ISBN: 978-1-315-16309-3 (Set) (ebk)
ISBN: 978-1-138-74578-0 (Volume 1) (hbk)
ISBN: 978-1-315-18053-3 (Volume 1) (ebk)

BANKRUPTCY AND INSOLVENCY IN LONDON DURING THE INDUSTRIAL REVOLUTION

Ian P. H. Duffy

Garland Publishing, Inc.
New York & London ★ 1985

Library of Congress Cataloging-in-Publication Data

Duffy, Ian P.H.
Bankruptcy and insolvency in London during the Industrial Revolution.

(British economic history)
Revision of thesis (Ph. D.)—Oxford University, 1973.
Bibliography: p.
1. Bankruptcy—England—London—History. 2. Great Britain—Industries—History. 3. Great Britain—Economic conditions—1760–1860. I. Title. II. Series.
HG3769.G73L63 1985 332.7′5′09421 84-45999
ISBN 0-8230-6679-0

All volumes in this series are printed on acid-free, 250-year-life paper.

Printed in the United States of America

BANKRUPTCY AND INSOLVENCY

IN LONDON

DURING THE INDUSTRIAL REVOLUTION

by

Ian P. H. Duffy

PREFACE

This is a modified version of a study which was accepted as a thesis for the degree of Doctor of Philosophy by Oxford University in 1973. Since then, a small part of the material has appeared in The American Journal of Legal History, volume XXIV, 1980, and in The Economic History Review, second series, volume XXXV, 1982. I am grateful to both journals for permission to publish it here.

Above all, I would like to express deep gratitude to my former supervisor, Dr. P.G.M. Dickson, for his encouragement and expert advice over a period of many years. My debt to him is enormous. Thanks are due also to the staffs of numerous libraries and record repositories, including particularly the Bank of England Museum, the Bodleian, the British Library, and the Public Record Office. At different times, my work has benefited from the generous financial assistance of Linacre College, the American Bar Foundation and, at Lehigh University, the Office of Research and the Lawrence Henry Gipson Institute. Finally, I would like to give thanks to Pauline, without whose patience, understanding and support this work could not have been written.

CONTENTS

Abbreviations

B.I.H.R.	Bulletin of the Institute of Historical Research.
B.P.P.	British Parliamentary Papers.
Ec.H.R.	Economic History Review.
C.H.J.	Cambridge Historical Journal.
Bull. of Bus. Hist. Soc.	Bulletin of the Business Historical Society.
Hist. Journal	Historical Journal.
J.H.C.	Journals of the House of Commons.
J. Pol. Econ.	Journal of Political Economy.
L.Q.R.	Law Quarterly Review.
New C.M.H.	New Cambridge Modern History
P.R.O.	Public Record Office, London.
Rev. Econ. Stats.	Review of Economic Statistics
T.R.H.S.	Transactions of the Royal Historical Society.
U.B.H.J.	University of Birmingham Historical Journal.
Vict. Studies	Victorian Studies.

INTRODUCTION

Historians have paid little attention to the evolution of the laws relating to debt and credit during the industrial revolution. E. Welbourne has examined the bankruptcy law before Victoria's reign in a brief, undocumented article;[1] E. Jenks catalogues, even more briefly, the major statutory changes in that law from its origins to the twentieth century;[2] and W.H. Winder discusses the growth of courts of request for small debt cases.[3] Apart from these specific studies, information can be gleaned from scattered references in W.S. Holdsworth's massive History of English Law[4] and from numerous but imprecise allusions, by a variety of authors, to the chaos of the bankruptcy process, the inhumanity of the insolvency laws and the defects of small debt procedure.[5]

This cursory treatment of the debt laws is symptomatic of the failure of historians to examine closely not only the legal system itself but also the service sector as a whole.[6] In this case, however, the omission is surprising because

---

1 E. Welbourne, 'Bankruptcy before the Era of Victorian Reform,' C.H.J., iv (1932), 51-62.

2 E. Jenks, A Short History of English Law (4th edn., 1928), pp. 382-8.

3 W.H. Winder, 'The Courts of Request,' L.Q.R., lii (1936), 369-94.

4 Sir W.S. Holdsworth, A History of English Law (1938), vols. i, v, vii, xi, xiii.

5 E.g. for bankruptcy, L.S. Pressnell, Country Banking in the Industrial Revolution (Oxford, 1956), pp. 71, 445-8; for imprisonment for debt, M.D. George, London Life in the Eighteenth Century (2nd edn., 1965), pp. 297-301; for small debts, B. Abel-Smith and R. Stevens, Lawyers and the Courts (1967), pp. 10-35.

6 For a discussion of this, see R.M. Hartwell, The Industrial Revolution and Economic Growth (1971), pp. 201-25.

research in other fields has emphasized the fact that, during the industrial revolution, financial collapse posed a constant threat at all levels of society. It has frequently been suggested that the expansion of business activity in the late eighteenth century was accompanied by a disproportionate increase in the risks which it involved. R.M. Hartwell, for example, argues that 'If industrialization enhanced the chance of gain, it also increased the chance, and the cost, of failure.'[7] H. Heaton even goes so far as to state that, for many enterprises, 'while death and taxes alone were inevitable, bankruptcy was probable.'[8] T.S. Ashton points out that the widespread use of credit may account for the extension of retail trade in the eighteenth century, but that it was also responsible for the high failure rate of shopkeepers.[9] Similarly, it seems, irregular employment and pay were responsible for the constant indebtedness of the lower classes and their susceptibility to imprisonment for debt.[10]

Since economic activity was so precarious, the legal procedures designed to deal with its victims deserve more attention than has usually been accorded them. This work examines two aspects of financial collapse during the industrial revolution. Part one deals with the legal and institutional framework which defined and regulated it. Following contemporary legal practice, this is divided into three parts: chapter one examines the bankruptcy laws, chapter two the insolvency laws and chapter three the small

---

7 Ibid., p. 307.

8 H. Heaton, 'Financing the Industrial Revolution,' Bull. of Bus. Hist. Soc., xi (1937), no. 1,6.

9 T.S. Ashton, An Economic History of England: The 18th Century (1959), pp. 69-70, 209.

10 See ibid, pp. 206-9; George, op. cit, pp. 362-3, 299-300.

debt laws. Each chapter traces briefly the pre-industrial origins of the respective laws, analyses their major weaknesses and describes their development in the late eighteenth and early nineteenth centuries. It will be shown that the major structural defects which were prevalent in all three sectors of the debt laws were exacerbated by the strains imposed by economic expansion towards the end of the eighteenth century, and that the consequent movements for reform, led by practical, theoretical and humanitarian critics, were followed in the 1830s and 1840s by radical changes not only in the law itself but also in basic attitudes to the relationship between law and the economic system. In chapter four, the evidence of change is interpreted in the light, first, of the major influences which determined its course and, second, of the connection between the law and economic growth. Part two focuses attention on bankruptcy alone, examining the causes of its dramatic increase at the start of the nineteenth century. Chapter five discusses the major economic influences upon bankruptcy levels between 1795 and 1826 and chapters six to ten the particular economic crisis of 1810-11, attempting to explain both its causes and the mechanism by which large-scale failures in overseas trade affected the stability of other sectors of the economy.

Although the study pays most attention to the situation in London, the largest centre of population and the hub of the country's financial activity, its significance cannot be understood without frequent references to provincial developments. This applies particularly to the small debt laws, which are considered in a national context, and to the general economic discussion, in which provincial bankruptcies are examined in order to show the influence of events in London.

PART ONE

THE LEGAL FRAMEWORK

CHAPTER I

THE BANKRUPTCY LAWS

I

> A BANKRUPT, is one that has broken or wasted his Stock, or hath failed in the World, being derived as some say, from the *French* Words *Banque* and *rumper*, signifying to break the Bank; or rather from *Banqueroute*, that is, a Person broke or decayed: In *Latin* such a Man is called *Decoctor*, for consuming and spending his Estate in extraordinary and delicate Living.
>
> *The Law for and against Bankrupts. By a late Commissioner of Bankrupts* (1743), p. 1.

The development of bankruptcy law in England was a product of the inflexibility of medieval Common Law and its procedure. The basic assumption of Common Law was that land was the source of all wealth and it obliged creditors individually to pursue remedies against the land and the bodies of their debtors. As English overseas trade grew in the middle ages, these remedies became increasingly inappropriate to large and often complicated mercantile concerns, requiring a different legal process which not only rendered commercial property liable for debts but also facilitated equal treatment of all creditors. As T.F.T. Plucknett says, 'It is typical of the middle ages . . . that this law should be not the law of the land but the law of a particular class of people, developed through their custom and enforced through their own organisation.'[1] This chapter examines the origins of bankruptcy law, its procedure and defects during the industrial revolution and its reform during the fourth and fifth decades of the nineteenth century.

---

1 T.F.T. Plucknett, *A Concise History of Common Law* (5th edn., 1956), p. 67.

The bankruptcy law and procedure which operated during the industrial revolution were products of legislation dating back to 1571. Unlike its only predecessor,[2] the Act Touching Orders for Bankrupts of that year restricted the bankruptcy process to merchants and traders. It empowered the Lord Chancellor to appoint 'wise and honest discreet persons' as commissioners who could imprison the bankrupt, if necessary, and take steps to seize all his assets and share them among his creditors. A formal procedure was established by which a creditor could petition the commissioners claiming that his debtor had committed an act of bankruptcy.[3] Bankrupts who did not surrender to the commissioners after due notice were proscribed and those who concealed property were fined and gaoled. All property acquired subsequent to the act of bankruptcy was liable for former debts.[4]

In the first quarter of the seventeenth century, the commissioners' powers and jurisdiction were enlarged. In 1604, the formal examination of the bankrupt on oath was introduced and the commissioners were empowered both to compel the attendance of witnesses to the bankruptcy and to collect debts owing to the bankrupt. Bankrupts who refused to answer the commissioners' questions were to be gaoled

2 34, 35 Henry VIII, c.4 (1542) had entrusted the collection and division of bankrupt estates to the Lord Chancellor, Keeper of the Great Seal, Lord Treasurer, President of the Council, Lord Privy Seal, the Privy Council and chief justices.

3 The acts of bankruptcy, which were considered to be proof of the debtor's intention of defrauding his creditors, were keeping house, being arrested for debt, yielding oneself to prison, departing the realm and taking sanctuary.

4 13 Eliz., c.7.

until they were prepared to co-operate and perjurors were to be pilloried and to lose an ear.[5] In 1624, aliens were made liable to become bankrupt and obstacles to the rapid acquisition of a bankrupt's estate were reduced by the stipulation that commissioners could break down the door of his house if necessary. In addition, bankrupts who fraudulently concealed property worth more than £20 were to be pilloried.[6] The only other seventeenth-century modification of importance was the arrogation of some control over disputed cases by Lord Chancellor Nottingham and his successors, after 1676.[7]

The basic assumption of these early attempts to deal with the problem was that bankrupts were dishonest, fraudulent and profligate. The act of 1604, for example, noted that

> Frauds and deceits, as new diseases, daily increase amongst such as live by buying and selling to the hindrance of traffic and mutual commerce, and to the general hurt of the realm, by such as wickedly and wilfully become bankrupts.8

Consequently, sixteenth- and seventeenth-century statutes were designed to prevent fraud and abuse of legal procedure by providing the commissioners with adequate coercive powers. As Holdsworth points out, the Council frequently intervened in bankruptcy cases, appointing commissioners to investigate people imprisoned for debt, encouraging creditors to accept compositions in lieu of debts and ordering them to give debtors time in which to pay.[9] After

---

5 1 Jac. I, c.15.

6 21 Jac. I, c.19.

7 Previously, disputed cases had been heard in the common-law courts. Nottingham began to hear appeals, as a judge, in Chancery.

8 1 Jac. I, c.15.

9 W.S. Holdsworth, <u>A History of English Law</u> (1938), viii, 233.

the abolition of the Council in 1641, however, no such relief was available and, as will be shown in chapter two, parliament itself began to intervene to relieve the more unfortunate imprisoned debtors, including bankrupts.

At the start of the eighteenth century, the spirit of the law was profoundly altered. The new policy did not seek to reduce the punitive powers available to commissioners in cases of fraud and evasion. Indeed, they were increased. In 1705, fraudulent disposal of goods by a bankrupt and non-surrender within thirty days of receiving notice of the commission (at the bankrupt's dwelling house and in the <u>London Gazette</u>) were declared non-clergyable felonies, and bankrupts who concealed property were to be fined £100 and twice the value of the property concealed.[10] In 1706, concealment and embezzlement of property by the bankrupt was made a capital crime if its value was over £20.[11] It sought, however, to minimise the prevailing dread of bankruptcy and to encourage bankrupts to co-operate with the commissioners by granting them rewards for honesty and assistance.[12] The statute of 1705, for example, stipulated that co-operative bankrupts would be given an allowance of five per cent of the assets if their estates produced dividends of eight shillings in the pound (up to £200 maximum). They could also receive from the commissioners a certificate of discharge from all debts owing at the time of bankruptcy, provided that the creditors did not object. Another concession to the bankrupt forbade commissioners to extract food and drink bills from estates. In 1706, further changes were effected which, with those of 1705, substan-

---

10 4, 5 Anne, c.17.

11 5 Anne, c.22.

12 The new policy was attributed to the failure, because of the French wars and storms, of honest traders, many of whom had fled the country. See <u>Remarks on the Bill to Prevent Frauds Committed by Bankrupts</u> (1706).

tially erected the bankruptcy process which was to operate until 1831. The vagueness of the 1705 act about the procedure for granting the certificate was now replaced by a definite stipulation that the consent of four-fifths of the creditors was required. The petitioning creditor's debt must amount to more than £100 (or £150 if there were two petitioning creditors and £200 if more than two). The majority of creditors in number were to choose assignees who would collect the bankrupt's estate (previously a function of the commissioners) and who were empowered to enter into compositions with the bankrupt's debtors. The assignees were to be subject to the equitable jurisdiction of the Chancellor when suits were filed against them.

That the legislature was becoming increasingly lenient towards bankrupts is further evidenced by the fact that in 1718 they were, for the first time, protected from arrest for debt during journeys to and from meetings with commissioners. This statute also attempted to reduce the incidence of frauds committed after proceedings had commenced by authorizing the Lord Chancellor to dismiss unsuitable assignees and ordering (apparently for the first time) that bankruptcy proceedings be recorded.[13] In 1719, it was enacted that imprisoned bankrupts would be released after receiving their certificate of discharge.[14] A year later, creditors who held bills of exchange which were not due at the time of the acceptor's bankruptcy were allowed to prove them in his commission.[15]

The mass of bankruptcy statutes was consolidated in 1732 by the <u>Act to Prevent the Committing of Frauds by Bankrupts</u>, which Edward Christian in 1818 called 'the most

---

13 5 Geo. I, c.24.

14 6 Geo. I, c.22.

15 7 Geo. I, c.31.

important existing statute in the system of bankrupt law.'[16] The act also effected a number of amendments in the law. The commissioners, whose fees were now specified, were to appoint three meetings with creditors within 42 days of the opening of the commission, in which time the bankrupt was to surrender to the commission. Assignees were to be chosen by the majority in value of creditors whose claims amounted to more than £10. The provision of allowances to co-operative bankrupts was extended.[17] Certificates were to be granted by four-fifths in number and value of creditors who were owed over £20, provided that the commissioners certified to the Lord Chancellor that the bankrupt's conduct, after the commencement of proceedings, had conformed to statute and that his evidence had been valid. In addition, the act ordered that the bankrupt should be free from arrest throughout the whole period of his examination.

By 1732, therefore, a procedure had been established which, in theory at least, facilitated the equitable division of bankrupt estates among creditors and provided incentives for the bankrupt to act honestly. In practice, as Lord Chancellor Hardwicke pointed out in 1737, because of its abuse by bankrupts, the law had become 'the accidental occasion of great frauds.'[18] In the following century, the legislature, accepting that bankruptcy law was now basically sound in principle, periodically sought to clarify controversial points and abolish opportunities for abuse. Many of

---

16 E. Christian, The Origin, Progress and Present Practice of the Bankrupt Laws (2nd edn., 1818), ii, 294. The act is 5 Geo. II, c.30.

17 If the estate paid less than 10s. in the pound, the bankrupt received up to 3% at the assignees' discretion; more than 10s., 5% (£250 maximum); more than 12s. 6d., 7-1/2% (£250 maximum); more than 15s., 10% (£300 maximum) and a discharge from his debts.

18 Quoted by B. Montagu, Digest of the Bankrupt Laws (1805), i, 49.

the more blatant frauds were committed by bankrupts who continued trading after their acts of bankruptcy, in the knowledge that creditors would be forced to forfeit property thus received when the commission was opened. In 1746, this loop-hole was closed by the stipulation that no creditor would be liable to refund any property received before notice of the bankruptcy.[19] A similar statute, in 1806, stated that a commission was not invalidated by the disclosure of a secret act of bankruptcy committed before the bankrupt had contracted his debt to the petitioning creditor.[20] Parliament responded similarly to other abuses of the law, declaring void certificates signed by creditors who had proved fictitious debts (1751),[21] requiring assignees to swear on oath that the estate had been collected honestly before paying dividends (1809)[22] and enabling creditors to apprehend witnesses to the bankrupt's trading and act of bankruptcy, where necessary (1823).[23] Other statutes concerned the bankrupt's property: estates which were sold were freed from auction duty (1779),[24] bankrupts could be compelled to transfer stock to the assignees (1796),[25] a deceased bankrupt's lands were rendered liable (1807),[26] annuity creditors were allowed to prove for the value of the

---

19 19 Geo. II, c.32.

20 46 Geo. III, c.135.

21 24 Geo. II, c.57.

22 49 Geo. III, c.121.

23 3 Geo. IV, c.81.

24 19 Geo. III, c.56.

25 36 Geo. III, c.90.

26 47 Geo. III, s.2, c.74.

annuity (1809)[27] and restrictions were placed on the amount of farming stock which could be sold (1816).[28]

In addition to these statutory changes, the law of bankruptcy, like other branches of commercial law, was clarified by Mansfield, L.C.J. in the Court of King's Bench, which dealt with cases sent by the Lord Chancellor and with common-law suits initiated by assignees attempting to collect bankrupts' estates. Mansfield rationalised one of the most vexatious problems of the bankruptcy law, that of a trader who transferred property on the eve of his bankruptcy. In Alderson v. Temple (1768) and Rust v. Cooper (1777), he established the principle that a fraudulent contrivance (or preference) on the eve of bankruptcy, designed to defeat the majority of creditors, was illegal and void. The property thus transferred was returned to the estate.[29]

The content of the law could, therefore, be changed, and was changed during the century after 1732. Despite the alterations, however, the law contained serious defects at the end of the eighteenth century, when the whole system started to crack under the increasing volume of bankruptcy business.[30] These defects must be examined in detail before turning to the growing tide of suggestions for reform and the radical legislation which followed in the 1830s and 1840s.

---

27 49 Geo. III, c.121.

28 56 Geo. III, c.50.

29 See C.H.S. Fifoot, Lord Mansfield (Oxford, 1936), pp. 85-6, 220.

30 See below, chapter V.

III

At the start of the nineteenth century, the bankruptcy process was relatively simple.[31] In London, the creditor's solicitor satisfied himself that the debt was valid, that the debtor was a bankrupt and that no other solicitor had commenced proceedings against him. The creditor made an affidavit before a Master in Chancery:

> Charles Jones of - in the County of - , maketh oath and saith, that A.B. of - , merchant, is indebted to this deponent in the sum of £100 and upwards, and that the said A.B. is become Bankrupt within some or one of the statutes, as this deponent is informed and now believes.

This was taken to the 'Bankrupt Office' in Chancery Lane, where the creditor gave a £200 bond as security that the bankruptcy would be proved and the bankrupt's name was entered in the Docket Book (this stage was called 'striking the docket'). The affidavit, bond and a petition, containing the fiat ('Let a commission issue as prayed, and be directed to . . .'), were sent to the Lord Chancellor, who signed the petition after a few days and the commission was sealed (all commissions bore the date of sealing). The solicitor then asked one of the seven messengers of the Bankruptcy Court, at Guildhall, to summon a private meeting

---

31 The following description is based on: B. Montagu, Bankrupt Laws and Precedents (1807), vol. iv; E. Christian, Practical Instructions for Suing Out and Prosecuting a Commission of Bankruptcy (1816); and interpretation of the series of commissions files stored at the Public Record Office (B.3). The files are compilations of documents relating to individual bankruptcies. Unfortunately, many have been destroyed; for the numbers which have survived for the period 1797-1826, see Table 1.1 in the statistical supplement.

of three commissioners, who examined the case and, if appropriate, declared the debtor bankrupt.[32]

The debtor normally heard of the process in one of three ways: through an advertisement in the London Gazette, through notification from the commissioners, to whom, on pain of death as a felon, he must surrender within forty-two days, or through the commission's messenger who came to reside in his house in order to supervise his property and effects. The advertisement in the Gazette notified the bankrupt's creditors of the dates of three public meetings appointed by the commissioners. At the first, the bankrupt usually surrendered; at the second, creditors who had proved debts of over £10 appointed two or three assignees, usually though not necessarily from their own body, to take over collection of the estate from the petitioning creditor; at the third, the bankrupt submitted to his final examination, during which he was interrogated by the commissioners on details relevant to his estate and effects. At all three meetings, creditors proved their debts. In the ensuing months, dividends were paid to the creditors as and when the assignees gathered in the estate (the first dividend must, legally, be paid after four and within twelve months of the date when the commission was issued, and the second dividend within eighteen months). Four-fifths in number and value of the creditors could grant the bankrupt's certificate of discharge at any time, thus immunising his future property from liability for former debts and allowing him to set up in business again with no deficit.

The bankruptcy procedure described above operated, with minor modifications, from the early eighteenth century until 1831. It contained a number of remarkable features. First, although its scope was extended during this period (as will

---

32 From the early eighteenth century, there were seventy commissioners, divided into fourteen lists of five. Their status and activities are examined in sections VIII and IX of this chapter.

be demonstrated), it remained a privilege exclusive to a minority of the indebted population. Many debtors did not qualify for its benefits since they were not 'traders' who owed at least £100 to one creditor. Second, the entire responsibility for prosecuting cases lay with the plaintiffs (i.e. the creditors) both because their solicitors initiated the commissions, which the Lord Chancellor was obliged to grant, and - a fortiori - because they controlled the appointment of assignees and the granting of the certificate of discharge. Third, the system was not uniform, the mode of electing provincial commissioners contrasting sharply with the use of official appointees in London.[33] Fourth, although originally authorized only to appoint commissioners, the Lord Chancellor had acquired domination of the process and was able to dismiss assignees and to hear appeals as a judge.

In theory the system was fairly straightforward. It was, however, complicated in practice and open to fraud and abuse. The major defects are discussed below, first in relation to the confusion in the definition of a bankrupt, second and third in relation to procedural and administrative weaknesses.

IV

In the eighteenth century, it was increasingly accepted that autonomous economic circumstances, and not just fraud or incompetence, could plunge a trader into financial difficulties. Bankruptcy thus came to be viewed as an act of mercy for the innocent victim of the uncontrollable workings of the economy. Formally, it was open to traders

---

33 In the provinces (more than 40 miles from London), the solicitor, who sued out the commission before a Master Extraordinary, nominated the commissioners. Two of these were supposed to be local barristers but, if no barristers resided within 20 miles, the solicitor chose five other solicitors.

only because, according to Sir William Blackstone, the laws of England were 'cautious of encouraging prodigality and extravagance by this indulgence to debtors' and because 'that set of men (traders) are, generally speaking, the only persons liable to accidental losses, and to an inability of paying their debts, without any fault of their own.'[34] It was, however, extremely difficult to put the restriction into practice. On the one hand, general definitions of trade, necessarily vague, inevitably provoked controversy over specific occupations. On the other, attempts to overcome such difficulties by drawing up catalogues of occupations which were within the law were vitiated by the fact that they were belated responses to legal disputes and, therefore, liable to become outdated as the economy developed.

The initial definition of people liable to the bankruptcy process was brief and general:

> any merchant, or other person using or exercising the trade of merchandize, by way of Bargaining, Exchange, Rechange, Bartery, Chevisance, or otherwise in Gross or by Retail, or seeking his or her trade of living, by buying and selling . . . 35

In succeeding centuries, this description continued to operate (with slight changes), although its implications were periodically clarified by statute. In 1624, scriveners were rendered liable to bankruptcy.[36] An act of 1662 excluded stockholders in privileged trading companies, specifically the East India, Guinea and Virginia Companies and the Royal Fishing Trade.[37] Stockholders in the Bank of

---

34 Sir W. Blackstone, Commentaries on the Laws of England (Oxford, 1766), ii, 473.

35 13 Eliz., c.7.

36 21 Jac. I, c.19.

37 13, 14 Car. II, c.24.

England were similarly excluded in 1696.[38] Bankers, brokers and factors were included in 1732, when farmers, graziers, cattle drovers, labourers, hired workmen and receivers-general of taxes were excluded.[39] Members of Parliament who traded were included in 1764.[40]

The intermittent and minor character of statutory clarification of a problem of such magnitude imposed an enormous burden of interpretation upon the courts of law. The frustration felt by the legal fraternity is shown in Mansfield's assertion that 'It is a pity that the Legislature should be silent, and should force the courts, in order to attain the ends of justice, to invent legal subtleties which do not come up to the common understanding of mankind.'[41] A good example of this in the early nineteenth century is the confusion over the status of scrivening, which, despite its specific inclusion in 1624, raised two problems of interpretation. The first arose from the legal differentiation between the scrivener and the attorney. When an attorney was employed to transfer money for his client to a borrower, he was not subject to the bankruptcy procedure, but, when the money was entrusted to him to find a borrower, he was scrivening and could therefore become

---

38 8, 9 Will. III, c.20.

39 5 Geo. II, c.30.

40 4 Geo. III, c. 33 acknowledged the difficulty of compelling M.P.s to pay debts because of their freedom from arrest in civil processes while parliament was sitting. The statute enabled the creditor of a trading M.P. who owed £100 to file an affidavit of debt in any court at Westminster and sue out a summons. If the M.P. failed to pay within two months, he was adjudged bankrupt and a commission issued. This was extended, in 1805, to clarify the procedure when the bankrupt did not pay after entering into a bond to do so (45 Geo. III, c.124) and, in 1812, to vacate for 12 months the seat of any bankrupt M.P. unless the debt was paid (52 Geo. III, c.144).

41 Wyllie v. Wilkes (1780) Doug. 519, 523.

bankrupt. The second was a product of the gradual disappearance of scrivening as the money market became more specialized during the eighteenth century. In 1814, Gibbs, C.J., declared that 'there is now no living character engaged in that occupation,'[42] alleging that the last scrivener was Jack Ellis, referred to in Boswell's Life of Johnson.[43] Nevertheless, scriveners went on appearing in the Bankruptcy Court and their continued existence was acknowledged when the Consolidating Act of 1825 defined them as traders.[44] Despite this, however, Gibbs's statement was still being used in the early 1830s to dispute the bankruptcies of scriveners.[45]

Many occupations whose existence was unquestioned caused constant problems and numerous examples could be cited of conflicting judicial interpretations of the status of individual 'trades.' A special case was that of innkeepers, who were often excluded from bankruptcy on the grounds that they functioned as public officers, who were legally obliged not only to receive travellers in their capacity as communis hospitator but also to deliver goods to their guests when requested (not by a trading contract) and at a reasonable price. As early as 1690, Holt, C.J., had pointed out that 'where a man buys and sells under a Restraint and particular Limitation, tho' it is for his Livelihood, yet he is not within the statutes.'[46] Thus, innkeepers could become bankrupt only if they traded outside their inns and, as Lord Eldon said in 1811, 'The question depends not on the quantum of dealing, but the intention, and it is enough if a man will sell to anyone who comes to

42 Malkin v. Adams (1814) 2 Rose 28, 29-30.

43 Under date of 5 April 1776.

44 6 Geo. IV, c.16.

45 E.g. Ex parte Bath (1832) Mont. 82.

46 Newton v. Trigg (1690) 3 Mod. 327, 329.

buy; it must be left to a Jury to say whether there is enough of that outdoor dealing to evidence the intention.'[47] The major problems arising from the insistence upon buying and selling are shown in two fine distinctions which the courts sought to apply. The first was that between those estate owners who sold the produce of their land and others who also bought produce for resale. Thus, dealers in stone, bricks, alum and other minerals extracted from their estates were excluded, as were farmers selling their own dairy produce or fruit and dealers in cider made from their own apples. But if, for example, the farmer could prove that he bought horses for resale, rather than to work his land, and the cider-maker could prove that he also bought large quantities of apples to mix with his own, both might be within the laws. In such cases, as Basil Montagu said, the decisions of the courts seemed 'to depend on the proportion between the produce and the purchased ingredients.'[48] A second distinction was drawn between tradesmen who acted as servants and tradesmen who, by buying and selling, acted as traders. In the wool trade, for instance,

> A Clothier, that buys Wool, and has it made up into Cloth, or if he works the same into Cloth himself, may become a Bankrupt: but a Tailor, that makes Garments only, as a Servant to his Customers, shall not be a Bankrupt.49

By the same token, many other occupations, including ship-builders, ship-owners, and proprietors of coaches and waggons, could not become bankrupt; builders were liable

---

47 Ex parte Magennis (1811) 1 Rose 84.

48 B. Montagu and S. Ayrton, The Law and Practice of Bankruptcy (1837), i, 20.

49 The Law for and against Bankrupts, op. cit., p. 9.

only if they sold movables, like loose bricks, and carpenters, cabinet-makers and other artisans only if they sold freely to prospective purchasers.

In order to get within the laws, many 'traders' were obliged to call themselves 'deal and chapman' as well (for example, 'builder, dealer and chapman') since, if one of a man's two or three occupations was within the law, he could become bankrupt. Despite widespread use of this fiction, it is evident that many commercial men were unable to become bankrupt in practice as well as in law. The Select Committee into the Bankruptcy Laws in 1818 emphasised

> the impropriety of excluding from the operation of the Bankrupt Laws, persons who are not traders according to the present construction of the law, because they do not buy and sell; but who nevertheless are really and substantially engaged in trade, which they carry on by means of the extensive credit which that very trade enables them to obtain.[50]

John Smith, reporting the committee's findings to the Commons, contrasted the large number of non-traders who had used the process with the equally large number of 'persons absolutely exercising trades (who) were declared not to be subject to the bankrupt laws.'[51] The committee recommended that, in order to overcome the confusion, the law be extended 'to all persons engaged in any trade, business or calling, whose dealings require that credit should be obtained by means of Bills of Exchange or otherwise.'[52] Seven years later, in 1825, parliament responded by broadening the scope of the bankruptcy laws to include individuals who sought their living 'by buying and letting for hire, or by the workmanship of goods and commodities.' The same statute included specifically bleachers, builders, calenderers,

---

50 B.P.P. Bankrupt Laws (1818), p. 4.

51 Hansard, P.D., 1819, xxxix, 1382.

52 B.P.P. Bankrupt Laws (1818), p. 12.

carpenters, cattle and sheep salesmen, coffee-house keepers, fullers, hoteliers, innkeepers, insurers of ships, packers, printers, scriveners, shipwrights, victuallers, warehousemen and wharfingers. Farmers, graziers, labourers, hired workmen, tax-receivers and subscribers to incorporated companies established by Act of Parliament were still, equally specifically, excluded.[53] Despite this act, problems of definition continued to vex legal minds after 1825. In 1840, for example, the Commissioners into Bankruptcy and Insolvency stated that

> It is often a matter of great difficulty to determine whether purchases made by a farmer are ancillary to the profitable expenditure of the product of his farm, or whether the direct object of them be a profit on the resale, the smallness of the profit being no consideration, and one instance of buying and selling being sufficient to constitute the trading.54

The justification for the consistent exclusion of farmers, like that of artists, attorneys, butlers, schoolmasters and many artisans, was that their livelihood was obtained by manual or mental labour, which involved neither buying and selling nor the use of extensive credit. Although, as will be shown later, further additions were made to the statutory list of occupations liable to bankruptcy in 1842, the problems were not finally eradicated until the trader/non-trader distinction was abolished in 1861.[55] The distinction, which probably lasted so long because of legal conservatism, clearly affects the composition of bankruptcy statistics. While these automatically contain the largest mercantile and commercial failures, they exclude a considerable number of traders whose status was controversial.

---

53 6 Geo. IV, c.16.

54 B.P.P. [Report of the Commissioners for Inquiring into] Bankruptcy and Insolvency (1840), [XVI], p. xii.

55 24, 25 Vict., c.124.

V

In addition to the problems of definition, other, more important defects were produced by bankruptcy procedure and administration. Mansfield complained in 1781 that there was not one bankruptcy statute which 'had not been grossly abused and which, instead of producing good, had not produced a considerable deal of fraud and villainy.'[56] The major procedural defects concerned the act of bankruptcy, the collection of the bankrupt's estate and the method of granting the certificate of discharge.

In order to satisfy the commissioners that a commission should issue, the petitioning creditor was obliged to prove not only that the debtor was a trader but also that he had committed an act of bankruptcy. At the start of the nineteenth century, there were seventeen such acts, only three of which were in frequent use: staying indoors for an unusually long time, leaving home for a similar time and lying in gaol for two months after being imprisoned for debt.[57] The operation of these acts of bankruptcy varied from case to case. Frequently, the bankrupt simply ordered his clerk to 'deny' him to any creditor who called by stating 'The Master is not at home.' In such instances, the bankrupt was often hiding in the house, the denial constituting nothing more than a legal formality, after which the creditor struck a docket and opened a commission. Once the commission was opened, the bankrupt could not be arrested until after his final examination. This rather civilised mode of proceeding was, however, uncertain and could be difficult to prove to the commissioners, because it was the intention of the act which was significant, not the denial

56 Hansard, Parl. Hist., 1781, xxii, 629.

57 Reduced to 21 days in 1825 (6 Geo. IV, c.16).

itself.[58] Misunderstandings could be eliminated if the bankrupt arranged for one of his creditors to call at a certain time in order to receive the denial. But, although in frequent use,[59] such concerted acts of bankruptcy were illegal and were often invalidated by the Lord Chancellor. Understandably in the circumstances, most creditors preferred to use imprisonment for debt, the only act of bankruptcy over which they had control, and, equally understandably, bankrupts tried to avoid it. In many cases, the commissioners were told that, after stopping payment, the bankrupt had gone into hiding. They heard, for example, that, on 29 November 1809, John Rogers, a merchant and jeweller in the Strand, had fled to Cadiz to avoid arrest and had not been heard from seven months later. Similarly, on 8 March 1810, Charles Grant, a Broad Street merchant, had stopped payment and fled to the Isle of Wight, where he remained until December, corresponding under the name of 'Mr. Ritchies.'[60] The unfortunate consequences of the debtor's inability to declare himself bankrupt are shown in a letter sent by Mayson Wilson and John Williams, Liverpool merchants, from their retreat in the Wirral, to the solicitor who had sued out writs for their arrest:

> Dear Sir, we wrote to you two days ago requesting you would take out immediately our commission and send us our protection down, as you must be well aware that our absence cannot be advantageous to our concerns.61

This was partly corrected in 1825, when traders were allowed to file a declaration of insolvency at the Bankrupt Office,

---

58 Smith and Another v. Currie (1813) 1 Rose 365.

59 B.P.P. Bankrupt Laws (1818), p. 46, Germain Lavie, a London solicitor.

60 For Rogers, P.R.O. B3/4177, 26 May 1810, Charles Fewell; for Grant, P.R.O. B3/1883, 18 Dec. 1810, Henry Mitchison.

61 P.R.O. B3/5179, 22 Nov. 1810.

which, when advertised in the *London Gazette*, constituted an act of bankruptcy.[62] Nevertheless, the problem was still vexatious throughout the 1830s and, after the abolition of arrest on mesne process in 1838, it was considered virtually impossible to establish an act of bankruptcy against an intransigent debtor until months after his credit had failed.[63] Montagu's suggestion, in 1840, that 'instead of Acts of Bankruptcy, acts of non-payment ought to be sufficient to warrant the issuing of a process,'[64] mirrored contemporary opinion. As will be seen later, this principle was established in the bankruptcy act of 1842.[65]

VI

The procedure by which a bankrupt's estate was collected gave rise to an equal number of problems. It has been noted that the solicitor responsible for taking out a commission chose a messenger of the court who arranged a private meeting of commissioners. After the commission had been opened, the same messenger was usually appointed by the commissioners to be the provisional assignee who took charge of the bankrupt's effects. The messenger then sent one of his men to the bankrupt's house, where he stayed until the creditors chose their assignees. This system contained many defects. Frequently, the messenger was commanded by the solicitor, upon whom he was dependent, not to occupy the bankrupt's house. In some cases, this was justified since the bankrupt's creditors considered him unfortunate and

62 6 Geo. IV, c.16.

63 *An Exposure of the Injurious Effects of the Present System of Bankruptcy Law. By a Barrister* (1841), p. 49.

64 B.P.P. *Bankruptcy and Insolvency* (1840), p. 151.

65 1, 2 Will. IV, c. 56.

honest but, in others, solicitors who were friendly towards the bankrupt were able to provide him with opportunities for fraud. In addition, the solicitor was able to control the choice of an appraiser to take account of the bankrupt's assets, although this was legally the messenger's mandate.[66] When messengers did occupy the bankrupt's premises, their agents were often unable to carry out their duties. Joseph Vandercomb, a London solicitor, told the 1818 Committee into Bankruptcy that messengers' men were 'of the lowest degree' and described their activities:

> The man goes with the warrant of seizure, and he becomes one of the family directly: he is placed, according to his station in life, in the kitchen with the servants, and what is going on upstairs he knows no more than I do, who am standing here, and . . . that I believe to be the time when the greatest peculation prevails. All the relations and friends of the insolvent come to condole with him, and I believe most of them take away something with them.[67]

Messengers were in an awkward legal position and were often prosecuted for trespass after commissions had been superseded.[68] John Tringer Nixon, for example, was obliged to pay between £5-£600 damages for seizing the barge of Marinas Price, whose commission had been invalidated.[69]

The most important stage in each commission was the appointment of assignees by the creditors, since their responsibilities included the collection and division of the estate and the presentation of the bankrupt's accounts at his final examination. The law presupposed that the creditors, who possessed intimate knowledge of the bank-

---

66 B.P.P. [Report from the Select Committee appointed to Consider of the] Bankrupt Laws (1817), [V], pp. 92, 94, Henry Page, a messenger.

67 B.P.P. Bankrupt Laws (1818), p. 41.

68 B.P.P. Bankrupt Laws (1817), p. 98, John Billing, a messenger.

69 Ibid., p. 107.

rupt's affairs, would control the estate closely and ensure that equitable dividends were paid to all. Unfortunately, the majority of traders were loathe to waste their time on such gratuitous pursuits. Their reluctance is typified by the assignees of Kensington and Co., the Lombard Street bank which failed in 1812, who told the commissioners that 'having under their immediate care and management extended commercial concerns of great importance they were extremely unwilling to undertake the office of assignees and were induced to do so at the pressing solicitation of many of the principal creditors.'[70] As a result, it was considered that most estates were collected inefficiently and dividends were invariably small (averaging about five shillings in the pound)[71] and paid extremely slowly. For example, the estate of Brickwood and Co., Lombard Street bankers who failed in 1810, produced six shillings over more than fifty years; that of Dawes, Noble and Co., bankers in Pall Mall (also in 1810), yielded 8s.10-1/2d. over 53 years; that of Wilson and Williams, Liverpool merchants (also in 1810), produced 4s.1d. over forty years.[72] In the circumstances, it is understandable that creditors paid little attention to the proceedings. In 1826, the secretary of the Bankruptcy Court filed 334 certificates of unclaimed dividends worth £219,978.[73]

---

70 P.R.O. B3/2825, 29 Aug. 1815, John Carstairs, John Doxeat and George Sandeman; cf. B.P.P. Bankrupt Laws (1817), p. 90, James Hunter.

71 B.P.P. Bankrupt Laws (1817), p. 40, Phillip George, a Bristol merchant.

72 These bankruptcies are examined in chapters VIII and IX, below.

73 B.P.P. Accounts and Papers (1826-7), xix, 48, 'Report of Mr. Pensam.' The total amount was probably larger since many assignees had not filed the unclaimed dividends. Pensam was unable to specify when the unclaimed dividends had been declared because most of the certificates were not dated.

A second consequence of the assignees system was the frequency with which their election was the occasion of dishonesty, as an interested minority sought to control the estate. The commonest method of influencing the election was by proof of fictitious debts.[74] Once a debt had been proved, the commissioners could not expunge it, the only recourse being a petition to Chancery which was described, in 1818, as 'a remedy often worse than the disease.'[75] John Billing, a messenger of the court, was convinced, in 1817, that much of the fraud was attributable to the London Jewish community. He maintained that when, in 'Jewish commissions' (involving a Jewish bankrupt whose creditors were predominantly Christian), there was a danger of the choice of assignees falling into the hands of the bona fide creditors, the solicitor recruited proofs, for a small consideration, from the army of laggards in the hall of the court.[76] Joshua Mayhew, who had served as a solicitor in Jewish commissions for fifteen years, was equally critical, stating that 'Jews are always attending on commissions, for the purpose of seeing how many frauds are detected . . . you never find a commission executed, if it is a commission of any moment at all, but the Jews are there, receiving their education.' During a three-year investigation in the Bankrupt Office into the affairs of a Jewish bankrupt named Braham, Mayhew had uncovered an 'amazing interchange of proofs' between a group of Jews, using accommodation paper and fictitious bills of exchange. He had even heard of an office in the City where such bills were manufactured and used for the purpose of electing assignees to defraud the

---

74 B.P.P. Bankrupt Laws (1818), p. 39, Joseph Vandercomb.

75 Hansard, P.D., 1818, xxxviii, 984, John Smith.

76 B.P.P. Bankrupt Laws (1817), p. 104.

general creditors.[77] Similarly, it was alleged in 1819 that 'there were three or more houses in London where persons upon being paid a percentage undertook to prove debts to any amount.'[78]

After election, dishonest assignees had the whole estate at their mercy. Some used their power to protect the bankrupt, and it was well-known that 'where assignees are adverse to a Bankrupt, there is always a better dividend.'[79] Others used the bankrupt's assets for their own commercial speculation. In 1743, Isaac Panchaud's assignees sold his debts for four shillings in the pound and then refused to have anything more to do with the estate.[80] Elijah Pitt's assignees, in 1760, took £848 'to their own use in trade and business and have made considerable profits.'[81] In 1832, a legal process issued against the assignees of John Leigh 'in respect of moneys belonging to the said Bankrupt's estate alledged to have been received and retained or misapplied.'[82] Assignees' usual pretext for non-payment of dividends was the difficulty they were experiencing in recovering the bankrupt's assets or selling his estate,

---

77 Ibid., pp. 81-2; cf. ibid., p. 53, Samuel Sweet; B.P.P. Bankrupt Laws (1818), p. 32, Montagu.

78 B. Montagu, Some Observations on the Bills Submitted to the Legislature (1819), p. xli.

79 B.P.P. Bankrupt Laws (1818), p. 88, George Grote.

80 Bankruptcy Court Order Books, P.R.O. B1/18, 1 March 1743. Panchaud, a member of the Vaudois merchant-banking family, had established his merchant house in London about 1730. His son established a bank in Paris which was the precursor of the Bank of France. He, also, went bankrupt in 1769. See H. Lüthy, La Banque Protestante en France (2 vols., Paris, 1959, 1961), ii, 420-39, 447-9, 458-63, 693-6.

81 P.R.O. B1/38, 21 Jan. 1760.

82 P.R.O. B3/2942, 19 Nov. 1832. The first dividend (worth 3-1/2d.) in Leigh's bankruptcy, which was opened in 1811, was paid in 1831.

which forced them to take the causes to law. Such suits, said Montagu, 'are frequently instituted for the very purpose of supplying a pretence for not dividing the property.'[83] The regularity with which creditors prosecuted corrupt assignees indicates how loosely statutory controls were applied.[84] The regulation of 1732 that no dividend was to be paid before the assignees' accounts had been audited seems to have been disregarded frequently and it was constantly necessary for the Lord Chancellor to prompt commissioners to be more vigilant in order to limit opportunities for peculation. In 1794, Lord Loughborough ordered assignees, whose creditors did not designate a bank for deposit of the assets, to use the Bank of England. Fifteen years later, commissioners were ordered to allow no dividend 'upon admission only of a certain sum in the hands of the assignees' but to scrutinize their accounts and conduct.[85] If the assignees had failed to divide property they were to be fined twenty per cent of the sum retained.[86]

Despite such regulations, fraud, embezzlement and peculation by assignees continued. The reason why they could not be controlled lay not only in the apathy of creditors and the remoteness of the Lord Chancellor's authority, but also, and more importantly, in the incompetence and laxity of the commissioners of bankruptcy, whose functions are examined later.

---

83 B. Montagu, Enquiries Respecting the Administration of Bankrupts' Estates by Assignees (1811), p. 6.

84 These cases are recorded in the Order Books of the court (P.R.O. B.1).

85 For the orders, see E. Christian, The Origin, Progress and Present Practice of the Bankrupt Law (2nd edn., 1818), ii, 2-3, 26.

86 49 Geo. III, c.121.

VII

The third major procedural defect in the law - the mode of granting the bankrupt his certificate of discharge - offered an even more tempting inducement to corruption than the procedures for opening the commission and dividing the estate. The right of the creditors to withhold a certificate was supposedly 'based upon a presumption that such power would be tenderly and but seldom exercised, and only in notorious cases.'[87] However, the magnitude of the favours which the certificate granted (immunity of the bankrupt and his property from future liability for former debts) inevitably inhibited creditors, who were frustrated by the bankrupt's failure and suspicious of his intentions, from consenting to it. Montagu, in 1809, considered that

> This law . . . has originated in the supposition that pecuniary satisfaction may not be a sufficient compensation to creditors, but that, as they may suffer by subtle and inexplicable fraud, they should be armed with the power of private vindictive satisfaction.[88]

In this sense, it may be compared with the insolvency laws which, as will be shown, gave creditors similar powers to punish their debtors. Like imprisonment for debt, the creditor's control of the certificate aroused immense hostility. In 1759, a Commons committee complained that one large creditor could frustrate the intentions of the rest (the consent was required of four-fifths in number _and_ value of creditors). Edward Green suggested to the committee that the remedy was 'to oblige such creditor to make his objection within a certain time before the commissioners' who

---

87 B.P.P. _Bankruptcy and Insolvency_ (1840), p. 67, Montagu, citing a petition from uncertificated bankrupts.

88 B. Montagu, _An Enquiry Respecting the Expediency of Limiting the Creditor's Power to Refuse a Bankrupt's Certificate_ (1809), p. 11.

would grant the certificate if that objection was unjustified.[89] The committee also noted the ambiguity of a law which forced the bankrupt to obtain his certificate at his own expense after ostensibly forfeiting all his property. Unfortunately, parliament was prorogued before the committee's recommendations could reach the statute book and the subject lay dormant until the 1770s. An act of 1772 liberated all uncertificated bankrupts who were not guilty of fraud and entitled every bankrupt to a certificate unless his creditors dissented with justification.[90] This and a similar measure of 1778, however, applied only to commissions which were being prosecuted when the statutes were enacted, not to future bankruptcies. After 1778, the subject was again dropped until 1809, when the necessary consent was reduced from four- to three-fifths.[91]

According to Montagu, the failure of the legislature to tackle the basic evil of control by interested parties led to two unfortunate consequences in the early nineteenth century. On the one hand, fraudulent bankrupts obtained their certificates easily by bribing intransigent creditors to sign and by acknowledging fictitious debts of friends. On the other, as many as forty per cent of all bankrupts remained undischarged.[92]

VIII

It has been shown that, by concentrating in the creditors' hands the power to open the commission, to collect the estate and to grant the certificate, the bankruptcy process

---

89 J.H.C., 1759, xxviii, 603.

90 12 Geo. III, c.47.

91 49 Geo. III, c.121.

92 B.P.P. Bankrupt Laws (1818), pp. 98-100; cf. ibid., p. 70, William Cooke, a solicitor; Hansard, P.D., 1817, xxxvi, 819, John Smith.

offered considerable opportunities for corruption, which could be detrimental to both sides. The potential restraint to dishonest practices was the authority of the seventy commissioners who were frequently exhorted by general orders from Chancery to root out fraud and punish corruption.[93] It was therefore unfortunate that, although some were conscientious and well-informed, most commissioners were inadequately qualified for such a post. One of the commissioners described his colleagues, in 1829, as 'the worst constituted court of justice that can well be imagined.'[94] To some extent, this is explained by the fact that the commissionerships were treated as political sinecures. When Erskine became Lord Chancellor in 1806 he received hundreds of applications to become commissioner.[95] Sir George Trevelyan describes Macaulay's appointment, in January 1828, as 'a rare piece of luck at a time when, as Lord Cockburn tells us, "a youth of a Tory family who was discovered to have a leaning towards the doctrines of the opposition, was considered a lost son".' (Macaulay, however, explained later that, as he was appointed between the resignation of Lord Goderich and the acceptance of the premiership by the Duke of Wellington, he could consider it as not obliging him politically).[96] A more important reason for the low ability of many commissioners, however, was their inadequate remuneration. Commissioners' fees, which did not increase in the century before 1831, were neither commensurate with the labour demanded of them nor sufficient to attract men of

---

93 For the general orders, see B. Montagu, Bankrupt Laws and Precedents (1807), iv, 4-6; Christian, op. cit., ii, 2-3, 26, 100, 202-3.

94 Reform of the Bankruptcy Court. By a Commissioner of Bankrupts (1829), p. 7.

95 See ibid., p. 41.

96 G.O. Trevelyan, Life and Letters of Lord Macaulay (1893), p. 101.

ability. The average annual earnings of each of 55 commissioners between 1 March 1828 and 1 March 1831 were £380.5.0d., derived from the exaction of a fee of £1 at every meeting.[97] As a result, the most able lawyers were said to avoid this sector of legal practice[98] which, according to one commissioner in 1829, had become the preserve of

> young or unoccupied men who have much leisure . . . those who are in business and have little leisure . . . (and) old men, alack, wanting the pastime of a little business and the dignity of a little brief authority . . . few, very few were appointed on account of their fitness for office.99

The large number of old commissioners was also attributed to the absence of a retirement plan.[100] The second consequence of their low pay was that commissioners appeared to be more interested in accumulating business (hence fees) than in dispatching it. Many of their meetings were considered totally unnecessary, while others, involving complicated points of law, were adjourned after two hours, regardless of the state of the case.[101] Adjournments increased fees greatly since, as Montagu pointed out in 1820,

> There is scarcely an adjournment of the Bankrupt's examination, where the commissioners at the adjourned meeting are the same commissioners by whom the adjournment was ordered, in which case the business is, as it were, to begin again, to the vexation of the bankrupt, and the expense of the estate, and of his friends.102

---

97 B.P.P. Accounts and Papers (1831), xv, 74-5. The other 15 had either kept no accounts or retired.

98 B.P.P. Bankrupt Laws (1817), p. 120, Ralph Blackiston, a solicitor.

99 Reform of the Bankruptcy Court, op. cit., pp. 36, 48.

100 J.S.M. Fonblanque, Observations on the Bill now before Parliament for Consolidation and Amendment of the Laws relating to Bankrupts (1824), p. 32.

101 Ibid., p. 38.

102 B. Montagu, A Digest of New Decisions in Bankruptcy (1820), p. 36.

This was because three out of the five commissioners in each list were needed to form a quorum; hence, a rotation system was adopted which excluded two from hearing the evidence at each meeting. As a result, litigants frequently received contradictory decisions at different meetings of the same commission.[103] Also, because of the contrasting abilities of commissioners, the decisions of different lists were not uniform. This is reflected in Christian's description of a common practice: 'If a commission was directed to any list, and the commissioners thought it their duty not to find the party a bankrupt, the solicitor would probably get the commission superseded and try an experiment with another list.'[104] Montagu demonstrated the inconsistency by citing the number of bankrupts gaoled by each list between January 1810 and July 1824:

Total Bankrupts imprisoned by each list of the Bankruptcy Court, Jan. 1810 - July 1824

No. of List	1	2	3	4	5	6	7	8	9	10	11	12	13	14
No. imprisoned	1	7	1	4	0	4	4	5	5	0	1	0	0	41

Source: B. Montagu, Suggestions Respecting the Improvement of the Bankrupt Laws (London, 1824), p. 33.

A related problem, affecting the dispatch of business and judgment of the commissioners, was the physical environment in which they worked. John Smith considered, in 1818, that 'The Guildhall on a busy day could be compared to nothing but a cock-fight; it was difficult to conceive of a scene of greater confusion.'[105] Because of the crowding and babble,

---

103 Idem, Suggestions Respecting the Improvement of the Bankrupt Laws (1824), p. 30.

104 E. Christian, The Origin . . . of the Bankrupt Law, op.cit., ii, 4.

105 Hansard, P.D., 1818, xxxviii, 984.

many creditors found it impossible to establish their claims and the commissioners were unable to scrutinize the papers laid before them.[106] It is tempting to attribute the chaos to the smallness of the building but, as was pointed out in 1818, the responsibility lay with the poor organisation of business by the commissioners, who reserved only one or two days each month for final examinations.[107] It is not therefore surprising that, although a statute of 1821 established a new, spacious bankruptcy building in Basinghall Street, with a separate room for each list, it made little impression: 'The evil of the system retained . . . almost all its magnitude, though it shook off some of its deformity.'[108]

It is clear that contemporary criticism of the maladministration of the commissioners was justified. It is less reasonable, however, to blame them alone for the fraud and corruption which characterised commissions of bankruptcy, for two reasons. First, their jurisdiction was circumscribed. One of the greatest inducements to dishonesty was the fact that, except when a trader had gone bankrupt more than once, the courts could investigate his behaviour only after proceedings had commenced, not his misdemeanours before the commission opened. In 1811, a bankrupt who had fraudulently obtained £30,000 before stopping payments was granted a certificate because his crime was committed prior to the period which the commissioners could investigate. The case was sent on appeal to Chancery, where Lord Eldon said

> I have often had occasion to observe . . . that it does not belong to me to look into the moral life of the bankrupt and the nature and quality of his acts before

---

106 B.P.P. Bankrupt Laws (1817), p. 98, John Billing.

107 B.P.P. Bankrupt Laws (1818), p. 42, Joseph Vandercomb; p. 66, Robert Waithman.

108 Reform of the Bankruptcy Court, op. cit., p. 21. The act is 1, 2 Geo. IV, c.115.

> the bankruptcy. The Legislature has left it entirely to the caprice of the creditors, who may be under a moral, but are certainly under no legal, obligation to sign his certificate. It is not so with the commissioners. I hold them bound, if the Bankrupt has acted conformably, to certify; and if after the creditors do not bring forward any wilful concealment by the Bankrupt, while Bankrupt, the Great Seal is bound to follow.[109]

Inevitably, many failing traders took advantage of the restrictions upon the commissioners' powers of investigation. Samuel Sweet, an attorney, told the 1817 Committee into the Bankrupt Laws of one species of fraud which damaged trade considerably. Traders who were in difficulties, he said, frequently purchased large quantities of goods on credit and sold them immediately, often at a great loss, in order to raise cash. When their credit finally dried up they became bankrupt or compounded.[110]

In most cases, however, even misdemeanours committed after the commencement of proceedings were exempt from punishment because, until 1820, such offences were legally punishable by death.[111] The ineffectiveness of capital punishment as a deterrent is revealed in Romilly's calculation that, of five thousand people who had warranted prosecution in bankruptcy cases in the 81 years since 1732, only five had been convicted as felons.[112] The aversion of creditors to using this facility is exemplified by the account by Thomas Tilson, a London solicitor, in 1817, of a bankrupt who had passed his final examination, when property worth £400 was found secreted in the roof of his cottage. His wife admitted helping him to put it there. When asked by the assignees whether they should prosecute, the majority

---

109 Ex parte Joseph (1811) 18 Ves. Jun. 340, 342.

110 B.P.P. Bankrupt Laws (1817), p. 56.

111 1 Geo. IV, c.115.

112 Hansard, P.D., 1813, xxvi, 303.

of creditors decided 'that the severity of the punishment, and the uncertainty of conviction, were so great, and the expense of prosecution so heavy, that they determined not to prosecute, though the case was clear.'[113] It is, of course, possible that in many cases like this the creditors' aversion to prosecuting was the product more of a desire to acquire dividends than of a tender conscience. The second factor which tempers, to some extent, one's criticisms of the commissioners is the fact that their investigations were hampered by current mercantile practices. Efficient book-keeping and accounting were, evidently, the exception rather than the rule. The resultant difficulties were not easy to solve since, as Joshua Mayhew pointed out in 1817, penalisation of bankrupts who did not keep books (for example, by refusing their certificates) 'would carry so much severity against illiterate persons, that I cannot possibly say how the law could lay down in what way such a man should conduct his business.' That the situation was abused frequently is suggested both by Mayhew's calculation that books were produced in only one out of fifty fraudulent bankruptcies[114] and by the allegations of others that, after bankruptcy, traders systematically destroyed or hid their books in order to facilitate false proofs.[115]

This problem was still acute in 1840 when, it was reckoned, about half of all traders, even in London, never took stock.[116] As a London solicitor said in the same year, 'There is actually a bonus on a man keeping no books - for

---

113 B.P.P. Bankrupt Laws (1817), p. 66; cf. B. Montagu, Thoughts on the Abolition of the Punishment of Death in Bankruptcy (1821), p. 38.

114 B.P.P. Bankrupt Laws (1817), p. 81.

115 B.P.P. Bankrupt Laws (1818), p. 67, Robert Waithman; p. 62, Samuel Amory, a solicitor.

116 B.P.P. Bankruptcy and Insolvency (1840), p. 496, J.H. Elliott, a trader.

it is then said that he has no books and can give no better account and is entitled to pass his examination: thus it is a premium on fraud.'[117] Evidently, some of the commissioners in the new Bankruptcy Court, erected in 1831, were more vigilant than their predecessors. Commissioner Evans's refusal of unsubstantiated claims worth hundreds of thousands of pounds was a pointer towards the inevitable insistence upon precise recording of financial transactions.[118]

IX

Lastly, we must consider the expense and delay of bankruptcy commissions. Like other sectors of the debt laws, particularly those relating to small debts, the costs of the procedure were disproportionate to the size of the debts involved. Although the Consolidating Act of 1732 had regulated the fees which could be levied at each sitting, the expense of opening a commission was considered to be at least £50, in 1743,[119] a basic cost which still obtained in the early nineteenth century.[120] In addition, because the number of sittings and exactions by lawyers and assignees had not been restricted, interested parties were able to multiply fees at will. In 1770, for example, the assignees of Zachary Hubberty, a solicitor from Kendal, charged £7,747.12.9-1/2d. for collecting the estate, leaving only £1,998.16.4d. to be divided amongst the creditors.[121]

---

117 Ibid., p. 57, Isaac Sewell.

118 Ibid., p. 203, Patrick Johnson, an official assignee of the Bankruptcy Court.

119 The Law for and against Bankrupts (1743), p. 166.

120 The solicitor's bill could amount to £60, the messenger's to £17. E. Christian, Instructions for Suing out and Prosecuting a Commission of Bankruptcy (1820), pp. 172-3, 175.

121 P.R.O. B1/51, 23 March 1770.

Montagu's comments on expense were the most critical. He considered that it increased

> from the nature of the tribunal, from the delays and difficulties in procuring decisions, from there being so many professional men concerned, from the litigation not being checked by a fear of expense to the individual on whose behalf the process is instituted, and from the uncertainty attendant upon the decisions not being the judgment of any permanent judges.

He estimated that the annual cost to bankrupts' estates of the fee system, messengers' and accountants' bills, superfluous litigation, mismanagement of assets, petty legal charges and delays by assignees amounted to £240,000 and recommended the erection of a permanent tribunal which would perform more efficiently for £40,000.[122] The figure of £240,000, spread over an estimated 1,200 bankruptcies a year, suggests a mean expense at this period of about £200. Even after Brougham's reforms in the 1830s, bankruptcy continued to be marked by high costs, especially in smaller cases. Commissioner Merivale's analysis of 180 estates in his division of the court between 1832 and 1839, shown in Table 1.2, indicates that, while ten per cent of assets worth more than £3,000 was spent on costs, seventy per cent was needed to collect assets worth between £130 and £200. Expense, indeed, seems to have increased with time for, of assets collected in England and Wales between 1853 and 1855 worth £1,978,325, 54 per cent was paid in dividends, 32 per cent went in expenses (12 per cent to solicitors) and 14 per cent was paid in court fees.[123]

Nor could the justice dispensed by the Bankruptcy Court be described as speedy. The slowness of the commissioners in complicated cases has been described; of greater significance were the interminable delays in the process of appeal

---

122 B. Montagu, Suggestions Respecting the Improvement of the Bankrupt Laws (1824), pp. 14-15.

123 J. Rayner, Bankruptcy Law Reform (1859), p. 6.

to Chancery, which seem to have increased greatly in the early nineteenth century. In 1832, Montagu harked back to the good old days, when all bankruptcy business in Chancery was concluded on Saturdays by Thurlow, Rosslyn and Eldon, and one day each week was too much. In Eldon's Chancellorship (1801-6, 1807-27), however, bankruptcy business increased until, said Montagu in 1824,

> I have known the Lord Chancellor sit during the time appointed to Bankruptcy petitions, from ten in the morning till eleven at night, with the daily interval of only two or three hours, for a fortnight together, but these exertions have been found in vain.[124]

There were two main reasons for the delays. First, Chancery procedure was not flexible. Evidence by affidavit, often extremely complex and filed by both parties in order to obscure the facts, necessitated extensive investigation by one, or all, of the Chancery Master, Jury, Vice-Chancellor and Lord Chancellor. Second, in some cases, it was difficult for any decision to be made either way, since the corpus of bankruptcy law was so complicated and obscure. Christian considered, in 1818, that 'there is no branch of the law of England that exhibits such extraordinary specimens of contrariety of opinions, and irreconcilable decisions as the Bankrupt Law.'[125] Eldon, indeed, was alleged four years earlier 'to have said that he had read the Bankrupt Laws seventy-two thousand times, and did not understand them yet.'[126] Many cases remained in Chancery for months and some for years.[127] The delays were particularly detrimental in cases concerned with the opening of

---

124 B. Montagu, Suggestions Respecting the Improvement of the Bankrupt Laws (1824), p. 61.

125 E. Christian, The Origin . . . of the Bankrupt Law, *op. cit*., i, iii.

126 Hansard, *P.D.*, 1814, xxviii, 798, Earl Stanhope.

127 For examples, see Montagu, *op. cit*., p. 27.

commissions. So summary and secret was the procedure for adjudicating a debtor bankrupt that a speedy process of relief for the innocent was essential. Hence, it was unfortunate that the trading and the act of bankruptcy were amongst the more controversial aspects of bankruptcy law. The most celebrated case of all was that of a Mr. Chambers, who spent more than twenty years and £20,000 trying to disprove his act of bankruptcy.[128] Equally difficult were problems associated with partnership cases. The technical defects of the law of partnership have been described elsewhere[129] and it is only necessary here to mention its effect on bankruptcy. The basic problem was that the law accepted as valid the first commission opened against a partnership. If that commission had been prosecuted against only one of the partners, litigation was inevitable both because the partnership creditors required joint dividends and because joint and separate commissions could not run concurrently. Chancery, in fact, tended to ignore the law, by superseding separate in favour of joint commissions.[130] Even when this stage had been reached, however, division of the estate was scarcely equitable, since the assignees of joint estates were still obliged to distinguish between the partners' private and partnership property. As Fonblanque asked in 1824, 'is it not absurd, to give the Estate, Stock in the Funds, Houses, Equipages, Plate, Jewels etc., of a great Banker, to his private creditors, and refer his great commercial correspondents for payment, to the fixtures, old

---

128 B.P.P. Bankruptcy and Insolvency (1840), p. 73, Montagu.

129 H.A. Shannon, 'The Coming of General Limited Liability,' in Essays in Economic History (ed. E.M. Carus-Wilson), (1954), i, 362-4.

130 See ex parte Rawson (1813) 1 Ves. & B. 160, 163.

pens, and ledgers of his counting house?'[131] Partnership cases posed many additional problems. It was frequently difficult, for example, for creditors to prove that all the partners had committed acts of bankruptcy. When only one partner failed, his assignees were obliged to enter complicated negotiations to ascertain his share in the partnership. Finally, when a bankrupt had participated in more than one partnership, organisational problems could become extremely complicated. Examples are cited in chapter eight. It is not surprising that Chancery was clogged with petitions demanding fair treatment in such commissions.

X

From the later eighteenth century, the annual number of bankruptcies increased sharply, more than trebling between the 1780s and the decade 1811-20.[132] The strain which this placed upon the whole fabric of bankruptcy law and administration led to an increasing flow of suggestions for structural reform. The major defects in both the bankruptcy and the insolvency laws were brilliantly exposed in 1783 by Sir James Bland Burges, whose suggestions provide an interesting example of practical, common-sense solutions deriving from within the system.[133] Burges pointed out that previous modifications in the bankruptcy laws, which he called 'an engine of villainy and deceit,' had been piecemeal and superficial:

> The Legislature in vain attempted to restrain abuses by partial and imperfect provisions; wherever they felt an

---

131 J.S.M. Fonblanque, Observations on the . . . Laws relating to Bankrupts (1824), p. 51, fn.

132 See below, chapter V.

133 Sir J.B. Burges (1752-1824) was called to the Bar and appointed commissioner of bankrupts in 1777, entered parliament in 1787 and was later appointed Marshal of the Marshalsea prison.

> immediate evil, they applied occasional remedy; they laboured to correct an effect, when they ought to have enquired into the cause.134

The laws were defective in two ways. First, their principle was erroneous, accepting as it did that there was a difference between the debts of traders and non-traders. Second, the practice of the law encouraged fraud, deception and perjury. Burges attacked especially the secret mode of opening commissions and the creditors' control of the choice of assignees and of the certificate. He suggested many reforms which would eradicate these and other faults: commissions of insolvency should be open to all classes of debtor; time should be allowed, before the commencement of proceedings, for the debtor to pay the debt or to defend himself against the plaintiff's accusations; the court should consist of nine, not seventy, commissioners, composed of perhaps five barristers of three years' standing and four merchants, thus creating a balance between law and trade; fraudulent bankrupts should not be put to death but employed in the navy or factories; certificates should be granted by the commissioners; and county courts should be established under the supervision of a central board.[135]

Although most of Burges's solutions were eventually adopted,[136] parliament, before the second quarter of the nineteenth century, continued its traditional policy of

---

134 Sir. J.B. Burges, Considerations on the Law of Insolvency (1783), p. 317.

135 Ibid., pp. 320-90.

136 E.g. the abolition of the death penalty in 1820 (1 Geo. IV, c. 115), the erection of a regular bankruptcy court in 1831 (1, 2 Will. IV, c.56), the provision of legal defence for the debtor before proceedings opened and judicial control of the certificate in 1842 (5,6 Vict., c.122), the erection of a county court system in 1846 (9, 10 Vict., c.95) and the abolition of the distinction between traders and non-traders in 1861 (24, 25 Vict., c.134).

attacking only specific grievances in the law and studiously avoided plans for its wholesale reconstruction. Proposals to effect radical changes were usually defeated or amended extensively. In 1808, for example, Lord Redesdale vainly attempted to abolish abuses of the assignees system by establishing a permanent body of three professional assignees to control bankrupt estates. The most persistent advocate of bankruptcy reform in the early years of the nineteenth century was Sir Samuel Romilly. His criticisms, however, were confined to technical defects of the system, indicating his realisation that the time was not ripe for substantive changes in the law. The tenor of his successful bills has been noted above and it is pertinent here to examine the attitude of the legislature to them. That his first statute (46 Geo. III, c.135) passed with only minor amendment was, according to Henry Brougham, explained by the fact that he was Solicitor General at the time.[137] The second (49 Geo. III, c.121) was severely mutilated. Clauses reducing the creditors' power of withholding a certificate (by allowing the bankrupt to appeal to the Lord Chancellor after two years) and enabling a certificated bankrupt to act as a competent witness for his assignees were both rejected. Romilly considered that the amendments made by the Lords to his bill were so great 'that, if they are right in themselves . . . it cannot be right that they should become law, without passing, in both Houses, through all regular stages of a Bill.'[138] Despite a temptation to abandon the bill, Romilly concurred in the alterations simply because he considered limited reform to be better than none at all.

---

137 Contributions to the Edinburgh Review by Henry Lord Brougham (Glasgow, 1856), iii, 104. Romilly was Solicitor General in the Ministry of All Talents from 12 Feb. 1806 to 25 March 1807.

138 Memoirs of the Life of Sir Samuel Romilly (ed. by his Sons), (1840), ii, 280.

The inability or unwillingness of the legislature to devise remedies for a problem which was becoming increasingly urgent inevitably provoked widespread extra-parliamentary agitation. The restlessness of the City was reflected in a petition presented to parliament, in 1817, by London bankers and merchants, complaining of the frauds perpetrated in bankruptcy proceedings.[139] A year later, a select committee, appointed in response to the petition, catalogued the enormous errors and injustices contained in the system, and, on 2 April 1819, John Smith sought to implement its recommendations in his Bankrupt Laws Amendment Bill. The bill proposed to define bankrupts as insolvent traders whose livelihood depended upon credit, excluding those who used manual or mental labour (artisans, artists, attorneys, butlers, farmers, schoolmasters, etc.). The commissioners were to be empowered to expunge dubious debts and to look into the bankrupt's conduct before bankruptcy in deciding whether to allow a certificate. A professional agent was to be appointed to supervise the bankrupt estate. In addition, the death penalty was to be abolished, a new Bankruptcy Court building established and bankrupts were to be encouraged to assist the collection of estates by receiving five per cent of everything gathered in.[140] Like many other measures designed to reform the debt laws, Smith's bill failed in the Lords, although, as noted above, the death penalty was abolished and a new court building erected in 1820.

In the 1820s, parliamentary resistance to legal reform began to dissolve. The work of Robert Peel as Home Secretary included two measures designed to ease the difficulties

---

139 Hansard, P.D., 1817, xxxvi, 819-20, John Smith.

140 Ibid., 1819, xxxix, 1380-8. Other suggestions included reform of the law of partnership, restrictions on the use of the supersedeas and consolidation of the bankruptcy laws.

confronting bankruptcy reform. In 1825, his Commission of Inquiry into the Court of Chancery examined the vexed problem of appeal. Chancery had long been clogged with bankruptcy cases, which constituted about a quarter of its business, and many thought the two antithetic. In 1813, a Vice-Chancellor's court had been established, but had failed to take the weight off the Lord Chancellor or to speed up the process, because appeals from the Vice-Chancellor's court to the Chancellor took just as long as the previous procedure.[141] The Chancery commissioners, however, rejected the separation of bankruptcy petitions from the Lord Chancellor on the grounds that they frequently involved the most important points of law and equity which were best handled by a high judicial authority versed in the whole range of equitable jurisdiction; they also considered that bankruptcy business was too small to occupy the whole time of a specially erected court.[142] Peel's second measure was more productive: at Eldon's suggestion, the confused and chaotic bankruptcy laws were brought together in a Consolidating Act.[143] After this, the problem could be tackled with a fuller understanding of the points at issue. Here, as in other legal fields, the work of Henry Brougham, Lord Chancellor from 1830 to 1834, was to be a watershed. His initial bankruptcy statute, in 1831, was a response to widespread mercantile dissatisfaction with the law. The Common Council of the City of London had been investigating the bankruptcy procedure since 1825 and, on 14 December 1830, presented a petition to parliament, signed by virtual-

---

141 In 1811, 114 cases were pending; in 1819, 289. B. Montagu, Inquiries Respecting the Courts of Commissioners of Bankrupts (1825), p. 77.

142 Idem, The Evidence in Bankruptcy before the Chancery Commission, with the Report (1826), p. xxii.

143 Hansard, P.D., n.s., 1823, viii, 705-6, Eldon; the act is 6 Geo. IV, c.16.

ly every trader of importance in the City, recommending the replacement of the fourteen lists of commissioners by 'such a Court . . . as will give the Public that Confidence which it ought to feel in the administration of so important a branch of the laws of the realm.'[144] Brougham's subsequent Act to Establish a Court of Bankruptcy entirely changed bankruptcy administration. It erected a new court with one chief judge, three puisne judges and six commissioners, forming two sub-division courts of three, all of whom were experienced serjeants, barristers or special pleaders below the Bar. Cases were conducted by one commissioner, elected by ballot, accompanied by a registrar who took minutes of proceedings. Appeals were now assigned to a Court of Review, consisting of the chief judge or the three puisne judges, subject to appeal to the Lord Chancellor on matters of law and equity if one of the judges approved. Also, Brougham selected thirty official assignees, experienced as merchants, brokers or accountants, who were divided equally among the commissioners, to collect the bankrupts' assets. However, sale of the estates and the appointment of solicitors were left in the hands of assignees appointed by the creditors. Further clauses in the act legalised concerted bankruptcies, established salaries of court officials and stipulated penalties for bribery of £500 and exclusion from all government posts thereafter. The old London bankruptcy system was extended to provincial areas, where 140 courts were established, each consisting of five commissioners appointed from local barristers, solicitors and attorneys.[145]

Brougham's court was not novel in conception. As noted earlier, Burges had advocated a reduction of commissioners

---

144 Minutes of the Proceedings of the Court of Common Council, vols. 1826-9, pp. 17, 42, 54, 72; 1830-2, p. 176.

145 1, 2 Will. IV, c.56.

as early as 1783 and official assignees were the brain-child of Redesdale in 1808. Nor had Brougham intended to effect radical changes of legal principle. As he explained,

> I will reform the Bankrupt law, and the Bankruptcy tribunals, but I will reform the tribunals first; for the reformed tribunals will be themselves the instruments of reforming the law, by the information they will acquire and communicate, and the suggestions which experience will enable them to furnish.[146]

Thus, as Fane pointed out in 1838, Brougham was initially concerned with 'making the Court of Bankruptcy respectable, which it never can be so long as members of that Court appear degraded in the eyes of the profession.'[147] Despite the limited scope of the statute, Montagu, the most knowledgeable and experienced bankruptcy practitioner in the 1830s, praised it highly.[148] His only major complaints were the failures to eliminate the creditor's control of the adjudication of bankruptcy and to provide a viable process of appeal (the Court of Review was burdened with the old system of presenting evidence by affidavit).[149] Jeremy Bentham was more critical, referring to the new tribunal as a 'pickpocket court' because of the superfluous expense incurred by the appointment of four judges to do the work of one and of other redundant offices which merely increased the Lord Chancellor's patronage. He also condemned the

---

146 Quoted by R.G.C. Fane, A Letter Addressed to the Lord Viscount Melbourne (1837), p. 4.

147 Idem, Bankruptcy Reform (1838), p. 15.

148 B.P.P. Bankruptcy and Insolvency (1840), p. 74; B. Montagu, The New Bankruptcy Court Act (1831), p.v. Basil Montagu (1770-1851), second son of the Earl of Sandwich, friend of Mackintosh and Romilly, was called to the Bar in 1798, appointed commissioner in the old system (1806) and accountant of the new Bankruptcy Court.

149 The Court of Review was abolished in 1847, when its functions were transferred to one of the Vice-Chancellors (10, 11 Vict., c.102).

appeal procedure, the fee system (official assignees received one per cent of assets collected) and the imprecise procedural stipulations of the statute.[150]

Bentham's attack on Brougham was unjustified. Brougham had not attempted to solve all the problems at once. He had, in fact, reduced the personnel of bankruptcy tribunals, established a single, professional court, abolished some fees and facilitated official interference in the collection of assets. That the new system was popular with the trading community was conceded in 1842 by Lyndhurst, who pointed out that the official assignees had collected more than £2,000,000 of outstanding debts, including between £3-£400,000 of the debts of old commissions going back to 1810.[151] Nevertheless, it was inevitably incomplete and defects survived throughout the 1830s. These were catalogued by the Commissioners for Inquiring into Bankruptcy and Insolvency in 1840. They criticised the fact that many traders were still excluded from the bankruptcy process by inadequacies of legal definition, the difficulty of forcing a debtor to commit an act of bankruptcy before he had dissipated his property and the minimum petitioning creditor's debt of £100 which excluded smaller traders from the process. They also condemned the length of time for which a petitioning creditor controlled proceedings after striking a docket (fourteen days in London and twenty-eight elsewhere), the unnecessary use of fiat, bond and affidavit, the secret adjudication of bankruptcy, the creditors' control of the

---

150 'Observations on the Bankruptcy Court Bill, 1832,' in The Works of Jeremy Bentham (ed. J. Bowring), (1843), v, 565-71.

151 Hansard, P.D., 3s, 1842, lxv, 226; for the success of the new court, see also ibid., 1836, xxxv, 68, Lord Chancellor; 1838, xliii, 1250-1, Sir William Follett; 1841, lvi, 482, Benjamin Hawes; B.P.P. Bankruptcy and Insolvency (1840), p. 562, Memorial of City Merchants.

certificate and, especially, the corruption of country commissions.[152]

Many of the commission's proposals for bankruptcy improvement were effected two years later by Lord Campbell's Bankruptcy Law Amendment Act.[153] The jurisdiction of the court was extended in two ways. First, more 'non-traders' were added to the list of occupations which could use the process.[154] Second, the minimum debt which a petitioning creditor could claim in order to institute proceedings was lowered from £100 to £50 (or £70 for two claimants and £100 for three or more), thus allowing smaller traders to become bankrupt. The acts of bankruptcy, which were clearly specified, included non-payment of a debt within fourteen days of the creditor's demand and a new method of opening commissions was devised. The creditor could now file an affidavit, swearing that he was owed more than £50 by the trader, and send particulars of his demand to the trader. The court then issued a summons for the debtor to appear before it in order to confirm or deny the claim. If the defendant admitted liability, he filed a schedule confessing the debt and was allowed fifteen days to pay, after which the fiat was issued against him (if he denied liability, he filed a deposition for adjudication by the court). The fiat process itself was both cheapened, by dispensing with the bond, and strictly regulated: if a petitioning creditor failed to open the commission within three days of taking the fiat to court, the commission could be opened in the name of another creditor after two weeks. The act declared that bankruptcies were to be advertised in the Gazette only

---

152 Ibid., pp. vii-xxviii.

153 5, 6 Vict., c.122.

154 The new definition included alum-makers, apothecaries, auctioneers, brick-makers, coach-proprietors, cow-keepers, livery stable-keepers, market gardeners, millers and shipowners.

after the bankrupt had been notified of the proceedings and given five days to deny their validity. Other clauses granted the bankrupt protection from all legal processes for debt until his certificate of discharge (not, as before, until his final examination) and eliminated the use of fraud as a means of obtaining discharge by stipulating that the certificate would now be granted by the court, which could investigate the bankrupt's conduct before, as well as after, his failure. Objections made by creditors to the certificate were to be adjudicated by the court, which could annex conditions when granting it. Finally, the corruption which plagued country commissions was tackled by the establishment of district courts of bankruptcy, controlled by barristers or serjeants at law of seven years' standing, in Manchester, Leeds, Liverpool, Birmingham, Bristol, Exeter, and Newcastle-on-Tyne.[155]

Although this second bankruptcy statute was not introduced by Brougham, it was undoubtedly designed to extend the work which he had instituted ten years earlier. His intention had always been to effect changes in the law in the light of experience acquired in the working of the court and he gave both the principle and the detail of the bill his whole-hearted support.[156] To many commentators, its most important provisions were those extending the London system to country areas. This may be compared with the growth at this time of other provincial facilities, including joint-stock banks, stock exchanges in Liverpool, Manchester and Glasgow and, as will be shown later, county courts.

In the 1840s, Brougham promoted two further bankruptcy acts. The first, in 1842, allowed small traders and all non-traders to use the Bankruptcy Court in a more summary

---

155 For the location of the courts, see R.R. Dees, The Law and Practice under the Statute for the Relief of Insolvent Debtors (1843), p. xlv.

156 Hansard, P.D., 3s, 1842, lxii, 3.

process than had existed before.[157] Seven years later, he abolished the fiat and reduced the number of commissioners to four.[158]

The process of reform instituted by Brougham was cautious and pragmatic. Ten years after the eradication of the major administrative defects of the Bankruptcy Court the more obvious procedural and technical faults were attacked in the light of experience. In 1844, Eldon's biographer considered that Brougham's statute had 'so facilitated the dispatch of business and the recovery of dividends, that hardly any desirable object is now left unaffected in the Administration of Bankruptcy.'[159] This, of course, was going too far since even Brougham did not anticipate that the system would work perfectly. Its continued defects included the problem of expense, the difficulties experienced by the court in detecting fraud and the fact that the new district courts covered over-large geographical areas until their amalgamation with county courts in 1861.[160] Despite these defects, however, as Bennett Abrahall, a barrister, pointed out in 1859, most traders and lawyers considered it to be a vast improvement on its predecessor.[161] The major mercantile criticism of it was that the official assignees system took judicial control of the collection of estates too far.[162] In view of the mismanage-

---

157 See below, chapter II.

158 12, 13 Vict., c.106.

159 H. Twiss, Life of Lord Chancellor Eldon (1844), iii, 140.

160 R.G.C. Fane, Bankruptcy Law Reform (1848), pp. 16-17; Bankruptcy and Insolvency. By a Registrar of a District Court of Bankruptcy (Liverpool, 1847), p. 7.

161 Sir B.H. Abrahall, Bankruptcy Law Reform (1859), pp. 31-2.

162 See Fane, op.cit., p. 4; J. Rayner, Bankruptcy Law Reform (1859), p. 5.

ment and corruption which characterised the collection of estates by creditors before 1831, however, it is difficult to sympathise with the mercantile argument that they should control it again. The legal fraternity considered official assignees to be the cornerstone of Brougham's system. Indeed, Abrahall advocated an extension of their duties, because much of the unnecessary expense was incurred in the sale of the estate by solicitors appointed by the creditors themselves.[163]

It does not lie within the scope of this study to analyse in depth developments in the latter half of the nineteenth century. It is sufficient to note that in 1861 the Chancellor's jurisdiction was vested in the Bankruptcy Court and the trader/non-trader distinction terminated,[164] and that in 1869 Brougham's official assignees were abolished, being replaced by creditors' assignees or trustees supervised by a committee of inspection.[165] Not until Joseph Chamberlain was President of the Board of Trade was the folly of the latter statute rectified by the establishment of control over a debtor's property and creditors' interests by an official receiver.[166]

---

163 Abrahall, op. cit., p. 43.

164 24, 25 Vict., c.134.

165 32, 33 Vict., c.71.

166 46, 47 Vict., c.52 (1883); 53, 54 Vict., c.71 (1890).

CHAPTER II

THE INSOLVENCY LAWS

I

Josiah Dornford suggested, in 1786, that

> Debtors may be considered of three classes. The first under the description of Merchants and capital Traders. The second of Tradesmen, Mechanics and Artificers, in the middle walk of life. The third, of the lower orders of Journeymen, of Labourers and Domestics.[1]

In theory, the first category was subject to the Bankruptcy Court, the second to the insolvency process, and the third to the small debt courts. However, in practice, this neat classification was rapidly becoming obsolete at the end of the eighteenth century, when increased economic activity was blurring occupational boundaries. This was for three main reasons. First, the narrowness of the legal definition of 'trading' excluded from bankruptcy many occupations which might, realistically, have been included in it. Second, it was possible for some individuals who were specifically excluded to use the bankruptcy process by convincing the court that their collateral dealings constituted trading. Third, bankruptcy was a privilege exclusive to 'traders' of relative substance. The legal stipulation that the petitioning creditor must be owed at least £100 and the general expense of bankruptcy proceedings ensured that the insolvency courts were flooded with smaller traders.

For these reasons, any occupational analysis of defendants in the bankruptcy and insolvency courts reveals close parallels. Butchers, builders, farmers, innkeepers, tailors and victuallers were some of the occupations which

---

1 J. Dornford, Seven Letters upon the Present Mode of Arresting Debtors (1786), p. 9.

appeared in both. Table 2.1 examines the occupations and debts of 500 insolvents in 1814-15. Obviously, some of the categories were automatically excluded from the bankruptcy process: the professional, labouring and 'gentlemen' groups, for instance, were not considered to be traders. However, the majority of the occupations listed could and did appear in the Bankruptcy Court (as will be shown in chapter six). In some of these cases — especially the merchant group — imprisonment was clearly being used as an act of bankruptcy. In others, exclusion from bankruptcy is probably explained by the controversial nature of the occupation (notably the artisans and farmers) and, above all, by the size of the debts involved. Although the range of aggregate liabilities of all debtors in the table is broad, a minority owed fairly large amounts: nine per cent owed more than £1,000 and 25 per cent over £500. In the artisan and shopkeeper categories, these proportions are larger: 15 per cent of artisans and 31 per cent of shopkeepers owed more than £500. But in each case it seems likely that debts owed to individual creditors were small. Eighty-nine per cent of plaintiffs' claims against artisans were for less than £100 as were 83 per cent of those against shopkeepers. The evidence suggests therefore that, in cases involving occupations which were often interpreted as trading, the plaintiffs were unable to use the Bankruptcy Court either because their claims were too small or because the expense of that procedure did not warrant its application.

Twenty-five years later the Commissioners into Bankruptcy and Insolvency of 1840 noted that, despite the specific inclusion of many controversial occupations within the bankruptcy laws, the situation was similar. The 3,691 petitioners to the Insolvent Debtors Court in 1839 were composed of 1,056 non-traders, 2,388 traders whose estates were too small to use the bankruptcy process and 247 whose occupations were classified as 'doubtful.' The latter included 65 farmers, 42 surgeons, 40 attornies, 20 auctioneers, 19 market gardeners, 14 surveyors, 12 master mariners and 10 artists.[2] This evidence suggests again that, while bankruptcy statistics give an increasingly accurate picture of large trading failures in the first half of the nineteenth century (because of the statutory inclusion of controversial trades), they are not completely adequate since they exclude both small traders and certain types of occupation, notably in agriculture and the professions. This chapter examines the legal process to which these excluded debtors were subjected from three points of view. The next two sections explain its harshness towards the debtor, which resulted from both the summary nature of legal procedure and the inequities of the prison system. The fourth and fifth sections deal with the ways in which its worst features could be evaded because of loop-holes in the system and parliamentary interventions on behalf of the debtor. The final two sections discuss the movements for reform of the insolvency laws, which culminated in their wholesale reconstruction in the 1830s and 1840s.

II

In order to understand the nature of the insolvency process at the end of the eighteenth century it is necessary to trace briefly its origins, which were influenced greatly by the vested interests of the English legal fraternity.[3]

---

2 B.P.P. Bankruptcy and Insolvency (1840), pp. viii - ix.

3 The following account is based on E. Farley, Imprisonment for Debt (1788); J.F. Archbold, The Practice of the Court of King's Bench (1819); M. Hastings, The Court of Common Pleas in Fifteenth Century England (New York, 1947); M. Blatcher, 'Touching the Writ of Latitat: An Act "of No Great Moment",' in Elizabethan Government and Society (ed. S.T. Bindoff, J. Hurstfield and C.H. Williams), (1961), pp. 188-212.

Originally, the Court of Common Pleas alone was responsible for deciding pleas for debt between subject and subject. In the fourteenth and fifteenth centuries, however, its monopoly was challenged successfully for two reasons. First, the fact that its procedure by original writ was expensive, slow and cumbersome made plaintiffs amenable to alternative modes of action. Second, the other superior courts developed more expedient procedures based upon the long-established principle that any subject with a cause of action against an officer or person in custody of a court could open proceedings in that court. In the Court of King's Bench, which originally determined actions of trespass (involving criminal matters, fraud and breaches of the peace), procedure was by Bill of Middlesex, which ordered the sheriff of Middlesex (in which the court sat from the early fifteenth century on) to arrest the defendant. Such a summary process was necessitated by the nature of the crimes involved. If the sheriff could not find the defendant, a _latitat_ ('he lurks') was issued, ordering the sheriff of the appropriate county to bring him to court. This was justified by the number of offences committed in Middlesex by transient persons. As soon as the defendant was delivered to the court by this process, which was far easier and cheaper than Common Pleas' original writ, any other cause of action (e.g. debt) could be opened against him. In Henry VI's reign, it was decided that a defendant who had obtained bail was technically still in the court's custody. The process by bill which thus became possible in the King's Bench was as follows. The plaintiff filed a bill of complaint for trespass against the defendant, whom the sheriff of Middlesex then attempted to arrest by a Bill of Middlesex. If he failed, a _latitat_ was issued to the sheriff of another county and, when the defendant had been either committed or had obtained bail, the action of debt was opened against him. In the sixteenth century, Bills of Middlesex and _latitats_ alleging fictitious trespasses became common. In addition, latitats, containing both the Bill of Middlesex and the sheriff's reply ('non est inventus'), were used as first process in civil actions wherever the cases occurred. The Court of Exchequer had adopted a similar fiction in the fourteenth century by issuing its writ quominus, stating that the defendant had committed a misdeed against the plaintiff 'whereby he is less able' to pay his debt to the King. The defendant's plea that the plaintiff did not owe anything to the King, and that therefore the court had no jurisdiction in the matter, was ignored. As a result of these developments, the Court of Common Pleas suffered a considerable loss of business, most of which had been transferred to other courts by the middle of the seventeenth century. Consequently, Baron Guilford, appointed Lord Chief Justice in 1674, invented a similar writ of trespass quare clausum fregit for breaking the plaintiff's 'close, vi et armis,' based on Common Pleas' control of jurisdiction of trespass to land, which authorised a capias ordering the sheriff of the appropriate county to arrest the defendant. If he was not in that county, a testatum capias issued to another sheriff and, after appearance, the plaintiff could declare for debt.[4] All three courts avoided the regulation of 1662 - that processes which forced defendants to find £40 bail must stipulate the cause of action - by the use of the clause 'ac etiam; and also a bill for debt.'[5] A corollary of these developments was the abandonment, from the late sixteenth century on, of the original writ in all actions. The plaintiff, instead, began the action by taking out a judicial writ, ordering the sheriff to arrest the defendant,

---

4 R. North, Lives of the Norths (ed. A. Jessop), (1890), i, 128-31.

5 13 Car. II, c.2.

which like the *latitat* presupposed that the previous stages of procedure had been completed.[6]

As a result of these developments, the procedure for opening debt cases in the eighteenth century was simple.[7] Having taken out the appropriate process, the plaintiff's solicitor took it to the sheriff's office and obtained a warrant for arrest, at the cost of one shilling, which he handed to the sheriff's officer. The warrant stated the cause of action, the sum for which the defendant was to be held to bail, and the names of the plaintiff and the solicitor who had sued out the process. The sheriff's officer then arrested the defendant (any slight touch of the latter's body constituted the arrest), and took him either to his own house for twenty-four hours and then to gaol, or straight to gaol if the debtor refused to go to the officer's house.[8] As soon as the debtor was detained, the plaintiff made an affidavit of the cause of the action and sum specified in the writ. After twenty-four hours, the debtor was given the choice of paying the debt, paying bail or remaining in detention.

The bail procedure was rather complicated. Initially, the defendant could give the sheriff the names of two sureties who, by entering into a bond with the sheriff for twice the amount of the debt, guaranteed his appearance in court on the return day of the writ (usually in the same or

---

6 Debtors could be arrested on a *capias ad respondendum*, after an original writ, after 1352 (25 Ed. III, c.5).

7 The uniformity of process provided by these developments was recognised in the *Uniformity of Process Act* which instituted a single writ of summons for all personal actions (2 Will. IV, c.39).

8 These were called 'spunging-houses' because of the extortionate fees they charged.

the following legal term).[9] If no detainers had been lodged against him by other creditors he was allowed to go free on what was known as 'bail below.' On the return day, the appearance of the defendant was not made personally. If he was free on bail bond, appearance was effected by putting in and perfecting special 'bail above' in court. If he was in prison, the sheriff returned a writ stating that the defendant was in custody and the only way he could be discharged was by putting in and justifying special bail above. This, again, involved two sureties who undertook that, if the defendant was condemned in the action, he would satisfy the costs and condemnation or render himself to prison. As soon as special bail above had been justified, the bail below (that given to the sheriff) was terminated.

After the return of the writ, the plaintiff was required to deliver to the court or to the defendant, before the end of the following term, a declaration stating the cause of the action, to which the defendant must plead. Consequently, the defendant could lie in gaol on mesne process for months before the declaration was made and the case brought to trial.[10] Many plaintiffs procrastinated for as long as possible before making the declaration, because, after the case had been tried, they could be made to contribute to the cost of the debtor's subsistence in prison, under the Lords' Act of 1759 (so-called because it originated in the House of Lords).[11]

---

9 Bail was often hired from professional bailers. Because of the preponderance of Jews amongst them, this was called 'Jew bail.' Farley, op. cit., p. 34.

10 Approximate legal terms were: Hilary, 23 Jan. - 12 Feb.; Easter, 23 April - 18 May; Trinity, 25 May - 15 June; Michaelmas, 6 - 18 Nov.

11 See below, section IV.

Plaintiffs in non-bailable actions[12] or who did not wish to imprison their debtor before judgment used a serviceable process. In this, the creditor issued a writ commanding the debtor to appear in court on an appointed day. If the debtor did not appear, the plaintiff produced an affidavit, stating that the defendant had been served regularly, entered appearance for him, and proceeded as if the defendant were present in person.

When finally taken to court, the defendant made his plea to the action (cognovit actionem, general issue, special plea in bar, demurrer, issue of fact, etc.), after which the judge summarised the case and the jury decided if the defendant was liable or not. If he was found liable, the plaintiff issued a writ of execution within two terms. Unfortunately, until 1838[13] writs of execution limited the plaintiff's distraining power over the debtor's property,[14] excluding much of his land, stock in public funds, shares, negotiable instruments, bonds, bank notes, annuities and debts due. The immunity which this gave to the debtor's estate induced many creditors to resort to a capias ad satisfaciendum, by which the debtor, irrespective of the size of the debt, was gaoled until he relinquished sufficient property to pay it. This writ originated in the legal principle, established in Edward III's reign, that a defendant who could be imprisoned on mesne process was also liable to imprisonment on final process. The distinction between the two lies in the fact that, whereas mesne process

---

12 The minimum debt to which mesne process could be applied was £10 in superior and 40s. in inferior courts in 1725 (12 Geo. I, c.29), £10 in all courts in 1779 (19 Geo. III, c.70), £15 in 1811 (51 Geo. III, c.124) and £20 in 1827 (7, 8 Geo. IV, c.71).

13 1, 2 Vict., c.110.

14 In the case of a fieri facias, goods and chattels; a levari facias, goods and profits of land; an elegit, chattels and profits of half of land.

was designed to get the debtor to court, the final *capias* was designed to satisfy the debt, representing imprisonment for debt *per se*. Creditors gaoling their debtors in execution lost the right of execution against the debtors' property.[15] As a result, debtors in execution sometimes remained in prison for life. The effectiveness of the *capias ad satisfaciendum* - as a deterrent to non-payment and as an instrument of vengeance - accounts for the popularity of the courts at Westminster and the relative insignificance of local courts, which could only command distraint but not sale of the defendant's chattels.

In general, it seems that the majority of debtors in prison at any particular time during the late eighteenth and early nineteenth centuries had been put there by mesne process and were awaiting the trial of their cases. In 1792, for example, gaolers' returns to parliament indicated that 1,251 out of 1,957 debtors had been imprisoned on mesne process and the remaining 706 on final process (35 per cent).[16] Thirty years later, the situation was similar. Of 2,836 debtors in prison in England and Wales on 19 April 1826, 1,878 had been gaoled on mesne process and 958 on final process (34 per cent).[17] Some debtors were successively imprisoned by both procedures. This is exemplified by the experiences of 'Dr. Syntax,' the satirist. On 18 October 1785, he was taken into the custody of the sheriff of Middlesex for debt and one week later entered the King's Bench prison. His trial was held in the following January, when he was returned to the King's Bench 'in execution for the damages aforesaid, there to remain until he satisfy the said John Palmer.' In May 1787 he was released. On 4 May 1799, he was again detained, for want of

15 *J.H.C.*, 1792, lxvii, 644, Report on Debtors.

16 *Ibid.*, p. 647.

17 B.P.P. *Accounts and Papers* (1826-7), xix, 203-29.

bail, and tried on 13 May for a debt of £40.11.6d. After the trial, he was taken back to the King's Bench prison, where he remained until his death on 19 June 1823.[18]

III

It is undeniable therefore that the insolvency laws provided creditors with extremely rigorous powers over their debtors. In addition to being imprisoned at the mercy of their creditors, however, many debtors were punished further by the intolerable conditions to which they were subjected in the debtors prisons. As will be shown later, these conditions closely influenced the insolvency legislation of the eighteenth and early nineteenth centuries and it is necessary to examine them briefly in this section.

The problems which afflicted the prison system in the early eighteenth century were not, of course, new; penal abuses had been attacked for centuries.[19] Despite periodic legislation, however, the worst defects lived on. They included gaol fever, the physical suffering of the poorest prisoners in contrast to the relative comfort of the wealthier,[20] overcrowding and corrupt administration, which, as Oglethorpe's committee of inquiry pointed out in 1729, resulted from the feeble remuneration given to prison officials.[21] Towards the end of the century, the iniquities of the prison system and the plight of debtors were sub-

---

18 H.W. Hamilton, Dr. Syntax (1969), pp. 139, 202.

19 See, for example, W.L. Clay, The Prison Chaplain (Cambridge, 1861), pp. 1-39; W.E. Hooper, History of Newgate (1935), pp. 142-4; R.H. Condon, 'The Fleet Prison,' Hist. Today, xiv (1964), 454-6.

20 See M. Pitt, The Cry of the Oppressed (1696); The Piercing Cryes of the Poor and Miserable Prisoners for Debt (1714); cp. E. Hughes, North Country Life in the Eighteenth Century (Oxford, 1952,), i, 2.

21 Hansard, Parl. Hist., 1729, viii, 706.

jected to concerted humanitarian pressure. John Howard contended that the main evils were the retention in prison of inmates who could not afford to pay discharge fees, gaol fever and the general corruption of morals produced by idleness and bad company. His suggestions included the construction of better prison buildings with improved sanitation and medical facilities, the classification and segregation of prisoners according to offence, employment of prisoners, abolition of the tap, and appointment and close supervision of humane and active gaolers.[22] According to W.H. Render, Howard's investigations in the 1770s and 1780s marked the turning point when 'the nation was at once aroused to the fearful condition of its system of dealing with transgressors of the law, and the House of Commons set itself to the task of vigorous reform.'[23] This is correct in the sense that Howard's evidence sparked off the work of other reformers (including Alexander Popham, John Jebb, Josiah Dornford and, later, Lord Althorp and Elizabeth Fry) and a succession of prison statutes.[24] But progress was inordinately slow. In 1812, James Neild admitted that most prisons were still appalling.[25] That this verdict was particularly pertinent to London debtors prisons is revealed in the evidence presented to a series of parliamentary committees between 1810 and 1820. The abuses which they

---

22 J. Howard, <u>The State of Prisons</u> (3rd edn., 1784), pp. 25-31.

23 W.H. Render, <u>Through Prison Bars</u> (1894), p. 69.

24 E.g. 13 Geo. III, c.58 (1773), ordering the appointment of chaplains; 14 Geo III, c.59 (1774), concerning sanitation, medical attendance and segregation of the sexes; 24 Geo. III, s.2, c.54 (1784), ordering segregation of different types of prisoner and banning liquor and gambling; 31 Geo. III, c.96 (1791), attempting to regulate fees and prison administration.

25 Cited by A. Griffiths, <u>Chronicles of Newgate</u> (1884), ii, 148.

uncovered may be summarised as inequity, ill-health and immorality. To take inequity first. As a result of the fee system, the living conditions of debtors were determined by their financial status. As will be shown, debtors of sufficient wealth were allowed to live in luxury outside the walls of the Fleet and King's Bench prisons. Debtors living inside the Fleet, Newgate and the Marshalsea were housed either in the relatively comfortable Master's side or the more squalid Common side, according to the fees they could afford. In these prisons and the King's Bench, destitute debtors were isolated from the rest and allowed to use the begging grate.[26] The problem of ill-health, a product of overcrowding, was particularly acute in Newgate and King's Bench. Newgate, which could accommodate 110 debtors and 317 criminals, was, according to its surgeon, a health hazard when 500 prisoners were detained. In January 1813 it held 822.[27] The average debtor population of King's Bench was 700, despite the fact that it had been built to hold 220.[28] This and the absence of bedding, coals, blankets and medical attendance explains why 96 debtors died there between 1805 and 1815. The third problem - that of immorality - resulted from the unlimited sale of liquor and admission of loose women to the Fleet and King's Bench. Nicholas Nixon, the deputy warden, described 'scenes of riot, drunkenness and disorder' in the Fleet, which he considered 'the largest brothel in the metropolis.'[29] The revelry of the Fleet was more than matched by what the 1815 committee into debtors

---

26 B.P.P. [Report from the S.C. into King's Bench, Fleet and Marshalsea] Prisons (1814-15), [IV], pp. 4-23.

27 B.P.P. Report from the S.C. into the State of Gaols in the City of London (1813-14), IV, p. 3.

28 W.R. Minchin, The Present State of Debtor and Creditor Law (1812), p. 57.

29 B.P.P. Prisons (1814-15), pp. 21-2.

prisons called King's Bench's 'vice and debauchery' which also included drunkenness and prostitution.[30]

Clearly, these abuses show the ineffectuality of legislation pertaining to prison discipline. The basic reason for this, throughout the eighteenth century, was the fact that its administrative mechanism was insufficiently developed. As A. Griffiths says, the legislation failed because of

> the remoteness of the pressure it exercised. The onus for improvement lay upon the magistracy, the local authorities administering local funds, and they were not threatened with any particular penalties if they evaded or ignored the acts.31

As a result, many late eighteenth-century statutes merely attempted to enforce previous acts which had not been effected.[32] The solution to this problem had been advocated as early as 1702 when the Society for the Promotion of Christian Knowledge recommended the appointment of a committee, composed of aldermen, common councillors or members of the society, to visit prisons and ensure that regulations were being enforced.[33] In 1776, William Smith more clearly anticipated Bentham's idea of the inspector's role on a national scale:

> The law is not deficient; but all the acts of Parliament, rules of court, or orders of magistrates will not avail against the evasions, chicanery and oppressions of mercenary, avaricious and tyrannical gaolers, without inspectors frequently to go into every part of a gaol with ample powers to remedy every grievance, and an entire abolition . . . of all fees.34

---

30 Ibid., pp. 13-14.

31 Griffiths, op. cit., ii, 149-50.

32 E.g. 24 Geo. III, s.2, c.54 (1784); 29 Geo. III, c.67 (1789); 31 Geo. III, c.146 (1791).

33 See R.S. Hinde, The British Penal System (1951), pp. 21-6.

34 W. Smith, State of the Gaols in London (1776), p. 45.

Seventeen years later, Alexander Wedderburn reiterated Smith's plea for constant inspection of prisons and demanded that a general system of discipline and regulation be imposed on all prisons in the country.[35] Similarly, in 1815, a Commons committee stated that 'a mode of visitation going much farther than that which has hitherto been practised should be considered the duty of the visitors.'[36] Inspectors were not appointed, however, until 1835.[37]

Even if the magistracy had been uniformly diligent in the eighteenth century, it is unlikely that penal defects would have been eradicated, for the simple reason that the prisons were not large enough to house the number of debtors committed to them. This applies especially to the King's Bench. Although the problem had been eased in 1725 by the reduction of small debtors gaoled on mesne process, the prison was still said to be incapable of holding a third of its population of 657 in 1730.[38] Later in the eighteenth century, it is likely that this problem was exacerbated, throughout the prison system, by the rising tide of insolvency and criminal committals produced by the growth of population and of the economy as a whole. Unfortunately, statistics of total debtors gaoled in England and Wales in this period are not available. Returns made by gaolers to parliament in 1818, shown in Table 2.2, suggest that the number of imprisoned debtors rose sharply in the early nineteenth century, but the statistics are unsatisfactory because many provincial gaolers had no knowledge of committals prior to their appointments. The total of 8,238, in 1818, which is accurate, however, is more than three

---

35 Observations on the State of English Prisons by Lord Loughborough (1793), p. 8.

36 B.P.P. Prisons (1814-15), p. 15.

37 5, 6 Will. IV, c.38.

38 Hansard, Parl. Hist., 1730, viii, 808, Third Report on Gaols.

times the size of Howard's total for 1776 (2,437).[39] In the absence of aggregate statistics, committals to King's Bench may be used as a barometer of general trends which is probably reasonably accurate because of the size of the prison and the fact that it catered for debtors from all parts of the country. Annual committals, shown in Table 2.2, grew from an average 223 in the 1750s to 357 in the 1760s and 537 in the 1770s. Discounting the statistics for 1780-1, which are probably inflated as a result of the Gordon Riots,[40] the annual totals continued to rise in the 1780s (averaging 622), after which they declined slightly to 587 in the 1790s. The upward trend from the late 1760s is paralleled in bankruptcy statistics, although the latter do not flatten in the 1790s. Between 1800 and 1820, however, both series rise sharply, average annual bankruptcies increasing from 764 in the 1790s to 938 in the first decade of the nineteenth century and 1,664 in the second; King's Bench totals at the same dates rose from 587 to 753 and 1,414. In the first half of the 1820s, bankruptcies declined slightly (averaging 1,357 p.a.) and the increase in King's Bench committals slowed (1,684 p.a.), possibly as a result of the return to more stable, peacetime conditions. In the whole period 1750-1820, the average annual totals in both series increased more than six-fold, the sharpest rise occurring between 1800 and 1820. The major contrast between their respective growths is that the King's Bench series is apparently unresponsive to economic

---

39 Howard calculated 2,437 debtors in a prison population in England and Wales of 4,084 in 1776; 2,078 of 4,379 in 1779; and 2,197 of 4,439 in 1782. Howard, op.cit., pp. 17, 492.

40 The prison was fired during the riots (June 1780) and statutory permission for debtors to live at home during the two years rebuilding may have encouraged an influx of debtors to the prison (20 Geo. III, c.64; 21 Geo. III, c.1).

fluctuations while, as will be shown in chapter five, the bankruptcy series reacts sensitively to economic crises.

Statistics of criminal committals in England and Wales are available only from 1805, when they were roughly equal to the number of committals for debt (see Table 2.2). After that date, they rose sharply both quantitatively and in relation to the growth of population. The annual average rose from 4,801 between 1806 and 1810 to 6,657 between 1811 and 1815 (a proportion over the five years of one committal in 1,210 of the crime-committing population over the age of ten), 13,150 between 1821 and 1825 (one in 707), 20,746 from 1831 to 1835 (one in 513) and 27,894 from 1841 to 1845 (one in 442).[41] After about 1815 the number of criminal committals consistently outnumbered those for debt.

Inevitably, the massive increase of criminal committals and imprisoned debtors in the first third of the nineteenth century imposed a great strain upon the prison system, which was reconstructed from the mid-1830s on. In addition to administrative reforms, a large-scale building programme was instituted; by mid-century new prisons had been constructed at Brixton, Dartmoor, Holloway, Pentonville and Wandsworth. This was merely the latest of a series of alleviations of the problem. C.W. Everett, for instance, argues that after Cook's discoveries the need for a programme of prison building was obviated by transportation.[42] As the number of criminal committals rose, this ceased to provide the necessary relief; in the 1830s, when annual criminal committals averaged more than 20,000, the number transported averaged 1,658.[43] However, it may be suggested that, as long as half or even more of the prison population consisted of debtors, parliament was provided with a safety valve

---

41 B.P.P. Accounts and Papers (1850), xvii, 470.

42 C.W. Everett, Jeremy Bentham (1966), pp. 42-3.

43 Clay, op. cit., p. 85.

against overcrowding: the fact that many considered imprisonment an unenlightened method of dealing with debtors allowed parliament to release them periodically, as it could not release criminals.

IV

It has been shown that debtors in the eighteenth century were vulnerable to both legal oppression and extreme physical discomfort. Understandably, they exploited every opportunity to evade the detrimental consequences of imprisonment. This section examines some of the methods employed by debtors to evade punishment and parliamentary attempts to alleviate the worst features of the system. It will be apparent that the legal machinery, though in theory efficacious, was not consistently so in practice and that creditors as well as debtors had just cause to demand its reform.

Debtors were able to evade their liabilities in three main ways. The first - by fleeing the country - clearly defeated the whole purpose of mesne process, which was designed to prevent evasion of legal process. A statute passed in 1729 noted that fears of the 'miseries of a Gaol' had driven abroad 'great numbers of workmen skilful in the several Trades and Manufactures of this Kingdom, and also many able Seamen and Mariners' and offered immunity to imprisonment for all returning fugitives who had served a one-year apprenticeship or been employed in manufacturing for a year. A year later, it was said that 600 fugitives had returned to use the act.[44] In 1783 the Earl of Effingham, no doubt exaggerating, estimated that there were 13,000 fugitives from the debt laws; the fact that many were

---

44 Hansard, Parl. Hist., 1730, viii, 810. The act is 2 Geo. II, c.20.

'mechanics' was detrimental to the economy.[45] Second, so summary was the arrest procedure that debtors could anticipate and avoid it by themselves imprisoning their creditors for fictitious debts. The extent of this practice cannot be gauged but many contemporaries were familiar with it and the forms of the law made such counter-attack an obvious expedient.[46] The third method of evasion was a consequence of laxities in the prison system. Just as creditors could imprison their debtors for life, so too the latter could stay in prison and avoid ever having to pay their debts. Geoffrey Sykes, a special pleader in law, reckoned in 1819 that such malicious debtors far outnumbered vengeful creditors.[47] The practice was encouraged by the existence of the Rules in the Fleet and King's Bench, the only prisons with such royal, privileged precincts. The Rules were the areas around the prisons where debtors who could afford the fee and find good security for their debts were allowed to live in order to prevent overcrowding and illness within the prison walls.[48] Debtors who could not afford to live in the Rules were allowed out of the prisons on 'Day Rules,' on payment of a fee, in order to negotiate with their creditors.[49] Theoretically a justified institution, the Rules, like most privileges, succumbed to the prevalent venality. Debtors from all over England were said to remove themselves to the

---

45 Ibid., 1783, xxiii, 1099.

46 Farley, op. cit., p. 23; Minchin, op.cit., p. 6.

47 B.P.P. [Report from the S.C. ... into the law respecting] Insolvent Debtors (1819), [II], p. 84.

48 In the Fleet, the fee was 3% of the debt; in King's Bench, 8 guineas for the first £100 and 4 guineas for each additional £100.

49 Day Rules could be used three times between the start of each legal term. In the Fleet, the fee was 5s.; in King's Bench, 5s. for the first and 3s.10d. for the subsequent two days.

King's Bench by a habeas corpus in order to use them.[50] Richer debtors treated them as a place to establish new lodgings and a pleasant social life evolved, centred around the 'Belle Sauvage' public house and the 'London Coffee House' near the Fleet. As Burges said in 1790,

> Every man had it in his power to procure his being arrested, and might say "I like to live on Ludgate Hill; I think it the pleasantest part of London"; or he might carry on any trade at St. George's Fields, to the amount of many thousands of pounds, and set his creditors to utter defiance, by being able to tell them, "I am in prison already; I choose to live there, and you may do your worst, I won't pay you a shilling."[51]

The Rules were rarely subject to strict supervision. Some debtors evidently left them during the long vacation to go hunting and shooting,[52] and it was alleged in 1816 that a Mr. Best had been in the Rules for ten years spending £2,000 p.a. 'and he is now living within the Rules, keeping his horses and servants, going out to the seaside for a fortnight at a time.'[53] William Combe, between 1803 and 1808, violated regulations nightly by walking to the City and working as editor of The Times. After five years the Marshal of the King's Bench moved him back to the prison and he lost his job.[54] Such violation of the regulations seems to have been fairly typical since Lord Ellenborough was reported to have refused an application for an extension of the Rules on the grounds that 'to his certain knowledge the

---

50 J. Britton, Picture of London (27th edn., 1826), p. 229.

51 Hansard, Parl. Hist., 1790, xxviii, 383.

52 B.P.P. Insolvent Debtors (1819), p. 112, Henry Dance, a solicitor.

53 B.P.P. [Report from the S.C. . . . into Acts for the Relief of] Insolvent Debtors (1816), [IV], p. 21, Peter Laurie, a sadler.

54 H.W. Hamilton, Dr. Syntax (1969), pp. 228, 234-5.

Rules already extended to the East Indies.'[55] The largest influx of debtors to the Rules usually occurred in November, during the Michaelmas term. Between 1814 and 1826, the average Rules population during each November was 102.[56]

This was one aspect of the softening of a harsh corpus of law in practice. Another was parliamentary interference. Throughout the eighteenth and early nineteenth centuries, parliament sought to ease the suffering especially of the smallest debtors. As was noted in section two of this chapter, the minimum debt to which mesne process could be applied was raised in 1725 (£10 in superior courts and 40s. in inferior courts), 1779 (£10 in all courts), 1811 (£15) and 1827 (£20). In addition, parliament provided facilities for the release of imprisoned debtors in two series of statutes. The first, starting in 1729,[57] allowed a debtor imprisoned in execution for under £100 to present a schedule of effects to the court which gaoled him and notice of proceedings to each creditor and, fourteen days later, to petition the court, which summoned and examined the creditors. If the creditors were satisfied with the debtor's schedule, the court could order the appointment of assignees, as in bankruptcy, to gather and divide the estate, the debtor was released and could not be arrested again for the same debts. But, if any one creditor objected, the debtor was obliged to stay in prison providing that the creditor paid his 'groats' of 2s.4d. per week (raised to 3s.6d. by 37 Geo. III, c.85). As soon as the creditor failed to pay groats the debtor was released. The

---

55 Britton, op. cit., p. 230. In fact, the Fleet Rules extended up part of Fleet Market and Ludgate Hill, covering 3/4 square mile; those of King's Bench encompassed St. George's Fields and most of the Borough.

56 B.P.P. Accounts and Papers (1826-7), xix, 351-3, 363.

57 2 Geo. II, c.22.

initial statute of 1729 was made permanent by the Lords' Act (1759)[58] which operated until 1823. After 1786, it was applied to debtors owing under £200 and, after 1793, to those under £300.[59] Although the Lords' Act released many debtors, the procedure was not a solution to the problem of lengthy imprisonment both because creditors often refused discharge and because, as John Howard pointed out in 1784, most debtors could not afford the costs of two or three guineas to obtain relief under the act.[60]

Parliament's second series of statutes - the temporary insolvent debtors acts - was rather more effective. These ordered sheriffs or gaolers to send to the justices of the peace at the next Quarter Sessions alphabetical lists of debtors who had been in gaol for over six months for debts beneath specified amounts and to pin duplicate lists on the prison gates. The prisoner then petitioned for release, inserted notice of proceedings in the London Gazette, delivered a copy of his estate to the Quarter Sessions and, in court, took an oath to the veracity of the schedule and to the fact that he had been in gaol for over six months. If the oath appeared unimpeachable, the debtor was discharged and could not be arrested again for debts contracted before he was gaoled. His subsequently-acquired property, however, was liable to further executions to satisfy former debts.

It is tempting to draw parallels between these acts and bankruptcy legislation in the eighteenth century, since both showed an awareness that financial ruin could result from misfortune as well as profligacy. Statutory justification of the earlier acts was fairly consistent, adhering to the preamble of the 1725 act:

---

58 32 Geo. II, c.28.

59 26 Geo. III, c.44; 33 Geo. III, c.5.

60 Howard, op. cit., p. 5.

> Whereas many persons, by losses and other misfortunes, are rendered uncapable of paying their whole debts; and though they are willing to make the utmost satisfaction they can, are nevertheless detained in prison by their creditors; and whereas such unhappy Debtors have always been deemed the proper Object of Public Compassion, and by several Acts of Parliament have been discharged . . .[61]

The analogy, however, can be pressed too far, for three reasons. First, while parliament was prepared to free debtors from prison, it made no provision for releasing them from their debts. Second, although the maximum limit of debts to which the acts applied was raised throughout the eighteenth century to include most debtors, the largest debtors were always excluded.[62] Third, unlike the bankruptcy laws, insolvency legislation was not designed to provide permanent facilities for release of debtors and was intermittent. Fifteen acts were passed between the first in Charles II's reign[63] and 1760, nine between 1760 and 1781, none from 1781 to 1794, and seven between 1794 and 1811. Indeed, far from representing a consistent policy of relieving unfortunate debtors, the acts, especially in the second half of the century, were usually passed as ad hoc solutions to temporary problems. A minor example is that of 1761, which was a response to the need for soldiers and sailors in the Seven Years War.[64] Most of the later acts, however, were designed simply to alleviate overcrowding in the prison system. From the 1760s on, this was often stated

---

61 11 Geo. I, c.21.

62 The maximum limit was raised from £100 to £500 in 1729 (2 Geo. II, c.20), £1,000 in 1761 (1 Geo. III, c.17), £2,000 in 1774 (14 Geo. III, c.77), returning to £1,000 after 1774 and rising to £1,200 in 1797 (37 Geo. III, c.115). Debtors owing more than the limit could be released only with the creditors' consent.

63 22, 23 Car. II, c.20.

64 1 Geo. III, c.17.

bluntly in the preambles, which were similar to that of the 1806 act:

> Notwithstanding the great Prejudice and Detriment which occasional Acts of Insolvency may produce to Trade and Credit, it may be convenient in the present crowded state of the prisons and gaols in England and Wales, that some of the prisoners confined therein, truly surrendering their effects to their creditors, should be liberated.[65]

The purpose of the temporary legislation therefore was to ameliorate prison conditions by releasing debtors who were victims of economic misfortune. In intention the system was admirable. It fell down, however, on a number of counts. Having obtained the right to be discharged under an act, many poorer debtors were not released because they were unable to pay their gaolers' fees.[66] In addition, the system failed to distinguish victims of financial distress from the less honest debtors and the self-seekers who went to gaol simply to take advantage of an imminent act. It was common knowledge that the periodic influxes of debtors into prison were the result of newspaper and other reports that parliament was contemplating a temporary insolvency bill.[67] Further, the system made a mockery of the law. Burges argued in 1783 that 'nothing can be stronger proof of the inexpediency of the practice of imprisonment for debt than the introduction of these occasional laws.' If, he said, imprisonment for debt was illegal, no man could commit another to gaol and insolvency acts were nugatory; if imprisonment for debt was legal, the insolvency acts were

---

65 46 Geo. III, c.108.

66 J. Neild, Account of the Society for the Discharge and Relief of Persons Imprisoned for Small Debts (1802), p. 297.

67 See Hansard, Parl. Hist., 1783, xxiii, 110, Earl Bathurst; 1806, vii, 146, Ellenborough.

unjust.[68] Thomas MacDonald, a barrister, agreed with Burges, in 1791, and noted the irony of the system: 'The laws of civil imprisonment strike promiscuously at all, least they should miss the guilty; and acts of insolvency operate indiscriminately in favour of all, least they should miss the innocent.'[69] The only plausible justification of such acts was Lord Holland's assertion that innocence should not be punished because guilt was confounded with it.[70] This, however, was to accept, perhaps incorrectly, the predominance of the innocent over the fraudulent debtor. It also indicates how far parliament was swayed by humanitarian pressure for, as Lord Mansfield pointed out in 1781, the acts were the product of 'mistaken compassion which . . . got such possession of the minds of men, that the edge of the law was frequently turned against the honest and deserving creditor in order to protect . . . the fraudulent debtor.'[71]

V

So far we have examined ways in which some debtors avoided being imprisoned and others obtained relief from their incarceration. It is clear that for less fortunate debtors discharge could not be guaranteed by either the Lords' Act or the temporary insolvency acts. Towards the end of the eighteenth century, when the problem of prison conditions was becoming increasingly acute, private philanthropy sought to relieve the poorest debtors. The

---

68 Sir J.B. Burges, Considerations on the Law of Insolvency (1783), pp. 177-8.

69 T. MacDonald, A Treatise on Civil Imprisonment (1791), p. 118.

70 Hansard, P.D., 1806, vii, 149.

71 Hansard, Parl. Hist., 1781, xxii, 628-9.

most effective effort in this direction was the Society for the Discharge and Relief of Persons imprisoned for Small Debts (or Thatched House Society),[72] of which the Earl of Romney was president and James Neild treasurer. Founded in 1772 on the strength of £81.11.0d. collected after two sermons, and existing on annual benefactions of about £1,800, its object was to release unfortunate debtors: 'they shall be persons actually imprisoned, whose respective debts, or the composition for whose debts, shall not exceed the sum of £10,' with preference given to the old and to those with large families.[73] Between 1772 and 1802, 19,063 debtors, 11,399 wives and 32,871 children were discharged at an average cost per debtor of £2.11.5-1/2d.[74] The necessity of this type of work is emphasised by Lord Moira's estimate that, of the seven hundred released by the society each year, 130 were unable to pay the costs of suing for their groats under the Lords' Act, and about 50 could not afford to sue for the supersedeas to which they were entitled.[75]

In view of parliamentary and private attempts to release them, it may be asked, finally, how long debtors remained in prison at the turn of the nineteenth century. It is indisputable that some were incarcerated for years, as gaolers' returns to parliament in 1792 indicate (see Table 2.3). In some cases, creditors refused to grant discharge under the Lords' Act or to agree to compositions proposed by the Thatched House Society; the debts of others were too large to use either the Lords' Act or insolvency acts; some were unable to pay gaolers' fees for discharge; and others

---

72 Two smaller debtors relief societies were The Philanthropic Society and the Society at the Sign of the Blind Beggar.

73 Neild, _op. cit_., p. 32.

74 _Ibid_., pp. 354-5.

75 Hansard, _P.D._, 1808, x, 1069.

stayed in gaol, or in the Rules, voluntarily. But lengthy imprisonment was probably not the norm. It is true that, in periods when no insolvency act was passed, some stayed in gaol for years. Of a sample of 300 debtors imprisoned in 1785 (nine years before an act), for example, 57 (19 per cent) were incarcerated for more than a year, including 14 for more than two years and two for more than four (these were gaoled for nine and eleven years respectively).[76] These debtors were eventually discharged either by their creditors or by the Lords' Act. The remaining 81 per cent were released within a year and 50 per cent within six months, generally by their plaintiffs, the Lords' Act or bail. A similar sample for 1800 is instructive since an insolvency act was passed in August 1801. Of the 300 debtors in the sample, 35 per cent were released by the act after staying in gaol for more than a year in anticipation of it. The remaining debtors were released by the other channels (especially by plaintiff). Only two debtors who stayed in gaol for more than a year failed to use the act.[77] Generally, this evidence suggests that, when no insolvency act was passed, a minority of debtors stayed in prison for a long time; when the acts were passed, most debtors could obtain their discharge. This is confirmed by evidence given to the 1816 committee on the insolvency laws by Nicholas Nixon, deputy warden of the Fleet, and by Bernard Brooshooft, deputy marshal of King's Bench, about the length of imprisonment in the first decade of the nineteenth century, when such acts were passed frequently. Nixon considered that most of the debtors who stayed in gaol for lengthy periods did so voluntarily.[78] When asked whether he

---

76 King's Bench Commitment Books, P.R.O. Pris. 4, No. 10, 1 Jan. - 28 July 1785.

77 Ibid., No. 16, 1 Jan. - 20 July 1800.

78 B.P.P. Insolvent Debtors (1816), p. 47.

knew of any debtors confined for a long time at the mercy of their creditors, Brooshooft replied: 'Between the times of the Insolvency Acts passing no doubt of it; but they have been so frequent of late years, we could hardly call it a long imprisonment, unless where the sum was beyond the limits of the Act.'[79]

VI

Agitation for reform of the debt laws in the latter half of the eighteenth century was closely influenced by the changing political climate. In the 1760s and 1770s, much of the agitation stemmed from the liberal, constitutional ideas of the Wilkite and pro-American groups outside parliament, in whose diatribes legal and penal reform was associated with constitutional theories. Major John Cartwright, John Jebb and Richard Price were all enthusiastic advocates of a more enlightened legal code and John Howard owed much to the latter two.[80] This is not surprising since the severity and arbitrariness of the legal and penal systems seemed, to many, just as much a violation of constitutional 'fundamentals' as George III's alleged interference in politics. The analogy of imprisonment for debt and general warrants was frequently drawn. In 1788, for example, Edward Farley considered that

> The great national evil of imprisonment for debt . . . . calls aloud for the exertion of every independent mind to restore the constitution to its original purity, to reconcile the interests of the creditor with the personal liberty of the debtor, and to give the blessings of a free constitution equally alike to all the subjects of the British Empire.

Farley went on to say that his criticisms of the debt laws had received such general approbation that he would perse-

---

79 Ibid., p. 50.

80 See C. Robbins, The Eighteenth Century Commonwealthman (New York, 1968), pp. 369-71.

vere 'in hopes that, like Mr. Wilkes, in the case of General Warrants, I may see that power annihilated, which is contrary to those laws handed down to us by our glorious ancestors, and which it is our duty to leave uncorrupted to our posterity.'[81] Farley's polemic echoes the popular constitutionalism of the latter half of the eighteenth century. The association in radical minds of imprisonment for debt and other constitutional abuses was reflected, perhaps, in the Gordon Riots and, certainly, in the ultra-Jacobin agitation against debtors prisons in 1816, when they were evocatively called 'Bastiles.'[82] Just as, in the latter case, imprisoned debtors rallied to the standard of political and constitutional agitation so too, throughout the late eighteenth and early nineteenth centuries, they periodically adopted violent tactics to escape their constraint. A statute of 1772, for example, noted that debtors in the King's Bench 'have lately unwarrantably, and without colour of law, conceived that Imprisonment for Debt at the suit of a subject was contrary to the law, and have therefore formed many dangerous schemes to set themselves at liberty.' On 19 November 1770 and 13 May 1771, sixty and one hundred prisoners respectively had broken out of prison using fire-arms.[83]

---

81 Farley, op. cit., pp. i-ii.

82 Rudé argues that the Gordon Riots were motivated by 'a groping desire to settle accounts with the rich . . . and to achieve some rough kind of social justice.' It is possible that the preponderance of debtors amongst the released prisoners indicates a desire to redress legal injustice. G.F.E. Rudé, 'The Gordon Riots: A Study of the Rioters and their Victims,' T.R.H.S., 5s, vi (1955), 93-114; for 1816, see E.P. Thompson, The Making of the English Working Class (2nd edn., 1968), p. 692.

83 13 Geo. III, c.23.

Similarly, in 1785, many prisoners were convicted for attempting to blow up the prison walls.[84]

However, like the Wilkite movement, which dissolved fruitlessly in the 1770s, arguments like Farley's had little impact upon a legislature whose willingness to tamper with the law was at best mild.[85] On the question of debt in the eighteenth century this may be explained by two factors. First, society was not yet ready for radical change. As W.L. Clay says, during a talk on the Lords' Act of 1759, 'Dr. Johnson swung some bludgeon logic at the folly of wholesale imprisonment for debt; but his notions were far too big for that generation.'[86] Second, important political groups had a vested interest in opposing reform. J. Brooke considers that 'the problem of imprisonment for debt was never tackled as a whole: there was too much opposition from the commercial interests for any attempt at changing the system to stand much chance of success, and all that could be done was to pass periodical acts, often in the teeth of strong opposition, for the relief of insolvent debtors.'[87] This was doubly unfortunate because, as early as 1783, Burges, as in the field of bankruptcy, had analysed the principle and practice of imprisonment for debt and suggested practical remedies which would have been useful for creditors as a class. His major criticism of the debt laws in general was levelled at the 'unjust and impolitic Distinction between Debtors Bankrupt and Not Bankrupt,' since non-payment of debt was just as much an offence when

---

84 Their convictions are recorded in P.R.O. Pris. 4, No. 10.

85 For the contrast between the radical ambitions of the agitators and the mildness of their parliamentary allies, see Robbins, op. cit., p. 376.

86 W.L. Clay, The Prison Chaplain (Cambridge, 1861), p. 39.

87 J. Brooke, The House of Commons, 1754-1790: Introductory Survey (Oxford, 1968), p. 267.

committed by a trader or non-trader.[88] He also condemned the inconsistency of the laws in practice: 'The honest Insolvent is permitted to be a victim while the dishonest Bankrupt triumphs in his uncorrected villainy, and insults those laws which he glories in having evaded.'[89] In the system which he advocated - the Court of Commissioners of Insolvency - no person, trader or non-trader, would be liable to imprisonment for debt. When the creditor opened proceedings in the new court, the commissioner would issue one warrant to a messenger, who would occupy the defendant's house and supervise his property, and another to the defendant, enjoining him to attend a hearing and defend himself against the charge. If the debt was proved, a warrant would be issued for the seizure of the debtor's property, all of which would be liable, the case would be advertised in the Gazette and three meetings would be arranged as in bankruptcy.[90]

After his election to parliament in 1787, Burges, conscious of the strong legal resistance to radical change, attempted limited reforms, designed to make mesne process more speedy and more certain, to ensure that innocent debtors were not gaoled for long before their cases were heard, and to apply the Lords' Act to all debtors, not only those gaoled in execution. His suggestions, however, were resisted by Thurlow in the Lords. Other attempts to reform mesne process, by Moira in 1793 and 1808 and by Stanhope in 1814, were opposed by Ellenborough and rejected. Similarly, Lord Holland's attempt, in 1806, to give creditors the right to acquire the whole of a debtor's present and future

---

88 Burges, op. cit., pp. 320, 342.

89 Ibid., p. 316.

90 Ibid., pp. 370-90.

property was defeated in the Lords.[91] The principal reason for the resistance was that, although individual politicians appreciated that legislative interference alone could reform the debt laws, the 'correct' path to reform was difficult to find. Some politicians suggested that, as insolvency was no crime in itself, the presupposition of the law was that every imprisoned debtor was solvent and had been gaoled for deception. Moira, for example, recommended in 1793 that 'If the debtor is guilty of fraud, punish him as a fraudulent agent; if not guilty of a fraud, do not punish insolvency as a crime which should rather be commiserated as a misfortune. To punish insolvency as criminal is to confound all moral distinctions.'[92] However, in contemporary minds the debt problem was more difficult than this. How could one recognise a fraudulent debtor? What was an unfortunate one? What was dishonesty? Lord Ongley reckoned that nineteen out of every twenty debtors in gaol were fraudulent and would have no scruples about gaining liberty through perjury.[93] The difficulty of choosing an appropriate approach rendered any positive action difficult. Samuel Romilly's response in 1807 to a petition from the King's Bench prison, requesting that he bring a bill to revise the laws, reflects the frustration in legal minds:

> I have no intention whatever to bring in a Bill on the subject. I think the law, as it at present stands, very defective and oppressive. I have long thought it so; but I have not been able to discover the proper remedy for those defects, and for that oppression.94

91 For Burges, Hansard Parl. Hist.., 1788, xxvii, 153-5, 547-50; 1790, xxviii, 381-2; for Moira, ibid., 1793, xxx, 647-8; P.D. x, 1068-70; for Stanhope, ibid., 1814, xxvii, 618, 739-40, 959-62; for Holland, ibid., 1806, vii, 148-50.

92 Hansard, Parl. Hist., 1793, xxx, 647.

93 Ibid., 1780, xx, 1404.

94 Memoirs of the Life of Sir Samuel Romilly (ed. by his Sons), (1840), ii, 203-4.

Romilly's caution was typical of contemporary unwillingness to tamper with the issue of legal principle.

Although the legal hierarchy resisted fundamental changes in the law, it did accede reluctantly to humanitarian measures designed to alleviate the worst consequences of imprisonment for debt. In addition to the series of temporary insolvency acts in the first decade of the nineteenth century, parliament passed three permanent relief measures. In 1808, prisoners owing under £20 who had been in gaol for a year were allowed to apply to the courts of Westminster for discharge.[95] Three years later, the minimum debt to which mesne process could be applied was raised from £10 to £15.[96] The third statute - Lord Redesdale's Act for the Relief of Insolvent Debtors in 1813[97] - shows the small extent to which the Benthamite, or indeed any other, impulse to study the principles of the debt laws had yet affected the legislature. The act was far less ambitious than the proposals of Burges and Stanhope for abolishing imprisonment for debt. It established a permanent Insolvent Debtors Court in Portugal Street, Lincoln's Inn Fields, with one judge, to whom debtors who had been imprisoned 'upon any process whatsoever issuing from any court whatsoever, for or by reason of any Debt . . . and who shall have been in actual custody upon some process for some or one of the said Debts during the span of three calendar months' could petition for discharge. The debtor was required to surrender all possessions except clothes, bedding, working tools and implements to the value of £20. A copy of his petition and schedule of effects was circulated amongst his creditors unless they were numerous, in which case notice of the petition was inserted in the

---

95 48 Geo. III, c.123.

96 51 Geo. III, c.124.

97 53 Geo. III, c.102.

London Gazette or two or more newspapers designated by the court. If the creditors could justify their opposition to discharge, the court remanded the debtor. If they could not, he was released, assignees were appointed to supervise his books and judgment was entered against his future estate, which was liable. If, within the ensuing year, creditors could prove that the discharge had been obtained fraudulently, the court was empowered to void it. Similarly, if creditors could prove that a released debtor could pay his debts but did not, discharge was to be revoked. Apart from these two qualifications, a discharged debtor could not be arrested again for the same debts. In effect, the act represented an extension of the principles which underlay the insolvent debtors acts and Lords' Act. Indeed, four years earlier, Redesdale had stated that his intention was to pass 'a sort of perpetual insolvency bill.'[98] It thus marked a watershed in the development of the debt laws, diminishing the draconic power of creditor over debtor, who was now assured of relief after three months if he could afford to sue for it and prove that no fraud had been committed.

The objects of Redesdale's act were to establish the cessio bonorum principle (that, on ceding his property, an honest debtor would be liable for discharge) and to ensure that no debtors would remain in gaol for life. In practice, the new system was at once 'universally reprobated as being ruinous to trade and public credit.'[99] It was pointed out that the creditor was given no opportunity of scrutinising his debtor's schedule of effects (which was presented at the end of three months in gaol) and that the debtor was provided with no incentive to pay large dividends or even to

98 Hansard, P.D., 1809, xiv, 889.

99 E. Christian, The Origin . . . of the Bankrupt Laws (2nd edn., 1818), ii, 530.

honour his liabilities after liberation.[100] In addition, it was still not possible for creditors to coerce debtors into using the act and, even if it had been, the volume of work thrust upon the court (over three thousand cases annually) was too great a burden.[101] Witnesses before a parliamentary inquiry into the debt laws in 1816 unanimously condemned the new system on the grounds that it encouraged debtors to avoid their liabilities by going to prison and using what became known as ' a security on Sergeant Runnington' (the commissioner of the court).[102] Dividends (if any) under the procedure were so minute as to mock their recipients since debtors were more concerned about paying off debts contracted after their discharge than in satisfying previous liabilities.[103] Between 1813 and 1816, debts of £5,597,859 produced a mere £1,460.[104] The effect of the new system on trade was considered disastrous, as tradesmen allegedly reduced the credit which they gave.[105] Peter Laurie, an Oxford Street sadler, estimated that, because so many people now refused to pay for goods, prices had risen ten per cent for those who did.[106] It was even reckoned that 'unless some modification took place in this law, there would be an end of the trade of this country altogether.'[107] It is interesting that the committee's conclusion that the act

---

100 Hansard, *P.D.*, 1813, xxvii, 233, John Lockhart.

101 *Ibid*., 1819, xxxix, 1010-11, Robert Waithman.

102 B.P.P. *Insolvent Debtors* (1816), p. 34, Samuel Oliver, a barrister.

103 *Ibid*., p. 21, Peter Laurie.

104 Hansard, *P.D.*, 1816, xxxii, 455, Lockhart.

105 B.P.P. *Insolvent Debtors* (1816), p. 16, Waithman; p. 43, James Punton, an attorney; Hansard, *P.D.*, 1815, xxx, 495, Mr. Sergeant Best.

106 B.P.P. *Insolvent Debtors* (1816), p. 21.

107 Hansard, *P.D.*, 1816, xxxiii, 287, Lockhart.

should be suspended and a new one prepared was not reported to parliament at the insistence of Romilly who argued that 'if it were repealed, it is quite certain that no other insolvent debtors act, however free from the defects of the present act, or however perfect, would have a chance of being passed.'[108] Instead, the committee recommended that another investigation should be conducted to consider alterations in the law and, in the meantime, a bill should be introduced to enable the commissioner to refuse discharge to debtors who had contracted debts rashly or squandered property.[109] The subsequent statute, stipulating that such debtors could not be discharged for five years unless all creditors consented, had little effect because its punitive clauses were too severe.[110] The fact that Runnington himself was loathe to apply them contributed to the notorious inconsistency of the court when dealing with dishonest practices.[111]

The facilities which the court provided for the release of debtors are reflected in the change, after 1813, in their mode of obtaining discharge. Whereas between 1798 and 1813 23 per cent of debtors had been released from the King's Bench and Fleet prisons by insolvency acts, 50 per cent were freed by the Insolvency Court between 1814 and 1818.[112] Analysis of a sample of 300 debtors committed to King's Bench in 1815 indicates that 144 used the Insolvency Court; 118 of these were released within six months of committal and 24 within a year. Of all debtors in the sample only ten

---

108 Memoirs of the Life of Sir Samuel Romilly, op. cit., iii, 252.

109 B.P.P. Insolvent Debtors (1816), p. 4.

110 56 Geo. III, c.102.

111 B.P.P. Insolvent Debtors (1819), p. 145, Runnington; cf. ibid., p. 162, George Heath, a barrister.

112 B.P.P. Accounts and Papers (1819), xvii, 163, 172.

stayed in gaol for more than a year.[113] This contrasts sharply with the 1785 and 1800 samples, examined earlier, in which 19 and 36 per cent respectively were gaoled for more than a year. The difference is, clearly, explained by the fact that, whereas before 1813 the modes of discharge were uncertain, Redesdale's court gave most debtors the guarantee of a speedy release. It did not, however, discharge every debtor automatically and a small number stayed in gaol for a long time after 1813, for three reasons. First, some debtors were not allowed to apply to the court (offenders against the revenue laws, crown debtors and prisoners in the Rules). Second, some debtors were remanded by the court for fraud committed either before committal or in the first year after discharge. As noted, this group was not large.[114] Third, some debtors remained in prison voluntarily, not wishing to forfeit their property in the court. This practice, encouraged in the Fleet and King's Bench by the luxury of the Rules, was said to be carried on in the late 1820s 'to a most scandalous extent.'[115] No debtor after 1813, however, could be kept in prison for a long time at the whim of a vengeful creditor.[116]

In view of their loss of power, it is scarcely surprising that traders put pressure upon parliament to reform the system, inducing the formation of another select

---

113 P.R.O. Pris. 4, No. 28, 11 April - 2 June 1815.

114 In its first four years, the court discharged 8,634 and remanded 411, B.P.P. Accounts and Papers (1817), xvi, 91-2.

115 Hansard, P.D., 2s, 1830, xxiv, 227, Waithman.

116 B.P.P. Insolvent Debtors (1816), pp. 46-50, Nicholas Nixon, Bernard Brooshooft. The poorest debtors used the court at the expense of the Thatched House Society (ibid., p. 34, James Nicholls, solicitor to the society).

committee on the debt laws in 1819.[117] This committee expressed approbation of the cessio bonorum principle of the law but criticised the procedure, fee system and small size of the Insolvent Debtors Court.[118] Its recommendations were effected in 1820, when Lord Althorp's Act for the Relief of Insolvent Debtors appointed a new court, in place of Redesdale's, consisting of three commissioners (barristers). In the new system, the debtor filed a petition for discharge within two weeks of arrest and was immediately ordered to deliver a schedule of debts and assets to the court. The petition was advertised in the London Gazette, after which creditors met to file claims and examine the veracity of his statements. Creditors could oppose discharge and, if fraud was discovered, the debtor's term of imprisonment could be extended for up to three years. The court sat twice a week and no fees were charged. Assignees were appointed to sell the debtor's effects and pay dividends.[119] In fact, Althorp's act was by no means as radical as he had intended. Because of opposition to his bill in the Lords, he had been obliged to dispense with two clauses: one empowering creditors to compel debtors to use the court and the other obliging debtors to sell their real property and divide the proceeds amongst their creditors. Nevertheless, in theory at least, the new act secured great gains, since the debtor's affairs could now be examined before his final examination and creditors could oppose his discharge.

In practice, however, Althorp's act failed to cure the faults of the insolvency system because the court was still unable to detect fraud. Many debtors in the 1820s underwent collusive arrests in order to use it.[120] Even Althorp

---

117 For petitions from traders, Hansard, P.D., 1816, xxxii, 349, Hart-Davis; xxxiii, 455, Brougham; 1819, xxxix, 515, Hart-Davis; 934, Brougham; 180, Waithman.

118 B.P.P. Insolvent Debtors (1819), pp. 1-5.

119 1 Geo. IV, c.119.

120 Hansard, P.D., n.s., 1823, vii, 540, Solicitor General.

himself conceded, in 1823, that 'instead of relieving the unfortunate debtor, it served to form the basis of a system of fraud, profligacy and perjury, such as had never before been witnessed.'[121] Although it is true that the proportion of debtors remanded by the court did increase during the 1820s,[122] the majority were able to secure their discharge within three months of committal (i.e. twice as fast as before 1820). The picture presented in Little Dorrit corroborates this judgment. On the one hand, referring to the late 1820s, Dickens states that 'a Marshalsea generation might be calculated as about three months.'[123] On the other, it is evident that a debtor like the Father of the Marshalsea, who was totally unable to explain his insolvency even to the 'sharpest practitioners' and whose affairs were tainted with fraud, had little prospect of speedy release.[124] The majority of debtors appear to have been more resourceful and the instant popularity of the new system was reflected in the increased business of the Insolvent Debtors Court after 1820, recorded in Table 2.4. Although some modifications were made to Althorp's court in the 1820s,[125] the verdicts passed on it in the next decade

---

121 Ibid., p. 609, quoted by Peter Moore.

122 Between 1820 and mid-1831, the court discharged 43,528 and remanded 3,652. B.P.P. Accounts and Papers (1831), xv, 89.

123 C. Dickens, Little Dorrit (Educ. Book Co. edn., 1910), p. 67. The Father of the Marshalsea was gaoled 30 years before publication in 1856 (p. 58).

124 For his inability to explain both the insolvency and the corruption involved in it, ibid., pp. 61, 65.

125 In 1822, the assignees' powers of acquiring property were increased (3 Geo. IV, c.123); in 1824, an extra commissioner was added and the court took over the functions of the Quarter Sessions in debt cases (5 Geo. IV, c.61); in 1826, the court was made a court of record and the various insolvency statutes consolidated. The court could now compel attendance of witnesses and the production of books, and fine debtors for unnecessary delay or expense (7 Geo. IV, c.57).

indicate that the evils were not eradicated. It was stated in 1837 that, on average, the 50,000 debtors who had used the court since 1820 produced a farthing in the pound.[126] Consequently, most merchants treated a notice from the court as tantamount to compulsion to abandon their claims.[127]

The debates of the 1820s indicate that the successive failures of their statutes had totally perplexed the majority of politicians, who were unable to devise constructive solutions in answer to the flood of petitions demanding further reform.[128] H. Grey Bennett, in 1823, bemoaned 'the perfect inactivity of ministers on Insolvent Debtors Bills, leaving it to others to devise remedies.'[129] Solicitor General Copley could think of no remedy for the problem of collusive arrests,[130] and Peter Moore stated that another committee on the subject would only produce the same solution as its two hundred predecessors: 'that they did not know how to remedy its evils.'[131] An indication of the parliamentary mentality is the reception accorded to Joseph Hume's demand, in 1827, for an inquiry into both debtors prisons and imprisonment for debt, which he wanted totally abolished.[132] While the necessity of a committee on prisons was generally accepted, his debt proposal was received with incredulity by the Attorney General, Sir Charles Wetherell, who sympathised with Hume's evidence of the plight of

---

126 Runnymede Secundus, The Prison House Unmasked (1837), p. 26.

127 E.g. B.P.P. Bankruptcy and Insolvency (1840), p. 103, John Kirkman; p. 17, Thomas Wood; p. 443, Messrs. Slee, Payne and Slee.

128 See Hansard, P.D. n.s. 1823, ix, 377, John Hobhouse.

129 Ibid., 1823, viii, 541.

130 Ibid.

131 Ibid., 1823, viii, 609.

132 Ibid., 1827, xvii, 233.

debtors committed on mesne process but considered his suggested abolition of imprisonment in execution to be preposterous: 'That was an extraordinary proposition. No person conversant with trade would listen to a proposition that imprisonment after process should be abolished . . . he conceived that the principle of arrest for civil debt could not be departed from with safety in a commercial country like this.'[133] Calcraft agreed that, in the present state of society, it was 'not prudent or proper to abolish imprisonment for debt' and Peel could think of no alternative to it.[134] The only product of Hume's endeavours was the Solicitor General's statute in 1827 raising the minimum debt to which mesne process applied to £20.[135]

The reason why the legislation of Redesdale and Althorp proved so unsuccessful was that it fell between two stools. On the one hand, it adhered to the doctrine, stated by Thomas MacDonald in 1791, that 'if the laws of imprisonment did not in their first operation proceed against debtors indicriminately, they would seldom proceed with effect . . . imprisonment for debt is indispensable.'[136] On the other, it failed in practice to ensure that dishonest debtors were not discharged easily. In addition, the immunity of much of a debtor's property from division frequently enabled him to avoid payment. The experiments of the first quarter of the nineteenth century reflect contemporary confusion about how the rights and interests of both parties in a debt dispute could be protected. Basil Montagu summarised the confusion in 1827:

> Extraordinary as it is how few fixed principles pervade society upon important questions of legislation, there

---

133 Hansard, P.D., n.s. 1827, xvii, 229-30.

134 Ibid., p. 230.

135 7, 8 Geo. IV, c.71.

136 T. MacDonald, A Treatise on Civil Imprisonment (1791), p. 57.

> was no question upon which it was more extraordinary than upon imprisonment for debt. If the subject was mentioned even in the company of lawyers, the want of fixed principles was obvious; one talked of the injured creditor; another of the oppressed debtor; one of the necessity of this power in the creditors for the sake of commerce; another that the counting-house had no alliance with the gaol. There was, however, one fixed principle which rendered all these discussions futile; let no man be judge in his own cause, and assign the punishment of his own pain.137

VII

In the late 1820s and the 1830s, attitudes to these apparently intractable problems underwent a transformation largely, as in the related sphere of bankruptcy, because of the work of Henry Brougham. Brougham's basic premise, similar to that of Montagu cited above, was 'that imprisonment should be the punishment of crime, and not the lot of misfortune.'[138] In his great law reform speech of 1828, he stated that the insolvency laws contradicted the three principles which should operate at the opening of a suit for debt. First, debtors should be prevented from wilfully absenting themselves in order to frustrate their creditors. Second, debtors should be given due notice of the creditors' allegations and the opportunity to defend themselves against them. Third, debtors should not be inconvenienced until the debt had been proved unless they seemed likely to flee. In addition, he considered that all a debtor's property should be liable for his debts.[139] In

---

137 B. Montagu, Reform (1827), p. 17.

138 Lord Brougham's Speech on Law Reform, 19 May 1845 (1845), p. 29.

139 H. Brougham, The Present State of the Law (1828), p. 65.

1831-2, the Commissioners into the Superior Courts of Common Law, appointed by Wellington's government in response to Brougham's speech, reported their findings, which were highly critical of the continued use of imprisonment on both mesne and final process.[140] Mesne process was detrimental not only to debtors in moderate circumstances, whose credit-worthiness was often ruined for life by the publicity attendant upon imprisonment, but also to creditors, who were often deluded by it into giving excessive credit. In practice, creditors gained nothing either by imprisoning a total insolvent or by threatening other classes of debtor with mesne process, since they simply went to gaol and used the Insolvency Act. In cases where mesne process was profitable, it benefited only the plaintiff at the expense of the general creditors. The commissioners noted that, as a result of the defects in mesne process, creditors increasingly favoured the use of serviceable process, which allowed the debtor to work in order to pay his debts before being taken to court. Almost half of the serviceable actions were settled without the case going to court. Nevertheless, it was equally unpractical to imprison debtors on final process unless fraud could be proved, since they were released by the Insolvency Court after about eight weeks. Consequently, the commissioners suggested that 'those who at present resort to arrest, and therefore wish to retain it, considering it to be their principal security, would willingly relinquish it (excepting in cases of fraud), provided readier means were substituted for getting at the property of the debtor by an execution.'[141]

In addition to these practical criticisms, the commissioners noted that, by presuming fraud, imprisonment

---

140 For the following account, B.P.P. Fourth Report of the Commissioners . . . into the Practice and Proceedings of the Superior Courts of Common Law (1831-2), XXV, 6-42.

141 Ibid., p. 11.

for debt was contrary to the spirit of English law. They suggested that future debt legislation should confine imprisonment to cases of actual or meditated flight, provide a cheaper and speedier process for recovering debts, induce debtors to cede property early, render all property liable, and prevent debtors from both staying voluntarily and being kept in prison for a lengthy period.[142]

After the report, which had elaborated upon Brougham's necessarily brief comments in 1828, the abolition (as distinct from limitation) of imprisonment for debt was virtually inevitable. In the subsequent parliamentary debates on the subject, it is evident that the majority of politicians, especially in the Commons, accepted the main principles laid down by Brougham and by the commissioners. Many considered the commissioners' investigations so comprehensive that further evidence was unnecessary.[143] Indeed the thin attendance during the Commons debates on the subject was attributed to this fact.[144] Nevertheless, bills introduced in response to the report in each of the succeeding four years were rejected, for three main reasons. First, as Brougham admitted in 1835, the abolition 'would perhaps, effect a greater change than had ever been made in the law of the country,'[145] and some members were averse to passing it without lengthy discussion.[146] The second rea-

---

142 Ibid., pp. 34-6. Of the five commissioners, four - Pollock, Starkie, Evans and Wightman - advocated abolition of imprisonment for debt. The fifth, Stephen, considered arrest a valid check on improvidence but thought that it should be abolished if a speedier and cheaper mode of recovering debts were found.

143 E.g. the Attorney General and Cottenham (Hansard, P.D., 3s, 1834, xxiv, 412; 1836, xxxv, 61).

144 Hansard, P.D., 3s 1835, xxix, 1094-5, Chancellor of Exchequer.

145 Ibid., 1835, xxx, 956.

146 E.g. ibid., 1836, xxxv, 74, Lord Abinger.

son, closely related to the first, was the opposition to the bills of the trading fraternity and some influential members of the House of Lords. In a sense, their respective objections contradicted one another. The argument of the former, presented in a series of petitions against the bills and by a small group of M.P.s led by John Richards, was that the abolition would 'annihilate' the country's trade.[147] Brougham, however, stated that the traders would discover that they were mistaken after the act had been implemented, since it provided them with an adequate substitute for imprisonment.[148] It was this substitute which provoked the greatest opposition in the Lords. The bills proposed to allow all property to be divided in order to prevent debtors evading payment as they had in the past. An initial encroachment was made upon the privilege of landed property in 1833, when the estates of deceased debtors were made liable for their debts,[149] but suggestions that this should be extended were met with stiff opposition, led by Wellington and Lyndhurst, in 1835 and 1836.[150] The third, and most important, reason for the delay was the fact that the bills were too ambitious, attempting as they did to abolish imprisonment on both mesne and final process and to grant a certificate of discharge to honest debtors as in bankruptcy. Although, as the commissioners had pointed out, many traders agreed with the principle of the bills and were prepared to relinquish imprisonment for debt provided an

---

147 For petitions, see _ibid._, 1835, xxvii, 1054, Peel; 1835, xxx, 955-7, Ashburton; for Richards, _ibid._, 1834, xxiii, 1227; 1835, xxvi, 1146; cf. _ibid._, 1228, Mr. Sergeant Spankie; 1835, xxx, 560, James Freshfield.

148 _Ibid._, 1837, xxxix, 576.

149 3, 4 Will. IV, c.104.

150 Hansard, _P.D._ 3s, 1835, xxx, 955, 1129; 1836, xxxv, 70; cf. _ibid._, 574, Lord Farnham.

adequate substitute was made available,[151] they were understandably cautious. Baring, for example, in 1834, wondered how it would be possible to acquire a debtor's property without proceeding against his person first.[152] Until the effects of extending liability to all property were felt, therefore, many people wished to preserve at least imprisonment in execution. In their attempts to abolish the latter the reformers could not draw effective parallels with the experience of other countries, as they could in their arguments against mesne process, since it was in common usage.[153] Despite the efforts of Brougham to persuade the Lords of the necessity of abolishing imprisonment for debt,[154] a committee of the House, after the bill's second reading, denuded it of its clauses relating to execution. Brougham played little part in the work of the committee because of the pressure of other business.[155] Nevertheless, when passed in 1838, as Lord Cottenham's Act (the Lord Chancellor had introduced the bill), it was generally considered to have stemmed from the work of Brougham himself[156] and Cottenham had depended greatly upon his support in the Lords. The act abolished arrest on mesne process and attempted to provide a process which would guarantee an equitable settlement for both

---

151 A deputation of London traders stated, in 1836, that they would relinquish imprisonment in execution 'if . . . they were furnished with power to seize his property' (ibid., 1836, xxxv, 63, Cottenham).

152 Ibid., 1834, xxii, 1226.

153 Lyndhurst admitted that mesne process did not exist elsewhere in Europe, although imprisonment in execution did (ibid., 1837, xxxix, 572).

154 See, especially, Hansard, P.D., 3s, 1837, xxxix, 576-95.

155 Ibid., 1838, xliii, 665.

156 See J.H. Elliott, A Remonstrance to Lord Brougham (1838), pp. 1-24.

debtor and creditor.[157] It stipulated that all actions would in future commence with a writ of summons and that no debtor was to be gaoled until his case had been tried and judgment pronounced, unless the creditor could prove to the judge of a superior court that he was about to flee the country. Debtors gaoled in execution could petition the Insolvent Debtors Court within fourteen days, demanding discharge and stating their willingness to vest all real and personal property in the provisional assignee. If the debtor had been in gaol for twenty-one days without paying the debt, the creditor could petition the court demanding that the provisional assignee start collecting the debtor's assets. After the petition (of debtor or creditor) the court appointed a meeting, within four months, at which it examined the debtor's schedule and witnesses for both sides and the creditors could cross-examine the debtor. If the court noted anything unsatisfactory in the debtor's schedule or conduct, the meeting was adjourned until a future date and the debtor was kept in custody. The object of the act was to ensure that the debtor's opportunities for fraudulent evasion of debts were reduced. Fraud was punishable by a maximum of three years in gaol and false declarations by three years hard labour. In addition, the act stipulated that, in future, all a debtor's property was divisible amongst creditors, whose hopes of full satisfaction would thus be fulfilled.

Although it is true that Cottenham's act eradicated some of the major defects of the debt laws (especially mesne process, the limited access to a debtor's property and the creditor's inability to compel the debtor to use the court), it was only a half-measure which reformers, like William Hawes, considered to be 'a contribution to a better state of things.'[158] Logically, the act of 1838 should have been

---

157 1, 2 Vict., c.110.

158 Hansard, P.D., 3s, 1838, xliv, 145.

accompanied by the abolition of imprisonment in execution, since its purpose was to make the property rather than the person responsible for satisfaction of debts. In fact, the gradual recognition that it could be abolished without causing undue problems was a product of the success of the new system. In 1839, Attorney General Campbell stated that 'he had received from all quarters the most gratifying intelligence of the operation of the bill for the abolition of imprisonment for debt. So beneficial was it found, that those who had been most opposed to it were now loudest in its praise.'[159] What was needed after 1838 was a system in which creditors had direct access to their debtors' property instead of being forced, first, through one of the superior courts and, then, through the Insolvent Debtors Court. The inefficacy of this round-about route was stressed by the Commissioners into Bankruptcy and Insolvency in 1840. They noted that, of 3,905 debtors imprisoned between 1 October 1838 and 1 December 1839, only 361 had been declared guilty of a criminal offence by the Insolvent Debtors Court. As the average cost of the remaining 3,544 cases was about £20, total wastage amounted to £66,900. The futility of the system was emphasised by the fact that in only five per cent of the cases were dividends paid to creditors.[160]

The evidence presented to the commissioners suggested that the abuses would be eradicated if, first, the debtor's property could be collected quickly and efficiently, second, the debtor was 'by the consent of a certain majority of his creditors . . . entitled to a total discharge from future liability,'[161] and, third, the 'fancied and generally delusive security (imprisonment on final process)' was abolished, thus 'throwing the creditor more on his own

---

159 Hansard, P.D., 3s, 1839, xlvii, 572-3.

160 B.P.P. Bankruptcy and Insolvency (1840), p. xxiii.

161 Ibid., p. ix.

caution in giving credit.'[162] Their conclusion, that most of these needs could be satisfied in a reformed Bankruptcy Court, was reinforced by their estimate, noted already, that over two-thirds of the petitioners in the Insolvent Debtors Court were traders.

The fusion of the insolvency and bankruptcy procedures was begun in two bills by which Brougham, who introduced them in 1842, intended to abolish imprisonment for debt completely.[163] The first, An Act for the Relief of Insolvent Debtors, stipulated that any non-trader, or trader owing under £300, could claim protection from arrest provided that he sent a schedule of debts to one-quarter of his creditors in number and value, presented a petition to the Bankruptcy Court containing a full disclosure of his debtors, creditors and property, and inserted a notice of insolvency in the London Gazette. The debtor's estate was then controlled and collected by an official assignee of the Bankruptcy Court and an assignee chosen by the creditors. If, on examining the debtor, the bankruptcy commissioner detected no fraud, the debtor was protected from all further processes and his future estate was exempt unless the court ordered otherwise.[164]

Brougham's second bill, enacted in 1844, extended the integration of the two procedures.[165] With the consent of one-third of his creditors in number and value, an insolvent non-trader could now petition the Bankruptcy Court setting forth a full account of his estate and proposing a composition with his creditors. A court commissioner, if satisfied that the debtor's demands were reasonable and not fraudulent, then summoned the creditors to a meeting, at

---

162 Ibid., pp. xxv-xxvi.

163 Hansard, P.D., 3s, 1842, lxv, 489.

164 5, 6 Vict., c.116.

165 7, 8 Vict., c.70.

which the consent was required of one-half in number and value (or nine-tenths in number or nine-tenths in value of those who were owed more than £20) to the debtor's proposals. At a second meeting, held between seven and twenty-eight days later, three-fifths in number and value of the creditors present (or nine-tenths in number, or nine-tenths in value of those who were owed more than £20) could resolve to accept the proposal which was binding if one-third of the creditors, in number and value, were present. The resolution was then filed by the bankruptcy commissioner, who granted the debtor's certificate of discharge and appointed a trustee to tend the insolvent's estate. Three days later (9 August 1844), the power of the small debt courts to imprison on final process for debts of under £20 was abolished unless fraud was proved.[166]

By the middle of the nineteenth century, imprisonment for debt had thus virtually been abolished. It is not intended here to analyse closely later developments. Briefly, the fusion of the bankruptcy and insolvency processes was continued. In 1847, the powers granted to the Bankruptcy Court in the preceding five years (insolvency cases and small bankruptcies) were transferred to the Insolvent Debtors Court in London and, in the provinces, to the newly established county courts, which also took control of the jurisdiction previously exercised in the Insolvency Court on circuit.[167] Fourteen years later, when the trader/non-trader distinction was finally ended, the Insolvent Debtors Court was abolished, its functions being transferred to the Bankruptcy Court and county courts, which also usurped the functions of the district bankruptcy courts.[168] Although this act effectively emptied prisons of

166 7, 8 Vict., c.96.

167 10, 11 Vict., c.102.

168 24, 25 Vict., c.134.

their remaining debtors, imprisonment for debt was not finally abolished until the Debtors Act of 1869.[169]

VIII

It may be suggested, in conclusion, that most of the problems associated with insolvency in the industrial revolution stemmed from the inflexibility of Common Law. As early as the sixteenth century, the legislature had acknowledged the fact that Common Law was inappropriate to traders, whose large estates demanded collective remedies against property which was not derived from land. As the economy grew, such property percolated throughout society and, by the nineteenth century, common-law forms were unsuited to a nation in which negotiable instruments, shares, bonds, book debts, funds, annuities and pensions were not the preserve only of the mercantile class. In the circumstances, the protraction of imprisonment for debt can be considered necessary, if only to blackmail the debtor into ceding property which was legally immune. But, as has been shown, statutory mitigation of the length of imprisonment left many creditors without a practicable legal sanction over either the property or the body of the debtor in the first half of the nineteenth century. Not until the 1830s and 1840s did parliament examine the law as a whole and attempt to adapt it to social and economic conditions by applying to all debtors remedies which had previously been exclusive to bankrupts alone.

---

169 32, 33 Vict., c.62.

CHAPTER III

THE SMALL DEBT LAWS

I

It has been shown that, from the sixteenth century, debtors were divided legally into two categories, the first composed of large traders, for whom a special bankruptcy system had evolved, and the second consisting of smaller traders and non-traders, who were subject to common-law remedies. In addition, the law had traditionally provided machinery for dealing with trivial debts which did not warrant the expense of common-law procedure and, in the eighteenth century, had sought to release the smallest debtors from the drastic operation of mesne process. The act of 1725, which raised its minimum limit to £10 in superior courts and 40s. in inferior courts, was designed to prevent 'frivolous and vexatious arrests;' that of 1779, raising it to £10 in all courts, was intended to remove an 'oppressive' power.[1] Two further acts in 1785 and 1786 restricted the creditor's power to imprison small debtors in execution in all small debt courts.[2] These statutes represent a reasoned response to economic conditions in the eighteenth century, when the lower classes were prone to indebtedness. This may partly be explained by contemporary accounts of their reckless expenditure which was encouraged by the credit facilities provided by retailers, especially

---

1 12 Geo. I, c.29; 19 Geo. III, c.70.

2 25 Geo. III, c.45 stipulated that courts of request could imprison for 20 days for non-payment of a debt of £1 and 40 days for £2. If fraud was discovered these limits were raised to 30 and 60 days. This was extended to all courts by 26 Geo. III, c.38.

in the tally-shops.[3] A more satisfactory explanation, however, lies in the nature of their economic position. As Ashton points out, the long pay which characterised eighteenth-century employment ensured that the worker was persistently forced into debt.[4] At the end of the century his position degenerated further, since the price rise produced by the French wars was not generally accompanied by a commensurate increase in wages, most of which must have been spent on food alone.[5] In 1802, James Neild noted that 'the distresses of the poor have greatly increased, perhaps in proportion to the increased price of provisions.' Neild advocated that, because of the inflation and the overcrowded state of debtors prisons, the minimum debt to which mesne process applied should be raised.[6] In 1811, this was done and the new limit of £15 remained until it was raised to £20 in 1827.[7]

While the economic conditions of the period justified statutory interventions to protect the small debtor, they also necessitated the provision of legal machinery to enable the creditor to enforce his claims. Neither debtors nor creditors, of course, should be viewed as a distinct class; the worker, for example, was both debtor to his shopkeeper and creditor of his employer. Nevertheless, because of the extent to which they were obliged to give credit, retailers, in particular, needed a viable process of recovery. This

---

3 See J.R. McCulloch, Dictionary of Commerce (1832), p. 421; cf. J.H. Elliott, Credit the Life of Commerce (1845), ch. 9.

4 T.S. Ashton, An Economic History of England: The 18th Century (1955), p. 207.

5 For the increase in the price of necessaries in the 1790s, see T. Tooke, A History of Prices (ed. T.E. Gregory), (1928), i, 228.

6 J. Neild, Account of the Rise, *op. cit.*, pp. 15, 303.

7 51 Geo. III, c.124; 7, 8 Geo IV, c.71.

was emphasized in 1845 by J.H. Elliott, a trader who had extensive dealings with shopkeepers and tradesmen. He cited the accounts of the unnamed 'largest wholesale grocer' in London, 76 per cent (517) of whose clients owed a balance of under £20 (averaging £5.18.0d.). The average debt owed by his 680 clients was pulled up by larger debtors to £15. Similar cases, cited by Elliott, were a newspaper agent, 6,000 of whose 7,000 accounts amounted to under £20, a wholesale ironmonger, whose 2,021 accounts averaged £10, a hardwareman with 300 out of 500 accounts below £20, and a wine and spirit merchant with 619 out of 738 accounts below £20.[8] The tenor of Elliott's argument - that the law provided creditors with feeble remedies against smaller debtors - echoed the complaints of many retailers in the previous half-century. The purpose of this chapter is to examine the nature of those remedies and the development of the laws relating to small debts in the late eighteenth and early nineteenth centuries.

II

The legal machinery which catered for small debt disputes at the end of the eighteenth century was totally inadequate. The old county courts had failed as early as the sixteenth century,[9] and those which survived were deficient for a variety of reasons.[10] Their jurisdiction was usually limited to debts of under forty shillings. The only way in which they could compel the debtor to attend

---

8 Elliott, op. cit., p. 84.

9 County courts had been granted jurisdiction of debts under 40s. in Edward I's reign.

10 The following account is based on B.P.P. [Report from the S.C. appointed to inquire into the Mode in which Debts amounting to less than] Fifteen Pounds [are recovered in England and Wales] (1823), [IV], pp. 2-4.

court was by distraining his property but, as they had no power to sell it, the creditor gained little and the property accumulated in the lumber rooms of the court. The county clerk, who was able to influence the jury (composed of freeholders), was a practising attorney, often on business terms with one of the litigants. The fact that the courts sat only in county towns frequently imposed heavy travelling expenses upon litigants. As they were not generally courts of record, pleas could not be heard in them for anything due on record and, when a case was removed to a superior court, four knights were required to travel to Westminster and recount what had transpired in the case thusfar. If a defendant left the county in which the court sat, the plaintiff was put to the expense of removing the case to another. Finally, proceedings in county courts were expensive. James Nicholls, solicitor to the Thatched House Society, told the 1823 Committee on Small Debts of costs amounting to £9.15.8d. to recover a debt of 19s.6d. in the county court at Colchester and of £4.2.10d. to recover £6 at Tiverton.[11] The cause of the expense was the fees, paid at each stage in the proceedings which began when the court served a writ on the defendant at a cost of two-and-a-half guineas. If the action was not settled quickly, a declaration was prepared, often costing £7, after which the defendant pleaded at his own expense, the plaintiff replied, and a record of the case was made.[12]

Two exceptions to the general ineffectiveness of the county courts were those in Middlesex and Lancashire. The Middlesex court was modified in 1753 to enable the county clerk, who was usually a barrister or attorney, to deal with debt cases by travelling through the various hundreds of the

---

11 B.P.P. <u>Fifteen Pounds</u> (1823), p. 39.

12 <u>Ibid</u>., p. 20, Francis Smedley, deputy high bailiff of Westminster.

county.[13] By the 1820s, the court was issuing four hundred summonses each week. Most of the cases which it heard consisted of defendants confessing their debts and waiting for the court to allow them time in which to pay by instalments.[14] In Lancashire, delays in procedure were eliminated by allowing cases to be entered during intervals between the regular days when the court sat as if they had been entered in the previous sitting.[15] A statute of 1794 stipulated that no cause could be removed from the court in Lancaster to Westminster in an action under £10 unless security was given for the debt, damages and costs,[16] after which date the court dealt with over nine thousand suits annually for debts under £10.[17]

In addition to the county courts, there were other inferior courts which dealt with small debt cases in the first half of the nineteenth century. The hundred courts and courts baron, like the county courts, usually possessed a forty-shilling maximum. Their defects are typified by the courts at Leeds, Bradford and Huddersfield which met twice a year and in which suits often continued for nine months.[18] The jurisdiction of borough courts generally encompassed larger debts. Established in towns which applied for the privilege of holding a court, they functioned in areas of large population like London (the Lord Mayor's Court), Bristol (the Tolsey Court), and Liverpool (the Court of

---

13 26 Geo. II, c.33.

14 B.P.P. Fifteen Pounds (1823), p. 59, George Heath, county clerk of Middlesex.

15 Ibid., p. 6.

16 34 Geo. III, c.58.

17 B.P.P. [Fifth Report of the Commissioners appointed to Inquire into the Practice and Proceedings of the Superior Courts of] Common Law (1833), [XXII], p. 7.

18 Ibid., p. 9.

Passage). Although inferior courts of record sometimes had jurisdiction over debts of any size, the ease with which larger cases could be transferred to Westminster dictated that most of their work was concerned with small debts.[19] This was the case, for example, in the Court of Passage[20] and in the Palace Court. The latter was the child of the old Marshalsea Court, which had been held before the Steward and Marshal of the King's itinerant household. Originally, its jurisdiction covered cases of trespass, within twelve miles of the royal court, in which one of the parties was a royal servant. In time, this jurisdiction was extended to cover all personal pleas and actions between any parties within twelve miles of Whitehall. Proceedings in the court, held before a jury in Scotland Yard every Friday morning, were simple. Only four counsel acted and the number of attornies was limited to five. Most of the debts adjudicated in the court were small and, by 1800, large debt cases were almost invariably removed from it to King's Bench. By the 1830s, the court was dealing with over six thousand cases each year under £20. Costs were £8.10.0d. for the plaintiff and £6.8.0d. for the defendant, the plaintiff receiving full compensation if his claims were proven. Five weeks usually elapsed between the start of each suit and final judgment.[21] The court was abolished in 1849.[22]

As we have seen, the jurisdiction of the superior courts of record encompassed debts to any amount. However,

---

19 The minimum debt which could be transferred from courts of record was raised from £5 (21 Jac. I, c.23) to £10 in 1779 (19 Geo. III, c.70) and £20 in 1827 (7, 8 Geo. IV., c.71).

20 B.P.P. <u>Fifteen Pounds</u> (1823), p. 66, William Statham, town clerk of Liverpool.

21 B.P.P. <u>Common Law</u> (1833), p. 10.

22 12, 13 Vict., c.101.

the expense of the superior courts, in which creditors were usually obliged to pay £18 before any security for costs was obtained (the writ cost £2 or £3 and attorney's fees the rest),[23] led to the development of a new system for small debts which provides an interesting example of institutional response to a pressing economic situation.[24] It involved the erection of more than 300 courts of request (or conscience) throughout England and Wales, between 1660 and 1846 (but especially 1750-1825), by special acts of parliament passed in response to petitions from communities which could justify the necessity of a new judicial organ. Their haphazard mode of erection ensured that the composition and jurisdiction of these courts varied from place to place. The latter was either exclusive or concurrent, in some courts based on law and in others on equity and conscience. The jurisdiction of earlier request courts was usually limited to debts under £2. However, those established after 1806 were competent to deal with cases up to £5 and some up to £10, the new limits designed to cater for the war-time inflation.

The original model for the courts of request was that established as early as 1518 at the Guildhall to try small debt cases quickly and cheaply, by eliminating attorneys, stamp duties, written pleadings and appeal. The process was simple. The plaintiff stated the sum he was owed in his application for a summons, which was issued promptly by a beadle. When the debtor appeared, two or three days later, his case was investigated by the commissioners and, if found

---

23 B.P.P. Fifteen Pounds (1823), p. 13, William Arroll, a boot-maker; cases involving costs of more than £100 were said to be common. See W.R. Minchin, Present State of the Debtor and Creditor Law (1812), p. 45, fn.

24 The following description is based on Debtor and Creditors Guide (1813); B.P.P. Fifteen Pounds (1823); Elliott, op. cit.; W.H.D. Winder, 'The Courts of Request,' L.Q.R., lii (1936), 369-94; B. Abel-Smith and R. Stevens, Lawyers and the Courts (1967).

liable, he was given the opportunity of paying by instalments. John Holmes, first clerk of the court in 1823, stated that one shilling a month for a debt of forty shillings was the lowest he had witnessed. The commissioners, who consisted of a voluntary group of aldermen, common councillors, principal inhabitants and merchants, usually numbered twelve to fourteen. Seven were required to judge cases between forty shillings and five pounds and three under forty shillings. By the nineteenth century, the court, which issued ten thousand summonses annually, had acquired a professional staff consisting of a principal clerk (£500 p.a. from fees), first assistant (£200), second assistant (£150), third assistant (£100), four beadles (£80), and four assistant beadles (£60).[25]

The Southwark request court, established by three statutes (the last in 1806), also possessed a £5 limit.[26] It consisted of two chief clerks, a high bailiff and 132 commissioners, appointed annually from the parish vestries, five of whom formed a quorum in cases over and three under forty shillings. In the latter, the summons cost 1s.8d. and the order for payment 2s.3d. If the defendant did not appear after the summons, a second (the attachment) was issued at an additional cost of 3s.0d. If he failed to pay after order of the court, an execution was issued against his body at a cost of 2s.6d. In addition, court fees of 2s.6d. were levied. Thus, the total expense, if all these processes were necessary, was 11s.11d. In cases over forty shillings, each item cost more, the total amounting to one guinea. All of these fees were charged to the defendant. John Meymott, clerk of the court, presented the following analysis of its work in 1821 as evidence of its popularity:

---

25 B.P.P <u>Fifteen Pounds</u> (1823), p. 26.

26 The following is based on <u>ibid</u>., pp. 28-30, John Meymott.

Litigation in the Southwark Court of Requests, 1821

Process	Total
Number of summonses under 40s.	10,051
Number of summonses over 40s.	3,331
Number of attachments under 40s.	1,623
Number of attachments over 40s.	683
Number of executions under 40s.	2,872
Number of executions over 40s.	1,375
Number of persons imprisoned	830
Number of executions returned not executed	425
Number paid into court when executed	1,553

Source: B.P.P. Report from the S.C. appointed to inquire into the Mode in which Debts amounting to less than Fifteen Pounds are recovered in England and Wales (1823), IV, 30.

A similar court in Westminster possessed a jurisdiction up to £2. It was composed of 242 commissioners, appointed by the parish vestries, three of whom formed a quorum. Summonses were issued on Monday, Tuesday, Wednesday and Saturday and cases heard on Thursday. It issued fifteen thousand summonses annually, of which ten thousand were tried.[27] Other request courts in London were held in Stepney, Piccadilly, Leicester Square, Southwark, Whitechapel, Edmonton, Wandsworth, Greenwich and Brentford.[28]

An analysis of sixty request courts throughout the country, presented to parliament in 1839, reveals the diversity of their jurisdiction, composition and activity.[29]

27 Ibid., p. 52, John Hodgson, clerk of the court.

28 Debtor and Creditors Guide (1813), pp. 6-17.

29 B.P.P. Accounts and Papers (1839), lxiii, 157-222.

As might be expected, those in the provinces were not as busy as those in London. In 1835, the Sevenoaks court, which met once a month, issued ninety-four summonses for debts under £5, fifty-two of which were heard and determined. The court at Folkestone, which also met once a month, issued seventy-six summonses for under £2, of which fifty-nine were heard. In contrast, the Southwark court met thirty-five times in that year, issuing 16,694 summonses for under £5 and hearing 11,812 cases. The court in Tower Hamlets met 104 times, issuing 13,891 summonses and hearing 10,516 cases. Of the sixty courts in the return, twenty-five dealt with cases under £2, one under £3, thirty-one under £5, two under £10, and one under £15; fourteen met once a month, fifteen twice, fourteen three times, three four times, ten five times and four more than five times monthly (the most frequent was 129 times in the year at Greenwich). The composition of the commissioners in the courts was less varied than their jurisdiction and activity. Although one or two were composed of people elected without qualifications by existing commissioners (e.g. Derby and Doncaster), the vast majority consisted by the terms of their foundation of propertied men (usually possessed of £40 freehold property or £1,000 personal estate).

Superficially, the courts of request appear extremely efficient and speedy instruments for the recovery of small debts, and statistics relating to them are impressive. In 86,812 cases heard in 32 courts in 1843, all except 15,365 debtors paid or settled their debts before execution was allowed to issue against their bodies. Of the 15,365, 11,814 paid as soon as it was issued, 1,573 shortly after imprisonment and only 1,978 stayed in gaol for the full term.[30] These statistics, however, should not blind us to the very real defects of request courts. For the smallest debts, the costs, which Griffiths calls 'the gallons of

---

30 Elliott, op. cit., p. 86.

sack to the penny-worth of debt,' were extortionate.[31] Neild, in 1800, cited instances of thirteen debtors, imprisoned by request courts in the previous three years, whose debts of about 2s.6d. had been quadrupled by costs.[32] In larger cases, there was further cause for dissatisfaction. The predominance of laymen among their personnel rendered the courts unpopular, especially because so much was left to their discretion. In 1834, for example, a barrister maintained that the courts were composed frequently of 'two or three hundred illiterate and unprofessional commissioners, acting in the capacity as judges' and described them as 'inexperienced persons, of little education, incompetent understanding, and sordid, mercenary occupations.'[33] As a result, they were frequently suspected of partiality.[34]

It is clear that, despite legislative attempts to deal with the problem, the various types of small debt court in the early nineteenth century were defective. A more important weakness of the system as a whole, however, derived from the limited jurisdiction of the courts, which was usually either £2 or £5. Creditors attempting to recover debts which were over that limit and under £15 (for which debtors could not be held to bail after 1811) were thus usually frustrated by the absence of appropriate legal machinery and were forced either to sacrifice the balance of the debt in order to recoup £1.19.11-1/2d. or £4.19.11-1/2d., depending on the jurisdiction of the local court (if there was one), or to give credit for more than

---

31 A. Griffiths, Chronicles of Newgate (1884), ii, 76.

32 J. Neild, Account of Persons confined for Debt (1800), p. 41.

33 W. Glover, Lord Brougham's Law Reforms (1834), p. 8; it is possible that the property qualifications were ignored. See Winder, op. cit., p. 376.

34 B.P.P. Common Law (1833), p. 12.

£15 in order to use the superior courts.[35] George Heath, county clerk of Middlesex, told the 1823 committee, 'I try many now up to £2. I think a seventh of the causes I try were for £1.19.11-1/2d.'[36] Such evidence corroborates Althorp's verdict, in 1823, that 'the present state of the law amounted to nothing less than an absolute denial of justice to almost all creditors in the country with regard to debts due to them under the value of £15.' Althorp went on to accuse tradesmen of frequently refusing to pay employees, relying on the fact that they had no feasible means of recovery.[37] Thus statistics which testify to the large number of cases tried in the small debt courts are more an indictment of the general legal system than a testimony to their efficacy. Robert Taylor, a boot-maker, told the 1823 Committee that

> If there were a law to enable us to recover from forty shillings to fifteen pounds, a number of people would not get into debt that do now, because they think that they can play with us tradesmen; now if they owe five, six or seven pounds, they can shift about from one place to another, they think we will not go to law with them.38

Others who testified to the committee in a similar vein included Donald Currie, a military hatter, the itinerant nature of whose clientele precluded almost all hope of recovery. 253 of his 560 debtors owed under £5, as did 300 of Robert Taylor's and one-third of Thomas Laidlaw's (both were boot-makers).[39]

---

35 B.P.P. Fifteen Pounds (1823), p. 13, William Arroll.

36 Ibid., p. 59.

37 Hansard, P.D., ns., 1823, ix, 543.

38 B.P.P. Fifteen Pounds (1823), p. 19.

39 Ibid., pp. 14, 18, 26.

III

The inadequacies of the small debt courts were apparent to all at the start of the nineteenth century, but, as with bankruptcy and insolvency, the problem of devising a viable alternative took a long time to solve. In 1823, the Select Committee into Debts under £15 rejected a suggestion that the jurisdiction of request courts be extended to £15 on the grounds that larger debts, often involving controversial points, required much closer examination than they could provide. It also vetoed a proposal to extend them to less populous areas because of the absence in such localities of men of sufficient intelligence and integrity. The committee recommended a new system, involving the appointment of a barrister of six years standing to preside over county courts, which would make annual circuits of each county, judging cases up to £15 before a jury of twelve.[40] Similar proposals, forwarded in the 1820s by Althorp and Redesdale, foundered because of opposition from local and central officials who demanded compensation for loss of business and forecast a lowering of legal standards in the provinces.[41]

As in bankruptcy and insolvency, the major stimulus to reform in the 1830s came from Brougham. In 1828, he advocated the revival of county courts[42] and, in 1830, criticised in detail the absence of a differential in the debt laws in the costs of large and small cases. In 1827, there had been 93,375 affidavits for debt over £10 in the

---

40 Ibid., p. 6.

41 Redesdale had first mooted a revival of county courts in 1809 (Hansard, P.D., 1809, xiv, 889). For his and Althorp's suggestions in the 1820s, see ibid., 2s, 1820, i, 742; 1823, ix, 543; 1824, x, 303; for the opposition of the legal vested interests, see W.S. Holdsworth, 'The Movement for Reforms in the Law (1793-1832),' L.Q.R., lvi (1940), 38.

42 Hansard, P.D., 2s, 1828, xviii, 190-1.

three superior courts, of which 30,000 were for under £20, 34,000 for under £50 and only 15,000 for over £100. In other words, 'a large proportion of litigation of the country . . . is of that kind to which he had first called the attention of their Lordships as being so moderate, not to say so trifling, in its intrinsic value, as to make the expense of it out of all keeping to the value of the thing litigated.' He recommended that the solution was to revive county courts whose judges ordinary (men of character and weight in the legal profession) would try cases of debt, trespass and trover up to £100 and other cases (assault, libel, seduction, etc.) up to £50.[43]

Brougham's bill on the subject was referred to the Common Law Commissioners on the suggestion of Lyndhurst. In their subsequent report, in 1833, the commissioners substantially agreed with Brougham. After stating that 'the rapid increase in population, wealth and commerce has given rise to extensive credit, and has thus naturally increased to a great extent the claims on public justice,'[44] they analysed at length the defects in the courts for recovery of small debts, concluding that

> the inadequacy of the present courts, in causes of action from forty shillings to at least £20, amounts almost to a denial of justice . . . creditors are, from want of sufficient means to obtain redress, obliged to abandon their just demands; . . . debtors are from the same cause tempted to a dishonest resistance, and . . . the result is great injury to public morals and private rights.[45]

It was essential, they maintained, that a uniform system of courts should be established throughout the country in market towns of over 20,000 people, no town of over 10,000

---

43 Legal Reform. The Speech delivered in the House of Peers by H. Baron Brougham (1830), pp. 14, 22-3.

44 B.P.P. Common Law (1833), p. 17.

45 Ibid.

should be more than ten miles from one, and every person should be provided with a court within 25 miles of his residence. The commissioners also recommended that the jurisdiction of the courts be extended to £20, that it should be exclusive, and that the judges should be barristers of ten years standing. The £20 limit was to be experimental and could be extended later.[46]

As in insolvency, the commissioners' suggestions did not immediately lead to far-reaching legislation. Brougham's second bill to erect county courts was defeated by Lyndhurst in the Lords in 1833. After that date, however, request courts were usually granted a jurisdiction of £15 and the presidency of a judge with professional experience (often a barrister).[47] In 1845 and 1846, steps were finally taken to erect a uniform system of small debt courts. The Act for the Better Securing the Payment of Small Debts (1845) proposed that, in future, the jurisdiction of all local courts with a professional judge should be extended to £20.[48] Before the act was put into operation, however, Lyndhurst, whose opposition had been wavering since the early 1840s because of the pressure for new local courts,[49] established the national network of county courts advocated by Brougham and many others for so long. The procedure, established in 1846, was modelled to a large extent on the Middlesex and Lancashire county courts. Five hundred courts were established by grouping the old request courts into sixty circuits and manning them with professional personnel (each circuit had one judge appointed by the Lord Chancellor from barristers of seven years

---

46 Ibid., pp. 18-20.

47 Winder, op. cit., p. 381.

48 8, 9 Vict., c. 127.

49 See Hansard, P.D., 3s, 1842, lxv, 230.

standing). Their jurisdiction covered debts of up to £20.[50] The act was not as radical as the suggestions of Brougham, who had wanted a jurisdiction covering debts up to £100 and local bankruptcy cases. This was partly remedied in 1847, when county courts took over insolvencies and small bankruptcies,[51] and in 1850, when their jurisdiction was extended to debts of £50, or more if both parties agreed.[52] In 1861 the functions of the district bankruptcy courts were entrusted to county courts.[53]

Although in its early years the county court system was criticised for its local prejudice and 'summary and vindictive' operations,[54] it has developed into a vital part of the legal system. A recent legal historian maintains that 'For routine business the English county courts have since become by the steady accretion of statutory powers the most important courts in the land.'[55]

---

50 9, 10., Vict., c.95 (The County Courts Act).

51 10, 11 Vict., c.102.

52 13, 14 Vict., c.61.

53 24, 25 Vict., c.134.

54 See W.L. Burn, The Age of Equipoise (1968), pp. 138-9.

55 A. Harding, A Social History of English Law (1966), p. 343.

CHAPTER IV

LAW REFORM AND ECONOMIC GROWTH

I

In the course of the first three chapters, it was shown that a drastic revision of the debt laws occurred in the 1830s and 1840s. It is evident that before 1830 not only were the bankruptcy, insolvency and small debt systems defective but also attempts to reform them were either unsuccessful or misguided; after that date reforms, which followed one another rapidly, appear to have been based upon consistent legal principles. The purpose of this chapter is to draw some conclusions about the course of reform and the significance of the debt laws during the industrial revolution. The discussion relates the specific developments in those laws to two questions raised by recent historians about social and legal reform in general. First, what were the most important influences which moulded the reforms of the 1830s and 1840s? Second, what was the relationship between the economy and the law during the industrial revolution?

II

By the middle of the nineteenth century a revolution had been effected in the administration of debt disputes in England. It is not suggested that all the problems confronting the legislature fifty years before had been solved, but the reforms of the 1830s and 1840s had, at least, replaced the old, haphazard and fragmented system with a uniform, national network of courts which, if handled intelligently, could be adapted to the rapidly changing needs of the Victorian economy. The courts themselves, however, were merely institutional products of a more fundamental revolution in attitudes to debt. One of the more remarkable characteristics of early thought on the subject is the fact that the three procedures - bankruptcy, insolvency and small debts - were persistently examined in isolation instead of being viewed as integral parts of the same basic issue. The most likely explanation of this is simply that legal tradition obscured the nature of the problem. The 1818 Bankruptcy Committee, for example, refused to recommend extension of the laws to non-traders on the grounds that 'such an extension would materially interfere with principles which have long been established, and are now interwoven with the law of the country.'[1] It is also likely that the complexity of the defects in each sector of the debt laws ensured that a broad view of the subject was virtually out of the question, especially for laymen.

Nevertheless, most lawyers and commercial men in the early nineteenth century were probably aware of the defects in the system. They could see the increasing irrelevance to economic conditions of the distinction between traders and non-traders. They were conscious of the inconsistency of a legal system which, on the one hand, virtually encouraged one man to flee from his home so that proceedings could be instituted which absolutely discharged all his property from liability and which, on the other, prevented another man from fleeing, by imprisoning him, in order to open proceedings in which discharge was never granted and only part of his property was liable. They were equally cognisant of the fact that the small debt courts, which were so important because of the nature and extent of retail trade, often forced creditors to sacrifice more than they actually claimed.

In a sense, the second quarter of the nineteenth century was a period of experiment, in which reformers

---

1 B.P.P. <u>Bankrupt Laws</u> (1818), p. 4.

appear to have stumbled inadvertently across the necessity of integrating the various parts of the system. Partial reform appears to have clarified contemporary perception of the whole problem. For example, after the abolition of arrest for debt on mesne process and the stipulation that the whole of a debtor's property was divisible, the fusion of the bankruptcy and insolvency procedures was logical and feasible. It was perhaps no accident that the first official inquiry into the possibility of co-ordinating the two was conducted as late as 1840. Similarly, when a uniform system of local courts had finally been established, the abolition of district bankruptcy courts and the Insolvent Debtors Court on circuit was logical. In another sense, the legislation can be considered the product of progressive reform in which the reformers, aware of the logistic and political difficulties of wholesale legal change, systematically eradicated sectoral defects in the law, with its general principles in mind.

The preceding examination of the way in which reform was achieved enables us to draw some general conclusions about the effectiveness of the various reforming impulses in the first half of the nineteenth century. The related field of social legislation during this period has recently been subjected to close and controversial scrutiny. Very briefly, the problem may be stated thus: did the so-called 'Benthamite' reforms after 1830 originate in and reflect the ideas of Jeremy Bentham or were they simply pragmatic responses to everyday problems? The issue is confused by the fact that, although the movement towards a centralised administrative state certainly occurred after Benthamites acquired positions of political importance, some of the reforms were initiated by non-Benthamites and many of them appear to have derived from notions prevalent long before 1830. The difficulty of proving whether or not a reformer - even a self-confessed Benthamite - was primarily motivated by doctrinaire principles is obvious and the debate has, to some extent, degenerated into an academic discussion of a thinker's relationship to his age. Did Bentham mould or merely reflect contemporary opinion? Is it plausible to suggest that individuals who had not read Bentham were influenced by his writings?[2] It is tempting to adopt B.A.M. Finlayson's compromise solution that 'Perhaps the safest and most satisfactory explanation of the changes in government and administration is one which allows for as many different forces as possible.'[3] As a generalisation this makes sense but, by extension, it is likely that Benthamism affected some areas of legislation more than others. In other words, what is needed is not broad generalisations about the significance of Benthamism but, rather, further specific investigation to ascertain which fields it did influence and which it did not.

Our investigation of legal reform of credit is pertinent to this controvery both because it was a subject in which Benthamites were keenly interested and because it overlaps prison reform. In relation to the latter field, even the 'Benthamites' concede that the notion of centralised control was not solely Benthamite[4] and it is indisputable, as Roberts points out, that the 1835 Prisons Act 'arose not from the ratiocinations of the Benthamites, but from the persuasions of the evangelicals,' supported by

---

2 The 'anti-Benthamite' case is stated most effectively by D. Roberts, 'Jeremy Bentham and the Victorian Administrative State,' Vict. Studies, ii (1959), 193-210, and by O. MacDonagh, 'The Nineteenth-Century Revolution in Government: A Reappraisal,' Hist. Journal, i (1958), 52-67; the 'Benthamite' case by H. Parris, 'The Nineteenth-Century Revolution in Government: A Reappraisal Reappraised,' Hist. Journal, iii (1960), 17-37, and by J. Hart, 'Nineteenth-Century Social Reform: A Tory Interpretation of History,' Past and Present, xxxi (July 1965), 39-61.

3 B.A.M. Finlayson, England in the Eighteen Thirties (1969), p. 72.

4 E.g. Hart, op. cit., p. 44.

some interested peers and local magistrates.[5] In fact, as has been already noted, the solution was much older than the Prison Discipline Society, cited by Roberts. It was suggested tentatively by the Society for the Promotion of Christian Knowledge at the turn of the eighteenth century and, more forcefully, by Smith and Wedderburn in the last quarter of the century and by the 1815 Committee on London Debtors Prisons. In the eighteenth century, however, when debtors constituted such a large proportion of the prison population, the legislature was able to alleviate the problem of prison conditions by periodic acts to release debtors. Indeed, as late as 1814, the comfortable delusion that overcrowding was the only fault in the prison system was still popular[6] and Redesdale's act, in the previous year, reflects its influence on parliament. After about 1815, both this interpretation of the problem and its solution ceased to be viable. On the one hand, a series of parliamentary inquiries pointed out the real defects in the prison system; on the other, the prisons were increasingly filled with criminals rather than debtors. The eventual adoption by the legislature of central inspection in the 1830s may have been partly a product of factors other than the persuasiveness of evangelical agitation at the time. There is much to recommend Hart's argument that, although experience taught that prison legislation was futile when entrusted to local magistrates, the central inspection solution was only adopted after Benthamites, 'the only consistent and systematic advocates of inspection in some form or other,' acquired positions of influence in government and on commissions of inquiry. She suggests that their specific contribution to the passing of the 1835 act might have been the product of their 'deep interest in

---

5 Roberts, op. cit., p. 205.

6 E.g. Hansard, P.D., 1814, xxviii, 70-85, George Holford, citing the Aldermen of the City of London.

punishment generally, and it seems at least likely that they had helped to clear people's minds about the purposes of punishment and the means to secure the ends intended.'[7] As early as 1813 Brougham had praised Bentham's theories on punishment as more comprehensive and perceptive than anything previously written on the subject,[8] and it is likely that his notions and those of James Mill circulated widely in the 1820s and 1830s, infecting humanitarians and pragmatists alike.

The danger for the 'Benthamites' in the above discussion is the temptation to adopt a post hoc ergo propter hoc line of argument. Their problem and that of their opponents is the difficulty of gauging personal motivation. The same can be said of the legal developments analysed in chapters 1-3 above. It may be suggested from this evidence, however, that the late 1820s marks the watershed between a century in which legislation was inhibited by a lack of understanding amongst politicians of the general issues applicable to the law of credit and a period in which it was fostered by the application to the various sectors of the law of consistent principles which derived, through Brougham, from Bentham. The period 1660-1830 had not, of course, been devoid of legal reform and innovation. Bankruptcy law had been changed radically in the first decade of the eighteenth century, consolidated in 1732 and periodically clarified by many statutes in the subsequent hundred years. Similarly, parliament had raised the minimum debt to which mesne process applied, periodically released insolvents from prison and established small debt courts in various parts of the country. But, from the late eighteenth century, the systems which operated

---

7 Hart, loc. cit.

8 Contributions to the Edinburgh Review by Henry Lord Brougham (Glasgow, 1856), iii, 145.

in all three sectors of the debt laws had become increasingly inadequate and suggestions for more radical legislation had grown. These suggestions were made by a variety of people, including humanitarian reformers like Howard, professional critics bred within the system like Burges and theoretical critics like Bentham. At this time, however, the majority of politicians resisted radical alterations not only in the debt laws but in most legal fields. Halévy argues that Bentham allowed his Introduction to the Principles of Morals and Legislation to be published first in French because 'the state of opinion in England at the end of the eighteenth century was unfavourable to the success of Bentham's programme of reform.'[9] In the early nineteenth century, Romilly's realisation that sweeping reforms were impossible is reflected both in the piecemeal and moderate nature of most of his work[10] and in his exhortations to the Commons to adopt Benthamite thought.[11] Parliamentary resistance to reform is explained by a variety of factors. One or two politicians were blindly reactionary, opposing all attempts to tamper with the legal code.[12] In contrast, most were simply apathetic when legal questions arose, considering them too technical for laymen and leaving reform to the lawyers.[13] This is understandable since most members were insufficiently versed in the law to contribute constructively to debates upon it. It is more difficult to explain the inactivity of politicians possessed

---

9 E. Halévy, The Growth of Philosophic Radicalism (Bath, 1952), p. 76.

10 Ibid., p. 300.

11 E.g. Hansard, P.D., 1811, xix, 659.

12 E.g. Hansard, Parl. Hist., 1797, xxxiii, 182, Lord Kenyon.

13 See B. Montagu, A Brief Statement on the Several Bills introduced with a View to the Amendment of the Criminal Law (1811), p. 1.

of legal training. According to one critic of the bankruptcy system, of thirty-two lawyers in the Commons in 1830, only two or three had attempted to promote legal reform,[14] with the result that reformers were constantly hampered by the absence of able supporters. Possibly, as Cullen suggested, this was attributable to the fact that lawyers were 'mechanics' not legislators.[15] Brougham argued similarly, in 1838, when assessing the effect of Benthamism on legal attitudes:

> Noone before him had ever seriously thought of exposing the defects of our English system of jurisprudence. All former students had confined themselves to learn its principles - to make themselves masters of its eminently technical and artificial rules; and all former writers had but expounded the doctrines handed down from age to age.16

It seems likely also, that polticial considerations obstructed radical legal change. The aversion of the more blue-blooded Whigs to their radical 'Jacobin' allies, like Romilly, Scarlett and Brougham, certainly inhibited a concerted opposition campaign.[17] Equally, the awareness of the average Tory peer that the attack on the judicial system emanated from the same source as the attack on the constitution induced uncritical opposition to most proposals before the 1820s.[18]

The suggestion that the change which occurred in the parliamentary attitude to law in the late 1820s is primarily attributable to Brougham needs modification. Logically, one

---

14 C.S. Cullen, Reform of the Bankrupt Court (1830), p. viii.

15 Ibid.

16 Speeches of Lord Brougham (1838), ii, 287-8.

17 For the Whig split, see A.S. Foord, His Majesty's Opposition (Oxford, 1964), pp. 439-40, 453-60.

18 See A.S. Turberville, The House of Lords in the Age of Reform (Oxford, 1958), p. 217.

cannot divorce the reforms of the 1830s from the legal work of Peel in the previous decade. Peel's importance in this respect must not be exaggerated. He was neither an original thinker on legal matters nor did he intend to institute sweeping changes in the law.[19] The general effect of his work was to consolidate rather than alter the law radically[20] and to abolish capital punishment for crimes to which it had not been applied for many years. The changes in bankruptcy law in the 1830s emphasize the limited nature of legal reform in the 1820s. Peel's attitude to the insolvency and small debt laws reveals a similar caution; he rebuffed the radical suggestions of Joseph Hume on the question of mesne process and refused to commit himself to reform of the small debt courts because of the problem of reimbursing displaced court officials.[21] Nevertheless, it is likely that Peel's acknowledgement of the need for legal reform contributed to the eventual success of Brougham's legislation. It did this not only by publicising legal defects and revealing the possibilities of state action in relation to law, but also by acclimatising his party to law reform. In 1828, Brougham acknowledged his debt to Peel, whose work had 'tended to silence the clamours that would otherwise have been raised against the reform of the law, and might possibly have proved fatal to it.'[22] Peel's intention, as Gash points out, was to make law reform a

---

19 See J.A. Gulland, 'The History of the Criminal Law Reforms of the Period of Peel's Home Secretaryship, 1822-7,' B.I.H.R., viii (1930-1), 183; cf. N. Gash, Mr. Secretary Peel (1961), pp. 336-9, 487.

20 E.g. the criminal law was codified and statutes relating to customs duties and juries consolidated.

21 Hansard, P.D., n.s., 1828, xix, 878; 2s, 1829, xx, 434; 2s, 1830, xxii, 267.

22 Ibid., n.s., 1828, xviii, 129-30.

practical, non-party issue.[23] Although he was only partly successful in this - the Whig legislation of the 1830s was constantly harassed by Conservative opponents - he had, by the late 1820s, made the necessity of law reform a widely accepted fact. The form which that reform should take, however, was still not apparent and it was Brougham who clarified the prevalent muddled thought and expounded the principles which were to guide legislation.

In his law reforms - perhaps, as his biographer suggests, in them alone - Brougham espoused Bentham's principles whole-heartedly: 'It was only in the field of law reform that he was even a Benthamite, and in that sphere he was to be Bentham's representative in action.'[24] This does not mean that Brougham swept away all the cobwebs in the debt laws with one master stroke. Indeed, his approach to legal problems reveals an almost pessimistic caution which fits ill with the expansive and optimistic certainty of Bentham. New takes pains to stress that Brougham was no philosopher or theorist and was not attracted by the general systems advocated by Bentham: 'Bentham was the basic theorist; Brougham the practical reformer.'[25] Even so, as will be shown, Brougham's work consistently reflected his debt to Bentham. The effect of his enunciation of Benthamism is apparent in the contrast between the confused parliamentary arguments on the debt laws before 1830 and their clarity afterwards.

This is illustrated by the development of bankruptcy legislation. Before 1830, alterations in bankruptcy law had been narrow in scope and had failed to tackle the fundamental causes of the defects in the system. The 1818 committee on bankruptcy maintained that most previous

---

23 Gash, op. cit., p. 314.

24 C. New, The Life of Henry Brougham to 1830 (Oxford, 1961), p. 154.

25 Ibid., pp. 400, 152.

proposals for reform had been rejected because parliament feared that reform might create more problems than it solved.[26] As a result, many politicians had shared Lord Holland's aversion in 1808 to 'innovation without taking a clear and comprehensive view of the whole of the bearings of the question.'[27] The gradual weakening of resistance during the 1820s is attributable to the fuller understanding of the problem acquired, first, from the criticisms and digests of bankruptcy law published by a small group of bankruptcy commissioners, including Edward Christian, Charles Sinclair Cullen, James Fonblanque and Basil Montagu, second, from dissemination of the evidence presented to the 1817 and 1818 committees and, third, from the clarity of the Consolidating Act of 1825. Nevertheless, Brougham could justifiably assert, in 1828, that 'After all that was lately done in arranging and simplifying this code, it remains full of contradictions, and the source of innumerable frauds and endless litigation.'[28] The success of his subsequent statute in 1831, in the face of strong Tory opposition to its patronage proposals,[29] is explained by the fact that its relatively narrow attack concentrated upon administrative abuses which were no longer defensible. Brougham was accused, initially, of attempting to rush the bill through the Lords at a time when Eldon was indisposed and Lyndhurst on circuit duty.[30] In this case, however, as Eldon acknowledged, Tory opposition was futile because of the

---

26 B.P.P. Bankrupt Laws (1818), p. 3.

27 Hansard, P.D., 1808, x, 1068.

28 Ibid., n.s., 1828, xviii, 241-2.

29 For the criticisms of Lord Wynford, Sir Charles Wetherell and Edward Sugden, see ibid., 3s, 1831, iii, 384, 917-20; viii, 25-33, 661-6, 817-8.

30 Ibid., 3s, 1831, iii, 389-90, Brougham.

universal disapprobation of the prevailing system, especially amongst merchants.[31]

Of the three sectors of the debt laws, bankruptcy was reformed first because the tenor of the criticisms of both merchants and reformers coincided. There was no initial clash over legal principle as in insolvency. The direction of bankruptcy reform in the 1830s and 1840s reflects Bentham's dictum that efficient procedure was the pre-requisite of good law.[32] In this, the necessary changes were less profound than in insolvency because bankruptcy already contained procedural forms which Benthamites were demanding for other courts. The opening of a suit, for example, was not encumbered by the forms of Common Law (declaration, pleading etc.) and was already speedy. Similarly, in bankruptcy, interested parties could be competent witnesses. Other aspects of procedure, however, induced reforms which reflect Benthamite ideas. The principal goal of the legislation appears to have been the eradication of self-interest in two areas. First, by abolishing the creditor's power to institute secret bankruptcy proceedings and to grant the certificate, the plaintiff's control of cases was destroyed. The institution of judicial control can be viewed as an attempt to provide 'proportionality' between punishment and offence (the new commissioners could annex discretionary conditions to the certificate). Second, the appointment of salaried officials abolished the 'fee-gathering' system so despised by Bentham. Other Benthamite aspects of the reforms include the institution of a single-judge system, the reduction of Chancery's participation, the further simplification of procedure (the abolition of bond and fiat), the erection of

---

31 See H. Twiss, Life of Lord Eldon (1844), p. 138.

32 According to Dicey, Benthamites concentrated upon procedure because 'A right which an individual cannot enforce is to him no right at all.' A.V Dicey, Law and Opinion (1905), pp. 204-5.

a uniform system of courts throughout the country and the gradual fusion of the bankruptcy and insolvency processes.

The contrast between the periods before and after 1830 is particularly marked in the insolvency laws, the unconstitutional nature of which had been attacked for centuries. Although, before Brougham, that attack had never converted more than a handful of politicians, insolvency legislation did provoke constant disputes amongst a minority. In 1783, Earl Bathurst told the Lords that, during his fifty-year political career, he had not witnessed one insolvent debtors act pass the house without arousing criticism of its detrimental effect upon credit.[33] As this implies, the insolvency question split interested politicians into two groups, which might be termed reactionaries and reformers. The former consisted largely of the merchant interest, anxious to retain its punitive powers, some country gentlemen, determined to resist encroachments upon the privileges of landed property, and a group of lawyers in the Lords who were concerned, with Eldon, not to allow sympathy for the sufferings of unfortunate debtors to outweigh the 'general interest of the empire and its commercial relation.'[34] The reformers were composed of what might loosely be called 'humanitarians,' concerned with alleviating the suffering of imprisoned debtors and including legal reformers anxious to abolish an abusive practice. Redesdale's statute represents a victory for this group and it is pertinent to examine the reasons for its successful passage.

It is tempting to compare the act with other humanitarian statutes of the early nineteenth century, which

---

33 Hansard, Parl. Hist., 1783, xxiii, 1100.

34 Hansard, P.D., 1806, vii, 146.

were the products of agitation by the evangelicals.[35] In this case, however, their influence must be doubted because none of the leading parliamentary critics of the insolvency laws - Burges, Effingham, Holland, Moira, Redesdale and Romilly - was an evangelical. Indeed, the domain of evangelical agitation tended to lie outside legal reform. This applies equally to the Methodists, whose political conservatism had always led them to reject constructive legal criticism in favour of philanthropy,[36] as to the leaders of the Evangelical Revival, whose reactionary social and political philosophies precluded association with radical legal reformers like Romilly.[37] The attitude of Thomas Fowell Buxton, the one evangelical who tackled legal questions with conviction,[38] is instructive. Briefly, he argued that, while imprisonment for debt was a necessary safeguard of the interests of the creditor, the debtor should not be punished further after being imprisoned.[39] His concern, therefore, like that of other evangelicals, was to improve the living conditions of debtors in prison rather than to change the law which put them there.

Although not a product of evangelical agitation, Redesdale's act was only a little more ambitious than this

---

35 E.g. legislation against the slave trade (1807), the pillory (1816), the whipping of women (1820) and cruelty to animals (1822).

36 See M. Edwards, After Wesley (1935), pp. 28, 236-8.

37 See F.K. Brown, Fathers of the Victorians (Cambridge, 1961), pp. 5, 66, 97, 111-3, 375; cf. S. Meacham, Henry Thornton of Clapham, 1760-1815 (Cambridge, Mass., 1964), pp. 140-2.

38 Buxton was a member of the Criminal Law Committee in 1819, before turning to the anti-slavery campaign. See Memoirs of Sir Thomas Fowell Buxton (ed. by his Son), (1848), pp. 118, 235-6.

39 T.F. Buxton, An Inquiry whether Crime and Misery are Produced or Prevented by our Present System of Prison Discipline (1818), pp. 2-5.

and it must be asked why reforming lawyers produced legislation which so obviously ignored legal principle. The answer lies in the strength of the resistance to radical legislation. Although admitting that the insolvency laws were in dire need of overhaul, Eldon was not prepared to institute an inquiry into possible solutions and was determined to prevent encroachments upon the immunity of landed property and the interests of creditors.[40] In his defence of the privilege of land, he was supported by the country gentlemen, whose concerted opposition in 1806 thwarted Romilly's attempt to make freehold estates liable for the simple contract debts of a deceased debtor.[41] Similarly, Moira and Redesdale vainly condemned mesne process in the first decade of the nineteenth century, after which the attack was conducted by isolated, radical Whigs like Earl Stanhope, Sir Francis Burdett, H. Grey Bennett, Peter Moore, and Joseph Hume. In the circumstances, revolutionary legislation was out of the question and reformers were obliged to promote humanitarian rather than legal reform. The underlying reason for their success in providing a permanent form of relief for debtors, in 1813, was the fact that temporary acts had ceased to be viable since, as Redesdale pointed out, the problem of overcrowded prisons was now perpetual.[42] The statute, therefore, was intended to save parliamentary time by obviating the necessity of passing frequent temporary acts.[43] It was said that the legal hierarchy gave way in order to allow the

---

40 E.g. Hansard, P.D., 1806, vii, 151; cf. Twiss, op. cit., p. 266.

41 Memoirs of the Life of Sir Samuel Romilly (ed. by his Sons), (1840), i, 38.

42 Hansard, P.D., 1812, xxi, 684.

43 Ibid., 1813, xxvi, 615, Romilly.

experiment to be tried and because the pressure for a permanent act had become so great.[44]

Thus, Redesdale's act, like the insolvent debtors acts, was the thin end of the wedge for the reformers. While the label 'humanitarian' is an apt description of the act itself, it is an inadequate description of the politicians responsible for it, many of whom had been forced to adopt a compassionate stance by their failure to effect drastic legal reform. Romilly, for example, rejected suggestions that the act should be more radical on the grounds that it 'would have to encounter every species of obstruction from those who are, on all occasions, the defenders of long-prevailing abuses.'[45] That his pessimism was justified is revealed in parliament's refusal to co-operate with Althorp, in 1820, by allowing the division of an insolvent's freehold estate and in the conclusions of the 1816 and 1819 committees on insolvency that imprisonment for debt was indispensable. As a result, during the twenty years after 1813, the only successful insolvency statutes were those which tinkered with Redesdale's court, attempting to make the system work rather than to rationalise its principles.

In the late 1820s, Benthamite influence transformed attitudes to the law, not least among the lawyers themselves. Bentham specifically examined the question of imprisonment for debt in 1827. Typically, and not without justification in this case, he attributed the defects of the laws to 'Judge and Co.,' stressing their culpability in previous centuries for perverting the course of justice by extending the use of mesne process in debt cases to serve their own financial ends. In fact, he said, imprisonment for debt could not be justified as an act of compulsion

---

44 Ibid., 1813, xxvii, 102, Redesdale; Memoirs of the Life of Sir Samuel Romilly, op. cit., iii, 109.

45 Memoirs of the Life of Sir Samuel Romilly, op. cit., iii, 110-111.

(since it forced some men to pay debts which they had not contracted and others to pay the debts of friends) or as an instrument of punishment (because debt was not an offence) or as a necessary institution (since trade did not benefit from it). It was the product of the greed and laziness of the judges who failed to investigate debt cases before committing defendants to prison. Judges should punish only those who were guilty of a misdemeanour. In addition, the distinction between bankruptcy and insolvency was unjustified since all men ought to be equally obliged to pay their debts.[46]

Fundamentally, Bentham's objection to the insolvency system was that, because the judiciary had abdicated its responsibilities in debt disputes, the plaintiff was able to control the case. The cessio bonorum principle provided no solution to this because it did not prevent debtors, who were not criminal, being imprisoned in the first instance. His basic notions were precisely the same as those of Brougham, who set out with the principle in mind that no man should be either judge or executioner in his own cause. In bankruptcy, as was shown earlier, this involved the destruction of the creditor's power to institute secret proceedings and to grant the certificate; in insolvency, it necessitated the abolition of arrest for debt first on mesne and then on final process. Of Brougham's speech in 1828, which expounded all Bentham's theories on the reform of adjective law, Holdsworth says:

> There is no doubt that his speech was the most learned and thorough criticism of the many defects of the Common Law that had ever been made since the Commonwealth period; and there is no doubt that the two commissions, issued as a result of it to some of the ablest lawyers of the day, to enquire into the practice and procedure of the Courts of Common Law and into the

---

46 J. Bentham, 'Of Imprisonment for Debt,' in The Works of Jeremy Bentham (ed. J. Bowring), (1843), vi, 176-80.

law of real property, effected more law reform than any of the commissions previously appointed.47

Given Bentham's preliminary spadework, the success of Brougham and the Common Law Commissioners in changing parliamentary attitudes to the insolvency laws is explained not only by the clarity with which they articulated legal principle but also by the practical nature of their approach. Basically, they demolished the popular myth that imprisonment for debt was an indispensable concomitant of English commercial wealth, by demonstrating both that the alleged benefits of the law were nugatory in practice and that creditors would benefit considerably if it were abolished. They were thus able to overcome one of the major weaknesses of earlier reform movements by associating legal principle, which had usually been expounded in isolation, and practical commercial advantage. Consequently, a campaign which had previously been conducted by radicals acquired the support, in the 1830s, both of Whig leaders, like Campbell, Cottenham, Lansdowne and Melbourne, and of most Whig politicians in the Commons, where George Grote, Benjamin Hawes, Thomas Spring Rice, Robert Rolfe and Henry Warburton stressed that mesne process not only violated legal principle but also was ineffective in practice. Although Peel played little part in the debates, the Conservatives offered concerted resistance to the bills. In the Commons, the opposition of, for example, John Richards, James Freshfield, Sir Robert Inglis and Sir Edward Knatchbull was overcome fairly easily because most members, including some merchants,[48] now disagreed with their basic contention that imprisonment for debt was essential to commerce. In the Lords, however, Conservative opposition

---

47 W.S. Holdsworth, 'The Movement for Reforms in the Law (1793-1832),' L.Q.R., lvi, (1940), 352.

48 E.g. Henry Warburton, Benjamin Hawes, Mark Phillips and William Ewart (Hansard, P.D., 3s, 1835, xxvi, 569, 1163-5).

was more fruitful. With assistance from Wellington, Farnham, Abinger and Ashburton, Lyndhurst was able, first, to delay and, later, to truncate Whig legislation, which consequently achieved rather less than was intended. It is indicative of their continued resistance that, in the early 1840s, Brougham adopted a round-about method of overcoming final process instead of Cottenham's more direct approach.[49] In his attack on the insolvency laws, in other words, Brougham was influenced by two considerations. On the one hand, his basic desire was to put into practice Benthamite legal principles. On the other, awareness of the continued political obstacles to radical change led both him and other Whigs to modify legislation and adopt expedients which, in practice, achieved reform approximating closely to their basic goals. Thus, imprisonment for debt continued but lost most of its force.

The movement for reform of the small debt laws contrasts sharply with those for insolvency and bankruptcy reform. The question did not arouse the wrath of humanitarians (except when small debtors were imprisoned in execution by the superior courts), because the fixed penalties of request courts did not appear barbaric and they did not allow creditors to control proceedings or debtors to evade their obligations. In addition, the mercantile sector was less concerned about small debt courts than about the bankruptcy process, which affected it more closely. As a result, the subject of small debt reform was supported neither by the passion which attached to the insolvency laws nor by the powerful pressure groups which advocated bankruptcy reform. This may explain the tardiness of the

---

49 Brougham acknowledged that one of his reasons for opening the Bankruptcy Court to non-traders was the stiff resistance to Cottenham's bill to abolish imprisonment in execution (*ibid*., 1842, lxv, 490).

legislature in tackling a problem which some European countries had solved in the eighteenth century.[50]

In this case, the problem was purely administrative: how to establish a court system which, in administering the law, could provide the two basic requirements of uniformity and respectability. In practice, this involved the provision of sufficient professional personnel to man a network of provincial courts. The reformers, led by the Benthamites who recommended a county-court system from the 1820s,[51] were confronted by resistance from the vested interest of the legal fraternity and the scepticism of politicians that the required number of legal officers was available. As long as the latter view prevailed, no solution to the problem was possible not only because Benthamite schemes were rejected but also because the request court system remained inadequate. In 1809, for example, Ellenborough, Eldon and Moira expressed their aversion to extending small debt courts because applications for them were thought to derive from the vested interests of local attornies.[52] The 1823 Committee on Small Debts also rejected their extension to the whole country because of the lack of able men in many areas. In the 1830s, this argument was used successfully to crush Whig bills which appeared to be designed to erect a centralized machinery to which most Conservatives were opposed.[53]. Indeed, Brougham's local courts bill of 1833 provoked a trial of party strength in

---

50 E.g. the reforms of Samuel Cocceji (1679-1755) in Prussia. See H. Holborn, A History of Modern Germany, 1648-1840 (1965), pp. 271-2.

51 As in bankruptcy, Brougham's insistence upon efficient administration and procedure mirrored Bentham's concern that the courts should enable all people to enforce their rights.

52 Hansard, P.D., 1809, xiv, 888-9.

53 See E. Halévy, A History of the English People in the Nineteenth Century (1950), iii, 103.

the Lords. After the bill had passed its second reading, Lyndhurst returned from circuit duty and rallied his party against its patronage clauses in the third reading, which consequently failed by five votes.[54] Hence, while other reforms were implemented, the small debt system lagged behind, becoming increasingly inadequate despite the enlarged jurisdiction of some request courts. The success of the humanitarians, in 1811 and 1827, in raising the minimum limit of mesne process, merely increased the volume of debts for which there was no legal remedy. Not until the 1840s did constant extra-parliamentary pressure lead to the erection of a co-ordinated system of courts, for which Brougham had campaigned for so long.

An admission that the Benthamite notions which were applied to the debt laws in the 1830s and 1840s represent little more than common sense suggests that the verdicts of Roberts and MacDonagh on the course of social legislation might apply to legal reform. Both argue that the administrative solutions which were applied to social problems would have been effected even if Bentham had not suggested them. Roberts contends that 'Had Bentham never written his epochal works, Victorian reformers would probably have contrived their poor laws, factory acts and educational schemes, all fitted out with central inspectors' and that the remarkable thing about Bentham was 'not his influence over men but the foresight, clarity and logic with which he expressed those truths which other forces, far stronger than his own ideas, would bring to pass.'[55] MacDonagh's investigation of the Passenger Acts leads him to a similar conclusion:

---

54 See Sir T. Martin, A Life of Lord Lyndhurst (1884), iii, 309-11.

55 D. Roberts, 'Jeremy Bentham and the Victorian Administrative State,' Vict. Studies, ii (1959), 209, 207.

> In fact, the whole process required little more than that men should have reacted reasonably intelligently to established facts, and with reasonable compassion for the sufferings of others. Given similar circumstances and stimuli - and similar circumstances and stimuli abounded in the nineteenth century - it is a safe assumption that things fell out in essentially the same fashion in many other areas of life.56

The fact that one or two non-Benthamite reformers - notably Burges - had previously advocated solutions to the debt problem similar to those eventually adopted reinforces the notion that Brougham's legislation was 'inevitable.' However, the evidence reviewed here suggests that, although this may be a valid interpretation in the long run, the reforms would not have occurred as early as they did and in the form that they did if Brougham had not clarified the thinking of contemporary lawyers and politicians. It is true that, in his speech in 1828, he described legal defects which lawyers had acknowledged for years but, as New says, 'that was one good reason for making the speech - lawyers might have talked of those matters for at least another generation, and if it had not been for Brougham's courage and enterprise nothing would have been done.'[57] The quietness of lawyers in the Commons during the preceding quarter of a century adds fuel to this argument. Indeed, in 1832, a well-informed commentator was still convinced that the traditional legal resistance to reform would lead the Common Law Commissioners to frustrate Brougham's plans.[58] Perhaps the major obstacle was the self-interest of the legal fraternity from Eldon down to the lowest attorney or

---

56 O. MacDonagh, A Pattern of Government Growth, 1800-60: The Passenger Acts and their Enforcement (1961), p. 9.

57 C. New, The Life of Henry Lord Brougham to 1830 (Oxford, 1961), p. 399.

58 J. Wade, The Extraordinary Black Book (1832), p. 327.

commissioner of bankruptcy.[59] Clearly, if the legal fraternity resisted change, parliament itself, dependent upon its lawyers for guidance, would adopt an equally reactionary attitude.

Thus, our interpretation of the influences upon reform of the debt laws is far closer to the theses of Hart and Parris than to those of MacDonagh and Roberts. Although the reforms were a response to current problems, their eventual form was a reflection of Benthamite influence. The latter was successful, as Parris says of Bentham's administrative theories, because 'they derived from the processes of change going on around him. He was working with the grain. But it does not follow that the same solutions would have been reached had he never lived.'[60]

III

In a suggestive, recent contribution, Hartwell raises some questions about the relationship between economic activity and the law during the industrial revolution.[61] He argues that, unlike the rigid, theoretical continental codes, English Common Law, independent of political control, responded empirically and flexibly to the needs of the influential merchant class in such a way that, by the early nineteenth century, it was dominated by commercial law. His concern is with the effect of legal change upon the rate of economic growth and the mechanism by which the two interacted. Did the law respond immediately or belatedly

---

59 For the hostility of bankruptcy commissioners to bankruptcy reform, see Hansard, P.D., 3s, 1831, iii, 391-3 Brougham; cf. B. Montagu, Inquiries Respecting the Courts of Commissioners of Bankrupts (1825), p. 6.

60 H. Parris, 'The Nineteenth-Century Revolution in Government: A Reappraisal Reappraised,' Hist. Journal, iii (1960), 36.

61 R.M. Hartwell, The Industrial Revolution and Economic Growth (1971), pp. 226-61.

to changing economic conditions? Was it influenced by non-economic factors? Was there, in the law, a conservative 'rationale' which inhibited its adaptability? Hartwell stresses the complexity of the relationship between the two variables, but suggests ways in which the law could influence economic activity:

> If one views the industrial revolution as the outcome, institutionally, of an increasingly efficient market, (i.e. of a market in which economic behaviour, rational, maximizing behaviour, could operate with expectations of reward and punishment according to the successful prediction of market needs and responses), then factors making for the efficiency of the market were of paramount importance for the industrial revolution. Those changes which enabled economic behaviour, whether by consumers or producers, to be satisfied and rewarded, and hence encouraged, gave the market an ongoing impetus.62

As examples, he cites the effects which modifications in the usury laws and the transferability of negotiable instruments had upon the mobility of short-term capital. In the context of Hartwell's general argument, the debt laws might be expected to bear some relation - positive or negative - to economic activity. Indeed, he suggests that the effect of legal changes before and during the industrial revolution was 'to incorporate into law the ideas and practices of the merchants and manufacturers, so that legal practice as regards contracts, negotiable instruments, bankruptcy, insurance, etc., was regularised and made certain.'[63]

The preceding study of the debt laws throws some light on these questions in the context of what is, admittedly, a narrow field. The problem will be examined from two points of view: the response of the bankruptcy, insolvency and small debt laws to economic growth and the effect of the three systems upon it. The evidence permits reasonably

---

62 Ibid., p. 258.

63 Ibid., pp. 245-6.

convincing conclusions about the first question but allows only tentative and hypothetical answers to the second.

The response of the law to economic growth was clearly belated in all three sectors. In bankruptcy, the foundations of a reasonable system had been laid in the early eighteenth century, but it failed to adapt to changing circumstances. This is illustrated by the two main problems posed by increased economic activity. First, the law rapidly became outdated, as evidenced especially by its persistent adherence to a narrow, anachronistic definition of 'trade.' Second, increasing pressure upon the bankruptcy system magnified its inherent technical and administrative faults. It is true that some of the technical modifications effected in the century after 1732 - particularly those of Mansfield and Romilly - clarified contentious points and added an element of sophistication but, on the whole, bankruptcy law before the Consolidating Act of 1825 was hopelessly confused and riddled with conflicting interpretations. Equally, its administration was seriously defective as a result both of the low quality and inadequate jurisdiction of the commissioners and of the illogical insistence upon entrusting the collection of estates and the granting of certificates to the creditors.

The failure of the legislature to respond to demands for inclusion of non-traders, judicial control of proceedings and the establishment of official assignees ensured that the law was unable to cope with the demands made of it by a rapidly developing economy. The eventual radical legislation of the 1830s and 1840s was largely a response to mercantile criticisms of the prevailing system, but the statutes themselves did not tally completely with merchants' demands. Indeed, in some respects, Brougham deliberately ignored the latter, as shown in his insistence upon instituting official assignees.[64] Thus, the response

64 For mercantile opposition to official assignees, see Hansard, P.D., 3s, 1831, iv, 316-7, Brougham.

of the bankruptcy laws does not fit Hartwell's suggested pattern. While it is indisputable that reform was the product of economic growth (which, by increasing bankruptcies, made the legal defects intolerable), it is also true that it was effected both belatedly and in response to legal criteria to which many traders took exception.

A similar verdict is applicable to the course of reform of the insolvency laws, which reveals close parallels to that of bankruptcy. In both, the system which operated before the industrial revolution provided reasonable certainty to creditors that their contracts would not be broken frivolously. In each, also, practical defects destroyed this theoretical efficacy. In addition, reforms of the two systems before the 1830s were invariably inadequate and the eventual solutions, although in the creditors' interests, ran counter to their desires. The efficacy of imprisonment for debt as a deterrent to non-payment was, to most contemporaries, self-evident. Its practical defects, throughout the eighteenth and early nineteenth centuries, were the product of institutional weaknesses: of the penal system, which facilitated evasion by allowing debtors to live in the Rules; of the legal system, which parties could manipulate in their own interests; and, above all, of legislative interventions on behalf of the debtor. It is evident that the effect of economic growth was to turn the legislative trend against the interests of creditors. Although the desires of the latter were not completely ignored in Redesdale's act, since imprisonment for debt was retained, the provision of speedy discharge and the defects of the system ensured that the trading community suffered greatly in the subsequent twenty years. Ironically, although the statutes of the 1830s and 1840s weakened further the creditor's powers of imprisonment, they were more advantageous to traders because they treated the question in relation to other aspects of the law. It would be unrealistic, however, to argue that the legislation reflected the desires of the trading community. The concurrence of some traders in it appears to have resulted from their disenchantment with the prevailing system and most seem to have considered that their powers of imprisonment should be strengthened. Indeed, in 1837, Brougham exhorted politicians to ignore the flood of traders' petitions against the abolition of imprisonment for debt.[65] It is thus clear that, throughout the industrial revolution, the influence of the trading classes upon insolvency legislation was not particularly significant. While their desires were never completely ignored, their influence was constantly superseded by stronger pressure which derived, before 1830, from humanitarians and, after, from Benthamism.

Like the other two sectors of the debt laws, those relating to small debtors also responded belatedly to the expansion of economic activity. The difference, in this case, is the fact that the system which existed before the industrial revolution was already inadequate and became increasingly ineffective as retail trade expanded. It is true that the erection of request courts, in the late eighteenth and early nineteenth centuries, represents a response to economic growth, but their jurisdiction was too small in relation both to geographical area and to the size of debts which they could adjudicate. As in both bankruptcy and insolvency, the resistance of the legal fraternity to a potential loss of business hampered reform in this sector. The eventual erection of a uniform county-court system occurred long after it was necessary.

---

65 Ibid., 1837, xxxix, 576.

IV

In all three sectors of the debt laws, therefore, economic growth posed problems to which the legislature responded belatedly. The inadaptability of the law has been explained by a variety of factors, including the reactionary mentality and enlightened self-interest of legal officers and political pressure groups and the ignorance of most politicians of the nature of the respective problems. However, the fact that reformers themselves were often unable to define the direction which legislation should take suggests that these explanations are only part of the answer. Perhaps a more fundamental cause of the inadequacy of most discussion of the subject was the absence of sufficient concrete information about the over-all defects of the law and its administration. As in many areas of social reform in the nineteenth century, this was not remedied until the evidence of parliamentary committees and royal commissions of inquiry had circulated widely in the second and third decades. The inquiries had a three-fold significance for debt legislation. First, they pierced the obscurity of the law by analysing its defects, the complexity of which had previously created confusion. The broad range of information and opinion which they elicited formed the basis of subsequent reforms even if Brougham's own interpretation of the evidence was not necessarily the same as that of the committees, as is indicated by the contrast between his bankruptcy reforms and the proposals of the 1818 bankruptcy committee. Second, the inquiries reduced the possible number of solutions by applying the basic common denominator of legal principle. Thus, both the Common Law and 1840 commissioners made Brougham's recommendations more palatable to parliament and public alike. Third, by advertising the principal illogicalities of existing administrative forms, the inquiries exposed a target which vested interest was no longer able to defend.

While the criticism was no doubt symptomatic of a growing general awareness of the need for higher standards of administrative competence, it is arguable that the debt laws could never function efficiently until other areas of society had been transformed. This is illustrated by the prolonged absence of national uniformity in the mode of recording commercial transactions. The difficulties of adjudicating and administering the bankruptcy of an illiterate or of the many traders who did not take stock have already been discussed. A solution to this problem was hampered by two factors. First, the educational and organisational obstacles to uniformity appeared insuperable. The answer of John Pollock, a solicitor, to Benjamin Hawes, in 1840, reflects the hopelessness of the task:

> Q . . . suppose every trader were required to use only books of account, which should be, before he commenced them, paged consecutively from beginning to end: do you think that would be at all a practicable regulation?
>
> A It would be a very good regulation in large houses, but I do not think you could ever introduce it into small ones. The idea upon the subject is exceedingly good if it were practicable.[66]

The second factor is the continued disorganisation of the professions and the absence of both scientific techniques and consistently high standards of conduct amongst, especially, accountants. The small size and unscientific methods of the accountancy profession during the early nineteenth century have been described elsewhere.[67] The eventual creation of a large, competent and professionally organised body of accountants appears to have resulted from the Railway Acts, the Companies Act of 1862 and,

---

66 B.P.P. Bankruptcy and Insolvency (1840), p. 289.

67 N.A.H. Stracey, English Accounting, 1800-1954 (1954), pp. 12-18.

ironically, the Bankruptcy Act of 1869.[68] The effects of poor accounting before the formation of professional bodies in the 1870s were probably felt at two levels in debt proceedings. Until accountants began to participate extensively in the collection of estates, bankruptcy administration may have been impeded. Also - and perhaps more important - low standards of conduct affected many cases. In 1817, Joshua Mayhew described the ingenious, undetectable frauds concocted by Jewish accountants in the books of their clients.[69] Isaac Sewell, in 1840, was similarly critical of the frequent dishonesty of accountants.[70] The absence of tight, professional regulations and well-defined accountancy principles must have added to the considerable problems of the courts, especially when dealing with large estates. Clearly, like the law itself, other components of the economy responded belatedly to economic growth. The faltering success of debt reform should thus be viewed as an example and, to some extent, a product of the problems which the industrial revolution posed for the tertiary sector as a whole.

V

While the belated response of the debt laws during the industrial revolution is relatively easy to demonstrate and explain, the question of their effect upon economic activity is complicated and difficult. The suggestion that law could influence economic growth appears incontestable. There is little reason to quibble with the eulogies frequently accorded to Mansfield's refinements of commercial law, which

---

68 Ibid., pp. 13, 22-3; cf. A.M. Carr-Saunders and P.A. Wilson, The Professions (Oxford, 1933), p. 210.

69 B.P.P. Bankrupt Laws (1817), p. 82.

70 B.P.P. Bankruptcy and Insolvency (1840), p. 56.

gave legal force to commercial contracts and established sound principles to govern trading disputes. As A.J. Youngson says, they 'enabled merchants very largely to confine their risks to the economic field. Enterprise, in this way, was given a share of that security which attached so firmly to property, and it could be carried on the more easily, and the more boldly, for the elimination of legal uncertainty.'[71] The debt laws are pertinent to this in two ways. On the one hand, they could reinforce or nullify the effectiveness of commercial law, the implementation of which was, obviously, dependent upon the provision of efficient legal machinery. The concept of fraudulent preference, for example, would be redundant if instances of it could not, in practice, be detected and punished. On the other, the laws could give security to financial contracts at all levels of society, thus providing a solid legal basis for economic activity. It is convenient to examine their influence upon economic growth in relation to two postulates. First, if the laws were to facilitate economic activity, it was essential that they should not impose excessively severe penalties for failure which would impede risk-taking. Second, if they were to encourage growth, they needed both to provide the creditor with the certainty of cheap and speedy redress in cases of default and to induce the debtor to act honestly before and after the collapse of his credit.

In bankruptcy, the first of these criteria appears to have been fulfilled by the legislation of the early eighteenth century. The privileges granted to the bankrupt - the certificate of discharge and a proportion of assets collected - eradicated the dread which bankruptcy may have previously instilled, by reducing the consequences of failure. It seems likely that if the previous repressive

71 A.J. Youngson, 'The Acceleration of Economic Progress in Great Britain, 1750-1800,' in Readings in the History of Economic Growth (ed. M.E. Falkus), (Oxford, 1968), p. 65.

system had continued to operate the exploitation of new or temperamental trades and markets would have been inhibited. In the context of Hartwell's suggestions, therefore, the foundations of a reasonable bankruptcy system, which at least did not discourage economic activity, had been laid before the industrial revolution.

The applicability to the bankruptcy laws of the second criterion is, however, questionable. In theory, the privileges which the bankrupt received and his obligation to submit speedily to the commissioners, on pain of death, encouraged honest dealings and provided creditors with reasonable certainty that broken contracts would not result in heavy losses. In practice, faulty law and administration encouraged dishonesty and prevented the speedy collection of estates. Malpractices were invited both by the excessive severity of the law and by the limited jurisdiction and inefficiency of the commissioners. One of the latter considered, in 1818, that most commissions were conspiracies between the bankrupt and petitioning creditor, designed to defraud the general creditors.[72] In addition, assets were rarely collected quickly and cheaply because neither the messengers nor the assignees maintained a tight hold on the estates. A solicitor reckoned, in the same year, that only one in twelve assignees acted fairly to the creditors and that dividends averaged about five shillings in the pound.[73] As a result, the bankruptcy laws were extremely unpopular throughout the industrial revolution. During the early nineteenth century, merchants, traders and bankers constantly remonstrated against them, complaining, above all, of the ease with which bona fide creditors were defrauded by fictitious claimants and of the inadequacies of the commissioners. The extent of the hostility is indicated

---

72 Hansard, P.D., 1818, xxxviii, 982, John Smith, citing Cullen.

73 B.P.P. Bankrupt Laws (1818), Montagu, quoting a letter from a solicitor.

by the fact that, in 1831, 4,500 people signed the parliamentary petition against the system within two and a half days, including 'all the powerful bankers, merchants, solicitors, and tradesmen of the city of London.'[74] A typical mercantile attitude was that expressed in a letter to Montagu in 1818: 'If it goes to a Commission of Bankruptcy, I will sell my debt for five shillings in the pound.'[75]

It is not unreasonable to assume that the universal condemnation of a system which clearly impeded the legal enforcement of commercial contracts indicates that bankruptcy law had a negative effect on economic activity. The smallness of dividends and the ease with which commissions were manipulated to the advantage of interested parties might be expected to make traders ultra-cautious in their selection of customers. There is, however, little indication in the available evidence that a fear of substantial losses incurred in bankruptcies actually restricted commercial activity. While it would be unrealistic to conclude from this that the activities of some traders were not hampered by the feebleness of bankruptcy administration, the simple fact has to be faced that aggregative economic growth occurred at a time when the law was totally inadequate. It is interesting that in America, where there was no law against fraudulent bankruptcies, de Tocqueville considered that 'The dread of being prosecuted as a bankrupt is greater in the minds of the majority than the fear of being ruined by the bankruptcy of others; and a sort of guilty tolerance is extended by the public conscience to an offence which everyone condemns in

---

74 Hansard, P.D., 2s, 1831, ii, 548, Brougham.

75 B.P.P. Bankrupt Laws (1818), pp. 9-10, Montagu, quoting a letter from a merchant.

his individual capacity.'[76] The apparent similarity between this and the attitude of English traders suggests that there is some truth in E.J. Hobsbawm's assertion that 'The cost of institutional inefficiency, high though it was, was little more than petty cash to the most dynamic industrial economy of the world.'[77] Indeed, while Adam Smith's contention that 'the number of prudent and successful undertakings is everywhere much greater than that of injudicious and unsuccessful ones . . .'[78] may have been true at the start of this period, it is arguable that the laxity of the system increasingly aroused, in a minority, a cynicism toward the prospect of bankruptcy. The commissioners were unable to investigate misconduct before failure and any resistance of the creditors to granting the certificate could easily be overcome by fraudulent means. Consequently, in 1785, bankruptcy was considered 'an infallible method for one in tattered circumstances to make himself whole again: It is called the Emetic of an undone man.'[79] John Ingram Lockhart, a commissioner, stated in 1818 that

> I have, in almost every commission in which I have been named, found that the Bankrupt had acted with great injustice towards his creditors, generally with dishonesty and fraud, and always with imprudence and carelessness of the wreck of his substance, which in fact was not his own, but their's, and this conduct I can only trace to one cause, and that is the facility with which almost every Bankrupt goes through the operation of his commission.80

---

76 A. de Tocqueville, Democracy in America (ed. P. Bradley), (New York, 1945), i, 239.

77 E.J. Hobsbawm, Industry and Empire (Pelican edn., 1970), p. 231.

78 A. Smith, The Wealth of Nations (Pelican edn., 1970), p. 442.

79 Fowler. Salisbury Scraps (Salisbury, 1785).

80 B.P.P. Bankrupt Laws (1818), p. 103.

Many of Lockhart's contemporaries were also aware of the prevalent cynicism.[81] It is thus possible that the defective bankruptcy laws contributed to the speculative activity and loose trading which characterised many of the overseas trade booms of the industrial revolution. Certainly, they did little to discourage dubious operations. The large increase in bankruptcies and the artificial trading conditions of the French war period possibly exacerbated this. In 1802, for example, Henry Thornton stated that, because of the way in which paper credit embroiled honest traders in the failures of dubious ones, 'to stop payment is considered too much a misfortune or accident, too little a fault; and thus a principal incentive to punctuality in mercantile payments is weakened, and an important check to adventurous speculation is in some measure lost.'[82]

At a general level, the role of bankruptcy law in economic growth may be compared with that of the banking system. Hartwell suggests that, although banks, especially in the provinces, were widely criticised for the rash credit which they granted, 'a liberal credit policy was more conducive to growth than a restrictive policy would have been, and so the banks provided essential and stimulating service to industry and trade at a critical stage of development.'[83] A similar verdict may be appropriate to the bankruptcy laws. If the latter had imposed excessive constraints upon traders who stopped payments, individual

---

81 E.g. B.P.P. Bankrupt Laws (1817), p. 63, Samuel Sweet; p. 82, Joshua Mayhew; p. 104, John Billing; p. 109, John Wilkinson; B.P.P. Bankrupt Laws (1818), p. 34, Basil Montagu; p. 69, Robert Waithman.

82 H. Thornton, An Inquiry into the Nature and Effects of Paper Credit in Great Britain (ed. F.A. Hayek), (1939), p. 188.

83 R.M. Hartwell, The Industrial Revolution and Economic Growth (1971), pp. 124-5.

enterprise would have been discouraged. If they had furnished a rigidly efficient instrument for punishing commercial 'misdemeanours,' speculation and risk-taking would not have been worthwhile. In other words, economic growth occurred within a legal (and financial) framework which did not discourage normal trading activity and which posed no obstacle to the frequently precarious entrepreneurial activity which characterised the industrial revolution.

It is more difficult to assess the economic effect of the insolvency laws. Many commentators were convinced that, by providing creditors with reasonable certainty that their contracts would be honoured, the laws had stimulated economic growth. Lord Kenyon, for example, stated, in 1797, that 'the law of arrest, as it at present prevailed, had conduced in an essential degree to the increase of commerce and the extent of trade.'[84] Forty years later, Wellington, agreeing with Lyndhurst, argued in a similar vein:

> one of the causes of debts being incurred in the country was, in a great degree, the power which creditors at present possessed to arrest their debtors on mesne process; and he still further believed that it was the facility which was thus given of obtaining credit which had been the cause of the great mercantile prosperity of the country.[85]

Neither Wellington nor the traders who concurred with this judgment suggested that imprisonment *per se* was a successful way of enforcing contracts. Indeed, all the available evidence pointed to the fact that prosecution rarely produced payment. What they did argue, however, was that the most significant - and incalculable - statistic was the number of debtors who paid because of the threat of imprisonment. As the merchants' champion insisted, in 1835,

---

84 Hansard, *Parl. Hist.*, 1797, xxxiii, 181.

85 Hansard, *P.D.*, 3s, 1837, xxxix, 597.

> there were a thousand instances in which the law, as it now stood, induced debtors to pay their debts, and this with great advantage to the community. The law operated silently and imperceptibly, but was not the less real for not being observed, while an instance of abuse was striking.86

Certainly, many traders appear to have pinned faith in the deterrent effect of the law. An opposite theme, running through the debates of the early nineteenth century, was that the abolition of imprisonment would suppress the rash and indiscriminate credit which was given. The implication here is that economic growth was accelerated by the psychological effect of the law upon creditors: the right to imprison was 'good security.' Brougham reckoned, in 1828, that it encouraged creditors

> to speculate upon the chance of payment from insolvent persons; so that they enter into a competition . . . in the credit they give to the needy and profligate, or suspected and extravagant men, unable to pay anything like the whole amount of debts, which the rashness or cupidity of tradesmen may allow them to contract.87

It is instructive in this context that, after the abolition of mesne process, a number of traders alleged that they had adopted a more cautious credit policy than before[88] and Elliott reckoned, in 1845, that the effective repeal of imprisonment for debt had 'broken down the commercial gates and fences of the nation.'[89]

If some contemporaries were convinced that legal sanctions justified the widespread credit facilities of the early nineteenth century, others were not so sure. There is substantial evidence that the 'escape hatches' provided to debtors by humanitarian legislation produced a flippant

---

86 Ibid., 1835, xxix, 1090, John Richards.

87 Ibid., n.s., 1828, xviii, 194.

88 E.g. B.P.P. Bankruptcy and Insolvency (1840), p. 447, Edward Swaine.

89 J.H. Elliott, Credit the Life of Commerce (1845), p. vii.

attitude towards the insolvency process. Many debtors appear to have sneered at the law in the same way as they did at the bankruptcy laws. The evidence, cited in chapter two, of the abuse of insolvent debtors acts and Redesdale's court is strong and convincing. As a result, Waithman maintained in 1819, 'it was notorious that this law gave birth to an extravagant spirit of adventure and gambling.'[90] Eleven years later, Alderman Thompson described its effect:

> the law, as it at present stood, operated with peculiar severity on the retail trader; the debts due to whom were of small amount, and who in vain incurred the costs of suing the debtor, as the latter, if the creditor recovered against him, merely went to gaol and took benefit of the act.91

The paradoxical conclusion emerges that the insolvency laws both encouraged traders to grant lavish credit, by giving them apparent security, and provoked excessive spending, by guaranteeing debtors a speedy release from prison. It is likely that each of these extreme interpretations contains some validity but that the truth lies somewhere between. Imprisonment for debt could deter a debtor from non-payment by raising the prospect, first, of a lengthy incarceration, second, of appalling prison conditions and, third, of the destruction of his financial well-being, reputation and future prospects. In the eighteenth century, all three of these threats were operative. The first two, however, became progressively less significant during the first half of the nineteenth century, as Redesdale's act dispelled the uncertainty of release which had characterised the temporary acts and humanitarian efforts gradually improved prison conditions. After 1813, the number of debtors imprisoned for years against their wishes decreased sharply and opportunities for evasion increased. A typical description of the effect of

---

90 Hansard, P.D., 1819, xxxviii, 517.

91 Ibid., 2s, 1830, xxiv, 229.

the new system is that of Peter Laurie, in 1816: 'under the old law, when a man was afraid of being arrested . . . he shook his feathers and endeavoured to make a compromise; but under the present law, he goes on to the last, ruins his morals and ruins his creditors.'[92] As a result, many traders stated that, after 1813, they had reduced the credit which they gave and others that they had raised their prices to provide what Brougham called 'a species of insurance on all bad debts.'[93] The effect of improved prison conditions was suggested by Sir Watkins Williams-Wynn, in 1835:

> Half a century ago, taking the state of prisons into consideration at that period, imprisonment for debt was a real and severe punishment. The condition of these receptacles of misfortune and crime had undergone such a change for the better since then that imprisonment for debt particularly was rather a change of place than a punishment.[94]

The consequence of humanitarian efforts was that, by the 1830s, the force of imprisonment derived largely from its detrimental financial effect and the ignominy of spending a couple of months in gaol. This, of course, should not be underrated. A specific manifestation of it was the shame felt by Charles Dickens at the incarceration of his father and family in 1824 and his later determination to conceal the episode from all but his closest friend.[95] Obviously, for the honest and the unwitting, imprisonment for debt could prove a tragedy. Such debtors, however, were the very people whom it was not worth imprisoning and the only possible justification for doing so was that their relatives might be forced to pay their debts for them.

---

92 B.P.P. Insolvent Debtors (1816), p. 24.

93 Hansard, P.D., n.s., 1828, xviii, 194.

94 Ibid., 3s, 1835, xxvii, 1162-3.

95 See A. Calder's introduction to Hard Times (Penguin edn., 1969), p. 7.

The evidence thus facilitates only a tentative answer to Hartwell's question. It is certain that the insolvency laws imposed an intolerable burden, especially upon those debtors whose financial resources were meagre and those whose credit collapsed unexpectedly. In addition, it is likely that the well-documented cynicism towards and abuse of the laws increased during the nineteenth century. The willingness of some traders to relinquish imprisonment for debt during the 1830s suggests that by then it had lost much of its force. But the effect of these factors upon both the aggregate volume of credit which was granted and the level of expenditure cannot be gauged. If the insolvency laws stimulated economic growth, they did so because creditors turned a blind eye to examples of abuse and because the majority of debtors were thought to be honest. If the dishonesty of debtors was as widespread as many suggested, it is clear that the law had little effect upon the level of economic activity which must have been determined primarily by market forces.

The relationship between the small debt laws and economic growth is more easily defined. Contemporary opinion was unanimous in asserting that the laws gave no certainty whatever to the creditor and that the small debt system was hopelessly inadequate to deal with the demands made of it. Every witness to the 1823 Committee on Small Debts stated that it was a waste of time and money to sue for debts under £15.[96] The jurisdictional restrictions on request courts prevented them from providing a remedy. Nevertheless, it is evident that, although some retail traders were very cautious in giving credit to their customers,[97] the majority granted it liberally. This is implied in the 1823 committee's assertion that

96 B.P.P. Fifteen Pounds (1823), p. 3.

97 Ibid., p. 34, John Cater, a hatter.

> The great extension of credit appears . . . to be an evil of considerable importance; and they have thought, when they are giving to creditors easier means of recovering their debts, it will not be unreasonable to require that they should not allow so long a period to elapse before they demand them, as is now frequently the case.98

There can be little doubt, in this case, that the development of credit facilities and economic growth was not inhibited by the defective legal system.

The evidence has suggested that the debt laws, in general, failed to protect the interests of creditors. This judgment is reinforced by the fact that, during the first half of the nineteenth century, merchants and traders sought to protect themselves by forming societies for the protection of trade against bad laws. By 1845, according to Elliott, six or eight of these societies had been founded in London and others in Birmingham, Bristol, Hull and other provincial towns.[99] Their diverse purposes included the formulation of credit registers of untrustworthy and fraudulent debtors, the detailed recording of bankruptcies and insolvencies, the provision of financial assistance to members embroiled in debt disputes and the investigation and improvement of the laws.[100] These instances of mercantile self-help provide an interesting commentary upon the validity of the two postulates by which, it was suggested, the relationship of the law and economic growth could be tested. On the one hand, they suggest that the threats of non-certification and imprisonment did not discourage

---

98 Ibid., p. 9.

99 Elliott, op. cit., pp. 62-3, fn.

100 For information about the societies, see B.P.P. Insolvent Debtors (1816), p. 20, Peter Laurie; B.P.P. Bankruptcy and Insolvency (1840), p. 22, John Dillon; Elliott, loc. cit.; P.R.O., C.114/34, Chancery Masters Exhibits, 'Society for the Protection of Trade.'

debtors from acquiring extensive credit. Economic growth was not, in practice, prevented by the imposition of excessive penalties for failure. On the other hand, they are clearly symptomatic of the failure of the laws either to provide the creditor with certainty of legal redress in cases of default or to prevent dishonesty. The very existence of the societies indicates that traders were anxious to restrict the widespread abuse of credit facilities. How far those facilities were actually restricted by creditors' consideration of legal defects is difficult to assess. The suggestion that some traders reduced their credit after Redesdale's act, for example, is counter-balanced by the insistence of many others that, regardless of the state of the law, credit was essential and inevitable. Similarly, the suggestion that aggregate economic growth may have been retarded by the unwillingness of some traders to grant credit is counter-balanced by the fact that the frantic speculation and overtrading which preceded early nineteenth-century crises was often attributed to the laxity of the law. The only certain fact is that, during the industrial revolution, the law was imperfect. Its effect on economic growth must remain a matter for speculation.

PART TWO

BANKRUPTCY

CHAPTER V

THE CAUSES OF BANKRUPTCY

I

Few economic historians would contest N.J. Silberling's assertion that bankruptcy statistics provide 'a fairly satisfactory barometer of business prosperity and depression.'[1] The presence of what might be termed a positive link between economic activity and bankruptcies has been suspected, at least, since the time of George Chalmers, who argued

> that in exact proportion as our traffic increased, from its infancy to its manhood, the number of bankruptcies, at every period, bore a just proportion to the amount of our trade . . . We might learn, from experience, that prosperity, generally, leads on to adversity, as the highest health is often the forerunner of the worst diseases.2

The task of testing this equation of business failures with increased economic activity in the later eighteenth century is impeded initially by two problems. The first - that of dating the industrial 'take-off' - has provoked a variety of conflicting solutions. It is likely, however, that, although advances occurred in some industries in the mid-eighteenth century, the major acceleration began during its last two or three decades when, according to P. Deane, 'the rate of growth in national product effectively out-stripped the rate of growth of population.'[3] The second problem is a product of the defects of bankruptcy statistics

---

1 N.J. Silberling, 'British Prices and Business Cycles, 1779-1850,' Rev. Econ. Stats. (1923), Suppl. 2, 236.

2 G. Chalmers, A Historical View of the Domestic Economy of Great Britain and Ireland (Edinburgh, 1812), pp. 224-5.

3 P. Deane, The First Industrial Revolution (Cambridge, 1965), p. 222.

derived from the London Gazette. It is certainly true that, as a source of short-term statistics (weekly or monthly), the Gazette is unreliable. It does, however, provide an acceptable indication of annual movements which can be used, with few reservations, in general macro-economic discussion.[4]

The calculations of Ashton and Silberling indicate that bankruptcies rose sharply during the last thirty years of the eighteenth century, when Deane detects the dramatic increase in the rate of growth of national production:

Average Annual Bankruptcies, 1732-1826

1732-39	208	1780-89	496
1740-49	202	1790-99	764
1750-59	227	1800-09	938
1760-69	254	1810-19	1,664
1770-79	456	1820-26	1,357

Source: for data, see Table 2.2.

The logical explanation of the increase is that commercial and industrial activity was more extensive during the last thirty years of the century than before and that bankruptcy statistics were in some way sensitive to that activity. By 1790, crises induced by economic factors (rather than by war or domestic conflict) were frequent. In the preceding twenty years, four major crises had been characterised by violent increases in bankruptcies after widespread speculative activity (1772, 1778, 1783, 1788). During the next thirty years, bankruptcy totals reached record levels. Taking the figures by decades, the annual average increased from 764 in the 1790s to 938 in the 1800s and 1,664 between 1810 and 1819; it then decreased slightly in the first half of the 1820s to 1,357. The largest actual annual total

4 For a discussion of bankruptcy statistics, see Appendix I.

before 1790 was 754 in 1788; that of 1793 was 1,377, of 1811, 2,112, of 1816, 2,145 and of 1826, 2,590. Although the figure for 1826 represents the highest peak, it is evident that, after 1810, the trend line flattens until the 1850s.[5] That the levelling occurred at a time when economic growth was probably proceeding at an increased rate and when a larger proportion of commercial men were becoming liable to bankruptcy proceedings is remarkable. It is beyond the scope of this work to examine all the possible causes of this change, but three contributory factors may be suggested. First, during a period of prolonged peace, economic activity was probably less hazardous and recovery from crises quicker than it was between the American Revolution and Waterloo. Second, the growing maturity of the banking system, after its rashness during the Napoleonic Wars, was reflected in the changes made in provincial banking during the 1820s and in the suppression of the Bank of England's real bills doctrine. The Bank, for example, never discounted as liberally after 1810 as before. Third, the bankruptcy reforms of the 1830s and 1840s, which have already been discussed, facilitated closer investigation and punishment of a bankrupt's trading operations. It is possible that the last two of these developments reduced the encouragement given to overtrading by defects in the financial and legal structure.

The purpose of this chapter is to examine more closely the causes of widespread bankruptcies between 1795 and 1826. Throughout, bankruptcies are treated as a dependent variable and an attempt is made to ascertain which independent variables appear to have influenced them most. What light can be shed on the causes of bankruptcy by examining its correlation with other economic indicators? The use of multiple regression analysis by computer to ascertain the

---

5 See A.D. Gayer, W.W. Rostow and A.J. Schwartz, <u>The Growth and Fluctuation of the British Economy 1790-1850</u> (Oxford, 1953), ii, 885.

correlation coefficients between bankruptcy statistics and the other variables was considered and rejected because of the smallness of the respective series. The following examination uses graphical representation which gives a reasonably clear picture of the relevant functional relationships.

II

In their analysis of trade cycles between 1790 and 1850, Gayer, Rostow and Schwartz note a sharp contrast between the stimulants to economic activity in the war period up to 1815 and afterwards. In the former, foreign trade dominated.[6] In the latter period, they note that, after the economy had adjusted to peacetime conditions, domestic investment increased producing a 'model instance of a major trade cycle' between 1819 and 1826.[7] Nevertheless, it is unlikely that the long cycle, characterised by long-term domestic investment, predominated before 1860[8] and it is likely that foreign trade statistics constitute the independent variables which correlate most closely to the bankruptcy series. The unsatisfactory nature of trade statistics is well known and it must be assumed that they afford only a rough guide to changes in the volume of trade.[9] Fluctuations in bankruptcies and foreign trade are compared in Chart 5.1.

---

6 Ibid., p. 647.

7 Ibid., p. 597.

8 W.W. Rostow, British Economy of the Nineteenth Century (Oxford, 1948), pp. 42-3.

9 The statistics used in this chapter are official values, which provide a poor indication of the value of overseas trade. They do, however, provide a reasonable guide to changes in the volume of trade and, certainly, of their timing, which is sufficient for our present purposes. See P. Deane and W.A. Cole, British Economic Growth, 1688-1959 (Cambridge, 1962), pp. 43-4; T.S. Ashton, Economic Fluctuations in England, 1700-1800 (Oxford, 1959), p. 53.

In theory, fluctuations in the series of re-exports and imports might be expected to correlate less closely with the bankruptcy curve than those of exports. Losses in the re-export trade would be sustained by London merchants and by overseas exporters who often financed it.[10] Similarly, losses incurred by importing were likely to affect the importers themselves and their overseas suppliers. In contrast, bankruptcies in the export trade would affect a host of domestic dealers and manufacturers who were dependent upon the exporters' ability to pay for produce. This, however, is a simplified picture which presupposes that the three trade curves can be treated in isolation. In fact, they were probably inter-related for two reasons. First, exporters of domestic manufactures frequently also imported produce aimed at both the domestic and re-export markets. Bankruptcy caused by reduced demand in either of the latter could obviously be transmitted to the domestic suppliers of exports. Second, at a more general level, the increasing dependence of the British economy upon export markets suggests that the supply of foreign goods was a reflex of overseas demand for British manufactures and re-exports. When foreign markets were accessible, for example, manufacturers were more likely to expand production and buy larger quantities of raw materials, whose price would rise, thus stimulating increased imports. The movement of imported commodity prices in Chart 5.1 is a little more complicated than this. The high freight charges and inflation of the war period probably obscure its general downward trend, which becomes more obvious in the 1820s. In addition, the actual timing of the movement of imported commodity prices is inconsistent. Whereas its sharp rise in 1808 anticipates the increase of exports, those of 1812-14 and 1817-18 coincide with it and that of 1825 follows it. Nevertheless, their general similarities

---

10 See Deane, op. cit., p. 58.

suggest that the price curve was a reflex of demand, actual or anticipated, in overseas markets. In turn, the movements of the import curve invariably coincide with or follow fluctuations in the imported commodity price series. While this may explain the simultaneous movements of the import and export curves, it does not account for the violence of their fluctuations, especially after 1808. The latter was probably a consequence of the nature of overseas trading in the early nineteenth century. As Sir Henry Parnell said, in 1827,

> It is when trade is in an unusually prosperous state that the temptation to an excess is so strong, that it is seldom suffered by merchants and manufacturers to revert quietly or gradually to an ordinary state, without first passing into a state of overtrading.[11]

The frequent saturation of overseas markets by British exporters was a characteristic of the inventory cycle.[12] The prevalence of a similar cycle in the import series is reflected in the frequency with which high imported commodity prices both stimulate and are reduced by increased imports.

In the light of these considerations, it is not surprising that the bankruptcy curve corresponds closely with the overseas trade series. During the war period, bankruptcies tend to rise in response to a preceding increase in exports and to reach a peak during years when the export curve declines (1797, 1811, 1816). After the war, the bankruptcy curve rises in response to decreased exports after previous high levels (1819, 1826). Thus there is a persistent lag, usually of one year, between the export and bankruptcy peaks. All the troughs in the bankruptcy curve coincide with rising or buoyant exports (1799, 1814, 1818, 1821-4). A similar correspondence is apparent between

---

11 Sir H. Parnell, Observations on Paper Money, Banking and Overtrading (1827), pp. 42-3.

12 See Rostow, op. cit., pp. 39-40.

the bankruptcy and import series. When both the import and export curves are relatively stable, the bankruptcy curve is also fairly steady (1804-8, 1821-4). It is also evident that bankruptcies respond to occasional fluctuations in the re-export curve. The connection is most pronounced in 1810-11 and 1815-16, when sharp reductions of re-exports are accompanied by a sharply rising level of bankruptcies.

Examination of the extent of failures during the peak years of 1811, 1816, 1819 and 1826 and of the length of time for which a large number of bankruptcies obtained reveals a marked contrast between war-time and peacetime conditions. The dramatic increases in failures initiated during the Napoleonic wars were large and continued for three or four years (1810-12, 1815-17). The peak of 1819, in contrast, was small, despite previous trading of comparable magnitude. Similarly, although the peak of 1826 was larger than those during the war, the high level of failures was relatively short-lived. The obvious explanation of this discrepancy lies in the fact that fluctuations in overseas trade were more violent during the wars than afterwards. Whereas war-time trading booms were exaggerated by the excessive mercantile response to high prices and inflated profits when overseas markets were available, the more stable post-war trading conditions and prices probably lessened the element of speculation in mercantile activity and, no doubt, shortened the period of recovery after economic crises.

It thus seems plausible to suggest that, between 1795 and 1826, bankruptcies reacted to changes in the volume of overseas trade. Which sectors of trade had the most influence? In Chart 5.2, the bankruptcy curve is compared with the series of sugar, coffee, tea and raw wool, which, with raw cotton, comprised the five largest imports.[13] It should be noted that the fluctuations of the coffee and tea

---

13 The raw cotton series is discussed later in relation to that of cotton exports.

curves are probably exaggerated because of their over-valuation in official values. With this reservation in mind, it may be suggested that the increased imports of coffee and sugar between 1808 and 1810 and of coffee in 1814 may have contributed to the bankruptcy peaks of 1811 and 1816. Their correlation with the bankruptcy curve at other times, however, is not pronounced. Similarly, the movements of the raw wool curve are only matched in the bankruptcy series in 1818-19 and 1825-6 and the tea and bankruptcy curves bear little resemblance. In general, the absence of a consistent correlation between the bankruptcy series and any of the four import curves suggests that none had a major influence on the level of failures for a considerable length of time.

It is convenient to discuss the fifth major import series - raw cotton - in conjunction with exports of cotton fabric and yarn, since the two were inter-related. The cotton industry grew rapidly throughout this period, its contribution to national income increasing from less than 1/2% in the 1770s to 4-5% in 1802 and 7-8% in 1818.[14] Its growth is attributable above all to international trade. Between 1793 and 1815, the volume of cotton exports rose at an annual rate of 10.6%.[15] Whereas, in 1800, cotton comprised 24% of exports and wool 28-1/2%, the relevant proportions in 1815 were 40% and 18% and, by 1830, cotton amounted to more than half of total exports.[16] While cotton was thus assuming the dominant position in the British economy, the woollen industry remained fairly static and, as late as the 1820s, still accounted for only 4-5% of national income.[17] There are two major contrasts between the two

---

14 Deane and Cole, op. cit., p. 184.

15 Rostow, op. cit., p. 15.

16 Deane, op. cit., pp. 63, 89.

17 Deane and Cole, op. cit., p. 199.

which are in a sense related. First, wool was much less dependent than cotton upon overseas markets. In 1805, 31% of wool raw materials were imported and 35% of the value of its final product exported.[18] Second, the demand for cotton was highly elastic, that for wool was not. Consequently, as soon as cotton out-stripped wool as the major industrial product, the health of the British economy would inevitably be influenced greatly by the fluctuations of cotton production. In addition, as the cotton industry itself became more dependent upon overseas demand for its products these fluctuations would become increasingly volatile. Both of these developments were completed in the first decade of the nineteenth century. By 1811-13, cotton had out-stripped wool in contribution to national income and, from 1807, overseas demand for cotton had greater significance than the home market.[19]

As might be expected, the bankruptcy curve conforms more closely to the cotton series than to that of wool exports. Fluctuations in the latter (shown in Chart 5.3) are mild throughout the period and its correlation to the bankruptcy curve is not pronounced. It is conceivable, however, that the decreased wool exports in 1797, 1811, 1816 and 1819 played a small part in the distress of those years. The two cotton curves, in contrast, are much closer to that of bankruptcies. Before 1809, all three are characterised by relatively gentle increases. After 1809, the correlation is marked. The sharp rise in bankruptcies in 1810 coincides with a flattening of the export curve at a time when imports continue to rise and the peak of 1811 reflects the dramatic downswings in both cotton curves. The rapid expansion of the cotton industry is mirrored in the general upward trend of its two trade curves between 1811 and 1826. During this

---

18 Ibid., p. 196.

19 M.M. Edwards, The Growth of the British Cotton Trade, 1780-1815 (Manchester, 1967), pp. 25, 50.

period, bankruptcies consistently increased during years when the expansion was impeded. In 1815-16 and 1819 the rise of both cotton curves is temporarily halted. In 1825, the cotton export curve declines while imports are expanding. In all three cases, the bankruptcy peak is recorded in the year after the trade peaks. It is noticeable that, of the two cotton curves, that of exports is consistently closer to the bankruptcy series. The import movements of 1808 and 1824, for example, do not appear to have affected bankruptcy levels significantly. In contrast, almost every movement of the export curve was accompanied or followed by inverse fluctuations of the bankruptcy curve. It seems clear that the dependence of the cotton industry upon overseas markets made the British economy acutely sensitive to fluctuations in export demand.

III

The investigation, so far, has suggested that the level of bankruptcies responded to fluctuations in overseas trade and especially in cotton exports. It is now proposed to examine three domestic series, the first of which - wheat prices - may have influenced domestic demand, and the second and third of which - the yield on consols and Bank of England discounts - probably affected the level of economic activity generally.

The influence of harvests upon economic activity is difficult to gauge. It may be suggested, briefly, that good harvests, by increasing the real wages and purchasing power of the non-agricultural sector[20] and by lowering raw material costs in many industries, stimulated industrial production and proved detrimental only to a small part of

---

20 Cp. Ashton's argument that increased employment would also expand the purchasing power of the agricultural sector. T.S. Ashton, An Economic History of England: The 18th Century (1955), p. 60.

the community, notably the farmers themselves. In years of bad harvest, these conditions were probably reversed. High food prices, by reducing real wages, decreased demand for manufactured commodities, while the cost of some industrial raw materials rose and unemployment of agricultural workers reduced their purchasing power. The effects of this upon business confidence were exacerbated by the necessity to import foreign grain which, as Thomas Tooke took pains to point out, raised prices disproportionately and seriously disturbed the money market.[21] Consequently, the only sector of society which benefited during years of dearth were the farmers. The effect which the above developments might be expected to have on bankruptcy levels is simply stated: a bad harvest, by thrusting the manufacturing and commercial world into difficulties, would induce a large number of failures. In years of good harvest, bankruptcies would be greatly reduced. The exclusion of most farmers from the bankruptcy process would lower this total even further.

Wheat prices and bankruptcies are compared in Chart 5.4. The evidence does not suggest that the anticipated, positive correlation of the two curves obtained consistently throughout the period. It is true that, during the post-war years, the general trends are similar, but the bankruptcy peak of 1819 is clearly not a product of harvest conditions. It is also true that, in some years, price increases were followed by a rise in bankruptcies (1796, 1808-10, 1824-5) and price decreases by a sharp drop in bankruptcies (1797-8, 1821-3). But in other years no such pattern is discernible. The price increases of 1798-1801 and 1805 were accompanied by a gently rising bankruptcy level and those of 1811-12 and 1817 by rapid decreases in failures. Similarly, bankruptcies did not drop during the good harvest years of

21 For a discussion of Tooke's views on the influence of agricultural prices, see T.E. Gregory's introduction to T. Tooke and W. Newmarch, A History of Prices (1928), pp. 15-19.

1802-4, 1807, 1815-6, and 1818. This erratic relationship lends weight to Rostow's assertion that, although harvests played a significant contributory role in the expansions and contractions of business activity, they cannot be considered a factor of prime importance.[22] It is possible that harvest conditions affected bankruptcy levels in agricultural areas but they cannot be considered a major autonomous influence upon aggregate bankruptcy statistics.

A steep rise in bankruptcies obviously represents a wholesale failure of mercantile credit, which is more likely to be produced directly by financial disruption than by overseas trade *per se*. An examination of the correlation between bankruptcies and, on the one hand, the yield on consols and, on the other, Bank of England discounts provides some interesting insights into the effect of the money market upon the bankruptcy level. The consols curve necessarily represents an objective index of business confidence, which is dependent upon other economic variables, while the discount curve represents a potentially independent variable which could seriously affect the level of both economic activity and bankruptcies.

Throughout most of this period, the yield on consols was abnormally high as a result of the large creation of new stock during the war and the typical persistence of high rates after it ended.[23] Nevertheless, it is likely that the yield on consols gives a reasonably accurate indication of the state of the money market. When it was low, money was plentiful, when high the market was usually stultified and capital scarce. Thus, upward movements in the consols curve indicate growing financial stringency and downward movements reflect improved monetary conditions. Throughout the period, an inverse relationship is generally apparent

---

22 Rostow, *op. cit.*, p. 51.

23 See Sir J. Hicks, *Critical Essays in Monetary Theory* (Oxford, 1967), pp. 83-102.

between the consols curve (in Chart 5.5) and those of overseas trade in Chart 5.1. The bankrupcy peaks represent inverse responses to movements of the latter and positive ones to fluctuations of the former. Thus the 1797, 1811, 1816, 1819 and 1826 bankruptcy peaks all follow sudden depressions in the trade series which are matched by upward movements in the consols curve. There are areas in the consols curve which do not correspond to fluctuations in the bankruptcy curve. The discrepancy in 1810 and 1815, when a rising bankruptcy curve accompanies a low yield on consols, is probably explained by the fact that war-time trading, generated by easy-money conditions, was frequently precarious; hence, the level of bankruptcies started to rise before the money market deteriorated. In addition, the fact that the consols fluctuations in 1801-3 are not paralleled in the bankruptcy series indicates, no doubt, the influence of political factors upon the money market (i.e. the temporary peace). It is evident that the largest number of bankruptcies occurred in years when factors of foreign trade and monetary disturbance combined. In other words, a financial crisis only induced a high bankruptcy level when it was itself the product of trading impediments; bankruptcies did not normally increase until excessive trading and marketing problems had induced a disruption of business confidence which was reflected in an increased yield on consols.

It was suggested that, unlike the yield on consols, the discount curve might act as an exogenous variable with an autonomous effect upon the bankruptcy level. In relation to peacetime conditions this hypothesis is rather less significant than during war. The function of the Bank of England as lender of the last resort would normally affect credit conditions only when the money market was tight and the refusal of private banks to discount bills had thrust responsibility upon it. During the war, however, the usual channels for discounts were, for a variety of reasons, very narrow and the Bank became the arbiter of credit conditions, able to influence closely the volume of commercial activity. The Bank's professed policy, during the war period, of catering to the 'needs of trade' implies that the discount curve represents a variable which was dependent upon the trade curves. However, an inverse relationship could obtain, as it did during the boom years of 1809 and 1810, when the volume of discounts operated as a permissive determinant of commercial activity.[24] This was particularly pertinent to the level of bankruptcies because a considerable portion of the trading facilitated by the Bank's liberal discount policy was conducted by marginal firms, which experienced a high failure rate not only because they were allowed to extend operations beyond their resources but also because, during the subsequent credit squeeze, their bills were the first to lose negotiability. The importance of the relationship between Bank policy and bankruptcy levels, however, is seen most clearly during periods of economic crisis. A contrast is evident in the chart between the relationship of the bankruptcy and discount curves before and after 1816. After the war, the Bank seems to have acted as a last resort, increasing its discounts when the trade curves turned down (1819, 1825-6) and, perhaps, reducing the extent of bankruptcies by alleviating pressure on the money market. Earlier, however, the bankruptcy peaks coincide with sharp reductions in discounting (1811, 1816) after previous high levels. It may be suggested that, at these times, having allowed trading to become excessive by its liberal discounting, the Bank aggravated the subsequent depressions by sharply restricting its accommodation when the crises set in.

---

24 Ths is discussed in chapter VI.

IV

The preceding discussion of macro-economic trends suggests that, at the time of its most startling rise during the Napoleonic Wars, the level of bankruptcies was related to the state of overseas trade, the volume of which was, in turn, influenced by the discount policy of the Bank of England. The implication is also that curtailment of overseas demand for British products (because of saturation or political prohibition) would tend to produce a commercial crisis, the severity of which would be (as in peacetime crises) conditioned by the Bank's willingness to continue liberal discounting. Chapter six is designed to test these hypotheses by reference to the specific crisis of 1810. As already noted, this year marks the watershed in Gayer's secular bankruptcy curve. It is also a year in which the apparent link between the overseas trade and discount curves is especially pronounced. The chapter examines the causes and course of the crisis, attempting to identify the factors responsible for the trade boom which preceded it, to assess the significance of Bank of England policy both before and during the crisis and to explain the timing and location of the widespread bankruptcies which it produced.

CHAPTER VI

THE CRISIS OF 1810

I

This chapter discusses the economic crisis of 1810 from three aspects. First, the general causes and course of the crisis are examined briefly. Second, an attempt is made to explain the uneven distribution of bankruptcies in England and Wales between April 1810, three months before the crisis broke, and July 1811, when the panic had subsided. The third aspect concerns the responsibility of the Bank of England for the trade boom after 1808 and its reaction to the widespread economic distress of 1810.

II

The fundamental long-term cause of the 1810 crisis was the disruption of British overseas trade during the Napoleonic Wars. In the previous decade a distinct trading pattern had existed, in which the leading export markets were Northern Europe, the United States and, increasingly, the British West Indies and Southern Europe; the major import markets were Northern Europe, the British West Indies, Asia and, to a lesser extent, Southern Europe and the United States.[1] After the resumption of hostilities in 1803, therefore, the political impediments to European and American trade threatened the two most important export markets and the leading source of imports. This was true especially after 1806, when attempts to restrict trade with Britain were pursued more forcefully. In the North American market, commerce, inhibited initially by the implementation in December 1807 of the Non-Importation Act (April 1806) and

---

1 See Mitchell and Deane, op. cit., p. 311.

by the Non-Intercourse Act of March 1808, resumed briefly between April 1809 (Erskine Treaty negotiations) and August 1809 (Non-Intercourse Act) and, again, after the latter's repeal in May 1810. Similarly, following the Berlin Decree of November 1806 European trade was difficult until the latter part of 1808, after which it fluctuated until 1810 in accordance with the accessibility of markets in the Baltic and Mediterranean. In April 1810, the Heligoland trade was stifled, and Bonaparte's annexation of Holland (July 1810) and his prohibitive tariff on colonial produce (August 1810) further reduced trade to the continent. In October 1810, the final and most profitable northern market, the Baltic, was closed.

The pattern of trade during this period, shown in Table 6.1, reflects the responses of British merchants to these problems. When the opportunity arose to trade with the traditional markets, commercial activity became intense as individuals sought to make capital out of the high prices of British manufactures and colonial goods on the continent and of foreign goods inside Britain.[2] Also, many merchants sought alternative markets in Central and South America, the possibilities of which had been revealed in Popham's prospectus of 1806.[3] The Spanish revolt of May 1808 provided the opening which merchants were seeking in both Europe and South America. On the one hand, it diverted French attention to the Peninsula, opening some Northern ports to the British (notably in Sweden). The subsequent opportunities were enhanced further by the deployment of the Grande Armée against Austria in 1809 (the Aspern-Wagram campaign), opening German ports and increasing greatly the

---

2 For continental prices in 1808, see F. Crouzet, L'Économie Britannique et le Blocus Continental, (1806-1813) (Paris, 1958), ii, 356; for British prices, see T. Tooke and W. Newmarch, A History of Prices (ed. T. E. Gregory), (1928), i, 290.

3 See Tooke, op. cit., i, 276-7.

volume of trade with Northern Europe. On the other, trade with the Foreign West Indies and South America received a boost as did that to the Mediterranean and the Peninsula itself (see Table 6.2). Mercantile eagerness to exploit these markets was a product both of a desire to acquire a more secure source of raw materials (especially cotton) than North America[4] and of the dependence upon foreign markets of the British cotton industry, which was characterised by a scramble to export whenever the opportunity arose.[5] The heaviest increases of both imports and exports were recorded in 1809. The volume of imports continued to rise in 1810, exports (including re-exports) reaching a peak in 1809 and slowly declining thereafter. In current values, the movements of the overseas trade series were as follows (in £ millions):

	IMPORTS (computed values)	DOMESTIC EXPORTS (declared values)	RE-EXPORTS (computed values)
1806	53.3	40.9	9.2
1807	53.8	37.2	8.3
1808	51.5	37.3	6.5
1809	73.7	47.4	14.3
1810	88.5	48.4	12.5
1811	50.7	32.9	6.7

Source: Mitchell and Deane, *op. cit.*, p. 282.
Note: The computed values of imports and re-exports are those of Imlah.

The flattening of exports in 1810 is explained not only by the more vigorous prosecution of the Continental System but also by the overstocking of foreign markets with British

4 B.P.P. [*Report from the S.C. appointed to inquire into the Cause of the High Price of*] *Gold Bullion* (1810), [III], p. 58, Charles Lyne.

5 See M.M. Edwards, *The Growth of the British Cotton Trade, 1780-1815* (Manchester, 1967), p. 74.

goods during the boom of 1809 and early 1810.[6] In South America the problem of overstocking was compounded by the difficulties of exploiting a new market. Much of the trade was conducted by speculators, ignorant both of South American conditions and of European demand for return cargoes.[7] In addition, returns from South America were inordinately slow, discouraging the more cautious traders from exploiting the market.[8]

Just as export markets were saturated, so too excessive imports glutted the domestic market. Of course, the two were closely related since decreased foreign demand for British manufactures and colonial goods automatically reduced internal demand for industrial raw materials and deflated the price of superfluous colonial produce. As early as the fourth quarter of 1809 many British merchants possessed large stocks of colonial and other imported goods which could not be sold.[9] Nevertheless, both European and colonial imports continued on a massive scale during the first half of 1810, many of them representing payments in kind for previous exports.[10]

The combination of glutted, domestic markets and losses sustained by exporters, especially in South America, bore the major responsibility for the widespread bankruptcies in

---

6 For the saturation of continental markets with colonial goods, see Crouzet, op. cit., p. 579; for the overstocking of South American markets, B.P.P. [Report from the S.C. appointed to take into Consideration the Present State of] Commercial Credit (1810-11), [II], p. 3.

7 B.P.P. [Minutes of Evidence . . . on the] Orders in Council (1812), [III], p. 483, John Gladstone.

8 Ibid., p. 189, William Drayton; cf. R.S. Fitton and A.P. Wadsworth, The Strutts and the Arkwrights, 1758-1830 (Manchester, 1958), p. 317.

9 Tooke, op. cit., p. 303.

10 Ibid., p. 301.

the commercial and industrial sectors during the latter part of 1810. However, a marked contrast was apparent between their respective fortunes in the first half of the year, when the industrial sector was fairly prosperous.[11] Overseas demand for manufactured cotton remained relatively strong for, although the European market was slowing, exports continued to South America. Also, from May 1810 to February 1811 the United States was open, exports to that market probably reaching a peak in the summer of 1810.[12] Other industries had not participated in the boom of 1809 and early 1810 to the same extent as cotton since they were more dependent upon the North American market, impediments in which had precluded a dramatic expansion of production. However, after May 1810, the woollen, iron, steel, pottery and other industries enjoyed considerable prosperity until February 1811 when they were all depressed.[13]

In contrast, the problems of over-supply increasingly afflicted the commercial sector in the first half of 1810. In March, five London merchants failed after dealing in Baltic hemp,[14] whose price in the London market had dropped consistently from early 1809 on. Colonial produce was especially affected for reasons which were later diagnosed by the Exchange Herald of Manchester:

> Since the end of the winter, there has been a general stagnation in the sale of colonial produce, the price of which has been falling from month to month. The price of coffee is particularly affected on account of the vast quantity on hand and the little disposition there appears to be with the inhabitants of Italy,

---

11 For the contrast, see Monthly Magazine (1810), i, 302.

12 Edwards, op. cit., p. 70.

13 B.P.P. Orders in Council (1812), pp. 7-8, Thomas Attwood; p. 127, Thomas Greenwood; p. 131, John Bailey; p. 166, Ralph Stevenson.

14 Monthly Magazine (1810), i, 301.

> Switzerland, the South of Germany and Austria, in particular, to purchase same, with cotton.15

As a result, the Monthly Magazine observed, in April, that numerous ships returning from the West Indies were certain to experience difficulty disgorging their cargoes in glutted markets.[16] Both these shipments and the 'frenzied importing of cottons' after the Non-Intercourse Act in May[17] were to exacerbate the problem of saturation. The effect of these developments on prices is shown in Table 6.3. Imported commodity prices, which had been rising since the middle of 1809, declined sharply between April and July 1810. The price of coffee was particularly affected. Very ordinary West Indian coffee fell from £4.16.0d. per cwt. in March to £3.11.0d. in April, £3.2.0d. in May and £2.17.0d. in June. Finest West Indian coffee similarly fell from £6.15.0d. in March to £5.19.0d. in May and £5.5.0d. in June. The price of sugar started to level out during the second quarter and fluctuated in the summer months before declining in the final quarter. Raw cotton was similarly affected. In addition to the price decrease in Bahia cotton, noted in the table, cotton from the West Indies fell by 3d. or 4d. per lb. between January and June 1810. By August, British cotton prices were said to have reached an all-time low.[18]

The growing difficulties of the economy were reflected in the high level of failures during the second quarter of 1810 when the bankruptcy total exceeded that for any similar period since 1793.[19] Although none of the failures was

---

15 See Exchange Herald. Aston's Manchester Commercial Advertiser, 12 July 1810, p. 2, col. 1.

16 Monthly Magazine (1810), i, 404.

17 Edwards, op. cit., p. 99.

18 Ibid.

19 N.J. Silberling, 'British Prices and Business Cycles, 1779-1850,' Rev. Econ. Stats. (1923), Suppl. 2, 251.

large enough to create panic, one or two foreshadowed later events. Four merchants failed in May at Liverpool. In the West Country, there were signs that financial stability could not be taken for granted. Country banks stopped payment at Wincanton, Somerset (Griffith) in May and Gosport, Hants. (Jukes, Langley) in June. In addition, the fall in Irish meat prices brought down three London houses engaged in the provision trade.[20] One of these - H. A. Bayley and Co. - led to the collapse of Mingay, Nott and Co., a small Smithfield banker and wine merchant which had given it credit.[21]

In July, the increasingly pronounced effects of over-supply were reflected in the failure of a cargo from Havannah, consisting of coffee, cotton and indigo worth £150,000, to find a buyer either in England or on the continent.[22] The most significant effect, however, was the bankruptcy which precipitated the crisis. On 6 July, Thomas Coles and Sons, West India brokers in London, stopped payment, followed immediately by their Lombard Street bankers, Brickwood and Co. The latter's failure was significant both because of its direct repercussions upon large mercantile clients and because of its impact upon the policies of the Bank of England and, consequently, upon the London banking fraternity.[23] The fate of Brickwood and

---

20 Crouzet, op. cit., ii, 615-6.

21 Mingay and Co.'s liabilities of £67,572 were largely owed to agricultural clients from East Anglia and Essex (P.R.O. B3/3223-4); for its links with Bayley and Co., see also Jones and Another v. Dwyer (1812) 1 Rose 339 and Snaith v. Mingay (1813) 1 M. & S. 87; 1 Ross 154.

22 Salisbury and Winchester Journal, 23 July 1810, p. 4, col. 1.

23 'The Moment that it is known that the Bank of England has resolved upon a Diminution of Discount, all private Bankers withhold a part of the Facilities which they are in Habits of giving to their customers,' B.P.P. Report from the Committee ... on the Outstanding Demands of the Bank (1797), XI, 37, Walter Boyd.

Co.'s clients is discussed in chapter eight and the reaction of the Bank later in this chapter. Briefly, the Bank's initial response was to reduce discounts sharply, a reversal of policy which induced panic in July. Down, Thornton and Co., the Bartholomew Lane bank, was subjected to a run[24] and, in the West Country, seven banks stopped payments in July, followed by two in August.[25] In Yorkshire, 27 traders failed in July, as did nineteen merchants and seven warehousemen in London. The discount restriction was so severe that the City was obliged to adopt a policy of self-help, stable merchants giving assistance to respectable houses which were in difficulties.[26] On 19 July, however, mercantile pressure induced the directors of the Bank to increase their accommodation, a change of heart which rapidly restored confidence. This was reinforced by the revival of commercial optimism in the second half of the month, when the five largest mercantile bankrupts and Jacob Bros., who failed on 18 July, attempted to prove that their embarrassments were temporary because returns expected from South America would cover their liabilities. The five produced balance sheets to confirm their solvency:

---

24 This was alleviated after Henry Thornton's friends poured funds into the bank. See H. Thornton, Paper Credit (ed. F.A. Hayek), (1939), p. 27.

25 The banks were Shaw, Hitchcock (Bath); Sturges, Gould (Bath); Wilcocks, Frazier (Exeter); Bowles, Ogden, Wyndham (New Sarum); Burrough (New Sarum); Bulkeel (Dartmouth); Phillips (Milford, Hants); Morgan, Jacobs (Shepton Mallett); and Stroud (Swansea).

26 Salisbury and Winchester Journal, 16 July 1810, p. 3, col. 2.

Balance Sheets of the Five Largest Bankrupts, July 1810

Bankrupt	Liabilities (£)	Assets (£)
Goodair	389,992	487,209
Greaves, Sharp, Fisher	508,000	632,592
Hardy, Ottley	286,898	330,444
Rowlandson, Bates	311,802	377,775
Rowlandson, Isaac, Brien	283,938	339,432

Source: Exchange Herald. Aston's Manchester Commercial Advertiser, 26th July 1810, p. 4, col. 3.

As a result of their promises of full satisfaction, the Bank of England and leading merchants and private banks (including Smith, Payne and Smith, Masterman and Co. and Newnham, Everitt and Co.) resolved to give the five extra time to honour their bills.[27] Public acceptance of the promises was, no doubt, encouraged by the arrival of the Brazil courier on 23 July with numerous remittances, some of which were due to the five firms in question.[28]

After these encouraging signs, the panic subsided and on 28 July it was reported that there would be no more large bankruptcies because the crisis had passed.[29] The failure of the West End bank, Dawes, Noble and Co., on 30 July, did little to disturb the optimism.[30] Indeed, in the middle of August, the publication of the Decree of Trianon, which regularised the licence system and was said to have 'in substance, though not in form, rescinded the Berlin and

---

27 Exchange Herald, 26 July 1810, p. 4, col. 4; The Times, 23 July 1810, p. 3, col. 1.

28 Crouzet, op. cit., ii, 619.

29 Salisbury and Winchester Journal, 30 July 1810, p. 2, col. 2.

30 The bankruptcy of Dawes, Noble and Co. is examined in chapter IX.

Milan Decrees,'[31] caused a minor sensation. On 16 August, The Times reported that, because of large-scale purchases, the price of sugar and other colonial produce had suddenly risen ten per cent.[32] The effect of the decree upon English commerce was, however, brief and insignificant.[33]

The renewed confidence of August and September was unrealistic. Although commercial failures in London declined, the over-all bankruptcy level remained high and the failure of six merchants in Manchester, where trade was said to be stagnant,[34] and of eight Lancashire textile manufacturers during the two months indicated that the economy was by no means healthy. In fact, the optimism was bound to be temporary because the basic problem of finding markets for manufactured and colonial goods was insoluble. By the middle of 1810 the home market for cotton goods was already over-supplied, the South American market was proving unprofitable and the European outlet was closing rapidly. The continued availability of the only alternative, the North American market, was uncertain, as Madison's government complained bitterly about British trade restrictions (which eventually provoked the Non-Importation Act of 1811 and the War of 1812). In any case, it is doubtful whether America could have compensated for the loss of other markets and many merchants were far from happy about the credit terms and general trading conditions in the United States.[35]

---

31 The Times, 16 Aug. 1810, p. 2, col. 4.

32 Ibid., p. 2, col. 5.

33 See F. Markham, 'The Napoleonic Adventure,' in New C.M.H., ix (1965), p. 328.

34 Monthly Magazine (1810), ii, 194.

35 Edwards, op. cit., p. 68.

The growing realisation of these facts is evidenced by the mounting tension in the City in September.[36] On 28 September, this was aggravated by the suicide of Abraham Goldsmid which threw the money market into confusion once again (the price of consols sank to 63-7/8 on 10 October). Although the government managed to cushion the immediate shock of Goldsmid's death,[37] confidence was severely shaken. In October, further poor returns from South America and the abandonment of both that and the European market for reasons of unprofitability and inaccessibility renewed the sense of crisis. The Bank of England again restricted discounts, commercial confidence evaporated and bankruptcies increased dramatically during the winter months. By December, it was said, 'Discounts (unless bills etc. of a few of the first houses of the city) can only be done through the medium of bill-brokers, at an extra commission, exclusive of regular interest.'[38] In February 1811, commerce was considered 'to be in a most deplorable way. Vast imports of East and West India produce in the market and no export for them to any part of the world, at present the home consumption being the only mode of getting rid of them.'[39] The closure of trade with America in February increased the distress in some districts and introduced it into others. In the following three months, thousands of operatives were unemployed in Birmingham, Glasgow, Manchester, Nottingham, Sheffield and other manufacturing towns.[40]

---

36 This is discussed in section IV of this chapter.

37 See S.R. Cope, 'The Goldsmids and the Development of the London Money Market during the Napoleonic Wars,' Economica, n.s., ix (1942), 205.

38 Monthly Magazine (1810), ii, 591.

39 Ibid., (1811), i, 197.

40 Ibid., 197, 304, 397.

The restoration of economic stability, which began in the summer of 1811, was attributed by contemporaries to two factors. In March, a Select Committee on the State of Commercial Credit, established in response to petitions from manufacturing areas and the City of London, recommended that relief should be provided by the issue of Exchequer Bills worth £6,000,000.[41] As in 1793, the bills were intended to provide sound firms with paper which could be discounted easily, enabling them to survive without selling stocks until prices had risen again.[42] Parliament sanctioned the issue on 5 April 1811 and 205 individuals applied for £2,083,451 of the bills. 119 applications were granted (worth £1,339,000), 48 were withdrawn (£387,000) and 38 rejected (£356,461). The commissioners appointed to administer the issue reported, in 1813, that the bills had removed commercial difficulties and enabled manufacturers to resume operations which had previously been suspended.[43] This possibly exaggerates the effect of the bills since, as W. Smart has pointed out, the fact that traders had applied for only about £2,000,000 suggests that few were able to furnish the necessary security.[44] Probably a more significant factor in the economic recovery was the improvement in commercial conditions in the middle of 1811 as a result of the expulsion of the French from Portugal, increasing South American demand for fine goods (the market for inferior goods remained glutted) and large orders for

---

41 B.P.P. Commercial Credit (1810-11), pp. 1-2.

42 Eighteenth-century crises had taught that an emergency issue of such paper allayed panic, reduced interest rates and restored confidence. See T.S. Ashton, Economic Fluctuations in England, 1700-1800 (Oxford, 1959), p. 111.

43 B.P.P. Accounts and Papers (1813-14), iii, 116.

44 W. Smart, Economic Annals of the Nineteenth Century (New York edn., 1964), p. 271.

British goods from the West Indies, where existing stock had been purchased by the Spanish.[45] Thus, on 1 July the Monthly Magazine noted that 'the manufacturies have revived in a great degree, chiefly owing to large orders for all kinds of woollen, linen and cotton, goods . . . for the markets of Portugal and South America. The goods of Birmingham and Sheffield are also in great demand in these markets - credit and confidence, we are happy to say, revives, and the towns of Manchester, Nottingham, etc. etc. feel vast benefit from the happy change that has taken place.'[46] Nevertheless, the continued impediments in North European and American trade throughout 1811 and 1812 ensured that the recovery was only partial. While it is true that the largest bankruptcies had occurred before the middle of 1811, many manufacturing districts were still acutely distressed during the second quarter of 1812.[47] It is unlikely that confidence was fully restored until 1813.

III

What was the regional and social impact of bankruptcy during the crisis? Table 6.4 and Chart 6.1 analyse the incidence of bankruptcies throughout England and Wales between April 1810 and July 1811. Although one cannot be precise about the average size of bankrupt estates in the early nineteenth century, it seems likely that, as in insolvency, a wide discrepancy existed between the minority of large traders and the majority whose assets and liabilities were fairly small. This was implied by Germain

---

45 Monthly Magazine (1811), i, 500, 600.

46 Ibid., (1811), i, p. 600.

47 See B.P.P. Orders in Council (1812), p. 2, Thomas Attwood; p. 131, John Bailey; pp. 157-8, Josiah Wedgwood; p. 178, Thomas Leach; pp. 196-8, William Midgeley; p. 327, Timothy Wiggin; pp. 299-303, John Honyman.

Lavie's statement, in 1818, that most bankruptcies involved trifling amounts and were barely able to support the costs of their commissions. He referred specifically to retail traders, who in recent years had flooded the Bankruptcy Court.[48] More detailed information was presented to the 1840 commission on bankruptcy and insolvency. Robert Hall, a barrister, observed that 'the greater number of bankruptcies in the country are very small matters, that is under £1,000,' intimating that the average London commission was in excess of that sum.[49] Specific evidence was presented to the commission by Commissioner Merivale. In addition to analysing the assets collected and legal charges in 180 estates between 1832 and 1839 (see Table 1.1), he reported the assets stated in the bankrupts' balance sheets. The average computed assets of the 180 amounted to £2,416. The largest twenty averaged £11,834 and the remaining 160 (89 per cent) under £3,000; 67 per cent averaged under £2,000, 44 per cent under £1,000 and 11 per cent under £500. Although Merivale's analysis is of a later date, and deals only with 180 of the 330 estates in his division of the court in which dividends were paid (an extra 200 paid no dividends), it confirms much other evidence that most bankrupt estates in the early decades of the nineteenth century were fairly small. A minority of estates, however, involved extremely large amounts. In fifteen of the major bankruptcies of merchants and warehousemen in 1810-11, total liabilities came to £3,149,035, averaging £209,935 per estate.[50]

---

48 B.P.P. Bankrupt Laws (1818), p. 44.

49 B.P.P. Bankruptcy and Insolvency (1840), p. 32.

50 The fifteen, all of which are examined later, were Bracken, Williams and Co.; Bull, Banks and Bryson; Duckham and Lankester; Goodair and Co.; Greaves, Sharp and Fisher; Harrison and Co.; Jacob Bros.; Laycock and Co.; Leigh and Co.; Parkin and Scobell; Rowlandson, Isaac and Brien; Vos and Essers; William Wilson; Wilson and Williams; and Winstanley and Hudson.

The general pattern of bankruptcies in 1810-11 reflects the economic developments which have already been described. After reaching a high level in the second quarter of 1810, they rose slightly in the third quarter and sharply in the fourth, remaining high in the first quarter of 1811 and declining thereafter. The sustained increase in the third quarter of 1810, which was boosted by the high July figure, is contrary to downward movements in all similar periods since at least 1779.[51] The upward movement in the winter, reaching peaks in November 1810 and January 1811, though more dramatic than in most years, was typical. As Ashton points out, bankruptcies traditionally increased in the winter perhaps in response, initially, to the high demand for money at the end of the harvest in the autumn and, later, to the fact that merchants and manufacturers balanced their accounts and sent out their bills around Christmas.[52]

Perhaps the most interesting feature of Table 6.4 is the uneven distribution of bankruptcies throughout the country. Generally, their density appears to have been dictated by the nature of regional, economic conditions. The obvious example is the contrast between the high failure rate in areas which concentrated upon cotton manufacture and overseas trade and the lower level elsewhere. In London, Manchester and Liverpool, where 54 per cent of all failures occurred, the rate was much higher than in the rest of the country, the two Lancashire cities experiencing the highest level of all. Examination of the experiences of individual areas adds weight to this suggested link between bankruptcies and local conditions.

Bankruptcies in London can be divided into commercial and non-commercial (or 'miscellaneous') categories. The

---

51 N.J. Silberling, 'British Prices and Business Cycles, 1779-1850,' Rev. Econ. Stats. (1923), Suppl. 2, 251.

52 T.S. Ashton, Economic Fluctuations in England, 1700-1800 (Oxford, 1959), p. 13.

former (which includes merchants, entrepreneurs and brokers) responded closely to the state of the money market, as shown by its increases in July and after September 1810. Throughout the period, this group constituted about thirty per cent of London failures, although in July 1810 this rose to 41 per cent as a result of Brickwood and Co.'s failure. In the fourth quarter, however, bankruptcies of both commercial and miscellaneous traders increased sharply, declining slowly during the first half of 1811:

Type of Bankrupt	1810 2nd quarter	1810 3rd quarter	1810 4th quarter	1811 1st quarter	1811 2nd quarter
Commercial	52	56	84	65	52
Miscellaneous	134	116	190	167	148

The miscellaneous group in London provided the largest number of bankrupts in the country (thirty per cent). As Table 6.5 shows, it consisted largely of shopkeepers and artisans, although its domain was broad, including essential services, food, clothing, housing, transportation and entertainment. The diversity of occupations within the group makes generalisation hazardous but a number of factors can be suggested which may have made its financial position insecure. As has been shown already, the defects in the debt laws ensured that tradesmen, who were obliged to give credit in order to retain their customers' good-will and to compete with neighbouring firms, experienced constant difficulty in enforcing their claims. In addition, many of the occupations involved were subject to seasonal fluctuations in demand for their services. This probably affected the more refined shops during the summer months, when the world of fashion was away from London, and artisans in the winter (work on houses, for example, was done during the summer).[53] In normal years, such fluctuations in demand

53 See M.D. George, London Life in the Eighteenth Century (Pelican edn., 1965), p. 263.

could be negotiated by the majority of tradesmen, the brisk business at some periods compensating losses which might be sustained at others. During the fourth quarter of 1810, however, the insecurity of the group as a whole was probably increased for a variety of reasons. First, the severe credit restrictions probably affected tradesmen even more than merchants, since the apparent reluctance of bankers to discount their bills at all times[54] would be accentuated. This problem was no doubt heightened by the bankruptcies of some wholesalers and the inability of others to give credit to the same extent during as before the crisis. Second, like merchants, tradesmen probably lost heavily as a result of the decline in price of stock accumulated earlier in the year. Third, at a time when money was scarce, customers were less able to pay their debts to shopkeepers while artisans were less likely to be paid for work done during the summer. The severe unemployment which afflicted, for example, the Spitalfields silk workers during the winter[55] further reduced the ability of customers to pay. Finally, all these problems were no doubt compounded by the fact that, like merchants and manufacturers, tradesmen sent out their bills at the end of the year.[56] The over-all significance of credit restrictions and refusals to pay is reflected in the increase of 'miscellaneous' bankrupts from 250 during the six months prior to 1 October 1810 to 357 in the subsequent six months and, perhaps, in the fact that 701 debtors were committed to the King's Bench prison during the latter period.[57]

---

54 See B.P.P. Bankrupt Laws (1818), p. 44, Germain Lavie.

55 B.P.P. Orders in Council (1812), John Honyman.

56 B.P.P. Fifteen Pounds (1823), p. 9.

57 The totals for similar periods are: 1806-7, 409; 1807-8, 518; 1808-9, 485; 1809-10, 514; 1811-12, 616 (calculated from King's Bench Commitment Books, P.R.O. Pris. 4, Nos. 20-25).

In Lancashire, the aggregate bankruptcy pattern was similar to that of London in the sense that thirty per cent of failures belonged to the commercial category. The rise in commercial failures here after 1 October 1810, however, was more marked than in London. During the previous six months they totalled 19 compared with 74 in the half-year after 1 October. Thus, it seems that the growing commercial difficulties of the capital throughout 1810 were not felt acutely in Lancashire until the fourth quarter, possibly because that area was less affected by impediments in European trade. A similar pattern is discernible in the bankruptcies of textile manufacturers, which rose from 19 between April and September 1810 to 66 in the next six months. Their relative immunity before October may be attributable to the intervention of the banking fraternity after Brickwood and Co.'s failure in July, which retarded the spread of bankruptcy from London commercial houses to their affiliated manufacturers. As noted above, the largest mercantile bankrupts were given time to honour their bills after stopping payments in July. In the fourth quarter of 1810, however, the commercial malaise in both London and Lancashire was inevitably transmitted to the manufacturing sector. The sensitivity of the cotton industry to the health of the commercial sector is explained by the dependence of manufacturers upon the acceptances of exporters and warehousemen, which ensured that they frequently collapsed together. The pyramidal pattern of bankruptcies emanating from the overseas merchants, which is examined later, is reflected in the spate of textile bankruptcies after September. In addition to Manchester, the smaller textile towns were depressed. For example, ten out of the fifteen failures at Stockport were of cotton manufacturers, as were seven of Bolton's eight and six of Chorley's eight.

As in London, the largest category of bankruptcies in Lancashire was that of miscellaneous traders. There is, however, an interesting discrepancy between their extent in Manchester and Liverpool and elsewhere in Lancashire. In the two cities they amounted respectively to 0.6 and 0.7 per thousand people (the proportion in London is 0.7) compared with 0.15 in the rest of the county. This suggests that retail outlets and demand for services were not as well-developed in less densely populated areas where tradesmen probably operated on a smaller scale. The increase of miscellaneous bankruptcies in Lancashire during the winter is, no doubt, explained by the same factors as in London. In both places, it is likely that credit problems were accentuated by the fact that the capital of local banks was locked up in the bills of mercantile bankrupts. As was pointed out by the 1811 Committee on Commercial Credit, this inevitably reduced the volume of credit available to traders as a whole and heightened the prevailing distress.[58]

Outside London and Lancashire, the area which was most severely distressed during the crisis was the West Country. Overseas trade difficulties probably account for the high level of failures at Bristol, which included eight merchants. Superficially, the distress elsewhere in the West Country seems to have been a product of the wave of country bank failures which followed the collapse of Bowles and Co. at Salisbury in July.[59] That these failures created difficulties is indisputable. In Exeter, for example, the collapse of Wilcocks and Frazier was followed by those of thirteen other firms in the town. At Bath, the stoppages of two banks were followed by thirty failures, that of Stroud, in Swansea, by nine and that of Jukes, Langley, in Gosport, by seven. However, the financial instability which was prevalent in the West Country in the first half of 1810 and the fact that only one of the banks which failed in July and

---

58 B.P.P. Commercial Credit (1810-11), p. 1.

59 For the failure of Bowles and Co., see chapter VIII.

August had used Brickwood and Co. as its London agent suggests that the financial panic was a symptom rather than a cause of economic malaise in the region.

What were the underlying reasons for the West Country's financial problems in 1810? L.S. Pressnell suggests that the country bank failures could be related either to harvest conditions or to economic activity.[60] Wheat was imported on a massive scale early in 1810 and prices rose from 100s. per quarter in February to 113s. in June, remaining high until the start of September.[61] This may have produced the shaken confidence during the summer months and it is, perhaps, instructive that as soon as wheat prices declined in September country bank failures in the West Country stopped for five months. This argument, however, is vitiated by the fact that only three country banks outside the West Country were docketed during the period under discussion.[62] While harvest conditions may have contributed to the crisis in this region, therefore, its root cause should probably be sought, as in London and Lancashire, in the nature of the local economy.

A comparison of the West Country economy and that of Yorkshire, the largest wool-producing region, provides a number of clues. There was a marked contrast between the raw materials which each used. West Country manufacturers were dependent upon the provision of high-quality Spanish wool, the scarcity and high cost of which throughout 1809

---

60 L.S. Pressnell, Country Banking in the Industrial Revolution (Oxford, 1956), p. 465.

61 Average wheat prices throughout the country in 1810: Jan., 101s.6d.; Feb., 100s.; Mar., 102s.3d.; Apr., 104s.11d.; May, 108s.2d.; June, 113s.2d.; July, 113s.4d.; Aug., 116s.2d.; Sept., 109s.11d.; Oct., 101s.1d.; Nov., 100s.9d.; Dec., 97s.1d. (The Tradesman, v, 1810).

62 The banks were Rowton, Morhall (Chester and Shrewsbury) in October; Seaton (Pontefract) in October; Gillett (Chesterfield) in November. Gillett's commission was not opened.

induced large increases in sale price and reduced demand. In 1810, when the scarcity was replaced by abundance, prices of woollen fabric fell quickly.[63] In September, it was reported that 'the fall in the price of English cloth is perhaps the greatest ever known. The finest sorts from Wiltshire, which last year sold at two guineas per yard, are not now worth twenty-eight shillings.'[64] The only West Country manufacturers to profit in 1810 were those who exported their product to America.[65] In contrast, the Yorkshire wool industry was fairly prosperous throughout 1810, production being stimulated by American demand. This probably nullified the initial effect of the crisis in July when 27 Yorkshire traders failed. In none of the following twelve months did Yorkshire bankruptcies exceed thirteen. Only at Hull, where sixteen merchants failed in the crisis, were overseas trade difficulties reflected in increased bankruptcies. In other towns the number of commercial and manufacturing bankruptcies was small. Seven merchants and six manufacturers failed at Leeds, one manufacturer at Bradford, one clothier and two merchants at Huddersfield, three manufacturers and one merchant at Halifax, and one merchant and three manufacturers at York. Nevertheless, the collapse of Seaton, Foster and Co., a Pontefract bank, in early October, sent a wave of fear throughout the county as indicated in the public pledges made in York, Leeds and Sheffield to honour the notes of the local banks.[66]

---

63 The Tradesman, v, 1810, 363, 413.

64 Salisbury and Winchester Journal, 10 Sept. 1810, p. 4, col. 3.

65 Crouzet, op. cit., ii, 512.

66 The Times, 9 Oct. 1810, p. 3, col. 3 (York); Cowdroy's Manchester Gazette, 6 Oct. 1810, p. 3, col. 3 (Leeds); Manchester Mercury, 16 Oct. 1810, p. 2, col. 1 (Sheffield).

It is thus likely that the economic insecurity of the West Country explains its lack of financial resilience and that the liquidity panic which forced so many bank stoppages in July and August was rooted in the depression of its woollen industry. The local failures during the following twelve months consisted largely of middlemen and retailers in the textile trade and of miscellaneous bankrupts. The low bankruptcy rate in the area (0.2 per thousand people) may be attributable to two connected factors. First, the relatively low density of its population suggests that the miscellaneous group was smaller than in London and Lancashire. Second, there is a noticeable absence, in its bankruptcies, of textile manufacturers, only fifteen of whom failed during the crisis period. This apparent immunity may reflect the organisation of the textile industry. During the eighteenth century, many of the larger merchants had transferred their centre of operations to London and the North. In addition, in the West Country, which did not cater to a mass market, manufacturing shops, with one or two exceptions, tended to be smaller than in Yorkshire. A group of wealthy merchants and clothiers dominated the industry, putting out their wool to hundreds of artisans, who performed the stages of manufacture, and sending the finished articles to London for export.[67]

Just as regional economic conditions may explain both the severity of the crisis and the density of bankruptcies in London, Lancashire, Yorkshire and the West Country, so too they probably account for the failure rates elsewhere in England and Wales. The evidence indicates that those areas which, like Yorkshire, were not severely distressed in 1810 also experienced a low level of bankruptcies in 1811. Only four hosiers failed at Nottingham and two at Leicester,

---

67 See R.G. Wilson, Gentlemen Merchants (Manchester, 1971), pp. 5,7, 52-4; J. De L. Mann, 'Clothiers and Weavers in Wiltshire during the Eighteenth Century,' in Studies in the Industrial Revolution (ed. L.S. Pressnell), (1960), p. 88.

where trade was active throughout 1810.[68] Derby suffered only seven failures and Coventry, Wolverhampton and Norwich six. The twenty-five bankruptcies in the North-East involved two coal-owners, two merchants, two anchorsmiths and nineteen tradesmen. The health of the iron and other trades in Birmingham and Sheffield[69] was reflected in a comparatively low number of failures (13 at Sheffield). In most of these areas, unemployment and depression were prevalent after the closure of American trade on 2 February 1811. As noted, however, their failure rates were low. This discrepancy between the experiences of Lancashire in 1810 and of other regions in the following year may be explained partly by the fact that the Non-Importation Act was soon followed by the revival of commercial confidence after the issue of Exchequer Bills and the re-opening of the Portuguese market. A more important factor, however, is the difference in the significance and nature of overseas trading in the respective areas. Industries which, like iron and steel, depended largely on the domestic market for their raw materials and for sale of produce were less sensitive than cotton to fluctuations in overseas trade.[70] It is true that, during the latter half of 1810, some regions, like Sheffield and the Potteries, were said to have exported as much as one-third of their produce,[71] but it is probable that, unlike the commerce of 1809 and early 1810, this trade was not exessive because American demand for iron, hosiery, wool and pottery was greater than British

---

68 B.P.P. Orders in Council (1812), p. 177, Thomas Leach.

69 Ibid., p. 2, Thomas Attwood; p. 131, John Bailey.

70 For the contrasting effects of fluctuations in overseas trade on the iron and cotton industries, see T.S. Ashton, Iron and Steel in the Industrial Revolution (Manchester, 1951), p. 151.

71 B.P.P. Orders in Council (1812), p. 131, John Bailey; p. 160, Josiah Wedgwood.

supply of those goods[72] and because the money market was already fairly tight. Thus, a contrast is apparent in the evidence presented to the Committee of the Whole House on the Orders in Council, in 1812, between the heavy mercantile losses which resulted from the earlier, marginal trading ventures and the more regulated and stable operations of later 1810 when profits continued to be high and the American market was not over-supplied. In the circumstances, it is not surprising that the transmission of bankruptcy through the bill mechanism, from the merchant to the manufacturer, appears to be less typical of the American than of the South American trade in 1810.

IV

The discussion so far has focused attention upon the course of economic developments before and during the crisis of 1810. It is evident that the general health of the economy was associated closely with the state of overseas trade. Equally, it seems that the extent of both aggregate and regional bankruptcies during the crisis was related to the nature of previous foreign trading which was in turn influenced by the credit conditions under which it was conducted. During the war period, the money market was particularly sensitive to fluctuations in the policies of the Bank of England, which thus may have constituted a fundamental determinant of overseas trading and, consequently, of bankruptcy levels. This supports the argument in chapter five that the similarity of their respective curves suggests a causal connection between the level of Bank discounts and both overseas trade and bankruptcies. In addition, it is possible that discounts operated as an autonomous variable which not only influenced

---

72 See <u>ibid</u>., p. 7, Thomas Attwood; p. 182, Thomas Leach; p. 128, Thomas Greenwood; p. 166, Ralph Stevenson.

the volume of overseas trade but also independently determined the level of bankruptcies. The rest of this chapter, which examines the policies of the Bank, seeks to answer two main questions. First, to what extent was the Bank responsible for the inflation and excessive trading which created the crisis? Second, does its reaction to the economic deterioration of 1810 suggest that the Bank possessed a crisis theory?

The first of these questions was hotly disputed by contemporaries. The policies of the Bank were subjected to criticism early in 1810, when there were distinct signs that the economy was not completely healthy. The most significant of these was the fact that the exchanges had been depreciating and the price of bullion rising for more than a year. After climbing from 34-4 to 35-5 between January and July 1808, the Hamburg exchange was close to par, after which it declined to 33 in October and 31-3 at the end of the year. The fall continued until June 1809, when it reached 28-6, and fluctuated between 28-6 and 29-6 for the remainder of the year. In 1810, it rose between February and April from 28-4 to 31 where it hovered before declining again to 28-6 in October.[73] The annual variations in the exchange and in the price of silver were as follows:

Price of Silver and Hamburg Exchange, 1807-11 (Par = 100)

Year	Price of Silver	Hamburg Exchange
1807	110.2	104
1808	107.1	106
1809	110.4	121
1810	113.9	120
1811	120.7	144

Source: Gayer, Rostow and Schwartz, op. cit., i, 106.

---

73 Crouzet, op. cit., ii, 526-7.

This problem, of course, called forth the Bullion Committee, which noted that, since the latter part of 1808, the market price of gold bullion had risen above £4 an ounce, fluctuating in 1809 between £4.9.0d. and £4.12.0d. (i.e. 15-1/2% above mint price).[74] It is pertinent to examine the causes of the depreciation and to relate them to contemporary explanations.

At first sight, it seems that the depreciation is adequately explained by the arguments of many anti-bullionists, since grain imports and government expenditure increased greatly in 1809 and 1810. However, it is difficult to substantiate the link between these factors and the initial depreciation in the latter part of 1808. Despite rising prices, corn imports in that year were negligible.[75] Government expenditure undoubtedly contributed to the general inflation of the war period[76] and it is true that, following five or six years at a relatively low level, it rose markedly after the Spanish revolt, coinciding with the downward turn in the exchanges and upward trend in gold price in 1808:

---

74 B.P.P. Gold Bullion (1810), p. 2.

75 Corn imports to Great Britain, 1808-11 (official values): 1808, £146,000; 1809, £1,137,000; 1810, £2,701,000; 1811, £466,000 (Mitchell and Deane, op. cit., p. 289).

76 See F. Crouzet, 'Bilan de l'économie, britannique pendant les guerres de la Révolution et de l'Empire,' Revue Historique, no. 234 (July-Sept. 1965), 83.

Overseas Expenditure of British Government 1801-1811 (£000,000)

Year	Bills and specie for British armies in Europe	Subsidies and Loans	Total
1801	1.7	2.2	3.9
1802	0.6	0.8	1.4
1803	0.2	0.1	0.3
1804	0.1	0.6	0.7
1805	0.8	1.9	2.7
1806	0.7	1.1	1.8
1807	1.7	0.9	2.6
1808	3.9	2.8	6.7
1809	5.6	2.7	8.3
1810	6.8	2.3	9.1
1811	11.6	2.2	13.8

Source: Gayer, Rostow and Schwartz, op. cit., pp. 77, 103.

However, the effect of the increased government commitments on exchange rates in 1808 is difficult to prove. F. Crouzet points out that nine-tenths of the governmental expenditure was paid in specie and gold and only one-tenth in bills of exchange on the Treasury, a fact which was to have serious consequences in the long run but which did not immediately influence the exchanges. Crouzet suggests that a more reasonable explanation of the initial depreciation was the fact that, although the balance of payments deficit was statistically small, the credit terms upon which trade was conducted rendered it large in practice.[77]

77 F. Crouzet, L'Économie Britannique et le Blocus Continental, (1806-1813), (Paris, 1958), ii, 539-40.

This interpretation - that the depreciation was initially a result of non-monetary factors - does not contradict the notions of moderate bullionists. Henry Thornton had always maintained that depreciation could be caused by adverse trading conditions[78] and the Bullion Report, which he influenced closely, conceded that

> the circumstances of the trade of this country, in the course of the last year, were such as to occasion a real fall in the exchanges with the Continent to a certain extent and perhaps at one period almost as low as the limit fixed by the expense of remitting gold from hence to the respective markets.79

This was explained both by the increased war-time cost of transmitting bullion (including insurance) and by the fact that advances had been necessary on imports from Europe as soon as the goods were shipped, while long credit was given on exports to the rest of the world.[80] The prevalent distrust of sterling and consequent demands for immediate payment by continental traders can largely be explained by the psychological effect of the Continental System and, especially, of the Treaty of Tilsit (July 1807). The Bullion Report noted that the depression of the exchanges in early 1809 was attributable to the effects of Napoleon's occupation of Northern Germany.[81]

Thus, the initial depreciation can be explained adequately by war-time trading conditions. Its protraction and increasing severity after 1808 are attributable to a variety of factors. The large-scale corn imports of 1809 and 1810 undoubtedly affected the exchanges adversely. In addition, the fact that, after 1808, government overseas expenditure was paid in bills, because bank reserves of

---

78 E.g. Paper Credit, op. cit., p. 225.

79 B.P.P. Gold Bullion (1810), p. 11.

80 Ibid., pp. 11-15.

81 Ibid., p. 16.

specie had declined, greatly increased the supply of bills on Britain.[82] It is doubtful, however, whether this explains the large depreciation of 1809 and 1810 when, Thornton considered, the pound had been devalued by forty or fifty per cent since the start of the war.[83] As Crouzet says,

> Si, en effet, la balance des paiements commerciaux courants avait été largement favorable, les dépenses du gouvernement n'auraient pas provoqué de dépréciation. Par conséquent le vrai problème est celui du deficit de la balance commerciale; il faut déterminer pourquoi ce déficit, faible jusque'en 1808, augmenta brutalement en 1809 et 1810.[84]

The adverse commercial balance is certainly not explained by export restrictions imposed by the Continental System, since throughout 1809 and early 1810 exports were strong. Crouzet considers that the most significant factor was the large price differential between England and foreign countries. This was caused at the end of 1808 by rising wheat prices and by scarcity of foreign goods (because of the Continental System and American embargo) at a time when industrial demand for raw materials was growing after remaining low since the start of the year. In normal circumstances, the price level and, consequently, the volume of imports would have declined in March 1809 when the previous scarcity of foreign goods had already been replaced by abundance. But, as Crouzet points out, the willingness of the Bank of England to increase its discounting (and note issues) in accordance with commercial demand 'transforma une simple

---

82 Crouzet, _op. cit_., ii, 543.

83 _Substance of Two Speeches of Henry Thornton on the Report of the Bullion Committee_ (1811), p. 21.

84 Crouzet, _op. cit_., ii, 544. Crouzet argues that, in the three or four years before 1808, the trade deficit had largely been alleviated by invisible transactions, including freight and foreign investments (_ibid_., p. 532).

poussée de fièvre spéculative en un puissant mouvement d'inflation,'[85] which protracted both the large importing, at a time when domestic and foreign markets were becoming saturated, and the depreciation:

> La livre fut dépréciée, en raison du déficit de la balance des paiements, dû lui-même au déficit de la balance commerciale, résultant de la disparité des prix, dont la cause essentielle était la situation inflationiste qui regnait en Angleterre . . . L'inflation ne fit pas baisser la livre, mais elle l'empêcha de se redresser.[86]

Although the country banks contributed to the inflation, Crouzet argues that their dependence upon the London money market ensured that ultimate responsibility lay with the Bank of England.[87] If the Bank had concentrated upon keeping the pound stable by contracting its issues, the exchanges would not have fallen beyond the gold points.[88] Thus, the inflation and depreciation are attributable to Bank policy.

This interpretation of the continued depreciation, like that suggested above to explain its outbreak, is close to the bullionist position. Thornton considered that, as long as paper was confined within its 'accustomed bounds,' any absence of gold induced by abnormal conditions, like one or two bad harvests, would prove temporary and would rectify itself.[89] However, an increased circulation would have the effect of

---

85 Ibid., p. 551.

86 Ibid., p. 547.

87 Ibid., p. 551; cf. Pressnell's account of the dependence of country banks on their London agents, whose policies were dictated by the Bank of England, op. cit., pp. 213-24.

88 Crouzet, op. cit., p. 547.

89 Thornton, Paper Credit, op.cit., pp. 158-9.

> enhancing the price of goods, which advanced price of goods affords employment to a larger quantity of circulating medium, so that the circulation can never be overfull. This advanced price of goods is the same thing as a reduced price of coin; the coin, therefore, in consequence of its reduced price, is carried out of the country for the sake of obtaining for it a better market.90

Thornton did not conclude from this that the circulation should be kept at a strictly specified level, because changing economic conditions could increase or decrease the velocity of circulation and the demand for money (i.e. fluctuations in liquidity preference).[91] But he did advocate that expansion and contraction should be effected cautiously (the main theme of Paper Credit is the danger of a rapid contraction) and that the Bank should allow its paper to 'vibrate' within certain limits.[92] By 1810, Thornton could see clearly that, as a result of the Bank's failure to manage its issues cautiously, the fallen exchanges of 1808 had not been redressed.[93]

William Huskisson, a co-author of the Bullion Report (with Thornton and Francis Horner), formed the conclusion that the Bank was responsible in a similar, non-doctrinaire manner. Like Thornton, he ascribed the initial depreciation of 1808 to political and commercial impediments to trade. But, after twelve months, he had begun to wonder whether 'the Bank, from too much indulgence to their customers at some particular moment, had somewhat imprudently extended their issues,' a suspicion which was confirmed, he said,

---

90 Ibid., p. 205.

91 Ibid., pp. 95-8. Bullionists in general stressed that the actual volume of paper in circulation was no indication of over-issue and depreciation; e.g. Lord King, Thoughts on the Effects of the Bank Restriction (1804), pp. 60, 115; R. Mushet, Enquiry into the Bank Restriction Bill (2nd. edn., 1810), p. 13.

92 Thornton, op. cit., p. 259.

93 Thornton, Substance of Two Speeches, op. cit., p. 15.

> when I found that the principle of regulating the issues and ascertaining the value of the pound by a reference to some fixed standard, and even the existence of such a fixed standard were either altogether overlooked by the Bank (they could scarcely be unknown to them) or utterly disregarded in their practice.[94]

The problem of establishing such a measure was not simple. In the absence of index numbers of the relative purchasing power of currencies, the bullionists were forced to rely on the market price of bullion as the gauge of depreciation. However, as they realized, this was an exceptionally difficult criterion for two reasons. First, they acknowledged the difficulties of assessing the price of bullion accurately (because of the need to ascertain the condition of foreign, metallic currencies, their degree of wear, the impediments to export, and the fact that, in practice, the British were on a gold and other countries on a silver standard). Thus, Thornton considered that, while the price of bullion 'distinctly established' the depreciation, the exchanges should also be adverted to for confirmation.[95] Second, how could they define a limit beyond which it could be asserted justifiably that there was over-issue? Hicks suggests that Thornton considered the limit to be the point at which it was no longer possible for gold coin to be drawn out of circulation for export (filling the gap in the balance of payments); after this, any further note issue, to replace the lost gold, would convert a depreciation useful to counter a temporary difficulty into

---

94 W. Huskisson, 'The Question Concerning the Depreciation of our Currency,' in Select Tracts (ed. Lord Overstone), (1857), p. 577.

95 Thornton, *op. cit.*, p. 70.

over-issue.[96] Like Ricardo,[97] Thornton was interested in measuring depreciation not against mint price but against the level which would have operated in convertible conditions. A price of £4 per ounce would, thus, not have worried most bullionists. The difficulty of finding a specific test of depreciation and the varying emphasis which individual bullionists placed on the importance of trade and political factors ensured the the Bullion Report was vague on this matter. After stating that non-monetary factors accounted for a depreciation of about seven per cent, it suggested that a large premium on gold and fall of the exchanges, 'for a considerable period of time, form the best general criterion from which any inference can be drawn as to the sufficiency or excess of paper currency in circulation.' The Bank, it contended, had failed to redress the initial fall by determining note issues in accordance with the state of the exchanges, as it would in convertible conditions.[98] It noted the fallacy of the 'real bills' doctrine which, at a time when commercial profits greatly exceeded the five per cent at which the Bank was obliged to discount, inevitably induced a large increase in the volume and the 'quickness' of circulation. This, in turn, lowered the relative value of the pound, creating adverse exchanges and a high price of bullion.[99]

The anti-bullionist argument, whose most eminent if not most persuasive advocates were directors of the Bank of England, was that, in inconvertible conditions, the

---

96 Sir J. Hicks, Critical Essays in Monetary Theory (Oxford, 1967), pp. 182-6.

97 See R.S. Sayers, 'Ricardo's Views on Monetary Questions,' in Papers in English Monetary History (ed. T.S. Ashton and R.S. Sayers), (Oxford, 1953), p. 78.

98 B.P.P. Gold Bullion (1810), p. 22.

99 Ibid., pp. 23-4, 26.

movements of the exchanges and of bullion price were controlled only by the balance of payments. The continued large exchange depreciation was, thus, the product of heavy government expenditure, war-time trade disturbances and, to a lesser extent, poor harvests,[100] and there was no relevance in exchange movements (like the gold export point in convertibility) as indicators of excess note issue. That the monetary ideas expressed by the Bank directors were singularly unenlightened has frequently been noted. As a body, they appear to have abandoned the wise policies of Samuel Bosanquet in the 1780s and, as late as 1819, were still denying the relationship between note issues and the exchanges.[101] Evidently, the exchanges were only adverted to as corroborative evidence of other criteria.[102] Having abandoned the exchanges, the Bank's only recourse was to the state of its cash balance, at a time when the suspension had made it irrelevant, and to general assertions of their duty to accommodate commerce by discounting 'real' bills. They considered that, by doing this, the Bank would be meeting the needs of trade and that its issues could neither be excessive nor play an active role in stimulating trade.[103] If, by chance, excess notes were issued, they would be redundant and quickly return to the Bank.

How was the real bills doctrine translated into practice? There were, of course, a variety of regulations defining the characteristics of real bills. They should not have more than sixty-five days to run; they should be drawn

---

100 Ibid., p. 90, John Whitmore; p. 143, Jeremiah Harman.

101 See J.K. Horsefield, 'The Duties of a Banker,' in Papers in English Monetary History, op. cit., pp. 1-36; for the position of the directors in 1819, see Idem, 'Bankers and Bullionists in 1819,' J. Pol Econ. (1949), 442-8.

102 B.P.P. Gold Bullion (1810), pp. 90, 96, John Whitmore and John Pearse.

103 Ibid., pp. 127, 157, Whitmore and Pearse.

on London; the Bank should know both the discounter and the acceptor; no bills should be drawn for under £20; no note was discountable which was designed to pay off other notes of the same customer which were falling due; and so on.[104] Although, logically, all bills which satisfied these requirements should have been discounted, it is evident that the directors were not blind to the necessity of limiting advances even on sound bills. In 1804, Deputy Governor Winthrop conceded that the discount of real bills could increase the currency beyond the 'proper Quantity' and that the Bank was used to rationing discounts.[105] Six years later, Governor Whitmore told the Bullion Committee that the directors 'do set limits to their advances according to circumstances, and as their discretion may direct them.'[106] The limits appear to have been set according to two criteria to which Harman alluded in his evidence to the Bullion Committee. He stated that 'though we have no precise limit, we constantly keep in view the aggregate amount, as well as the amount of every individual account' and that the Bank attempted to keep its paper 'at nearly its accustomed standard,' although variations in demand necessitated fluctuations from time to time.[107] Individual accounts were restricted by specific Bank regulations and total discounts by its judgment of market conditions. In 1804, the individual limits were established as follows: bankers' discounts were not to exceed £60,000 and those of other houses £30,000, though the Bank could extend each by £10,000

---

104 For a catalogue of the regulations, see Bank of England records, ADV/B 533 - 1, 'Extracts relating to Discounts.'

105 B.P.P. Report from the S.C. . . . into the State of Ireland, as to its Circulating Paper . . . (1804), III, 7.

106 B.P.P. Gold Bullion (1810), p. 80.

107 Ibid., pp. 142-3.

if necessary. The Committee on Discounts recommended that a committee should be established every six months to investigate the accounts of all persons whose discount account had exceeded £5,000 for more than three years.[108] Five years later (January 1809) the bankers' limit was raised to £100,000 and it was recommended that all large accounts should be reported weekly to the court.[109]

A clue to the criteria which influenced the Bank's policy towards aggregate discounting may be found in the evidence of Samuel Thornton to the Committee on the Resumption of Cash Payments in 1819. He stated that, at times when the demand for discounts was increasing rapidly, the Bank's policy was

> to consider the amount of bank notes out, and what could be the cause for a call for an increase. If it appeared to be at a period when trade and manufactures were flourishing, that seemed to me a sufficient inducement, but if trade was under any degree of check, the same inclination to accommodate the public, did not seem to me justifiable. I also felt it my duty to look at the state of the foreign exchanges and the price of bullion.110

The important determinant for Thornton was the state of trade.[111] Presumably, the restriction of discounts during difficult conditions was justified by the reasonable assumption that doubtful paper was more abundant then. Nevertheless, the implication of Thornton's statement (and of those of Whitmore and Harman, cited above) is that some, at least, of the directors were conscious of the danger of blind adherence to the real bills doctrine.

---

108 Bank of England, Special Discount Committee, ff. 11-14.

109 Ibid., f. 45.

110 B.P.P. Report from the S.C. on the Expediency of the Bank Resuming Cash Payments (1819), III, p. 85.

111 Thornton was not fully convinced of the usefulness of the exchanges and price of bullion as indicators. See J.K. Horsefield, 'Bankers and Bullionists in 1819,' J. Pol. Econ. (1949), 445.

Why, then, did the Bank discount so liberally in 1809 and, especially, early in 1810 (as will be demonstrated later)? There are two possible answers. First, the pressure on the Bank at that time was such that a restrictive policy designed to root out dubious paper was not feasible. The difficulty of detecting accommodation bills seriously hampered such a policy at all times and the problem afflicted the Bank throughout the Napoleonic period. The Discount Committee of 1804 emphasized 'the propriety of reducing the large amount of advances upon Bills and Notes' which had 'necessarily introduced a dispatch of business, inconsistent with the care and circumspection formerly bestowed . . . .' The committee reiterated the Bank's discount regulations, considering that 'if those Rules and Orders had never been departed from . . . the different accounts would have been smaller.'[112] In 1809, the problem was still vexatious since the recommendations of the 1804 committee had not been effected.[113] In 1810, another committee anxiously observed that

> the check endeavoured to be put upon too indiscriminate liberality in Discount, as well as upon the Acceptances of Bankers, by Reporting the high Accounts Weekly to the Court has fallen into disuse. It is possible that an unprecedented press of Business may have obliged the daily Committee in Waiting, and the Court to dispense with regulations . . . generally acknowledged to be useful and proper.[114]

The second explanation of the Bank's liberality in 1809-10 is the odium it incurred by rationing discounts in 1796, which, as Clapham suggests, may have made it averse to repeating the operation in 1810.[115] In January 1810, the

---

112 Bank of England, Special Discount Committee, f. 12.

113 Ibid., f. 22.

114 Ibid., f. 58.

115 J.H. Clapham, 'The Private Business of the Bank of England, 1744-1800,' Ec. H.R., xi (1941), 82.

Court rejected the Discount Committee's recommendation that discounts be reduced and stated that 'although the Discount Accounts of some Individual Houses may appear upon comparison to be unusually high, it does not seem expedient to have recourse to any extraordinary measures, to reduce the total Amount of Discounts . . . this Corporation being particularly interested in the prosperity of the Commerce of this Country, is peculiarly called upon to give every possible assistance and support to the Commerce and Credit of the City of London.'[116] In other words, during a period when trade was apparently flourishing, the Bank was prepared to ignore the reservations of some of its directors[117] and to pursue a discount policy designed to give maximum accommodation to commerce. It was neither willing to ration aggregate discounts nor, by its own private admission, able to detect dubious paper. The consequence of its indiscriminate liberality was not only a large increase in discounting during the boom years of 1809 and early 1810 but also, and perhaps more important, a stimulus to overtrading.

The cause of the initial increase in discounting in 1808 was the Spanish revolt, as a result of which, according to A. Feavearyear, 'sheer optimism, producing a reckless expansion of business, just drew the paper into circulation for purely commercial purposes.'[118] Huskisson considered that, after 1808, 'the Directors of the Bank appeared to have considered the increased eagerness for discount as

---

116 Bank of England, Court of Directors Minute Books, 12 April 1809 to 4 April 1811, ff. 206, 218-9.

117 The members of the Discount Committee in 1809 were Campbell, Davidson, Dorrien, Manning, Pole and Stamforth; in 1810, Campbell, Dorrien, Drewe, Maitland and Richards.

118 Sir A. Feavearyear, The Pound Sterling (1931), p. 174.

requiring some increased indulgence on their part.'[119] In parliament, Huskisson described the effects of the liberal credit upon trade:

> the race of old English merchants, who could never persuade themselves to go beyond their capital, was superseded by a set of mad and extravagant speculators, who never stopped so long as they could get credit . . . . In this way had commerce become a sort of wholesale gambling, such as had never before been seen in this country.120

These comments are corroborated by the Discount Committees of the Bank itself. The number of discounters at the Bank rose from 1,342 in July 1808 to 1,394 in January 1809 and 1,492 in January 1810. At the same dates, the paper under discount increased from £12,774,957 (1808) to £14,587,311 (1809) and £19,914,810 (1810).[121] The main beneficiaries were overseas merchants. The largest increases in the volume of discounts granted to individual branches of trade between January 1809 and January 1810 were: general merchants trading to the continent (increased by £1,088,553); Russian merchants (£399,458); wine and brandy merchants (£395,961); Spanish merchants (£360,004); America merchants (£355,820); and Irish provision dealers and merchants (£347,873). In domestic trade, the largest increases were granted to linen drapers (£534,349), Scotch factors (£193,365) and Backwell Hall factors (£232,124).[122]

---

119 W. Huskisson, 'The Question Concerning the Depreciation of our Currency,' in _Select Tracts_ (ed. Lord Overstone), (1857), pp. 657-8.

120 Hansard, _P.D._, 1811, xix, 340; for similar comments, see _ibid._, pp. 730-1, Huskisson; p. 530, Lord King; B.P.P. _Orders in Council_ (1812), p. 525, Robert McKerrell; p. 577, John Buckle.

121 Bank of England, Special Discount Committee, ff. 26, 41, 52.

122 By contrast, in 1810, the only overseas traders whose discounts increased substantially were West India Merchants (by £206,030). _Ibid._, ff. 41-2, 52-3, 63-4.

That many of the new discounters were inexperienced traders is evidenced by the 1809 committee's statement that

> the peculiarity of the present times, and the unhappy state of European Commerce, is without a Parallel; and . . . that large accommodation afforded to Persons hitherto unaccustomed to such extensive concerns, is likely to cause speculations founded upon Monopoly; which must in the end prove Injurious to some Individuals; and may give the Public cause to lament the too great liberality and Indulgence of the Bank.[123]

In January 1810, the committee similarly noted that the largest increases in demand for discounts by overseas merchants came from 'newly Established Houses' many of whom, like internal merchants, were suspected of using accommodation paper to speculate upon an anticipated rise in commodity prices.[124]

Nevertheless, the Bank continued to discount liberally and, in its eagerness to accommodate commerce, greatly extended its note issues, circulation rising from £17.1 million in August 1808 to 18.5 in February 1809, 19.6 in August 1809, 21.0 in February 1810 and 24.8 in August 1810.[125] Tooke considered the Bank's policy irresponsible in 1808 and 1809 when 'mercantile interests certainly, and the public finances probably, would have been gainers, if the Bank Directors, disregarding the applications for increased discounts or advances, had steadily adhered to the duty of preserving their paper in a sound state.' Had the Bank been more cautious, he maintained, merchants would have been less confident of discounts in succeeding years, the boom of 1809-10 would have been reduced and the exchanges would not have fallen as low as they did.[126]

---

123 Ibid., f. 43.

124 Ibid., ff. 56-7.

125 A.D. Gayer, W.W. Rostow and A.J. Schwartz, The Growth and Fluctuation of the British Economy, 1790-1850 (Oxford, 1953), i, 105.

126 Tooke, A History of Prices, op. cit., i, 354-8.

The evidence thus suggests that Bank discount policy played a part of some importance in bringing on the crisis of 1810. Does the Bank's record during the crisis itself indicate that, when faced with general commercial collapse, it could act with greater prudence? Had it, in short, a theory for crisis more impressive than its theory for prosperity? This question has proved controversial. M.A. Hudson contests Clapham's contention that, during crises, the Bank usually aided commerce by expanding discounts.[127] He detects two major influences on the Bank: a regard for the public interest and a very high degree of caution. During crises, he says, the latter predominated and 'given this attitude, it may be . . . concluded that the Bank would have been fairly unlikely to adopt an expansionary policy for its discounts at any time when over-all economic conditions were unfavourable.'[128] Consequently, the Bank's willingness to discount decreased as bankruptcies rose. His argument is difficult to sustain in the light of the large increase in discounts in the first quarter of 1810, when bankruptcies, after rising sharply in the previous quarter, continued to grow (see Table 6.3). It is also difficult to accept his explanation of the discounts of the second quarter of 1810, which is that their increase was slowing while bankruptcies were increasing. It is true that the rate of growth of discounts at that time (3.7%) was considerably lower than during the first quarter (15.7%), but the increase in bankruptcies had virtually halted (their rate of growth was proportionately lower than that of discounts). Hudson's theory for the second half of 1810, that the Bank slowed its discounts when bankruptcies increased in the third quarter and then reduced them when bankruptcies rose sharply in the fourth, is substantiated by

---

127 M.A. Hudson, 'The Bank of England and its Discounts,' Ec. H.R., n.s., xvi (1964), 536-8.

128 Ibid., p. 536.

the relevant statistics. This appears a more satisfactory general explanation than that of Clapham, which is rather too sympathetic towards the Bank:

> the Bank was giving help when the crest of the trade wave was toppling over. Its maximum of discounting was done in the third quarter, and the worst crashes came in the fourth . . . . As commercial bankers, it was their duty not to alarm a shaken City by acquiescing in any policy of sudden and drastic limitation of that assistance which only they could now give.[129]

However, neither theory adequately explains the reaction of the Bank to the 1810 crisis, since the use of quarterly averages of discounts obscures short-term changes in Bank policy and allows Hudson and Clapham to attribute to it a consistency which most contemporaries would have denied. In practice, the Bank's policies during the second half of 1810 suggest that it was far from sure of itself and seriously undermine any attempt to ascribe to it a crisis theory. As the weekly discount totals in Table 6.6 indicate, the maximum accommodation during the third quarter of the year was, in fact, granted before the crisis broke, in the first week of July. At this time it is likely that the money market became tense as a result of rumours circulating about the health of Brickwood and Co., which, no doubt, made other bankers less willing to discount commercial bills and thrust the burden onto the Bank.[130] When the crisis broke, on 6 July, the Bank immediately curtailed its facilities and threw the commercial world and money market into disarray. The discount fluctuations of the first two weeks in July indicate that both Clapham and Hudson are unjustified in asserting that the Bank adhered to a well-defined policy.

---

129 J.H. Clapham, <u>The Bank of England</u> (Cambridge, 1944), ii, 21.

130 Clapham argues that the issue of the Bullion Report, followed by the outbreak of the crisis, made country banks lose nerve and bankers in general tighten credit, thus forcing more borrowers onto the Bank. <u>Ibid</u>., 25-6, 29.

If, as Hudson argues, the Bank reduced its discounts as difficulties increased, why did it expand them so greatly when the City became tense in the first week? If, as Clapham says, the Bank was prepared to assist commerce during the difficult third quarter of 1810, why were discounts restricted so dramatically when the crisis, which had been brewing for some time, actually occurred? The probable answer to both questions is simply that the Bank had what E. Cannan calls 'the failings of the crowd' and that the contrast between its policies before and after Brickwood and Co.'s failure indicates that it

> was apt to change its policy too late, so that it continued liberal advances when drawing in was required, and began to draw in when it was no longer desirable to do so, with the natural result of disaster accompanied by confusing recriminations about the comparative advantages of the "restrictive" and "expansive" policies, both of which were right if only adopted at the proper time.131

Having adopted a tight money policy, the Bank was even prepared to disregard its real bills doctrine which, in theory, guaranteed accommodation to respectable traders during periods of financial difficulties. Solid firms were unable to obtain discounts and, in mid-July, it was recommended that immediate relief be given by the Bank to all traders and manufacturers who could make a deposit of real property as security.[132] On 17 July, a deputation of London merchants asked the Bank for relief, which was refused because some of the directors did not attend. The directors' reluctance to co-operate is, perhaps, mirrored in their statement that the Bank was anxious to assist commerce 'but with a firm conviction of the evils of the too extended system of country banking, feel much difficulty in an emergency so critical and delicate.' After a conference

---

131 E. Cannan, The Paper Pound (1919), pp. xx, ix.

132 Manchester Mercury, 17 July 1810, p. 2, col. 5.

between the merchants and the Chancellor of the Exchequer, the Bank promised, on 19 July, to extend discounts by £3,000,000 to save men of real property.[133] The subsequent increased discounting restabilised the money market.[134]

As Chart 6.2 shows, the Bank's discounts fluctuated throughout the remaining months of 1810. The temporary rise at the end of August was probably the product of dealings generated by the Trianon Decree. However, the largest increase and the most significant to the student of Bank policy is that of early October. The funds had fluctuated greatly throughout September, when borrowing was difficult because of the large sales of stock necessitated by the July bankruptcies. The growing insecurity of the City evidently persuaded banks to tighten their credit, again inflating the demand for discounts at the Bank of England. On 18 September, the Governor told the Committee of Treasury that 'a considerable alarm had gone forth on account of the number of Bills rejected within the last Ten Days by the Directors in waiting; and many of them on respectable Bankers.' The Committee, taking account of the large decrease in discounts since 21 July, resolved 'that at this period of embarrassment and want of confidence a liberal accommodation to the public in the way of Discounts, of undoubted good Commercial Paper, appears to them to be advisable.'[135] This explains the increase of discounts in late September. The more dramatic rise in early October represents a continuation of this policy at a time when the suicide of Abraham Goldsmid (28 September) had shaken confidence. The consequent pessimism was exacerbated by the

---

133 Salisbury and Winchester Journal, 17 July 1810, p. 2, col. 2; Exchange Herald, 26 July 1810, p. 3, col. 1.

134 On Thursday, 19 July, discounts totalled £1,613,765 compared with £914,620 on the previous Thursday (12 July).

135 Bank of England, Committee of Treasury Minute Books, viii, ff. 13-14.

further deterioration of the commercial situation in October. The Bank's reaction during October appears most puzzling since, within a month of expanding discounts in order to assist commerce during a difficult period, it sharply reduced them again in the middle of October, after which they remained relatively low for the ensuing twelve months.[136] In the light of this and the other fluctuations in its discounts, especially those of early July, it is difficult to accept the contention of both Clapham and Hudson that the Bank possessed a crisis theory to which it consistently adhered in 1810. Clapham's thesis is contradicted by the drastically reduced discounts of the second week in July and by the Bank's refusal of a large number of good bills in mid-September and Hudson's fails to explain the fact that the sharpest increases in discounts occurred at times when economic conditions had seriously deteriorated. The solution to this problem appears to be that there were, at the Bank, two schools of thought, one supporting its publicly stated policy of meeting the needs of trade and the other, acutely conscious of the dangers of such a course of action, advocating retrenchment. The two philosophies were not necessarily urged by different groups of directors since, as Hudson points out, it is possible, by reading between the lines, to detect both in the statements of Whitmore and Harman to the Bullion Committee.[137] The sharp fluctuations of the Bank's discounting in the 1810 crisis thus reflect the dilemma of an institution publicly committed to a policy about which it had serious, private doubts.

---

136 Weekly discounts in 1811 averaged £1.82 millions. The Bank did not again discount more than £3 million in one week until October 1811 and £4 million was not discounted in a week until 15-21 July 1815 (calculated from Bank of England, General Ledger, no. 18, 1 March 1805 to 29 Feb. 1816).

137 Hudson, op. cit., p. 536.

V

The analysis in this chapter provides considerable support for the general conclusions drawn in the preceding one about the factors which influenced bankruptcy levels. The suggested link between the pre-crisis increases in overseas trade and Bank of England discounts appears even closer than was suggested. At the simplest level we can say that war, the exogenous factor, set the upper and lower limits of commercial activity by expanding and contracting market opportunities. However, the actual volume of trade in 1809 and 1810 is mainly attributable to the unrestricted accommodation granted by the Bank to the trading fraternity in general and to new, marginal operators in particular. It is instructive that, in 1812, the Court of Directors stipulated that discount facilities would not in future be offered to wholesale traders who had been operating for less than two years.[138] An associated link between the level of trading and Bank policy was the way in which increased note issues sustained the rise of domestic prices, thus protracting the boom in 1809 and early 1810 and increasing the severity of the subsequent commercial crisis. During that crisis, in turn, Bank policy had a significant effect upon the timing and extent of bankruptcies.

The evidence also contributes to our understanding of the characteristic one-year lag of bankruptcy peaks after those of trade and discounts. First, and rather obvious, the full extent of trading losses (and the consequent curtailment of discounts) was not realised until the end of the year when the shipping season closed, producing a high level of bankruptcies which 'spilled over' into the succeeding year. Second, the ramifications of the largest failures upon the economy in general were experienced

---

138 Bank of England, ADV/B533-1, 'Extracts relating to Discounts,' ff. 11, 19.

belatedly because, although bankruptcy was extremely contagious, its gestation period could be fairly lengthy.

In addition, the investigation has indicated that, when the depression set in, some areas of the country suffered more than others. The explanation of this, which is obscure, may lie in the contrasting nature of regional economics. The greatest distress occurred in areas which were particularly vulnerable to fluctuations in overseas trade. In London and Lancashire, heavy mercantile losses were incurred both because of saturated overseas markets and because of drastic reductions in the value of colonial produce. The West Country depression was closely related to fluctuations in the supply and price of Spanish wool. Within the distressed areas, the level of bankruptcies seems to have been related both to the size of local manufacturing houses and to the density of population, perhaps because the hard core of bankruptcies belonged to the miscellaneous group, the size of which was influenced by demand for services and retail outlets. Also, it seems clear that the distress was accentuated by credit restrictions imposed by banks which had lost heavily through discounting mercantile bills of exchange. Indeed, it has been suggested that bills provided the main channel by which bankruptcy was communicated not only from the merchant to the manufacturer but also from one region to another. The remainder of this study examines the influence of the bill of exchange at this period both upon economic activity in general and upon the incidence and spread of bankruptcies.

CHAPTER VII

THE BILL OF EXCHANGE

It has been suggested that the communication of commercial distress during the crisis of 1810 was largely attributable to the widespread use of bills of exchange. Before illustrating this process it is necessary to discuss briefly the bill mechanism and to explain its popularity, abuse and status in bankruptcy proceedings.

Basically, the bill was an instrument by which a creditor demanded payment of a debt at some future date. If his debtor 'accepted' the bill, the creditor could await payment until it matured, discount it at a bank or pass it on to one of his own creditors. When the bill was passed on, it became

> an order addressed to some person residing at a distance directing him to pay a certain specified sum to the person in whose favour the Bill is drawn, or his order. In mercantile phraseology, the person who draws a Bill is termed the drawer; the person in whose favour it is drawn, the remitter; the person on whom it is drawn, the drawee; after he has accepted it, the acceptor. Those persons into whose hands the Bill may have passed previously to its being paid, are, from their writing their names on the back, termed indorsers; and the person in whose possession the Bill is at any given period, is termed the holder or possessor.1

In contrast to the bill, which was a request or order for payment, the promissory note was accepted as soon as it was issued since it represented 'a plain and direct engagement in writing, to pay a sum specified at the time therein limited, to a person therein named, or sometimes to his

---

1 J.R. McCulloch, Dictionary of Commerce and Commercial Navigation (1832), p. 520. The Bankruptcy Court used 'payee' instead of 'remitter.'

order, or often to the bearer at large.'[2] When it was indorsed, it resembled a bill of exchange, 'for then it is an order by the indorser to the maker of the note, who by his promise is his debtor, to pay the money to the indorsee.'[3] After indorsement, the indorser became the equivalent of the drawer of a bill, the maker of the note became the acceptor and the indorsee became the payee.

When introduced into England, probably by Italian merchants during the fourteenth century, the bill was a written authorization for a creditor abroad to receive payment from a debtor of the drawer in the same country.[4] The bill, of course, became the principal instrument of international payments and by the end of the seventeenth century a sophisticated foreign exchange market had developed in London.[5] More important for our purposes, however, is the use made of the inland bill, which appears to have increased greatly along with the gross national product in the latter half of the eighteenth century.[6] The bill was popular essentially because the alternative forms of payment were either inadequate or less well-developed. It is true that the chronic shortage of coin, produced by undervaluation of silver at the Mint and by the large

---

2 The Compting-House Companion (1810), p. 8.

3 Ibid., p. 13.

4 A. Harding, A Social History of English Law (1966), p. 318.

5 See T.S. Ashton, An Economic History of England: The 18th Century (1955), pp. 188-96.

6 The date of the increase is disputed. Pressnell notes the large growth during the Revolutionary Wars. Shapiro, using Bank of England discount income as a guide to market trends, suggests that discounting was heavy throughout the country between 1760 and 1830. L.S. Pressnell, Country Banking in the Industrial Revolution (Oxford 1956), p. 89; S. Shapiro, Capital and the Cotton Industry in the Industrial Revolution (New York, 1967), p. 83, fn. 16.

denominations of gold coins, was overcome in most areas by the use of local bank notes for small payments. But in Lancashire, as Ashton points out, distrust of local notes led to their replacement by bills of small denomination.[7] For commercial payments, which were often larger and more distant, notes and gold were unsuitable for two main reasons. The first is the obvious physical problem of carrying large amounts of money on unpoliced roads. The second is the fact that the notes of neither country banks nor the Bank of England circulated widely outside their immediate localities. One solution to this - the deposit transferrable by cheque - was firmly established in principle by the early eighteenth century but does not seem to have been practised widely before the second quarter of the nineteenth.[8] Instead, banking institutions concentrated upon bill finance which probably bore the major responsibility for their simultaneous growth in the provinces and in London during the second half of the eighteenth century.[9] The bill, indeed, possessed intrinsic qualities which added to its attractiveness. At a time when debts were not assignable (i.e. the right to sue could not be transferred) at Common Law,[10] the bill made them

---

7 T.S. Ashton, 'The Bill of Exchange and Private Banks in Lancashire, 1790-1830,' in Papers in English Monetary History (ed. T.S. Ashton and R.S. Sayers), (Oxford, 1953), pp. 41-3.

8 R. Cameron, Banking in the Early Stages of Industrialization (Oxford, 1967), p. 49.

9 See ibid., p. 24; J.H. Clapham, The Bank of England (Cambridge, 1944), i, 165; D.M. Joslin, 'London Private Bankers, 1720-1785,' in Essays in Economic History (ed. E.M. Carus-Wilson), (1962), ii, 346.

10 Until the Judicature Act of 1873 (36, 37 Vict., c.66).

assignable in commercial practice.[11] Further, the security which a bill's successive indorsers personified, the stability which contemporaries, rightly or wrongly, attached to it because it originated in a definite commercial transaction and the fact that it did not invite theft (because it was not payable to bearer) added to its popularity. In addition, the appreciation of its capital value between receipt and date of maturity rendered it a profitable investment and an ideal method of giving short-term loans.

The eighteenth-century bill system was by no means perfect. Ashton's description of the dealings of Peter Stubs illustrates its irksome practical defects.[12] Nevertheless, the absence of a sophisticated banking structure ensured that bills were used extensively. They were most important in industrial areas, especially Lancashire where, as late as 1825, nine-tenths of business in Manchester was still transacted by bill.[13] The precise volume of bills in circulation at the start of the nineteenth century is difficult to gauge since contemporary estimates appear to be inflated.[14] However, Tooke provided some interesting calculations pertaining to the middle of the century when, he estimated, the average bill circulation of about £150 million amounted to more than four times the circulation of all bank notes.[15] He also cast some light

---

11 In the early eighteenth century, statutory force was given to the assignability of bills and notes and the assignee's right to take action against the assignor. See R.B. Westerfield, Middlemen in English Business (New Haven, Conn., 1915), pp. 390-1.

12 T.S. Ashton, An Eighteenth-Century Industrialist. Peter Stubs of Warrington (Manchester, 1939), pp. 103-21.

13 Ashton, 'The Bill of Exchange . . .,' op. cit., p. 39.

14 See Cameron, op. cit., p. 44.

15 T. Tooke and W. Newmarch, A History of Prices (1857), vi, 587.

upon the obscure problems of the size of bills and their usance or tenor (i.e. the period between the creation and maturity of a bill). Tooke identified three categories of bills: small bills, drawn upon small retailers and drawn by those retailers upon consumers; medium bills, drawn by wholesalers and manufacturers on retailers and other dealers; and large bills, drawn by importers on manufacturers and wholesalers and by the latter two on exporters. Between 1830 and 1853, the average small bill was drawn for £22.11.0d. at 3.14 months, the medium bill for £127 at 3.45 months and the large bill for £1,055.18.0d. at 4.20 months. Over the same period, the volume of small bills had declined from more than £22.2 million per annum to under £18.6 million, while medium bills had increased slightly (from £87.7 to £105.99 million) and large bills sharply (from £87.3 to £201.7 million). By comparing fluctuations of bill circulation and bank rate, Tooke further concluded that the volume of bills created varied inversely with the state of the money market. In other words, when other means of payment were scarce bill finance was widely used.[16]

In order to appreciate the significance of the bill in bankruptcy cases, it is necessary to grasp its legal standing. The pure theory of the bill, as elaborated under Mansfield L.C.J. between 1756 and 1788,[17] was stated in 1843 in the following terms:

> that the Drawer has funds in the hands of the Drawee; that he sells or assigns to the Payee, for a valuable consideration, such part thereof as amounts to the sum payable by the Bill; that when the Drawee accepts to pay the amount, it is an appropriation of the funds *pro*

---

16 *Ibid.*, vi, pp. 587-92.

17 See J.M. Holden, *The History of Negotiable Instruments in English Law* (1955), p. 99; C.H.S. Fifoot, *Lord Mansfield* (Oxford, 1936), pp. 91-2.

> *tanto*, for the service and use of the Payee, or other person holding the Bill under him, so that the amount ceases henceforth to be the money of the Drawer, and becomes that of the Payee, or other holder, in the hands of the Acceptor. Hence it is, that after such acceptance, the Acceptor is treated as the primary or principal debtor of the payee, or other holder, and that the Drawer, and other parties on the Bill, are held to be collaterally liable only to the Holder upon the default of payment by the Acceptor.18

The significance of the final part of this statement cannot be stressed too strongly. The multiple liability of parties to a bill was a consequence of the fact that an indorsement was considered the equivalent of making a new bill, which the indorser guaranteed would be paid. When the acceptor stopped payment, the holder of the bill, after proving that he had demanded payment from him, could claim against all parties to the bill, either successively or simultaneously.[19] Because dividends of bankrupt estates were rarely paid rapidly, bill-holders often claimed against all previous participants as soon as the acceptor refused to pay (claims could be made before the bill matured). One example of the panic which could afflict parties to a dishonoured bill is sufficient. On 24 April 1810, Bowles, Ogden and Wyndham (Shaftesbury, bankers) drew a bill at seventy-five days to the value of £2,481 on Brickwood and Co. (Lombard Street, bankers) and paid it later to J.T. Deal and Co. (Shaftesbury, brewers). The latter indorsed the bill to John Goodair (a Cheapside merchant) who, in turn, indorsed it to Fermin de Tastet (Bishopsgate Street, merchant) 'for valuable consideration.'[20] Brickwood and Co., the acceptor, stopped payment on 6 July 1810 and Bowles, Ogden, Wyndham, the drawers, on 11 July. On 12 July, Deal, the payee, received a letter from Goodair stating that the

---

18 J. Story, *Commentaries on the Laws of Bills of Exchange* (1843), pp. 14-15.

19 *The Compting-House Companion* (1810), p. 30.

20 P.R.O. B3/252, 10 Nov. 1810.

bill had been dishonoured and on 14 July de Tastet, who had already claimed against all participants in the bill, became Deal's petitioning creditor.[21]

Such speed was imperative to bill-holders, for they would be liable themselves to similar calls for their own acceptances and faced the possibility of their bill-holders striking dockets against them. This occurred on numerous occasions in the 1810 crisis, for so many merchants drew upon only one or two acceptors that when the latter failed the drawers immediately suffered the same fate. The dependence of many provincial traders and country banks upon London houses and the popularity of London bills in interprovincial transactions[22] ensured that the national credit structure was extremely sensitive to fluctuations in the London money market. The 1810 crisis was characterised by the chain reaction of failures: acceptor (usually in London), drawer, payee and then, occasionally, some or all of the indorsees. Nine years after the crisis, John Beck, a Carlisle banker, stated that in bills accepted by John Goodair

> all the drawers, acceptors and indorsers of the said several drafts or bills of exchange, upon the credit of which said advance of eleven thousand, six hundred and thirty two pounds nineteen shillings was so made by this deponent and his said partners, became Bankrupt or were insolvent at the times or soon after the said several bills became due and payable, whereupon this deponent and his said partners could only receive dividends from the estates of such of the drawers, acceptors and indorsers of the said bills as had become Bankrupts.23

If the bill system was largely responsible for the contagious nature of bankruptcy, it was also dangerous because of the prevalence of what Rosser termed 'credit

21 P.R.O. B3/1294, 14 July 1810.

22 See H. Thornton, Paper Credit (ed. F.A. Hayek), (1939), p. 94.

23 P.R.O. B3/1880, 16 Oct. 1819.

pernicious:' accommodation bills.[24] These were bills for which the acceptors received no valuable consideration from the drawers, who agreed to pay the bills when due. In theory, such bills were nothing more than promissory notes with two securities instead of one, but, as Henry Thornton said, 'they have . . . in general, that shape communicated to them . . . which is thought likely to render them discountable.' Thornton went on to stress that accommodation bills were not, as commonly supposed, 'a species of false wealth, by which the nation is deceived . . . supplying imaginary capital' any more than the many real bills which were created in transactions involving one set of goods.[25] Nevertheless, in times of financial stringency, for the market in general or individuals in particular, accommodation bills were frequently created in order to raise short-term capital and to restore credit. Pressnell describes their employment in 1788 by Livesey, Hargreaves and Co. in its attempts to finance an ambitious calico printing project.[26] The use made of them for speculative purposes led Rosser to the conclusion that 'they are the surest indications of ruin possible in those who interchange them.'[27]

In bankruptcy proceedings, accommodation paper posed the problem of attributing liability. It was certain that 'the person for whose accommodation a note is drawn, or a bill drawn or accepted, cannot prove it under a commission against the person who drew or accepted it for his accommodation' (because no debt was due on it).[28] But

---

24 A. Rosser, Credit Pernicious (1823).

25 Thornton, op. cit., p. 87.

26 Pressnell, op. cit., pp. 91-2.

27 Rosser, op. cit., p. 28.

28 J.F. Archbold, The Law and Practice of Bankruptcy (3rd edn., 1829), p. 76.

problems arose when indorsees held accommodation acceptances of a bankrupt estate. In theory, the acceptor of an accommodation bill must have declared the drawer's liability as soon as the transaction was made. However, the effect of this was nullified by the fact that the declaration could be made verbally.[29] The result was that many indorsees were not aware that their bills originated as accommodation paper.[30] During the eighteenth century, the problems involved in claiming such bills were slowly eradicated and a definite procedure evolved. By the early nineteenth century, it was accepted that the holder of an accommodation bill should claim against both drawer and acceptor (as in normal bill claims) and the latter should claim the amount of the bill against the drawer's estate. In cases where mutual accommodation bills had been contracted and one of the parties failed, the solvent party was similarly obliged to pay off his acceptances before he could claim against the bankrupt's estate. If both parties failed, a financial adjustment was made according to the balance of accounts between the estates.[31]

This chapter has shown briefly the central importance of the bill of exchange as a means of payment during the industrial revolution and the legal reasons for its contribution to bankruptcy proliferation. The rest of this study is designed to throw further light upon both of these topics by examining some of the leading bankruptcies in the 1810 crisis. Chapters eight and nine analyse the ramifications of the failures of two London banks, Brickwood and Co. and Dawes, Noble and Co., and the final chapter draws some conclusions about contemporary commercial and financial practices.

---

29 Holden, op. cit., p. 155.

30 Thornton, op. cit., p. 89.

31 Archbold, op. cit., p. 76.

CHAPTER VIII

THE BANKRUPTCY OF BRICKWOOD AND CO.

I

It was shown in chapter six that the crisis of 1810 occurred in two stages. In July, the City was shaken by the failure of a mercantile bank, Brickwood and Co. of Lombard Street; confidence was temporarily restored by less stringent discount policies of the banking fraternity in August and September. In October, the crisis was renewed when returns from South America proved disappointing and the European market finally closed.

The initial panic in July, which revealed the dramatic effect one or two large failures could have on the money market, can be explained by three factors. First, it was common knowledge that much of the heavy commercial activity of the previous year had been risky and that markets were becoming increasingly difficult in the first half of 1810. The failure of some overseas merchants had been anticipated for months. Second, the realisation that such failures would disrupt the credit both of the merchants' domestic customers and of large sectors of the economy rendered commercial and financial houses acutely sensitive to any sign of distress. Third, doubts about the ability of the banking fraternity to cushion the impact of the crisis heightened the prevailing insecurity.

The effects of Brickwood and Co.'s stoppage were felt at two levels, which can be termed 'direct' and 'indirect.' The latter affected firms whose financial transactions were inhibited by the credit squeeze which followed the bank's failure. The direct effects were felt by firms whose credit was dependent upon Brickwood and Co.'s solvency. These included not only clients of the bank but also firms which were financially linked with those clients. The purpose here is to examine the extensive, direct ramifications of Brickwood and Co.'s stoppage and to demonstrate the responsibility of the bill of exchange for the spread of bankruptcies in a 'house of cards' effect emanating from the original bank failure.

II

The immediate cause of the crisis was the failure of John Brickwood, John Rainier, William Morgan and Joseph Starkey, Lombard Street bankers. This firm, founded in 1796 as Bowles, Beechcroft, Brown, Reeves and Collins in Exchange Alley, Cornhill, underwent the mutations and partnership changes so typical of the mushroom banking houses of the period. In 1800, Beechcroft and Reeves withdrew to join Bosanquet and Co. and a new partnership was formed, consisting of Bowles, Brown, Ogden, Cobb and Stokes. In 1802, Bowles and Ogden left to establish a bank, in Lombard Street, in partnership with George Wyndham (with whom they also ran a Wiltshire bank) and Brickwood. In 1808, this concern became Brickwood, Morgan and Starkey, when Bowles, Ogden and Wyndham retired to their bank in Wiltshire.[1] Like many country bankers they acted as receivers-general of taxes, which they remitted to Brickwood and Co. in London.[2]

---

1 F.G. Hilton Price, <u>Handbook of London Bankers</u> (1876), p. 20.

2 Country banks sought government accounts eagerly for two reasons. First, they could take poundage on money collected. Second, such accounts were viewed as insurance policies, enabling the bank to take out extents-in-aid (i.e. in aid of the crown debtor) against the property of its debtors. The extent gave the crown debtor precedence over other claimants and thus enabled him to avoid losses in bankruptcy cases (if the extent was issued before other creditors struck dockets). See L.S. Pressnell, 'Public Moneys and the Development of English Banking,' <u>Ec.H.R.</u>, n.s., v (1952-3), 391.

The bankruptcy of Brickwood and Co., on 6 July 1810, shocked London for it was considered 'perhaps as solid a house as any one in the city.'[3] Its stoppage was attributed to 'the failure for £300,000 of one of the first firms in general brokerage, but more especially concerned with West India dealings.'[4] This was William Coles, of Mincing Lane, who was said to have suffered because of recent restrictions upon the introduction of colonial goods to the continent[5] and to have lost £50,000 in a short time after speculating in Spanish wool, the price of which slumped dramatically in 1810.[6] Coles had certainly been trading in Spanish wool during June 1810 as well as in madder which he imported in large quantities during April.[7] Unfortunately, the records of Coles's commission have not survived and it is impossible to be precise about the amount claimed against his estate by Brickwood and Co. Some indication is provided by the instructions given on 10 October 1811 by the creditors of Brickwood and Co. to their assignees:

> to compromise or otherwise agree all accounts and differences depending between the assignees of the said bankrupts and the assignees of William Coles and to deliver up to the said assignees of William Coles certain Bills of Exchange to the amount of £70,000 and upwards on such terms as the said assignees of Brickwood's and Co. shall think fit, and to compromise and agree the amount of proof and claim to be made upon

---

3 'The Bank - The Stock Exchange - The Bankers' Clearing House,' quoted by L.S. Pressnell, Country Banking in the Industrial Revolution (Oxford, 1956), pp. 466-7.

4 The Times, 9 July 1810, p. 2, col. 4.

5 Salisbury and Winchester Journal, 16 July 1810, p. 2, col. 1.

6 The price of Leonessa wool fell from 15s. per lb. at the start of 1810 to 10s. in July. See F. Crouzet, L'Économie Britannique, op. cit., ii, 577.

7 In June, Coles imported six tons of Spanish wool and, in April, 45 tons of madder (The Tradesman, iv, 377, 473; v. 89).

> the estate of the said William Coles, and make such arrangements from time to time as to the liquidation of the said claims.8

These instructions suggest that the financial transactions of Brickwood and Co. and Thomas Coles and Sons (William Coles's firm) had been extensive. Although the nature of their bill dealings is not clear, it is possible that the £70,000 represents bills deposited by Coles at Brickwood and Co. as part-security for a loan which was not repaid. Certainly, the loss sustained by the bank must have been extremely large since, a few months earlier, Rainier, who owned extensive property in India, had invested £100,000 in the house and Brickwood himself had contributed £60,000 only a fortnight before the stoppage.[9] Despite these additions, Brickwood and Co. was acutely embarrassed by Coles and Co.'s difficulties in early July and evidently sought to ease its immediate problems since Down and Co., the Bartholomew Lane bank, was reported to have disposed of stock for it worth between £10,000 and £20,000. The immediate cause of the bank's stoppage was a run resulting from leakage of information about this transaction at a time when money was tight because tax revenues were due to be paid to the government.[10]

The combined effect of the failures of Coles and Sons and Brickwood and Co. was disastrous. The major bill creditors of Coles at the time of his failure are shown in Figure 8.1. The numbers in the diagram represent the value of a bill, or bills, in pounds. The names represent firms which participated in the bills. To the names of the firms are attached their occupations and, except where they operated in London, their locations. Those above line (a)

---

8 P.R.O. B3/254, 10 Oct. 1811.

9 <u>Salisbury and Winchester Journal</u>, 16 July 1810, p. 2, col. 1.

10 See Pressnell, <u>op. cit</u>., p. 467.

were debtors of Coles who had failed to honour their bills, those below line (b) were his creditors. Thus, the following segment of the diagram -

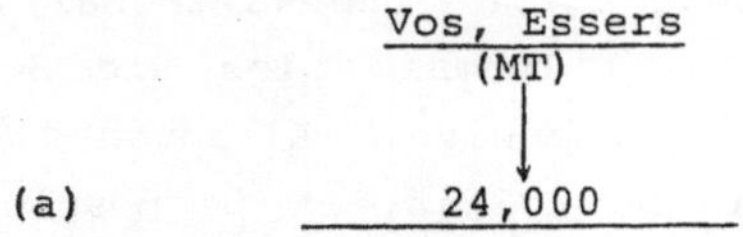

indicates a series of bills worth £24,000 drawn by T. Coles and Sons on Vos, Essers and Co., a London merchant. A similar segment -

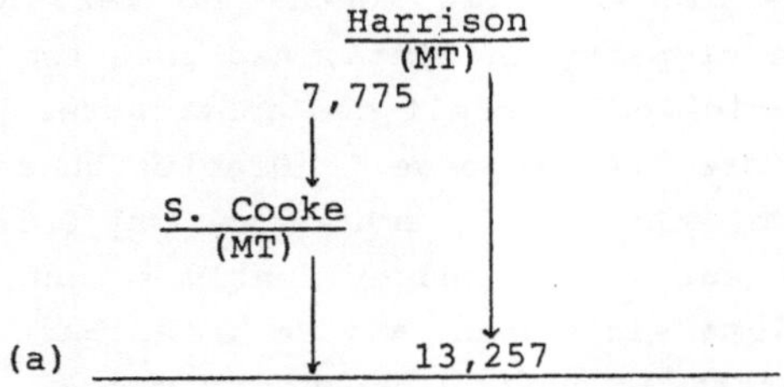

- represents two series of bills accepted by Harrison and Co., a London merchant: the first (£7,775) drawn by S. Cooke, also a London merchant, and paid to the bankrupt (Coles); the second (£13,257) drawn by Coles. Coles was responsible for paying all the bills below line (b). In almost every one, he was the acceptor, the other firms consisting of drawers, payees and indorsees. Thus, in the extract -

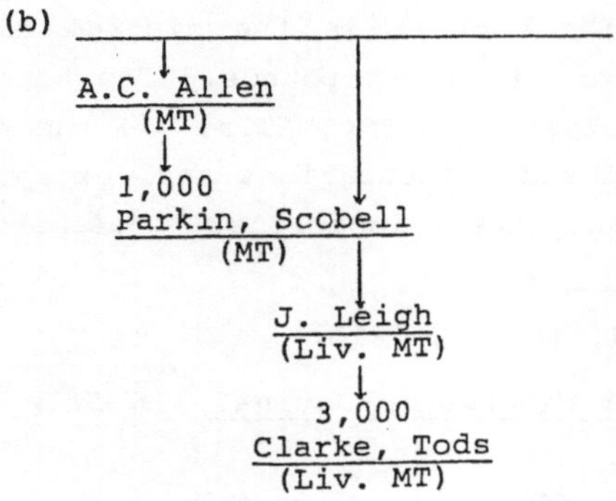

- A.C. Allen, a London merchant, drew a bill worth £1,000 on Coles and paid it to Parkin, Scobell and Co., also a London merchant; the latter drew bills to the value of £3,000 on Coles and paid them to J. Leigh, a Liverpool merchant, who indorsed them to Clarke and Tods, another merchant house in Liverpool. All the firms in this segment failed during the crisis (indicated by underlining of their names) though other bill creditors, like Splitgerber, survived. The firms referred to in this and the next chapter are alphabetically indexed, with their locations and occupations, at the end of the statistical supplement.

By using this format to indicate the largest bills transacted by leading bankrupts, it is possible to ascertain quickly the main ramifications of their stoppages. In this case, Coles's failure thrust liability for a large number of bills upon his drawers, including Parkin and Scobell (£20,000), Harrison and Co. (£10,000), Meir McNin (£23,915) and J.G. Gerard (£23,421). The liability was also transferred to the payees and indorsees of the respective bills: in the case of Parkin and Scobell, to J. Leigh (the payee) and to A.C. Allen, Clarke and Tods, Heywood and Brickwood (the indorsees); in the case of McNin, to Winstanley and Hudson, Edward Paine, Rowlandson, Isaac and Brien and John Goodair; in the case of J.G. Gerard, to Harrison and Brickwood and to Wistinghausen and E. and T. Ward. The majority of these firms failed during the crisis but, as they incurred greater losses as a result of other bankruptcies (notably that of Brickwood and Co.), they are examined later.

The main concern which suffered solely because of Coles and Co.'s stoppage was that of Hermanus Vos and Jan Christian Essers, merchants of New Court, London. Throughout the first six months of 1810, they had exported cloth and other manufactures to Holland and South America and imported West Indian goods.[11] Presumably they supplied much of the produce which Coles, in his brokerage business, distributed in the English market, Coles paying for it, as Figure 8.1 indicates, by large-scale acceptances of Vos, Essers and Co.'s bills. Coles's failure obliged Vos and Essers to pay £122,077 of his acceptances and, as a result, Vos and Essers stopped payment on 7 July, one day after Coles's docket was struck. In turn, the rapid collapse of Coles and Co. and Vos, Essers and Co. damaged Rowlandson, Isaac, Brien and Co. and Greaves, Sharp, Fisher and Co. Both, however, were more severely embarrassed by the failure of Brickwood and Co. and are dealt with below.

It was stated that Brickwood and Co. probably stopped payment because Thomas Coles and Co. failed to repay a large loan. As the credit part of Figure 8.2 indicates, Brickwood and Co. also discounted Coles and Co.'s acceptances, £25,845 of which were outstanding at the time of Coles's bankruptcy. The figure shows that Brickwood and Co.'s discount policies seem to have been careful. Only the £4,195 bills drawn on Goodair and, perhaps, the £5,405 on Wilson and Williams could be considered even remotely dubious.[12] As we shall see, even Goodair's bills involved little risk before Brickwood and Co. fell. It was, therefore, unfortunate that the only apparent injudicious transactions of the bank (with Coles and Co.) should bring it down, at a time when one or two other London banks survived despite consistently reckless policies.[13]

The reason why Brickwood and Co.'s bankruptcy was so important is that, as a large, commercial bank, the credit of its bill-drawers and of the payees and indorsees of the

---

11 P.R.O. B3/5106, 19 July 1810, Richard Dawson, clerk of Vos and Essers.

12 For the bankruptcy of Wilson and Williams, see chapter IX.

13 This is discussed in chapter X.

latter was dependent upon its ability to honour acceptances. It is true that the claimants against the estate included thirty-two non-traders who were owed £18,777 as balance of accounts for money deposited at the bank. But this type of client (including widows, 'gentlemen,' 'esquires' and clergy), who usually patronised West End banks, comprised an extremely small proportion of Brickwood and Co.'s business which was dominated by bill dealings. Bills drawn at short date on a substantial London bank were easily cashable and negotiable everywhere even in the worst credit conditions. The popularity of Brickwood and Co.'s bills is indicated in Table 8.1 which lists the major claimants against the estate (as in the figures, this refers to sums over £1,000).[14] Except for the bills held by the Bank of England, all those claimed against Brickwood and Co. had been accepted by the bankrupts and either immediately discounted by the drawers at other banking houses or paid to other traders for one of three reasons: 'for valuable consideration,' 'for money lent and advanced' or 'for goods sold and delivered.' About half of the bills claimed by John Sparkes Cox (clerk of the Bank of England) had been accepted by Brickwood and Co. (and discounted at the Bank) and the other half were bills of merchants and traders which Brickwood and Co. had received and rediscounted at the Bank of England. The wide variety of bill-holders, which included London firms claiming £195,663 of Brickwood and Co.'s acceptances, country banks claiming bills worth £49,311 and London private bankers claiming £150,976, indicates the general negotiability of the bank's bills. The table also shows that very few of the claimants failed during the crisis. The probable reason for this is that, as bill-holders, they were able to claim payment against previous participants in the bills and thus

14 The 'traders' category refers to commercial and industrial firms outside the other categories (banks, merchants, warehousemen and brokers).

to lose less than is actually recorded in the table. In other words, the contagious nature of bankruptcy affected, above all, the drawers of bills accepted by the bankrupts. This is illustrated by the failures of a number of Brickwood and Co.'s drawers (represented in the debit part of Figure 8.2). Dockets were struck against Robert Parker, a calico printer in Manchester (24 September 1810), W. Robertson, a London merchant (3 October 1810), L. Strickland, a Liverpool merchant (1 November 1810), W. Ford, a rope-maker at Beckington (2 November 1810), W. Fry, a Leicester Square linen draper (5 December 1810), John Kroger, a Plymouth merchant (31 January 1811), and William Grobekker, a Great Saint Helens shipowner, on 18 January 1811. However the most significant failures attributable to the stoppage of Brickwood and Co. are those indicated by asterisks in the table: Bowles, Ogden and Wyndham; Harrison and Co.; Bracken, Williams and Co.; John Goodair and Co.; and John Leigh and Co. The operations and failure of each are examined below.

III

The prime example of a bankruptcy caused by direct dependence upon Brickwood and Co. is that of a country bank. As noted already, William Bowles, Thomas Ogden and George Wyndham left Brickwood in 1808 to concentrate upon their Wiltshire house which had branches at Salisbury and Shaftesbury, where James Barrow conducted operations. Two of the partners took up residence in Wiltshire, where they were men of local standing. Ogden had, in 1786, established the Salisbury Commercial Society to promote local trade interests and Bowles was a man of property with an estate at Heal, near Salisbury. Wyndham remained in London, managing the bank's transactions with Brickwood and Co.[15]

---

15 H.A. Wyndham, <u>A Family History, 1688-1837</u> (Oxford, 1950), p. 332.

Bowles, Ogden and Wyndham issued circular notes, for £1, £5, £10 and £20, payable at Salisbury and Shaftesbury and also at Brickwood and Co.[16] Customers who required larger sums were given bills of exchange drawn by Bowles and Co. on Brickwood and Co. Hence, as soon as the latter failed, Bowles and Co., as drawers of over a hundred of its acceptances, also stopped payments.[17] On 7 July, Joseph Everitt, a New Sarum clothier, struck a docket against the bank. On the next day, the leading citizens of Salisbury rallied round and issued a declaration of confidence in the stability of the bank, whose notes they promised to accept as usual.[18] The optimism of the resolution was unfounded since the bank did not open its doors on Monday 9 July. The inability of Brickwood and Co. to honour bills drawn on it by Bowles and Co. imposed on the latter liability for thousands of pounds. In addition to these losses, Bowles and Co. lost their balance at Brickwood and Co. On 18 August 1810, John Hodding, solicitor to Bowles and Co.'s assignees, claimed £114,670.7.1d. as their balance of account at Brickwood and Co.

The effects of Bowles and Co.'s stoppage upon the local community were severe. Charles Lamb, on holiday in Wiltshire, noted that 'the city of Salisbury is full of weeping and wailing. The Bank has stopt payment; and every body in the town kept money at it, or has got some of its notes. Some have lost all they had in the world. It is the next thing to seeing a city with a plague within its walls.'[19] Nevertheless, the number of traders who sustained large losses was small. The local newspaper, on 16 July,

---

16 P.R.O. B3/259, 28 Jan. 1820, Richard Titt, clerk at the bank.

17 P.R.O. B3/258, 12 July 1810, Richard Titt.

18 Salisbury and Winchester Journal, 9 July 1810, p. 3, col. 2.

19 Quoted by W.J. Thorne, Banking (Oxford, 1948), p. 15.

reported that 'great inconvenience has been felt by persons of all descriptions, but we do not find that any of the sufferers are likely to be involved in bankruptcy by their losses.'[20] This was almost true, for only one of the bank's creditors definitely failed because of its stoppage. John Turl Deal, a Shaftesbury brewer, who was made liable for £12,243 of Brickwood and Co.'s bills (including the £2,481 noted in chapter seven), stopped payment on 12 July.[21]

The main effects of Bowles and Co.'s stoppage, however, were the results of its psychological impact. It was reported that the failure 'occasioned a suspicion that no house could be relied on; the immediate consequence was a run on Mr. Burrough, who has also stopped payment.'[22] Michael Burrough, a man's mercer and part-time banker at Salisbury,[23] was unfortunate since his balance at Kensington and Co. far exceeded his liabilities.[24] His collapse, a typical example of a country bank stoppage induced by panic and consequent high liquidity preference, was the prelude to a wave of similar failures throughout the West Country, all occasioned by the collapse of Bowles and Co. As the Exchange Herald of Manchester said,

> when the failures took place at Salisbury, all those persons who had no other money than Salisbury notes, were without the means of carrying on their trading concerns . . . persons, who had the notes of contiguous bankers, exchanged them with shopkeepers, for fear and at a hazard, for goods, which they did not want, and

---

20 Salisbury and Winchester Journal, 16 July 1810, p. 4, col. 4.

21 P.R.O. B3/1294, 14 July 1810, Samuel Durnford.

22 Salisbury and Winchester Journal, 16 July 1810, p. 4, col. 4.

23 P.R.O. B1/120, f. 188.

24 P.R.O. B1/123, ff. 183-5.

> the confusion thus occasioned in many villages and towns in the three most Westerly counties are indescribable.25

By 13 July 1810, it was said, runs had led to country bank failures in Totness, Plymouth, Shrewsbury and Exeter, where Mr. Luke, a grocer and part-time banker, committed suicide.[26] In this way, the failure of a London bank could, by arousing panic in provincial areas, cause the stoppage one after the other of banks which were completely solvent.

A failure similar to that of Bowles and Co. was experienced by Rowton and Morhall, bankers at Chester and Shrewsbury, who also banked with Brickwood and Co.[27] Like Bowles and Co., Rowton and Morhall acted as receivers-general of public money, which they remitted to Brickwood and Co. Their assets at the London bank also included a large amount of short bills. Justifiably anticipating repayment of both the short bills and the taxes, Rowton and Co. declared that their stoppage, which occurred as soon as Brickwood and Co. failed, was temporary and that cash payments would soon be resumed[28] and took out an extent-in-aid against Brickwood and Co. to recover the public money. On 18 August, when neither the latter nor the short bills had been received, Rowton and Co. petitioned the Lord Chancellor, complaining that it was unable to continue payments until Brickwood and Co. had honoured its obligations. The balance of accounts between the two banks is shown below:

---

25 Exchange Herald, 3 Aug. 1810, p. 3, cols. 3, 4.

26 Salisbury and Winchester Journal, 23 July 1810, p. 4, col. 4.

27 The following description is based on P.R.O. B1/124, ff. 192-3.

28 Cowdroy's Manchester Gazette, 14 July 1810, p. 4, col. 5.

Details of the Claim of Rowton, Morhall and Co. against the Estate of Brickwood and Co.

	£.	s.	d.	£	s.	d.
Short bills deposited by Rowton at Brickwood and Co.				20,591.	15.	4.
Bills accepted by Brickwood for Rowton and Co.	26,070.	11.	3.			
Cash deposited by Rowton at Brickwood and Co. (including £21,339 excise duty of the Cheshire collectors)	25,272.	12.	9.			
Balance due from Rowton to Brickwood and Co.	797.	18.	6.	797.	18.	6.
Sum claimed by Rowton (short bills minus balance due)				19,793.	16.	10.

Source: P.R.O. B1/124, f. 192.

Although Eldon ordered Brickwood and Co. to pay Rowton and Co. the amount claimed, the latter failed to resume business. It is likely that, during the months spent in litigation, public confidence in the country bank was destroyed. Its commission was opened on 2 October and it received a certificate of discharge on 23 February 1811.

IV

The third 'direct' bankruptcy is that of William Harrison, William Gorst, William Harrison Jr., John Fairweather Harrison and Samuel Cooke, merchants and shipowners of Tower Street, London. Their main activities involved coal-mining in Durham and shipping coal from

Sunderland.[29] From 1808, Rowland Wilson, their agent in Sunderland, had arranged for masters and owners of ships to convey each week over one thousand chaldrons of coal from Sunderland to Scottish ports, including Leith, Dundee and Aberdeen. In 1809 and 1810, the firm took a fourteen year lease on six collieries, which were managed by Cooke at South Heaton, Urpeth, Kibbleworth, Seefield, Harraton and Chattershaugh, in addition to their original one at Berwick. Ships were chartered, by Wilson in Durham and William Harrison in London, to transport coal to the London market. Thirty-four thousand chaldrons were sent in the year before the firm's failure.

In addition, Harrison and Co. conducted a variety of operations in the West Country. James Lathy acted as agent, drawing bills on Brickwood and Co. for the use of business associates in Exeter and Plymouth. The extent of his bill-drawings is indicated in Figure 8.2. The brothers, William and J.F. Harrison, also ran the Totness Union Bank and a number of other concerns. With John Teed, a banker, and John Kroger, a merchant, both from Plymouth, J.F. Harrison supplied fresh beef in the first half of 1810 to the navy and prisoners-of-war at Dartmouth.[30] Teed, in fact, left this operation after a month and was persuaded by the Harrison brothers to pour capital into the Durham mining concern. Teed stated later that 'he had reason to believe the said collieries were a very valuable and flourishing concern . . . .'[31] At a moderate estimate, he said, they were capable of producing two hundred Newcastle chaldrons of coal per day, worth £189, or £68,860 per annum, at a daily

29 The following description is based on the evidence of Rowland Wilson to Harrison and Co.'s commissioners. P.R.O. B3/2150, 1 Dec. 1810.

30 P.R.O. B3/2818, 4 Feb. 1811, John Kroger; 15 March 1824, J. Rowe.

31 P.R.O. B1/125, f. 161.

expense of £97.[32] On the strength of this potential, Teed advanced a loan of £35,000, receiving as security a mortgage of the leasehold collieries and farm at Urpeth and Harraton and a share in a colliery at Ledfield. Teed's optimism was not completely justified for two reasons. First, the collieries were not worked to full capacity, producing only 58 chaldrons of coal per day which was not sufficient to pay expenses.[33] Second, and probably connected with this, the firm's capital was inadequate. William Harrison later bemoaned 'the multiple liabilities of the concern, to which they were forced to resort, to raise money from defective capital.'[34] Nevertheless, it is unlikely that Harrison and Co. would have failed had Brickwood and Co. continued operations. William Harrison, William Gorst and Samuel Cooke all attributed their bankruptcy to the stoppage of the London bank.[35] The shock of the events of 6 July was reflected in the distress of Cooke: 'when he got up the morning before, he considered himself worth £100,000, and now he was ruined.'[36]

Harrison and Co.'s dependence upon Brickwood and Co. is explained by the large number of bills which they drew upon the bank and by the extremely close financial links of the partnership's various operations, which ensured that when one failed the others quickly followed. Their most important transactions were the bills drawn by Samuel Cooke to finance the mining venture. As Table 8.2 shows, Cooke used more than half of the bills to raise capital by discounting them at banks or with brokers. London bankers

---

32 Ibid., f. 162.

33 Ibid., f. 168.

34 P.R.O. B3/2150, 19 March 1811.

35 Ibid., 1 Dec. 1810; 19 March 1811; 28 May 1811.

36 Ibid., 1 Dec. 1810, Mark Pinkney, partner in the Ayrton Bank, Durham.

appear to have had no qualms about discounting his bills. Of the £114,427 claimed by Marsh, Sibbald and Co., in Table 8.3, £38,000 represented bills drawn by Cooke on Brickwood and Co. and indorsed to Marsh and Co. 'for money lent and advanced.' £32,000 represented bills drawn by Cooke on Brickwood & Co. and paid to J.F. Harrison of the Totness bank who, in turn, discounted them at Marsh and Co. and £10,000 represented bills drawn by Harrison and Co. on Thomas Coles and Sons and discounted at Marsh and Co. Newnham, Everitt and Co. of Mansion House Street were equally accommodating. Of the £113,885 bills which they claimed against Harrison and Co., £43,342 represented bills drawn by Cooke on Harrison and Co. or on Harrison and Gorst. Similarly, all the bills claimed by Freen and Co. of Bartholomew Lane were drawn by Cooke on Harrison and Co. and immediately discounted by Freen. It is clear that the discount policies of these London banks were by no means safe, since Cooke's bills had received no indorsement from any other substantial London firm. Henry Fauntleroy, a partner at Marsh, Sibbald and Co., later described the distress caused there in July 1810 by the sudden loss of £170,000 and the difficulty of concealing it from the public.[37] Their discounting for Harrison must have been largely responsible. In connection with Marsh and Co.'s discounts, it should be noted that the two series of bills drawn by Cooke on Brickwood and Co., worth £38,000 and £32,000, were claimed against both Harrison and Brickwood by Marsh and Co.

In addition to the bills which were discounted at London banks, Harrison and Co. in general and Cooke in particular transacted a large volume of bills in the course of trading. These transactions, which are shown in Figure 8.3, suggest that the firm had either given accommodation to

---

37 <u>A Full and Accurate Account of the Trial and Execution of Henry Fauntleroy for Forgery</u> (1824), p. 17.

overseas traders (for example, Rowlandson, Isaac and Brien) or had actually dabbled to a small extent in commerce.

A large number of the bill creditors of Harrison and Co. collapsed during the crisis. E. and T. Ward, Cheapside haberdashers, failed on 13 July after Harrison and Co.'s stoppage imposed liability for bills worth £14,264. Joseph Walker, a Castle Street broker, whose credit was injured by the loss of more than £40,000 on Harrison and Co.'s bills, failed on 3 October. Edward Paine, a Baltic trader from Dowgate Hill, who was embarrassed throughout the latter half of 1810 by liability for £10,300 of bills drawn by Walker on Harrison and Co. and £5,482 drawn by Coles on Harrison and Co., stopped payment on 2 January 1811.[38] Other bill creditors, who were less severely hurt by the stoppage of Harrison and Co., were forced to stop payments during the crisis. William Lucas, a Clapton underwriter, made liable for £6,101, fell on 17 October. Joseph Nailer, a merchant of St. Mary's Axe, lost £4,000 on Harrison's acceptances for Rowlandson, Isaac and Brien and failed on 25 February 1811. Some of Harrison's bill creditors were docketed but not declared bankrupt, probably indicating that they were damaged by their bill losses but were able to survive. John Walters, for example, a Webb Square victualler who lost £7,912 on Harrison's bills, was docketed on 22 November 1810. Alexander Mackenzie, a Manchester linen draper, liable for £3,864, was docketed on 30 October 1810. Meir McNin, a merchant of Haydon Square, liable for £12,731 of Harrison and Co.'s bills as well as £21,915 of Coles and Co.'s bills, was docketed on 11 and 14 July and 7 August 1810. In addition to the bill creditors, some of Harrison and Co.'s business associates were also embarrassed. The Totness Union Bank, which was dependent on the London firm, fell on 18 July. John Kroger, the Plymouth merchant who had

---

38 P.R.O. B3/3885, 26 Jan. 1811, Thomas Berry, clerk at Paine and Co.

managed J.F. Harrison's meat contract with the Navy and had indulged in mining operations in Cornwall,[39] was also hurt. The meat contract had not been as profitable as Kroger had expected because many oxen which were not 400lb. weight had been refused.[40] After Harrison and Co.'s failure, Kroger almost fell but managed to struggle on until stopping payments on 11 January 1811.[41]

As was the case in the bankruptcy of Brickwood and Co., few of the actual claimants against Harrison and Co. (shown in Table 8.3) went bankrupt. Most of the claims made by non-bankers against the estate were small. It should be noted that some of these claimed the same bills against Brickwood and Co. They include Dominick Oliviera, J. and J. Mackenzie, Cockerill and Traill, Samuel Williams, Adam and Robertson and Bourne and Monkhouse. The largest claims were, as usual, made by banks. The survival of Marsh, Sibbald has been described as fortunate and it is a pity that no record has survived of the difficulties faced by Newnham, Everitt and Co. in 1810. Like Marsh and Co., Newnham managed to survive until 1825 despite their losses on Harrison's and Brickwood's bills.

V

The fourth example of a firm which failed because of its direct dependence upon Brickwood and Co. is that of Richard and Lancelot Bracken and Thomas Williams, who manufactured flannel in Rochdale as 'Lancelot Bracken and Co.' and marketed their produce in London as 'Bracken,

---

39 See P.R.O. B3/2818, 13 Feb. 1824, Joseph Clemens, who had operated Kroger's mine at St. Blezzey, Cornwall.

40 P.R.O. B3/2818, 4 Feb. 1811, John Kroger.

41 <u>Ibid</u>., 15 March 1824, John Rowe.

Williams and Co.' It seems likely that the partnership was an amalgamation of manufacturer and London distributor.[42]

The records of the partnership are poor but it is possible to elicit information from their surviving Dividend Book, the Bankruptcy Court Order Books and from the files of other commissions. Bracken, Williams and Co. opened an account with Brickwood and Co. in September 1807, depositing bills and notes which they received in trade and drawing bills on the London bank. They agreed to leave a surplus at all times at Brickwood and Co., who would charge half of one per cent commission on all acceptances (this was reduced to one-quarter per cent in 1808). At the time of Brickwood and Co.'s bankruptcy, their acceptances for Bracken and Co. still circulating amounted to £24,000. As security, the latter had furnished a cash balance of £4,968, short bills worth £23,890 and title deeds to premises in London worth £2,961. In fact, when the short bills were paid upon maturity they produced only £15,069 in nine years.[43]

Acceptances by Brickwood and Co. constituted one of two series of bill transactions which caused the stoppage of Bracken, Williams and Co. They were drawn by Lancelot Bracken on the bank and paid to Bracken, Williams and Co., who, in turn, discounted them at London banks (these amounted to £8,500) or indorsed them to other traders: £8,200 to Bruce, Warren (Throgmorton St., brokers) 'for valuable consideration'; £700 to John Fisher (Angel Court, insurance broker) 'for money paid and advanced'; £800 to Robert Storey (Gracechurch St., merchant); £1,000 to Brockbank and Royds (Bucklesbury, factors); £800 to John Shaw (Cheapside, merchant); £600 to Bell and Grant (Angel Court, merchants); and £500 to Staines and Carpenter

---

42 Such amalgamations were common. See M.M. Edwards, The Growth of the British Cotton Trade, 1780-1815 (Manchester, 1967), p. 149.

43 From P.R.O. B1/123, ff. 121-2; Ex parte Waring (1814) 2 Rose 182.

(Ironmonger Lane, merchants). The last five were all exchanged for cash.

As in the case of Rowton and Morhall, the short bills were used to balance bills drawn by Bracken on Brickwood and Co. The latter's assignees kept separate accounts of the proceeds of the short bills when they were paid and made dividends from them to the holders of Bracken's bills on Brickwood. When these bills were satisfied, the residue of the short bills was paid to Bracken and Williams to be divided among their own creditors.[44]

The second series of bills was drawn by both 'Lancelot Bracken' and 'Bracken, Williams' on Tomas Laycock, a Minories slopseller. Laycock paid for Bracken, Williams and Co.'s produce by accepting for them short-dated bills, 42 of which were in circulation at the time of Laycock's bankruptcy on 11 July 1810.[45] Of these, Bracken, Williams and Co. had used £2,939 to purchase goods from five London firms (two hosiers, two warehousemen and a slopseller) and from a Manchester cotton manufacturer. The remainder, for £15,287, were discounted at a variety of London firms. The largest of these were: £1,497 at Richard Richards (Drury Lane, man's mercer), £1,990 at the Bank of England, £1,037 at John Hoppe and Co. (Minories, merchant), £1,297 at William Wilson and Co. (Fenchurch Street, merchant), £1,549 at Brickwood and Co., and £1,166 at George du Bois and Co. (London Wall, merchant).

Unfortunately, Laycock was one of the traders who lost heavily in South American ventures, his balance sheet indicating book debts of over £100,000 in Rio de Janiero and Gibraltar.[46] He experienced financial difficulties throughout the second quarter of 1810 and resorted to

---

44 P.R.O. B1/123, f. 123.

45 P.R.O. B3/2928-9.

46 P.R.O. B3/2928, 15 Dec. 1810.

dubious financial transactions to stave off failure. It was common practice, during periods of tight credit, for traders to provide each other with mutual accommodation and for manufacturers to assist their large London customers whenever possible. Laycock received assistance from both quarters. He agreed to give acceptances to John Haywood and John Jones, Minories linen drapers, in return for their own. The arrangement was contrary to normal practice in accommodation bills for, as Haywood told Laycock's commissioners later, 'the acceptances which we put ourselves under we were to pay, and the acceptances which they put themselves under they were to pay.'[47] Haywood's policy was to obtain cash immediately by discounting the bills at two provincial banks, Rishworth and Townsend of Wakefield and Ingham, Ikin of Huddersfield. Laycock used his bills to buy goods from London merchants. At the time of Laycock's failure, £15,494 of these bills were in circulation. Laycock also obtained accommodation paper from Bracken Williams and Co. In April and May 1810, the latter accepted three accommodation bills worth £3,036, drawn by Laycock, and eight others worth £5,225, drawn by Lancelot Bracken and paid to Laycock. Laycock used the former three bills to balance his accommodation account with Haywood and the latter eight were indorsed to other merchants. As a result of embarrassed trade and the fictitious nature of their capital both Laycock and Haywood failed during the crisis. Haywood survived until 10 September, but Laycock collapsed on 11 July, during the panic aroused by Brickwood and Co.'s stoppage, followed on 24 July by Bracken, Williams and Co.

The effects of Bracken and Co.'s bankruptcy are difficult to gauge because of the poor quality of their files, which provide no information about the reasons for individual claims. The majority of claims against the firm were small, the largest amounting to £7,552 (claimed by the

---

47 P.R.O. B3/2929, 3 May 1815.

Bank of England) and the total to about £50,000. Some of the creditors went bankrupt during the crisis. James Wainhouse, a cotton and twist dealer in Salford (who claimed £1,000), failed on 7 July, Richard Earnshaw, a Manchester merchant (£1,306), on 17 October, Living, Downes and Co., London merchants (£2,096), on 10 November, J. and J. Gaskill, Minories woollen drapers (£2,730), on 13 November, and Joseph Varley, a Houndsditch slopseller (£1,000), on 31 October. The relatively small size of all these debts, however, suggests that Bracken, Williams and Co.'s bankruptcy was only a contributory cause of the respective firms' stoppages.

VI

The fifth example of a bankruptcy directly induced by close financial dependence on Brickwood and Co. is that of John Goodair, a Cheapside 'merchant, factor, warehouseman, dealer and chapman.' Goodair's failure is the most interesting of all in the crisis since it precipitated the stoppages of five other large traders and aroused a chorus of criticism from the national press.

Goodair's activities included warehousing and exporting. His warehousing business centred upon the Manchester cotton trade, in which his brother, Francis, acted as factor and operated a warehouse at Stockport.[48] Their textiles, which were bought from William Anderton and Robert Lightollers, cotton spinners at Chorley, and from Robert Tipping and George Fleming, calico printers at Holden Clough, were paid for by large-scale acceptances of bills and by bills drawn on Brickwood and Co. Goodair sold his cotton to exporters, including Vos and Essers. However, in 1810, he also exported goods on his own account. In the

48 Goodair's assignees ordered the sale of the warehouse in 1812. P.R.O. B3/1881, 25 Dec. 1812.

second quarter of the year he sent cotton goods worth £36,615 to Cadiz, Lima and the River Plate in Fermin de Tastet's ship, the Cartella. Like many such shipments in the first half of 1810, de Tastet's suffered large losses because overseas markets were glutted with English manufactures. Returns on the whole cargo, initially forecast as £132,114, amounted to a mere £27,800. Goodair's share - £7,487 - entailed a deficit of £29,128.[49] He incurred similar losses in ventures to Curacao, in partnershp with Solomon Cohen, and to South America, with Antonio de Paiva.

During such appalling trading conditions, Goodair's sudden obligation in early July to pay £22,885 of bills drawn on Brickwood and Co., £11,092 on Vos, Essers and Co. and £14,241 on Thomas Coles and Sons could not be fulfilled (these bills are shown in the credit part of Figure 8.4). Samuel Rowlandson told his own commission that Goodair's credit was totally destroyed by the failure of Brickwood and Co.[50] As noted, however, Goodair was granted a temporary reprieve by his creditors and his commission was not opened until 27 October.

The major claimants against Goodair are listed in Table 8.4. As it indicates, claims against the firm amounted to under £200,000, in contrast to the inflated liabilities published in the press in July 1810 (£381,953). As usual, the largest category of claimants is that of banks which had discounted bills to which Goodair had been a party. Those claimed by Sharp and Co. included many bills indorsed by Goodair to Rowlandson, Isaac and Brien, whose bankruptcy is examined below. Those claimed by Pedder, Lomax and Co. of Preston had been drawn on Goodair by both Anderton and Lightollers and Tipping and Fleming and discounted at the bank. In addition to these bills, Pedder and Co. claimed a

49 P.R.O. B3/1880, 16 Feb. 1816.

50 P.R.O. B3/4182, 2 March 1812.

bond worth £12,000 which Goodair had given to Tipping and Fleming in February 1809 as collateral security for their bill dealings at the Preston bank. None of the commercial firms failed as a result of the specific transactions recorded in the table. The concerns which lost most because of Goodair's failure are shown in the debit part of Figure 8.4. Of these, Tipping and Fleming, who had consigned all their calico to Goodair, failed on 1 August, having lost £15,236 on his acceptances, and Anderton and Lightollers, liable for £36,317, failed on 29 October. E. and T. Ward, who also lost on the bills of Coles and Sons and Harrison and Co., failed on 13 July.

It was noted earlier that, in addition to Goodair, five other large speculators stopped payment in July 1810: Rowlandson, Isaac and Brien; Rowlandson and Bates; Greaves, Sharp and Fisher; Hardy and Ottley; and Jacob Bros. Ironically, not one of them was closely connected with Brickwood and Co. Their embarrassments, which illustrate the secondary and tertiary waves of the bankruptcy mechanism, were the product of the failure of John Goodair.

The firm most directly affected by Goodair's failure was that of Samuel Rowlandson, Edward Isaac and William Brien, merchants of Cheapside. The history of this partnership reveals an opportunist at work and illustrates almost every mistake which a commercial adventurer could make during the easy-money conditions which preceded the crisis of 1810. By inclination and ability, Samuel Rowlandson was a warehouseman. As William Brien told the commissioners,

> As a warehouseman and wholesale dealer I had a good opinion of him, and I told him as much on the day on which I agreed to dissolve the partnership. Upon that occasion I told him that I would prefer him as a partner to any man that I knew conducting the business to which he was brought up and with which he was acquainted.51

---

51 P.R.O. B3/4182, 24 Feb. 1812.

Rowlandson had started in business as a warehouseman in 1808, in partnership with Richard Rothwell and I.C. Kent, conducting one or two minor trading ventures to Spain. This partnership was soon dissolved and, on 14 April 1808, Rowlandson formed another with Edward Isaac, William Brien and Thomas Outhwaite, the last of whom retired on 27 October 1808. At the time of the formation of his second partnership, Rowlandson committed the first of his many indiscretions. Edward Isaac, an ex-army officer with little knowledge of, or aptitude for, business, had contributed £10,000 capital, Brien, a wealthy sleeping partner, brought in £9,500, and Rowlandson was expected to provide £5,000. Rowlandson raised the first instalment of this by a bill for £2,800 drawn by Joshua Bates, a Cheapside merchant, on Rowlandson, Isaac and Brien. Of this sum, £2,500 was given to Rowlandson to use as capital and £300 was used to pay off his private debt to Bates and his partner Thomas Rowlandson, who was probably a relative of Samuel Rowlandson. The latter subsequently admitted that the other partners were not informed of this transaction but 'that was the only bill which was not entered in the Books.'[52] The rest was raised by loans from the Cornhill brokers, Rainier, Ballard and Morgan.

After he had thus established a partnership backed by substantial capital, Rowlandson was tempted to exploit opportunities to export to any potentially lucrative market. After the Cadiz rising of early 1808, the surrender of Dupont at Baylen (22 July 1808) and the diversion of Soult's troops to Portugal in pursuit of Moore, ports in the southern part of the Iberian peninsula were open. These routes and the opportunities in Heligoland and South America attracted Rowlandson. In 1808 and 1809, shipments were sent to Gibraltar which impressed him because 'the returns were

---

52 Ibid., 2 March 1812.

quick and the profits great.'[53] He considered that the fifteen or twenty per cent profit was sufficient pretext for telling his partners nothing of his business methods or activities (Brien later stated that Rowlandson's reports always showed a huge profit anyway).[54]

Two episodes led to Brien's resignation. The first was his discovery, in July 1809, of an extensive shipment made by Rowlandson. He had sent £12,000 worth of linen goods through Mr. Solomonson, a broker, to a Mr. Vandermarck in Cadiz, which was besieged by the French on the landward side. Rowlandson knew Vandermarck only at second hand. Brien was told by a friend who had engaged in Iberian trade for a long time 'that the shipment was a very wild and dangerous one and that he never knew in his life a person bowl away, as was his expression, at such a rate, without bringing his house to ruin.'[55] Brien communicated this to Isaac and also told him that

> I could discover Mr. Rowlandson's object to be to attempt a large trade with the credit he had obtained by forming a partnership with us, and to endeavour to make a large fortune in a short period, and that if he failed in his attempt, and became bankrupt, he would be as rich as ever he was but that he would leave us poor indeed.56

Isaac's immediate promise to inform Brien of all future foreign ventures was sufficient to pacify him on this occasion but he again heard nothing for months. Although many people in the business world suspected the firm because of its speculations in the latter half of 1809,[57] Rowlandson continued to seek profits in overseas markets. He had heard

---

53 Ibid.

54 Ibid., 24 Feb. 1812.

55 Ibid.

56 Ibid.

57 Ibid., William Brien.

of the large profits gained by John Milford from a shipment worth £80 - £100,000 to South America and immediately invested £6,000 in a second shipment.[58] Very soon, he was exporting goods to Brazil, Cadiz, Canada, Gibraltar, Malta, the West Indies and West South America. Not only did Rowlandson extend his liabilities far beyond the partnership's resources but he also began utilizing its capital to finance another firm's ventures. This was the second discovery which annoyed Brien. On one of his rare visits to the counting house in February 1810, he happened by chance to notice the invoice of a consignment worth £50,000 to be sent to Saint Domingo. Brien was horrified not only by the size of the transaction but also by the fact that it was to be conducted jointly with Thomas Rowlandson and Joshua Bates, merchants of Cheapside:

> I believe that there was no example to be met with of one partner forming a new partnership and committing the credit as capital of the House without the concurrence of his other partners.59

The incident convinced Brien that he must leave the partnership, and arrangements were made with the petulant Rowlandson to repay Brien's capital in eighteen-month instalments. Rowlandson's pretext for not informing Brien of the business was even more dubious than the shipment itself. He stated that, after Isaac told him of Brien's displeasure at being restrained from drawing on the firm's bankers, he did not wish to anger Brien further. Rowlandson later claimed that Isaac had supported Brien's departure, as the only way to prevent Brien's constant complaints at the Exchange bringing the house into disrepute. However, Isaac's statement to the commissioners contradicted this: 'In consequence of the shipments and extremely extended concerns that the House was branching out into, taking into

58 Ibid.

59 Ibid., 2 March 1812.

consideration the small capital the House possessed compared to the vast extent of the Business it was doing,' he would have retired six months before Brien had he possessed any property outside the partnership.[60]

Many of the creditors, giving evidence to the commission, agreed that the firm was insolvent as early as 18 February 1810, largely because of losses incurred in ventures conducted with Rowlandson and Bates. In any case, it is apparent that few foreign shipments had much prospect of success in the first half of 1810. Brien's friends assured him of this and, commenting on another South American scheme in the Catherine, Brien 'thought it a very bad measure, as I did all such shipments unless the vessel sank in the River as soon as they were shipped.'[61] However, not even insurance could have saved a concern as poorly administered as Rowlandson, Isaac and Brien. Brien was appalled at the fact that 'their property was so dispersed and scattered over Europe, Africa and America that I never expected to see them return as they were calculated upon.'[62] Hence, he considered Rowlandson's claims that the firm was still solvent in February 1810 as mere sham. After Brien left, Rowlandson resorted to doubtful methods of acquiring credit. He began 'obtaining discounts in all quarters' and selling goods to merchants whose credit was dubious, thus running great risks.[63] Accommodation bills had been used sparingly before that date (amounting to between £5,000 and £6,000 from May 1809 to February 1810). Afterwards, they predominated, many being drawn on Rowlandson and Bates. Despite this, Rowlandson disclaimed responsibility for the bankruptcy, stating that after February 1810 the firm's

---

60 Ibid., 12 March 1812.

61 Ibid., 24 Feb. 1812.

62 Ibid.

63 Ibid., 5 March 1812, Edward Isaac.

finances deteriorated rapidly 'by events that I believe no man living at that time had ever contemplated' - the fall in price of colonial produce, and especially of coffee (returns in the Catherine were almost totally coffee).[64] Thus, when the house failed, he maintained that its assets 'would depend on other Houses' and drew up the following balance sheet:

Balance Sheet of Rowlandson, Isaac and Co., July 1810

ASSETS	Amount (£)	LIABILITIES	Amount (£)
Debts owing to Rowlandson, Isaac and Co.	44,459. 5. 5.	Debts owed by Rowlandson, Isaac and Co.	283,938. 7. 6.
Debts owing in Town ledger	80,216.17. 8.	Balance	55,493.12. 8.
Stocks in warehouses	43,408.18. 6.		
Bills in hand & Bank surplus	71,721.18. 5.		
Leases of warehouses	3,000. 0. 0.		
Half-share in Catherine	3,000. 0. 0.		
Half-share in Welcome (Schooner)	175.11. 6.		
Goods abroad (Gibraltar)	26,454.13. 3.		
Goods abroad (Malta)	46,244.11. 5.		
Balance of shipment to Haiti and Martinique on joint account with Rowlandson and Bates	20,750. 4. 0.		
	339,432. 0. 2.		339,432. 0. 2.

Source: P.R.O. B3/4182, 12 March 1812.

64 Ibid., 2 March 1812; 5 March 1812.

The size of Rowlandson, Isaac and Brien's operations compared to their relatively small capital needs some explanation. Overtrading of this nature was facilitated by the state of commercial credit and contemporary attitudes to it. During the first half of 1810, even the bills of notoriously unsound firms could be discounted. The Bank of England, for example, discounted the following acceptances of Rowlandson which contained only two signatures:

Date (1810)	Drawer	Acceptor	Amount (£)	Usance
18 April	J. Mawson	Rowlandson, Isaac, Brien	£1,416. 8. 0.	3m
14 May	Rowlandson, Bates	"	2,391.15. 0.	65d.
16 May	W. Bowdler	"	1,482. 7. 0.	3m
28 May	A.C. Allen	"	1,471.11. 0.	65d.
3 June	Duckham, Lankester	"	980. 2. 0.	2m
6 June	J. Mawson	"	1,951. 7. 0.	2m

Source: P.R.O. B3/4181, 11 Nov. 1810.

The fact that all the drawers except Mawson failed during the crisis shows the danger of failing to scrutinize bills offered for discount. The laxity of the Bank of England is revealed especially in its willingness to discount the second bill, drawn by Rowlandson and Bates, which involved two highly unstable firms and was almost certainly accommodation paper. For his own discounts, Rowlandson employed, on a part-time basis, Thomas Cornford who was confidential clerk at Langston, Timmins and Co., a large warehousing firm in Watling Street. Cornford, who received £600 p.a. for acquiring discounts for Rowlandson, took most of the bills to Joseph May, a bill broker. Between July 1809 and July 1810, May had discounted £463,737 of bills for Cornford, most of them deriving from Rowlandson. Cornford discounted the remainder of Rowlandson's bills at Newnham,

Everitt and Co., the Mansion House Street bank, Sharp and Co., a Southampton bank, Thomas Sharp and Co., a Portsmouth linen draper, and at his own firm, Langston, Timmins and Co.[65] It seems that Thomas Langston gave Cornford a free hand in discount operations, since he complained to Rowlandson and Co.'s commission that Cornford had greatly exceeded his credit limit in discounting Rowlandson and Co.'s bills.[66]

The ease with which credit was obtained gave hope to William Brien, who was prepared to sacrifice all his capital in order to escape from Rowlandson's clutches:

> I thought, by retiring, I had a chance, though a bad one, of escaping the ruin of the House. The chance was that as money was easily obtained by procuring bills discounted, that their credit might last till my liabilities were paid off, being only about eight or nine months the credit at which they bought their goods.[67]

In other words, Brien hoped that Rowlandson's inevitable failure would occur after acceptances of 'Rowlandson, Isaac and Brien' had been honoured. Of course, had the firm been a joint-stock company, Brien would have been able to avoid the failure by selling his shares on the market.[68] Normal partnerships held the participants in an iron grip. Unfortunately for Brien, Brickwood and Co. failed five months after his withdrawal and the consequent collapse of

---

65 P.R.O. B3/4182, 4 Sept. 1810, Thomas Cornford.

66 Ibid., 22 July 1812, Thomas Langston.

67 Ibid., 24 Feb. 1812. Of bills accepted by Rowlandson and Co., 62 per cent were drawn at between six and twelve months and the remaining 38 per cent at less.

68 By the Bubble Act, a partnership legally constituted a joint-stock company if its shares were transferable. See A.B. Dubois, The English Business Company after the Bubble Act, 1720-1800 (New York, 1938), p. 4.

Goodair destroyed Rowlandson's credit completely.[69] The two firms had exchanged bills in the Catherine venture:

> the bills drawn upon Goodair to the amount of £30,000, I believe, were drawn in consequence of his having drawn for the same amount on Rowlandson and Bates upon the joint shipment in the Catherine.[70]

As a result, Goodair's failure involved Rowlandson in demands which he could not meet.

The history of Rowlandson's estate after his stoppage sheds light both upon the attitude of the commercial world towards failures of large houses and upon the difficulties involved in conducting the commission of a bankrupt who had participated in more than one partnership. In early July, Rowlandson stated that his financial difficulties were only temporary and that he should be given time to pay. A subsequent mercantile commission of investigation, after

Bankruptcy Proceedings against Rowlandson and Co., 1810-1811

	Docket (1810)	Commission sealed	Commission opened	Bankrupts
(a)	13 Aug.	14 Aug.	18 Aug.	S. Rowlandson, E. Isaac, W. Brien
(b)	15 Aug.	17 Aug.	18 Aug.	S. Rowlandson, E. Isaac, W. Brien
(d)	16 Aug.	-	-	T. Rowlandson, J. Bates
(d)	18 Aug.	31 Oct.	-	T. Rowlandson, J. Bates
(e)	20 Oct.	22 Oct.	23 Oct.	T. Rowlandson, J. Bates, S. Rowlandson, E. Isaac, W. Brien
	(1811)			
(f)	29 May	30 May	31 May	T. Rowlandson, J. Bates

Sources: P.R.O. B4/29, 30; London Gazette, 1810, 1811.

69 Rowlandson commented on the ironic fact that, although he had drawn only one bill, worth £1,000, on Brickwood and Co. and had received only £5,000 of Coles's bills, 'the stoppage of those houses led to all the injury.' P.R.O. B3/4182, 2 March 1812.

70 Ibid., Rowlandson.

many meetings, advised Rowlandson on 10 August that he was in fact bankrupt.[71] The chronology of proceedings against the three estates (on page 269) indicates the difficulties involved in adjudicating such a complex group of failures. Commission (a) was superseded because of a technical defect. Although Rowlandson, in arranging for a petitioning creditor to call at his house in order to be denied, was acting in compliance with the mercantile commission's instructions, the Lord Chancellor adjudged that the bankruptcy was concerted and, consequently, void.[72] The remaining dockets represent attempts to find a satisfactory solution to the problem of collecting and dividing the assets of each of the estates. The confusion is recorded in a series of petitions sent to the Lord Chancellor. Some creditors wanted the estates of S. Rowlandson and Isaac to be combined with that of Brien.[73] Others wanted the estates of S. Rowlandson, Isaac and Brien to be combined with that of T. Rowlandson and Bates.[74] Others complained that, after proving debts worth £13,652 due from S. Rowlandson in Commission (e), they discovered that they could not prove the same debts in commission (b), which was paying a dividend of four shillings in the pound.[75] Such complaints were justified since creditors who did not prove their debts before the second dividend was paid (within eighteen months of the issue of the commission) were legally entitled to receive only future dividends.[76] The problem was eventually solved

71 P.R.O. B1/124, f. 149.

72 <u>Ibid</u>., f. 152.

73 P.R.O. B1/123, f. 315.

74 P.R.O. B1/124, f. 153.

75 P.R.O. B3/4182, 26 Aug. 1812.

76 In practice, later claimants were usually paid the first dividend but not the second. B. Montagu, <u>Bankrupt Laws and Precedents</u> (1807), iv, 250.

when commissions were allowed against, first, S. Rowlandson, E. Isaac and W. Brien, second, T. Rowlandson and J. Bates, and, third, S. Rowlandson, E. Isaac W. Brien, T. Rowlandson and J. Bates.

The major claimants in the commission against S. Rowlandson, E. Isaac and W. Brien are recorded in Table 8.5. The largest was Newnham, Everitt and Co., which had both discounted bills delivered by Cornford and May and granted Rowlandson short-dated acceptances in return for the deposit of long-dated bills. Many of the latter, claimed by Newnham and Co. against Rowlandson's estate, were drawn at eight or nine months by Rowlandson on other firms which stopped payment in 1810 and then deposited with Newnham and Co. These included £18,347 of Goodair's acceptances. Thus, Newnham and Co. sustained heavy losses as a result of the bankruptcy of Rowlandson as well as that of Harrison. Nevertheless, it managed to survive, as also did the majority of other claimants against Rowlandson and Co. Two exceptions were Lee, Martineau and Co., warehousemen from Temple Bar, who failed on 25 February 1811, and Bowdler, Gilgrest, Cheapside warehousemen, who were docketed on 8 February 1811.

Some of the bill creditors of Rowlandson and Co., shown in Figure 8.5, were acutely embarrassed during the crisis. Charles Bedford, a Manchester merchant, was docketed on 18 August 1810, Hancox and Cooper, Liverpool merchants, on 19 October 1810, A.C. Allen, a merchant from Ironmonger Lane, on 1 December 1810 and J. Lyon, a Leadenhall Street insurance broker, on 4 May 1811. Hardy, Ottley and Co., the Cheapside warehousing concern which was one of the five large firms to stop payments in July 1810, also lost a considerable amount as a result of the failures of Rowlandson, Isaac and Brien and Rowlandson and Bates. Unlike the other four, however, Hardy, Ottley and Co. managed to survive the crisis without a commission of bankruptcy being opened against it.

Less fortunate was the largest firm that failed because of Rowlandson and Co.'s stoppage: that of James Pierrepoint Greaves, Hercules Sharp and Francis Fisher, merchants of King's Arms Yard. In addition to the partnership dealings, both Greaves and Fisher conducted individual trading ventures. The former purchased goods from Pierrepoint Greaves, a cotton manufacturer at Chorley, and from Hugh Greaves, a Manchester merchant, and dealt with Charles Greaves, a calico printer from Stratford, Essex. He also acted as agent shipping other firms' goods to South America[77] and exported, on his own account, goods bought from various warehousemen, including Daniel Haigh of Aldermanbury and J.R. Lawson of the Poultry, and from manufacturers, including John MacFie, a Glasgow calico printer. The files provide some interesting information about Fisher's arrangement with Masterman and

Bills deposited by Francis Fisher at Masterman and Co.

Date (1810)	Drawer	Acceptor	Amount (£)	Usance (m)	Indorsee
1 March	Greaves, Sharp, Fisher	Rowlandson Isaac, Brien	3,000	7	-
7 March	"	"	10,000	7	-
17 March	"	Rowlandson Bates	300	6	-
22 March	"	"	2,348	6	-
14 May	Rowlandson Isaac, Brien	"	2,841	6	Greaves, Sharp, Fisher
23 May	"	"	3,095	8	"
12 June	"	"	2,500	6	"
			24,284		

Source: P.R.O. B3/1879, 26 Jan. 1811.

77 P.R.O. B3/1874, 8 Jan. 1812.

Co., bankers of White Hart Court. Like the similar arrangements of Bracken at Brickwood and Co. and Rowlandson at Newnham, Everitt and Co., Fisher's involved the deposit of bills in return for short-dated acceptances. At the time of Greaves, Sharp and Fisher's bankruptcy, £50,675 had been deposited in this way. Most of the bills had been indorsed by Greaves, Sharp, Fisher and many accepted by Rowlandson, Isaac and Brien or Rowlandson and Bates, (such as those listed on page 272). It seems clear that, during the first half of 1810, Masterman and Co. did not scrutinize the bills which they received as security for their own acceptances.

The joint concern of Greaves, Sharp and Fisher concentrated on trade with South America. They bought large quantities of goods from domestic wholesalers to ship for themselves, exported for other firms and sold imported colonial produce. The extent of their dealings with Rowlandson, Isaac and Brien indicates that their policies were less than realistic since rumours of Rowlandson's impending collapse circulated through the City for months. Greaves's activities, however, appear just as hazardous as Rowlandson's since he attempted to purchase part of the Catherine from Rowlandson before it sailed.[78] The interchange of paper between the two firms is represented in Figure 8.5. As it shows, they had drawn a large volume of bills on each other and it is not unlikely that some of it was accommodation paper. When Rowlandson failed, Greaves, Sharp and Fisher were made liable for more than £40,000 of his acceptances, ensuring that their own collapse was virtually inevitable. In addition, Greaves and Co. were damaged by the failures of other firms. That of Coles and Sons made them responsible for bills worth £15,585 (shown in Figure 8.1) and other losses accrued from the acceptances of Bull, Banks and Bryson, a wholesale linen draper

78 P.R.O. B3/4182, 24 Feb. 1812.

(£4,186), Jacob Bros., a merchant (£5,642), and John Goodair (£1,950).

The bankruptcy of Greaves and Co. illustrates well the house of cards effect, since it was the fifth link in a chain of failures emanating from Coles and Sons and successively destroying the credit of Brickwood, Goodair, Rowlandson and Greaves. This can be extended to a sixth stage by examining the firms which were injured by Greaves and Co.'s failure. Aldebert, Becher and Co., merchants of St. Paul's Churchyard, for example, lost a balance of £17,847 at Greaves and Co. and failed on 12 October. Archibald McNair, who proved £2,411 against Greaves's estate, fell on 26 September and William Naylor, a calico printer at West Ham who claimed £3,000, was docketed on 27 September. Joshua Barnsley, a Manchester cotton merchant who proved £1,550, was docketed on 13 August and Foden, Slatter and Co., a Chester linen draper who lost £1,976, on 14 November. Richard Percival Moulson and Peter Fawcett, manufacturers in Manchester, lost heavily because of bill dealings with both Greaves and Rowlandson. Bills claimed against the respective estates include £9,985 drawn by Moulson and Co. on Greaves, Sharp and Fisher and £14,248 drawn by Rowlandson on Greaves and Co. and paid to Moulson and Co. In addition, bills were claimed worth £54,594, which had been accepted by Rowlandson, Isaac and Brien and paid to Moulson and Co. by Charles Bedford, a Manchester merchant (£6,243), Williams and Burford, London calico printers (£3,957), Hardy, Ottley and Co. (£15,971) and Rowlandson and Bates (£28,423). Other bills claimed against Moulson and Co. included £2,600 accepted by Brickwood and Co., £3,206 by Benjamin Aspinall, a Wigan manufacturer who failed on 20 December 1810, and £2,654 by Samuel Holland, a Liverpool merchant, bankrupt on 26 October 1810.[79]

---

79 Moulson and Fawcett also lost heavily on bills accepted by Dawes, Noble and Co. See below, chapter IX.

VII

A further example of the sixth stage in the 'house of cards' mechanism is the complex of firms involved with William Jacob, a Member of Parliament, and his brother, John, merchants in Newgate Street. Like many mercantile houses, Jacob Bros. was ruined in mid-1810 by lack of remittances and the increasingly embarrassed state of their trading to South America.[80] Because of the failure of Greaves, Sharp and Fisher, Jacob Bros. was obliged to honour bills worth £26,907 (see Figure 8.6) and they stopped payment on 18 July. Like the other July bankrupts, Jacob Bros. requested time to pay their debts since their assets were locked up in South America and Heligoland.[81] Although some creditors refused, bankruptcy proceedings were delayed. As a result, although the three largest firms in this complex - Bull, Banks and Bryson, Jacob Bros. and Richard Jones - stopped payment on 17, 18 and 19 July respectively their dockets were not struck until 6 November, 15 October and 19 October.

The pattern of trade conducted by firms in this group is identifiable in their mutual bill dealings. At the centre was Jacob Bros., exporters who bought textiles from various concerns, including Hodson and Quarrell, calico printers in Radcliffe, and Matthew and Peter Longsdon, Manchester fustian manufacturers. The goods were paid for by acceptances of the manufacturers' bills. During the first half of 1810, Jacob Bros. turned for financial assistance to Hodson and Quarrell who gave them a series of accommodation bills which they discounted at London houses:

---

80 P.R.O. B3/2677, 23 Oct. 1810, Joseph Bishop, clerk at Jacob Bros.

81 <u>Salisbury and Winchester Journal</u>, 23 July 1810, p. 2, col. 2.

Date (1810)	Drawer	Acceptor	Amount (£)	Payee	Usance (M.)	Indorsees
27 Mar.	Hodson, Quarrell	J. Hodson	1,298	Jacob Bros.	4	Merle & Co. (The City, bank)
12 Apr.	"	Winstanley, Hudson	2,315	"	6	J. Roberts (London, merchant)
14 Apr.	"	"	1,283	"	4	F. de Tastet (London, merchant)
14 Apr.	"	Bull, Banks, Bryson	994	"	3	"
18 Apr.	"	"	992	"	3	"
21 Apr.	Hodson Quarrell	Winstanley, Hudson	2,000	"	6	Newnham, Everitt (Lombard St. bank)
17 May	"	"	1,505	"	3	F. de Tastet (London, merchant)
30 May	"	J. Hodson	2,498	"	3	V. Stuckey (Sloane St. broker)
9 June	"	Bull, Banks, Bryson	1,350	"	2	Bank of England
30 June	"	Winstanley Hudson	943	"	3	V. Stuckey (Sloane St. broker)

Source: P.R.O. B3/2677-9.

Most of these bills were drawn by Hodson and Co. upon their warehousemen for large amounts at short date. Although the two bills drawn on Jonathan Hodson were clearly accommodation paper, Jacob Bros. was able to discount them in London, probably because the weakness of its own financial position was not yet suspected. Jacob Bros.'s credit was finally destroyed by the effect on the money market of Brickwood and Co.'s stoppage although, as already noted, the firm was allowed to struggle on until mid-October before actually being taken to the Bankruptcy Court. In the intervening period, Jacob Bros. accepted eight bills, at between six and twenty months, for Richard Jones (£2,355) and Ebenezer Leathley, a Hackney merchant (£2,355). Apart from these bills, the firm did not engage in trade between July and October, by which time the continual harassment by creditors drove John Jacob to flee to Bristol.[82]

The major claimants against the firm are listed in Table 8.6. As usual, a large proportion of the claims were made by banks holding Jacob Bros.'s bills of exchange. Examination of these indicates the ease with which the firm's bills were discounted during the first half of 1810 despite its increasing commercial and financial difficulties. This applies equally to the accommodation paper which, as noted above, Jacob Bros. received from Hodson and Quarrell as to the firm's own acceptances. The Bank of England, for example, discounted four bills worth £5,927, drawn by Longsdon on Jacob, and two worth £3,777, drawn on the firm by John Goodair. Jacob and Co.'s acceptances for Longsdon were also discounted by Bosanquet (£2,800) and Haddock (£4,735), and Lloyd and Co. discounted £10,637 of their acceptances for Hodson and Quarrell. Such transactions suggest that, before July, the acceptances of overseas merchants were easily negotiable at London banks even if their only other signature was that of a provincial manufacturer. The largest of the trading claimants - Fermin de Tastet - suffered heavy losses from bill dealings. In addition to the £29,277 which Goodair failed to pay, he lost on bills indorsed to him by Jacob Bros. These included £4,861 accepted by Greaves, Sharp, Fisher for Richard Jones, and paid to Jacob Bros. and £8,299 of Hodson and Quarrell's

82 P.R.O. B3/2677, 23 Oct. 1810, Joseph Bishop.

bills on Bull and Co. and Winstanley and Hudson. Nevertheless, de Tastet, like all the claimants against Jacob and Co., except Bowman and Spencer, managed to avoid bankruptcy during the crisis.

A different picture emerges from the list of bill creditors, represented in Figure 8.6. Thomas Eastman, for example, a merchant in Clement's lane, made liable for £14,121 by Jacob Bros.'s collapse, was docketed on 6 November after spending two months hiding from his creditors.[83] Matthew and Peter Longsdon, the manufacturers, who had drawn £38,431 of bills on Jacob and Co., failed on 19 February 1811 after five dockets had been struck against them in the previous six months. The two other leading drawers who failed were Richard Jones and Hodson and Quarrell.

Jones, a merchant and warehouseman in the City of London, was probably typical of the large number of small traders who rose and fell in the wave of South American speculation after 1806. Born in 1783, the son of William Jones, an affluent Wrexham leather seller,[84] he was apprenticed at the age of fourteen to Charles Poyser, a mercer in Wrexham. At nineteen he was apprenticed to William Waithman, a linen draper in Blackfriars, and in the same year moved on to Messrs. Tapp, Wilson and Waller, Cheapside wholesale linen drapers. One year later he joined the warehousing firm, Robert Harris and Son, in Watling Street, where he stayed for eighteen months. He then joined James Crossley, a Cheapside warehouseman, who traded with Halifax and Manchester. After Crossley went bankrupt in November 1807, Jones established a warehousing business at Bow Church Yard, banking at Bosanquet and Co. In October

83 P.R.O. B3/1527, 23 Nov. 1810, Mary Clements.

84 The following description is based on Jones's examination by the commissioners. P.R.O. B3/2680, 25 June 1811.

1808, he terminated the commission business and set up as 'merchant and dealer . . . buying and selling . . . cotton, woollen and other kinds of goods and merchandizes, and also . . . exporting the same to Cadiz and other parts beyond the seas.'[85]

Jones explained to his commission that, on establishing the warehousing concern in 1807, he did not need any capital because some of Crossley's clients began consigning goods to him instead of to the defunct Crossley and Co. At that time, he said, he did not possess £5,000, 'or any such other sum to the amount of £100 of his own property after payment of his debts.'[86] Nevertheless, Jones was able to acquire sufficient credit to conduct extensive trade. When he failed, his assets included goods shipped to Pernambuco, Prussia and Konigsberg. In addition, in March 1809, he contracted with the Earl of Aboyne for the sale of timber from the forest of Glantanner, 34 miles North of Aberdeen, where he erected a sawmill, cottages and stables, constructed a new road and bought horses and conveyances. The timber was sold in Liverpool, Swansea and London. Jones stopped payment on 19 July, the day after Jacob Bros. Although, like that of Jacob, his commission was not opened until October, Jones left his counting-house during September to avoid arrest.[87] His bankruptcy was the result of Jacob Bros.'s stoppage which entailed a loss for Jones of £60,638. Some of the bills were accommodation acceptances, negotiated when Jones's finances deteriorated during the second quarter of 1810.[88] Of the firms to which Jones had paid Jacob and Co.'s bills, Newham, Oliphant and Co., factors in Mitre Court, failed on 18 January 1811.

---

85 *Ibid.*, Thomas Wheale, clerk at Jones and Co.

86 *Ibid.*, Richard Jones.

87 *Ibid.*, Thomas Wheale.

88 P.R.O. B3/2678, 25 Jan. 1812, Jonathan Hodson.

Unfortunately, the files of the commission of Jonathan Hodson and Charles Quarrell, calico printers at Radcliffe, have not survived. It is clear from the records of other commissions, however, that their solvency was dependent upon that of Jacob Bros. The latter paid for Hodson and Quarrell's produce by accepting bills, £31,229 of which were in circulation at the time of their stoppage (see Figure 8.6). Hodson indorsed many of the bills to Richard Winstanley and George Hudson, a warehousing partnership which operated as 'Winstanley and Co.' in London and 'George Hudson and Co.' in Manchester, buying and selling cotton and other goods on commission.[89] It is possible that Hodson and Quarrell purchased raw materials from Winstanley and Co. who, at the time of Hodson and Co.'s bankruptcy, held £13,547 of its bills drawn on Jacob Bros., £7,445 drawn directly on Hodson and Co., as well as £8,942 drawn by Richard Jones on Jacob. The chain reaction of failures originating with that of Jacob Bros. is clear. Winstanley and Hudson bought their manufactured goods from Hodson and Quarrell. Of debts claimed against their estate amounting to about £90,000, £34,353 derived from bills drawn by Hodson and Co. on Winstanley and Hudson and paid to a variety of firms, including John Goodair (£3,717) and Bull, Banks and Bryson (£11,644). Most of the claims, in Table 8.7, were made by banks, which had discounted both the acceptances of Winstanley and Co. for other traders and bills which Winstanley had presented. The claims by traders were relatively small, although Foden, Slatter and Co., linen drapers in Chester who claimed £4,978, failed on 14 November 1810.

The final bankruptcy in this complex was that of John Bull, William Banks and George Bryson. Bull, Banks and Bryson, who had started trading in August 1809, 'carried on

89 P.R.O. B3/5174, 8 Feb. 1811, James Lane, clerk at Winstanley and Co.

the trade of wholesale linen draper, together in co-partnership, and bought, from time to time, divers quantities of linens, cottons, muslins and woollens, hosiery and other goods, and sold the same goods again to various merchants, shopkeepers, retail traders and others for profit.'[90] They also exported and imported goods in partnership with Christopher Chryssell Hall, a Southwark merchant, using John Symonds as agent in Brazil. These consignments embarrassed Bull and Co. during the first quarter of 1810[91] when the firm resorted to an accommodation agreement with Richard Read, who was also in financial difficulties. Read was a Lothbury factor and owner of 'manufacturies' at Trowbridge and Falkam, which supplied a large proportion of Bull and Co.'s woollen goods.[92] The bills transacted between the two firms reveal how dangerous the bill mechanism could become for they were negotiated in an amazingly haphazard fashion. Over £40,000 was ostensibly drawn by Read's agent, John Wood, on Bull, Banks and Bryson. In fact, they were drawn by Wood's son, an occasional assistant whom Banks had never met. In return for these acceptances Bull, Banks and Bryson drew bills on Read. Many of them were drawn by Robert Colley, 'a lad between 16 and 18 who was in the employ of Bull and Banks - a boy who used to go on errands and assist in the Counting House.'[93] Despite their doubtful origin, Read was able to discount his bills at the Bank of England and at Down and Co. The Bank appears to have had no knowledge of the nature of the bills until mid-July when it rejected two as accommodation

---

90 P.R.O. B3/269, 6 Nov. 1810, Edmund Sturley, clerk at Bull and Co.

91 Ibid., 27 Dec. 1810.

92 P.R.O. B3/4180, 7 Nov. 1811, Benjamin Grobety, a carrier of Read's goods.

93 P.R.O. B3/269, 27 Dec. 1810, William Banks.

paper.[94] Peter Free, a partner in Down and Co., stated later that he had frequently discounted bills of Read which he 'thought irregular' but had not refused any until late July when he followed the Bank of England's lead.[95]

Bull and Co. dealt extensively with the other firms in this complex. Debts proved against the estate include £11,644 of bills drawn by Hodson and Co. on Winstanley and Hudson, £5,050 drawn by A. Hodgson, a Fenchurch Street merchant, on the latter and £6,686 drawn by Richard Jones on Jacob Bros. Like the other firms in the complex, Bull and Co. were not docketed until October. After their initial stoppage on 17 July 1810, 'Mr. Bull said there was plenty to pay everybody.'[96] Their stoppage was described later by Thomas Jackson as a 'partial suspension.'[97] Between 17 and 19 July Bull and Co. made no payments, but after the 19th proceeded to do business again. On 25 July 1810, Bull presented the firm's creditors, who had been summoned to the warehouse, with a statement of accounts which 'appeared sufficient to pay every creditor twenty shillings in the pound provided a reasonable time is given for that purpose.'[98] The creditors, without even referring to the firm's books, agreed to allow it time to pay its bills by quarterly instalments over the subsequent two years.[99] On 1 September, the agreement was renewed. Between 25 July and 31 October 1810, Bull and Co. made more than £20,000 worth of payments, transferred over £1,000 of goods to C.C. Hall, bought over £5,000 of goods from Sheldon, Cass and Co.,

---

94 P.R.O. B3/4179, 29 Sept. 1810, Samuel Wilson, clerk at Read and Co.

95 P.R.O. B3/4180, 7 Nov. 1811.

96 P.R.O. B3/270, 21 Jan. 1811, William Banks.

97 Ibid., 28 Nov. 1812.

98 Ibid.

99 Ibid.

warehousemen, some of which they shipped to Rio, and made 'sundry consignments' to other firms.[100] On the latter date, Bryson ordered their clerk, Edmund Sturley, to tell Mr. Hudson, a Basinghall Street woollen draper who was expected to call, that none of the partners was at home. This Sturley did when Hudson called half an hour later, though the partners were upstairs in the warehouse.[101] Their docket was struck on 1 November and the commission opened on 6 November.

Table 8.8 lists the major claimants against Bull and Co.'s estate. It is interesting that, like the bills of other firms which experienced dire financial problems in the first half of 1810, those of Bull appear to have been negotiable and easily discounted. The claims of both Newnham, Everitt and Co. and Smith, Payne and Smith, for example, derived from bills which had been drawn on Bull and Co. by Rowlandson, Isaac and Brien and then discounted. Similarly, both Down, Thornton and Co. and the Bank of England had discounted the accommodation paper negotiated by Read and Bull. The majority of the claims of traders were small. The largest of these was made by Thomas Jackson, a cotton manufacturer at Cheetham from whom Bull bought printed calicoes. Jackson lost £5,552 as a result of Bull's stoppage and failed on 28 February 1811.

VIII

The final example of a failure caused directly by the bankruptcy of Brickwood and Co. is that of John Leigh, a Liverpool merchant trading to Ireland and South America. After his stoppage, which occurred as late as 10 August 1811, Leigh's clerk told the commissioners that 'owing to

---

100 <u>Ibid</u>., 16 Jan. 1811; 28 Nov. 1812.

101 P.R.O. B3/269, 6 Nov. 1810, Edmund Sturley.

the losses he had sustained by the bankruptcy of Messrs. Brickwood, Rainier, Morgan and Starkey, Bankers in London, and of Messrs. Clarke and Tods, merchants in Liverpool . . . he was rendered unable to meet his engagements.'[102] The fact that Clarke and Tods did not fail until May 1811 indicates that, after Brickwood and Co.'s stoppage, Leigh was in financial difficulties throughout the latter part of 1810 and the first half of 1811. As Figure 8.7 shows, he was made liable for £20,785 of Brickwood and Co.'s acceptances, which he had discounted at Parr, Lyon and Hurst, the Warrington bankers. In addition, he lost heavily on other series of bills accepted by firms which failed during the crisis. The first of these was drawn on Coles and Sons by Thomas Parkin and Thomas Scobell, Broad Street merchants, who dealt in various goods including cotton, ironmongery and earthenware, 'exporting them to Spain, Saint Domingo, South America and other places beyond the seas, and importing from thence coffee, hides, tallows and other sorts of merchandize and selling the same.'[103] Like Vos and Essers, Parkin and Co. had supplied Coles with West India produce in return for bill acceptances. After Parkin and Co. failed on 7 January 1811, liability for £20,000 of Coles and Co.'s outstanding bills was thrust upon Leigh. The second series of bills which aggravated Leigh's financial difficulties was that accepted by Joseph Duckham and Robert Lankester, who 'exercised the business of warehousing by purchasing quantities of cotton and linen goods and selling them to diverse persons.'[104] Duckham and Co.'s stoppage, on 4 January 1811, imposed liability upon Leigh for £12,338 of their acceptances. Similarly, claims were made against

102 P.R.O. B3/2942, 16 Aug. 1811, John Kay.

103 P.R.O. B3/3889, 22 March 1811, Thomas Jones, clerk at Parkin and Co.

104 P.R.O. B3/1305, 12 Jan. 1811, Adam Davidson, clerk at Duckham and Co.

Leigh's estate for £14,408 of bills accepted by Benjamin Thomas, a Liverpool merchant, who failed on 6 July 1811. In addition, Leigh lost on the acceptances of Caron, Distell and Co., Samuel and Thomas Hinde, Sill and Watson and John Goodair (see Figure 8.7).

It is noticeable that many of the bills claimed against Leigh's estate had matured long before he stopped payment and that, in some instances, the other parties to the bills had gone bankrupt earlier. Sill and Watson, the Liverpool merchants, had failed on 31 October 1810, John McCarsley, also a Liverpool merchant, on 14 November 1810, Benjamin Aspinall, a Wigan manufacturer, on 20 December 1810, and Samuel and Thomas Hinde on 5 January 1811. The reasons for Leigh's survival until August 1811 are not clear since the fact that the bills were claimed against his estate as well as those of the other parties indicates that he had failed to honour his liabilities from mid-1810 onwards. It is possible that he managed to appease his creditors by lodging with them long-dated accommodation bills drawn on John Hodgkinson, in whose firm he was a partner, and especially on Clarke and Tods, whom he had partnered in the Rio trade for several years. The size of their mutual bill dealings suggests that Clarke and Tods and Leigh had financed much of their trading by accommodation paper. Many of the bills claimed by Fry and Co., Hurst and Co. and Heywood and Co. (in Table 8.9) had been drawn by Leigh on Clarke and Tods. This explanation certainly accounts for the significance attached by Leigh to Clarke and Tod's failure which, it seems, was the final blow to his credit.

IX

The direct effects of the failure of Brickwood and Co. provide an insight into the problems confronting traders at the start of the nineteenth century. It is evident that, despite the repeated failures of private banks in London, the commercial world still placed implicit faith in their stability. Many firms, like Harrison and Co., John Goodair and the country banks concentrated most of their capital in one bank. When the latter stopped payments, these comprised the primary wave of direct bankruptcies which resulted, and their failures can be considered inevitable. Equally inevitable was the phenomenon of secondary and tertiary bankruptcy waves. The secondary wave involved firms which conducted extensive transactions with the primary bankrupts. Their failures can be attributed to two forms of financial relationship with the latter: either they received, from the primary bankrupt, bills which he had drawn on the bank (J.T. Deal from Bowles, Ogden and Wyndham; J. Walker from Samuel Cooke) or they simply drew a large amount of bills on the primary bankrupt (Anderton, Lightollers and Co. on J. Goodair; Rowlandson, Isaac and Brien on J. Goodair). The tertiary wave was the product of a similar process, by which secondary bankrupts either indorsed bills of the bank or primary bankrupts (J. Goodair to Anderton and Lightollers to E. and T. Ward) or accepted bills for the tertiary bankrupts (Rowlandson, Isaac and Brien for Greaves, Sharp, Fisher and Co.). The waves could be extended further than this as the failure of Jacob Bros. and associated firms indicates. Logically, however, the further away a firm was from the centre of the 'explosion,' the greater were its chances of survival.

Obviously, the analysis presented in the above paragraph is simplified since the interchange of bills was vast and many firms were related to the initial bank failure in more than one of the ways described. It is clear, however, that the bill of exchange provided an extremely effective channel for the communication of bankruptcy not only from one trader to another but also from one geographical area to another.

CHAPTER IX

THE BANKRUPTCY OF DAWES, NOBLE AND CO.

During the 1810 crisis, two major London banks stopped payment. The collapse of Brickwood and Co. proved a disaster to the commercial world; that of Dawes, Noble and Co., a West End bank, had, as one might expect, less impact. However, an examination of the latter's affairs indicates that the contrast which is usually drawn between West End and City Bankers is not always completely valid.

Dawes, Noble and Co. was founded in 1756 by William Backwell who had retired, in the previous year, from Child and Co. after a legal dispute.[1] Like many banking partnerships of the period it experienced frequent changes of personnel. In 1765, Price informs us, the partners were Backwell, Hart, Darell and Croft, the last of whom had also previously been a partner at Child and Co. In 1770, it was called Croft, Hart and Backwell; in 1778, Croft, Backwell, Roberts and Croft; in 1779, Crofts, Devaynes, Roberts and Dawes; and, in 1782, Crofts, Devaynes, Dawes and Noble. Several changes occurred between 1782 and 1810 which Price does not record. In March 1804, the younger William Devaynes assumed his dead father's position at the head of the bank, which he controlled until his death on 29 November 1809, when the surviving partners were John Dawes, William Noble, Richard Henry Croft and Richard Barwick.[2]

Situated in Pall Mall, Dawes Noble and Co. functioned as a West End bank in the sense that most of its clientele consisted of non-commercial people whose wealth derived above all from rents. S.R. Cope cites a contemporary author who maintains that such banks generally had

---

1 The following description is based on F.G. Hilton Price, A Handbook of London Bankers (1876), pp. 48-9.

2 P.R.O. B3/1299, 19 Feb. 1835, petition of William Angus Devaynes.

> no interest whatsoever, nor acquaintance with Trade-Their occupation is to keep the Cash of people out of Business, and to employ in Stocks and Mortgages such part of it as they may venture to Employ; but whether Discount is easy in the City, whether merchants are able to execute the Commissions they receive, whether they are able to encourage Consignments to the Country by the necessary advances, are all objects in which they feel little immediate concern.3

The non-commercial character of the majority of Dawes, Noble and Co.'s clientele is reflected in the list of the largest claimants against the estate in Table 9.1. Most of the customers were peers, clergy, widows, spinsters and people variously described as 'gentleman' or 'esquire.' In addition, the table indicates that the bank catered for clients drawn from almost all over the country. The majority of their claims were for 'balance of account for money had and received by the said Bankrupts to and for the use and on account of this deponent.' As this suggests, most of the deposits consisted of simple cash accounts, although some also claimed stock. The executors of the estate of the deceased John Wrigglesworth, for example, claimed £15,843 of three per cent consolidated Bank annuities, i.e. consols. The claim of Somerset Davies (£2,482) represents the balance of £15,000 of consols used to secure a loan from Dawes and Co. Julius Hutchison, of Lincoln's Inn, similarly claimed £27,580 three per cent consols as well as a cash balance. When Dawes and Co. failed, such non-commercial customers lost the whole of their cash deposits. Their one consolation was that the estate paid dividends which were larger and quicker than those of Brickwood and Co.

Table 9.1 also shows that Dawes, Noble and Co. did conduct extensive bill dealings, which must be viewed either as an anomoly or as an indication that some West End banks

---

3 Quoted by L.S. Pressnell, Country Banking in the Industrial Revolution (Oxford, 1956), p. 82.

continued to dabble in mercantile transactions in the early nineteenth century.[4] Indeed, Dawes and Co.'s failure was caused by their excessive accommodation to Mayson Wilson and John Hesketh Fleetwood Williams, a large import and export concern in Liverpool.[5] The latter firm was founded in 1802, when Wilson, a former broker's clerk, entered into partnership with Williams and Mordaunt James Shipley as West India merchants and commission brokers. Shipley acted as agent in Nevis until his death in 1806 when he was replaced by Birch Harrison. In the same year, Nicholas Salisbury joined the commission broking side of the business, which was known as 'Shipley, Williams and Co.' in England and 'Wilson, Harrison and Co.' in the West Indies. In 1809, the broking business was dissolved by mutual consent, Williams and Wilson thereafter concentrating upon mercantile activity and, in 1809, joining John and Ashton Case as insurance brokers in Liverpool.

From 1806, Wilson and Williams banked with Devaynes and Co., who accepted thousands of bills of exchange which were paid to Birch Harrison by the parent firm. As security for their acceptances, Devaynes and Co. in April 1806 became half-partners with Wilson and Williams in the ships Shipley, Augusta and Fleetwood, which were registered at Liverpool in the names of Wilson, Williams, Devaynes, Shipley, Dawes, Noble and Barwick. Devaynes and Co. had, in fact, desired only a mortgage on (not property in) the ships, but their names were inserted in the registers without their

---

4 Most West End banks appear to have relinquished mercantile dealings in the eighteenth century. See D.M. Joslin, 'London Private Bankers, 1720-1785,' in Essays in Economic History (ed. E.M. Carus-Wilson), (1962), ii, 348.

5 The following description is based on P.R.O. B3/5177, 19 Jan. 1811, Mayson Wilson; B3/5179, 16 Nov. 1816, William Noble; B3/1299, 13 Aug. 1813, John Machel, James Penny and Robert Kitchen (Liverpool merchants); Ex parte Machel (1813) 1 Rose 447.

knowledge, thus making them liable for debts. The subsequent closeness of the financial links of the two houses was extremely dangerous for Dawes, Noble and Co., who naturally paid great attention to the state of West Indian commerce. By the middle of 1810, when it was apparent that Wilson and Williams's shipments might not achieve success similar to that of previous years,[6] Dawes, Noble and Co. began seeking support in other quarters. Pascoe Grenfell, the financier, was invited to join the bank but, after inspecting their books, refused and advised several country banks to withdraw their capital from it.[7] Grenfell's reaction precipitated the run which was to bring the bank down. As Edward Howell, one of the bank's clerks, said, 'for more than a week immediately previous to Monday the thirtieth of July last past there was a considerable run on the banking house.'[8] On the evening of the thirtieth, Dawes, Noble and Co. suspended payments.

The crash ruined Wilson and Williams who, as Wilson told his own commissioners, were 'deprived of their former resources, and the credit of the house being in consequence much shaken they were under the necessity of suspending their payments . . . at the time of the bankruptcy of the said Dawes Noble and Co., the Examinant and his said partners were indebted to them in the sum of £120,000 and upwards.'[9] After obtaining judgment in King's Bench on 8 November 1810, the bank issued an extent against the

---

6 At the time of its bankruptcy, Wilson, Williams and Co.'s assets included £147,618 at Nevis, £68,383 at St. Kitt's, £69,046 at St. Croix and £12,388 at Monserratt.

7 See F. Crouzet, L'Économie Britannique, op. cit., ii, 620.

8 P.R.O. B3/1295, 2 Aug. 1810.

9 P.R.O. B3/5177, 19 Jan. 1811.

Liverpool firm for £120,000 and Wilson and Williams were temporarily incarcerated in the Marshalsea.[10]

The bill liabilities of Dawes, Noble and Co. reveal that, in addition to its transactions with Wilson and Williams, this West End bank was heavily involved with two other firms: Moulson and Fawcett, manufacturers in Manchester, and Lowndes and Bateson, Liverpool brokers. At the time of the bankruptcy of Dawes and Co., £26,627 of bills drawn by Moulson and Co. were outstanding, which were secured by the deposit of £16,510 in short bills and a cash balance at the bank. Dawes and Co.'s assignees refused to deliver the short bills and cash to Moulson and Co. until the latter had honoured the bills which they had drawn on the bank.[11] Moulson and Co., who had also lost heavily because of the bankruptcies of Greaves, Sharp, Fisher and Rowlandson, Isaac and Brien, failed on 29 October 1810. Lowndes and Bateson were similarly affected by the bank's stoppage. At the time of Dawes and Co's bankruptcy, Lowndes and Co. had an overdraft at the bank of £37,462 and had drawn bills to the value of £105,535. They were obliged to satisfy both these liabilities before Dawes and Co.'s assignees would return short bills worth £68,073 which they had deposited at the bank.[12] Of the latter, £37,795 had been drawn on John Leigh. The embarrassments of Lowndes and Co. after Dawes's failure are evidenced by their acquisition on 24 August 1810 of a £100,000 loan from the Bank of England, secured by notes of London merchants.[13] This enabled the firm to survive until 11 July 1811. Consequently, most of the commercial claimants against Dawes

---

10 P.R.O. B3/5178, 15 Dec. 1810, William Noble.

11 P.R.O. B3/1296, 18 Sept. 1810.

12 P.R.O. B3/1295, 4 Sept. 1810.

13 Bank of England, Committee of Treasury Minute Books, ix, 6.

and Co. did not lose since Lowndes and Co. paid the bank's acceptances when they matured. Among the bill-holders who benefited from this (in Table 9.1) were Mitchell, Shepherd, Murray, Allen, Touchet, Rainier and Goodbihere.

The confusion which personnel changes and deaths could cause in the estates of large partnershps is illustrated by the chaotic litigation occasioned by the failure of Dawes and Co. After the death of William Devaynes Jr., on 29 November 1809, the new partnership of Dawes, Noble, Croft and Barwick was obliged to collect the old partnership's assets, pay off its debts and return the individual assets of Devaynes to his executors.[14] At the time of his death, as the following table shows, the bank's assets amounted to about £720,000 and its liabilities to about £700,000.

Assets and Liabilities of Dawes, Noble and Co., 1809

Assets	(£)	Liabilities	(£)
Due on bills, over-drawn accounts, bonds and other securities	575,799	Balance due on cash accounts	595,151
Cash in till	140,420	£3 per cent Consols	52,765
£4 per cent annuities	1,444	Exchequer bills	24,932
£3 per cent reduced annuities	1,083	£3 per cent reduced annuities	10,200
£3 per cent Consols	1,050	India bonds	9,530
		Bank stock	4,300
	719,796		696,878

Source: P.R.O. B3/1299, 19 Feb. 1835, petition of William Angus Devaynes.

Between November 1809 and the failure of the new partnership, the surviving partners were said, by their

14 The following description is based on P.R.O. B3/1299, 19 Feb. 1835, petition of William Angus Devaynes.

assignees, to have collected £345,676 of the old partnership's assets and to have discharged all their liability for Devaynes and Co.'s debts except £102,192. This residue could quite easily have been paid by the assignees, since they collected a further £127,028 of Devaynes and Co.'s assets. After payment of the debts, the balance of £24,836 should have been divided amongst the surviving partners according to their respective number of shares.[15] Unfortunately, the assignees failed to separate the two partnerships:

> though fully aware that these two distinct estates existed and that there were many creditors of the said partnership of Dawes, Noble and Co., who were not creditors of the said Testators' partnership, and who had no right or title to be paid anything out of the estate belonging to the said Testator's partnership at the time of his death, yet the said assignees blended and mingled together the said two estates and in their accounts . . . represented the whole assets received by them . . . as belonging to the estate of the said new partnership of Dawes, Noble and Co. only.16

Consequently, the £127,028 was divided amongst the creditors of both partnerships. In 1811, petitions were presented to the Lord Chancellor by the three interested parties, viz., the executors of the estate of William Devaynes Jr., the creditors of that estate, and the assignees of the estate of Dawes, Noble and Co. The first petition (i.e. of the executors) produced an order from Chancery, on 29 June 1813, that the executors should be allowed to prove their claims in Dawes, Noble and Co.'s commission. The second and third petitions resulted in orders from the Lord Chancellor (on 2 March 1812 and 27 July 1814) that the assignees and executors should produce accounts of all money received and

---

15 After the death of William Devaynes Sr. in 1804, the firm was split into 576 shares: 203 to William Devaynes Jr., 145 to Dawes, 116 to Noble, 64 to Croft and 48 to Barwick.

16 P.R.O. B3/1299, 19 Feb. 1835, petition of William Angus Devaynes.

paid, in order to ascertain how much was still owing from the bank to Devaynes's estate, and that the assignees should inform Devaynes's creditors of the state of his account when he died. Because of the confused nature of the two estates litigation continued until 1837. The conflict between the assignees of Dawes, Noble and Co. and the executors of William Devaynes degenerated into a slanging match in the Court of Chancery, while Devaynes's creditors were not paid. Dividends on the bank's estate were suspended by order of the Lord Chancellor between 13 August 1825 and 31 March 1831, pending the settlement of the dispute. They were continued again only because the three executors died. In December 1834, the case was resurrected by the Reverend Robert Roy of Fulham, on behalf of William Angus Devaynes. Finally, on 3 July 1837, agreement was reached that all suits in Chancery should be terminated and that £50,240 should be paid to the creditors of William Devaynes out of the estate of Dawes, Noble and Co.

CHAPTER X

CONCLUSIONS

I

In 1816, William Harris observed that

> Commissioners of Bankruptcy can bear the most decided testimony to the large speculations which have been carried on by great numbers of persons with the capital of others; some by taking the loan of money, but in most instances, by taking credit to a great amount . . . The numerous failures occasioned by rash adventure, and especially those in which the system has been maintained by long credit and bill transactions . . . admonish every tradesman to retrench, as much as possible, the credit he takes and allows.1

As this suggests, the availability of widespread credit facilities largely accounts for the looseness of trading and the extent of commercial crises during the early nineteenth century. It is, therefore, surprising that little is known about the credit instruments which were used at the time and the operations of financial institutions which had the power to control them. The purpose of this chapter is to shed light upon these problems by examining the implications of the evidence presented in part two of this study. The conclusions relate to three aspects of economic activity: the policies of the banking fraternity, the activities of commercial firms, and the employment of negotiable instruments in the normal course of trade.

II

As Pressnell has shown, the money market between 1710 and 1825 was prone to persistent failures.[2] This was

---

1 W. Harris, <u>The Present Distress of the Country and Suitable Remedies</u> (1816), p. 26.

2 L.S. Pressnell, <u>Country Banking in the Industrial Revolution</u> (Oxford, 1956), pp. 536-8.

probably a product of recurrent, perhaps cyclical, pressure upon a financial system which was inherently unstable. Our study of the causes and course of the 1810 crisis suggests that the instability resulted from weaknesses in both financial institutions and monetary theory. The Bank of England gave unity of a sort to the loosely organised banking structure since, directly or indirectly, it controlled the credit of both London and provincial banks. Through its function as lender of last resort and through the accommodation which it afforded to private individuals and, after 1797, to London bankers[3] the Bank was the arbiter of the country's credit, possessing the power to dampen excessive commercial activity by restricting discounts and to alleviate financial pressure by expanding them during crises. It was, therefore, unfortunate that its policies during the restriction period were not particularly enlightened. The theoretical defects of the real bills doctrine have been discussed and it has been suggested that, in practice, it was difficult to detect fictitious paper. In the early nineteenth century, however, this was disputed. Henry Boase, for example, claimed in 1804 that the directors could 'discover and distinguish, almost intuitively, between genuine and fictitious bills.'[4] Fifteen years later, Charles Pole, Deputy Governor, observed that the Bank could identify merchants who conducted real transactions based upon the prevalent market price, to whom discount facilities were granted, 'whilst to

---

3 Before the suspension of cash payments, bankers could open drawing accounts only, although it is possible that one or two favoured firms were allowed to discount. After 1797, discount accounts became common. See J.H. Clapham, 'The Private Business of the Bank of England, 1744-1800,' Ec. H.R.., xi (1941), 83.

4 H. Boase, Letter to Lord King in Defence of the Conduct of the Directors of the Banks of England and Ireland (1804), p. 11.

individuals who are purchasing up an article to hold merely as a monopoly of the trade, the Bank would not render assistance, conceiving that to be a speculative transaction.' He considered that speculation was easily detected,

> when a person goes so deeply into a concern that his own means are not adequate for the performance of it, and he is obliged to find a means of getting brokers' acceptances or such other as you are enabled to see through at the bank, or through your connexions on change.[5]

Many of Pole's contemporaries were not so optimistic. Critics of the Bank, like Lord King, considered that the real bills doctrine inevitably involved th Bank in discount of accommodation paper.[6] Indeed, the Bank's Special Discount Committee was acutely conscious of the mass of doubtful bills which the overworked committee-in-waiting discounted. In January 1810, the committee noted the frequency with which the Bank was asked to discount notes transacted between two importers,

> which has the appearance of mutual consent to support the price of an Article and to the prejudice of the public; whereas the regular Course of Trade would be, for the Commodities to pass from the Importer to the Middle-Man or Manufacturer.

The same type of bills were also said to be common in the home trade, where warehousemen used them to speculate upon an anticipated price rise.[7] The evidence indicates that, in practice, the Bank did discount bills of doubtful origin. In addition to those mentioned in chapter eight, many other imprudent discounts could be cited, including the following:

---

5 B.P.P. Report from the Committee of Secrecy appointed to Consider . . . of the Resumption of Cash Payments (1819), III, 37-8.

6 Lord King, Thoughts on the Effects of the Bank Restriction (1804), p. 21.

7 Bank of England, ADV/586-1, Special Discount Committee, ff. 56-8.

Date	Drawers	Acceptors	Amt.(£)	Usance	Indorsees
(1809)					
18 Dec.	T. Law	Jacob Bros.	1,000	7m	Bank of England
(1810)					
24 Feb.	J. Goodair	"	1,933. 3.-	6m	"
27 Mar.	Hodson, Quarrell	"	1,340. 7.-	4m	Winstanley, Hudson; Bank of England
16 Apr.	R. Jones	"	1,986	3m	Bull, Banks, Bryson; Bank of England
7 June	"	"	1,350	2m	"
24 Mar.	R. Read	Bull, Banks, Bryson	784.11.-	4m	Bank of England
1 May	M., P. Longsdon	"	865	3m	"
"	J. Goodair	"	805. 9.-	3m	"
"	A.C. Allen	"	978. 3.-	3m	"
11 May	Bracken, Williams	"	939. 3.-	3m	"
22 May	R. Read	"	799.18.-	3m	"
25 June	A.C. Allen	"	789. 1.-	65d.	"
2 July	M., P. Longsdon	"	702. 1.-	65d.	"
23 May	M. Abitbol	Coles & Sons	2,500	3m	Brickwood; Bank of England.

Source: P.R.O. B3/252, 18 Aug. 1810; B3/269, 6 Nov. 1810; B3/2677, 4 Dec. 1810.

It is clear that the Bank failed to scrutinize the acceptors of bills offered for discount and was prepared to accommodate bills containing only two names. This was extremely dangerous because of the large number of drawers who followed their acceptors into the Bankruptcy Court. Of the drawers in the bills cited above, for example, only Law survived the 1810 crisis. The bills drawn by Read on Bull, Banks and Bryson were accommodation paper. Those drawn by Longsdon on Bull and Co. represent a manufacturer drawing on a warehouseman whose credit was very dubious and the bills of Goodair and Jones on Jacob Bros. were drawn by one adventurer on another. It is not surprising that the Bank's General Ledgers, which record the dividends received from bankrupt estates, include payments from the assignees of many of the marginal firms which failed in 1810. Among the dividends received between mid-1810 and 1812 are those of Read, Rowlandson, Isaac and Brien, Jacob Bros., Bull, Banks and Bryson, Greaves, Sharp and Fisher, Vos and Essers, Thomas Laycock and John Teed.[8]

The Bank's liberality is not wholly explained by the difficulty of detecting fictitious or doubtful paper. Rowlandson's financial plight, for example, was well-known throughout the first half of 1810. Rather, it seems that the Bank's machinery and operations left a lot to be desired. This was conceded by the Special Discount Committee of 1810 which observed that the methods employed by the Bank were totally inadequate to cope with large increases in demand for discounts, that excessive accommodation had repeatedly been granted to individual traders and that the committee-in-waiting had discontinued the practice of reporting high accounts to the Court each week.[9] A year later, the committee reported that the latter practice, which had previously acted as a check upon excessive discounting, was still in disuse.[10]

As a result of its operational defects, therefore, the Bank failed to wield its power to restrict economic

---

8 Bank of England, General Ledger, No. 18, 1 March 1805-29 Feb. 1816, ff. 707-12, 349-50.

9 Bank of England, Special Discount Committee, loc. cit.

10 See above, chapter VI.

activity, by refusing individual discounts, until too late. Indeed, it seems that the committee-in-waiting only scrutinized bills closely after the crisis had commenced. This is confirmed by Samuel Rowlandson's statement that, after Brickwood's failure, 'the bankers in general became alarmed, and the Bank of England became alarmed, so that the discounts we were in the habit of receiving from the Bank of England were less than formerly.'[11] In July, the usual difficulty of detecting dubious bills was exacerbated by increased discount demand. The Bank's only recourse, therefore, was to impose blanket restrictions upon all but a select few clients, a policy which inevitably stagnated the money market as a whole. The conclusion which emerges is that, if the Bank's machinery had been more efficient, much of the frenzied trading which characterized the boom of 1809 and early 1810 would have been impossible and the subsequent crisis commensurately milder.

The second tier of the banking structure - London private banks - inspired even less confidence than the Bank itself. Traditionally, these banks have been divided into two categories corresponding to the nature of their business. West End banks generally made loans to the landed classes on mortgage and bond and, to a lesser extent, to the City on a variety of securities (Bank stock, East India stock, etc.). They also invested in such securities on their own account. Logically, these banks were more secure than their City counterparts because of the nature of their clientele and their avoidance of commercial discounting.[12]

---

11 P.R.O. B3/1482, 12 March 1812.

12 Joslin cites Richard Cantillon's statement that, because West End banks were less liable to sudden withdrawals, they could safely hold lower cash reserves than commercial banks. D.M. Joslin, 'London Private Bankers, 1720-1785,' in Essays in Economic History (ed. E.M. Carus-Wilson), (1962), ii, 349.

If, however, a run took place on a West End bank, the illiquidity of its assets made bankruptcy virtually inevitable. City banks, in contrast, were agencies for the discount of commercial bills and made advances by loans upon security and by accepting their clients' bills. The danger for both groups was not that of excessive notes, since the majority of banks had stopped issuing before the end of the eighteenth century.[13] It was, rather, the difficulty of employing assets in such a way that variations in demand upon the banks could be met. Certain precautions were essential and obvious, especially for the City banks. They include the retention of a healthy cash balance, the discount of sound paper, the avoidance of long-term overdrafts and of large advances on unsound security. They should have resisted the temptation to plunge capital into commercial enterprises and to accommodate individuals whose trade was hazardous.

The instability of London banks was basically a product of structural and operational defects. Their scale of operations was limited by the six-partner rule and individual withdrawals could create difficulties. In addition, it is apparent that they were sometimes administered injudiciously. This is exemplified by the anecdote, in Price, of Sir Matthew Bloxham, whose bank, founded in Southwark in 1795, survived until the appointment of a new clerk in 1809:

> The chap was a Yorkshireman, and at once saw how things were, and not having been used to "our ways", he told some friend, that friend told a third, and so we were run out. This, however, I will say for all the other clerks, we paid them well, dined them well once a week - they knew our secret, and kept it for full ten long years.14

---

13 J.H. Clapham, The Bank of England (Cambridge, 1944), i, 166.

14 F.G. Hilton Price, A Handbook of London Bankers (enlarged edn., 1890), p. 17.

The history of Marsh, Sibbald and Co. of Berner's Street illustrates both structural and operational weaknesses. Its embarrassments during the crisis of 1810 have already been described but it had been in difficulties since 1794 when the retirement of some partners, two years after the bank had been founded, incurred a loss of £20,000 which was never replaced. After 1800, the bank extended large advances to builders and, between 1814 and 1816, speculated with builders and bricklayers, losing £100,000. After 1815, Henry Fauntleroy, who had sole charge of the bank's business, forged signatures to a power of attorney for the sale of over £100,000 worth of consols which he credited to the banking house in order to preserve its credit. Before his execution for fraud, Fauntleroy maintained that the house had been almost without capital since the 1790s.[15] A third example of faulty management is that of Kensington and Co., of Lombard Street, who for eight years before their failure in 1812 advanced large sums to enable Alexander Learmouth, a West India merchant, to carry on business and to overcome temporary difficulties. Learmouth's failure entailed a loss of over £70,000 which was largely responsible for the bank's stoppage.[16] These three examples of banking failures suggest that London bankers during the early nineteenth century, like the Bank of England itself, were still groping to establish sound principles of administration. As a result of operational handicaps and crude banking theory, the practices of some of them appear to have been extremely loose. Further evidence of this is provided by the lack of caution shown by Brickwood and Co. and Dawes and Co., the one accommodating the transactions

---

15 For the history and trial of Henry Fauntleroy, see _A Full and Accurate Account of the Trial and Execution of Henry Fauntleroy for Forgery_ (1824).

16 P.R.O. B3/2868, 26 May, 8 Dec. 1819; 4, 7 Feb., 28 March 1820.

of a speculative broker, the other tying its capital to an unsound foreign merchant. Similarly, the discount policies of other bankers, like Newnham, Everitt and Co. in the case of Harrison, Masterman in the case of Greaves, Sharp and Fisher and Down, Thornton and Co. in the case of Read, were imprudent. To some extent, their liberality may be attributable to the lead which the private banks were given by the Bank of England. It is scarcely surprising that, as long as rediscounting facilities were large, private bankers would be prepared to extend their credit. This applies equally to the total volume of discounts which they gave as to their willingness to accommodate individual traders. Closely related to this was the natural eagerness of private bankers to profit from discounting and from drawing accounts. Rowlandson stated that bankers usually retained a surplus of bills in excess of the amount which they had accepted for individual traders.[17] This policy was not always followed faithfully, however, as in the case of Lowndes and Bateson's account at Dawes, Noble and Co. and Richard Read's at Down, Thornton and Co.[18] In addition, many of the bills which bankers discounted or used as security for their acceptances in 1810 were extremely doubtful. The effect of their laxity was three-fold. First, like the Bank of England, private banks bore a large responsibility for the excessive trading of 1809 and early 1810. Second, considerable losses must have been sustained in 1810 by many of them, including Newnham, Everitt and Co., Marsh, Sibbald and Co., Kensington and Co., Masterman and Co. and Smith, Payne, Smith and Co. Finally, it is understandable that liquidity panics, of the type which ruined Brickwood and Co. and Dawes and Co., should be

---

17 P.R.O. B3/1482, 12 March 1812.

18 In July 1810, Read was overdrawn by £1,200. P.R.O. B3/4180, 7 Nov. 1811, Peter Free.

set off by rumours about the banks' stability and that, during crisis periods, even those with the soundest of reputations, like Down, Thornton and Co., could be threatened.

The experiences of Brickwood and Co. and of the other banks cited above reveal the basic fact of life for bankers in the early nineteenth century. As long as public confidence could be maintained by projecting an appearance of stability, the banks were safe regardless of their structural weaknesses. This consideration was also uppermost in the minds of most country bankers because, as Pressnell points out, 'in a panic, practically no normal asset - quite apart from the mortgages and other assets not realised easily at the best of times - would fetch money.'[19] Normally, the public was well-satisfied with banks whose partners appeared to possess the attributes of local prestige, personal wealth, landed property or personal integrity. A veneer of respectability enabled many country banks to overcome their severe operational handicaps, which included the six-partner rule and the reluctance of the Bank of England to assist them during crises. To the problems raised by the awkward position of provincial banks in the money market were added those of note issues and local connections. As with London banks, their priorities are rather obvious: they should maintain a healthy cash reserve by moderate note issues and discounting, avoid investments which could not be liquidated rapidly, restrict long-term advances and involvement in local industry, and scrutinise all securities deposited by their customers. During the Napoleonic Wars, it is apparent that many country bankers were not cautious. Henry Burgess, their leading advocate, referred later to the 'really vicious times of Banking, previous to 1815' and, specifically, to 'the vicious

---

19 Pressnell, op. cit., p. 236. The following account is based on ibid., pp. 75-104, 213-4, 225-43, 284-309.

principles of indiscreet Bankers' in 1810.[20] The difficulty of refusing loans to well-known local clients and the absence, before railway stock was readily available, of a range of good liquid securities no doubt contributed to this. But, before 1815, advances were frequently made without any security at all, especially to farmers, and the practice of forcing issues was not uncommon.[21] Not all the country banks were badly run, but the acknowledged recklessness of some explains why frequent panics, like that in the West Country in 1810, forced even sound bankers into the Bankruptcy Court.

III

The second aspect of economic activity upon which the evidence reviewed earlier sheds some light is the nature of commercial operations in the early nineteenth century. The activities of individual firms during this period are not well-documented and hard commercial information, in the form of published accounts, is scarce. Although the bankruptcy files do not completely fill this gap, since they include balance sheets only occasionally, they do contain information which often facilitates the construction of a reasonably clear picture of a firm's trading activities. This includes the testimony of witnesses to the bankrupt's trading and of the bankrupt to the Lord Chancellor, the dividend warrants, which indicate total liabilities, and the claims made against the estate. The evidence pertains especially to marketing procedures and the structure of commercial firms.

The general impression which emerges is that marketing techniques were by no means specialised in the early

---

20 H. Burgess, A Letter to the Right Hon. George Canning (1826), pp. 40, 51.

21 Pressnell, op. cit., pp. 213, 303.

nineteenth century, particularly in overseas trade.[22] This applies not only to the fact that many of the merchants who have been studied indulged in both exporting and importing but also to the scope of their activities, which often encompassed a wide range of foreign markets and goods. Although exports were dominated by cotton, some merchants, like Parkin and Scobell, shipped a variety of manufactures. That many sold their goods in a multiplicity of markets, on two or even three continents, is indicated by the transactions of Goodair, Jones, Laycock, Parkin and Scobell, Rowlandson, Vos and Essers and Wilson and Williams. Return cargoes from these regions seem to have been diverse, importers concentrating more upon the general produce of a market or markets than on one particular commodity.

Domestic marketing procedures have been described at length elsewhere.[23] On the supply side, raw materials were usually sold by importers, acting either on their own account or as commission agents for planters and foreign exporters, to dealers who resold them to manufacturers by auction or private contract. Larger manufacturers, however, were turning away from dealers and using brokers instead, in order to by-pass the middleman and to obtain access to a wider variety of goods. Although the early history of brokerage is far from clear, it seems that, by 1800, it was playing a significant role in the supply of raw cotton. It is conceivable, as Edwards suggests, that the functions of brokers became specialised earlier in Lancashire than

---

22 For further evidence of non-specialisation, derived from statements made to parliamentary committees, see N.S. Buck, The Development of the Organisation of Anglo-American Trade, 1800-1850 (New Haven, Conn., 1925), pp. 10-11, 39.

23 See *ibid.*, pp. 31-49; M.M. Edwards, The Growth of the British Cotton Trade, 1780-1815 (Manchester, 1967), pp. 111-3, 119-22.

elsewhere.[24] Certainly, the activities of Coles and Sons, one of the largest West India houses, suggest that brokerage was less well-defined in London, for two reasons. First, Coles dealt in a variety of imported goods. Second, while it may be true that, in Liverpool, 'the opinion was developing that a broker's business depended for its success on the avoidance of personal speculation,'[25] Coles's Spanish dealings were not only large but also supported by a reputable London bank.

The marketing of manufactured goods seems to have been in a similar transitional state in 1810.[26] In the cotton trade, internal distribution was still largely dependent upon the use of fairs, local warehouse sales and salesmen travelling around the countryside. From the 1780s, however, the picture had been changing, as marketing was concentrated increasingly upon warehouse sales in Manchester, where easier access was possible to the London market. A variety of techniques was used for distributing goods in the capital. Some of the larger manufacturers, like Lancelot Bracken and Tipping and Fleming, were in partnership or agreement with London merchants. Some used commission agents who advised them of current market demand. In addition, for both London and other areas, the 'Manchester merchant' group was growing, possessed of sufficient capital 'to purchase grey cloth from the manufacturers, to pay for it to be bleached and finished in Manchester and then to resell it in the home retail market.'[27] Probably

---

24 Edwards, <u>op. cit</u>., p. 118.

25 F.E. Hyde, B.B. Parkinson and S. Marriner, 'The Cotton Broker and the Rise of the Liverpool Cotton Market,' <u>Ec. H.R</u>., s. 2, viii (1955-6), 77-8.

26 See Edwards, <u>op. cit</u>., pp. 147-81; R. Smith, 'Manchester as a Centre for the Manufacture and Marketing of Cotton Goods,' <u>U.B.H.J</u>., iv (1953-4), 47-65.

27 Smith, <u>op. cit</u>., p. 61.

the most important channel for the distribution of manufactured goods, however, was the group of London warehousemen who sold to London and provincial retailers. These wholesalers influenced greatly the kind of goods which were produced since they were aware of the state of the market. The criticisms, a quarter-century earlier, by S.W. Salte, a London warehouseman, when Samuel Oldknow's produce was not of sufficient quality reveals how important it was for the warehouseman

> to keep in constant and sensitive touch with the fluctuating demand of fashionable consumers on the one hand and with the technical resources and business capacity of an ever-changing body of manufacturers on the other. They had to be prepared to offer credit both to manufacturers and retailers and the extent to which this could be extended in any one case constituted perhaps the main problem of the business.[28]

This was a relatively new market function at the start of the nineteenth century and the delicate, specialized nature of warehousing business was realised very slowly. Some warehousemen, like Winstanley and Hudson, appear to have concentrated upon cotton alone. Others, however, distributed a wide variety of goods. Bull, Banks and Bryson, for example, dealt in cotton, muslin, woollen, hosiery and other goods, Duckham and Lankester in linen, cotton, muslin and calicoes and Richard Jones in both cotton and wool.

Overseas distribution was equally diversified. Some manufacturers evidently sold their own cloth abroad although the trend was towards a separation of the manufacturing and marketing functions.[29] Exporters derived their goods from a variety of sources. Some, like Jacob Bros., were in direct communication with the manufacturers (Hodson and Quarrell and Longsdon). Others, like Vos and Essers, bought goods

---

28 G. Unwin, Samuel Oldknow and the Arkwrights (Manchester, 1924), p. 56.

29 Edwards, *op. cit.*, pp. 178-9.

from middlemen (Goodair and Rowlandson). Others used two or three methods. Francis Fisher, for example, bought from manufacturers in Scotland and Lancashire (MacFie and Pierrepoint Greaves), a Manchester merchant (Hugh Greaves) and London warehousemen (Haigh and Lawson). It seems likely, however, that most exporters received goods from warehousemen, who were rapidly becoming the linchpin in the marketing chain between manufacturers and both domestic retailers and overseas merchants. Their operations could be extremely complex, a fact recognised by William Brien, who acknowledged Samuel Rowlandson's expertise as a warehouseman concentrating on the domestic market but forecast that his reckless ventures in the export trade would prove fatal. Nevertheless, many entrepreneurs were only too eager to follow Rowlandson's example. John Goodair similarly ruined his warehousing business by foreign speculations, as did Thomas Laycock and Bull, Banks and Bryson, while Richard Jones virtually abandoned warehousing altogether in favour of the richer profits of South American trade.

The instability of the economic system was increased by the frailty of many business concerns. As noted in chapter six, William Huskisson and the directors of the Bank of England commented upon the mushrooming of new commercial partnerships during the boom years which preceded the crisis, implying that the mortality rate of young houses was abnormally high. The best specific example is Bull, Banks and Bryson, who had been trading for only ten months prior to their stoppage. Rowlandson, Isaac and Brien had been operating for less than two years before they failed and both Bracken, Williams and Co. and Richard Jones for less than three. Some of these firms were able to generate extremely large-scale trading in spite of their small, initial capital. Richard Jones, for instance, started with nothing at the age of twenty-four and incurred debts of more than £70,000 within two years. Samuel Rowlandson sustained liabilities of more than £500,000 after starting with less than £25,000. This phenomenon, which was widely criticised, is probably attributable to a combination of commercial, legal and financial factors. The basic, commercial explanation lies in the large profits offered by overseas trade, which encouraged established houses to extend their activities and led to the creation of new partnerships. The appalling risks which characterised much of the trading reflect the wave of optimism produced by high prices and profit margins. It also probably reflects the cynicism of many traders towards the prospect of failure. This was suggested both by Brien's explanation of Rowlandson's carelessness and by the observation of a trader, at the height of the crisis, that 'Bankruptcy is nothing more than a new method of paying off old debts and living cheap in these hard times.'[30] Finally, the extent of the trading reflects the ease with which commercial operations were financed. A marked contrast is apparent between the long-term expectations and large fixed capital requirements of Harrison and Co.'s mining operations and the rapid profits of mercantile houses whose capital, tied to commodities with a relatively quick turnover, was far more liquid. For the latter, the bill of exchange was the perfect financial instrument since it allowed the buyer to resell the goods before he was obliged to pay for them. The evidence of our investigation indicates the vital part played in trade and in the proliferation of bankruptcy of bills drawn on London bankers, merchants and warehousemen. The importance of the London bill is explained by a number of factors. First, and rather obvious, the size and reputation of most London private banks ensured that their acceptances were the most coveted of all. Bills accepted by Brickwood and Co. were negotiated and discounted without difficulty throughout the country. Second, London was the

---

30 The Tradesman, vi, 9, 1 Dec. 1810, letter to the editor from 'Cursitor.'

largest market and the distribution centre for textiles. Although its marketing pre-eminence was declining at the start of the nineteenth century, the fact that London merchants and warehousemen probably had more capital than their Manchester counterparts ensured that their acceptances retained their popularity. It is difficult to estimate how far 'Manchester merchants' were independent and how far they were merely agents of London houses.[31] Third, the Bank of England discounted only bills drawn on London houses, refusing those merely payable in London. This, according to Thomas Joplin, rendered non-negotiable half of country bills during crisis periods.[32] In effect, it meant that larger firms, which had extensive dealings in the metropolis, could obtain discounts even in periods of tight credit, while smaller ones were forced either to stop payments or to use dubious paper.

While the bill was in some respects the ideal means of financing commerce, it also facilitated overtrading both because there were no limits to the volume of paper which a trader could manufacture and because the banking fraternity was loathe to restrict discounting until absolutely necessary. Bill finance could easily be abused. Contemporaries uniformly criticised the widespread use of accommodation paper to raise capital for speculative purposes. The process is described in the following explanation of the crisis, in November 1810 (possibly by Jeremy Bentham):

> It is an indisputable fact, that the numerous bankruptcies which lately occurred in the mercantile world have been in a principal degree, occasioned by unwarrantable speculations carried on by fictitious credit and the discount of accommodation bills to an immense amount. With this view, those speculatists form a variety of real or fictitious co-partnerships or both - one individual or more having different houses,

---

31 Edwards, <u>op. cit</u>., pp. 178-80.

32 T. Joplin, An Examination of the Report of the Joint Stock Bank Committee (1837), p. 114.

> under different firms, in different parts of the city or the Kingdom. One firm draws on another bills of exchange, which are perhaps indorsed by a third, all, in fact, the same concern; and thus the public are deluded into a belief that they have the ample security of three respectable houses . . . and among the late failures it would be easy to give some strong instances illustrative of these facts, as well as the difficulty of ascertaining the actual partners in the different firms.33

It is impossible to gauge the extent to which fictitious bills were used between 1808 and 1810. As this quotation suggests, some traders probably employed them to finance business activity throughout the boom period. Logically, however, accommodation paper would flourish during periods when trade was becoming difficult and remittances and profits were declining. The evidence of such bills in the preceding chapters relates, on the whole, to the first half of 1810, when many firms were suffering because of saturated overseas markets and declining domestic prices. Accommodation arrangements, designed to enable firms to continue trading during a period of temporary difficulty, took various forms. The bills drawn by Samuel Rowlandson on Rowlandson and Bates seem similar to those described above, as do those drawn by Samuel Cooke on Harrison and Co. Generally, a firm accommodated one of its clients by accepting bills which could either be discounted or used for trading purposes. Examples of such acceptances are those of Bracken, Williams and Co. and Haywood for Laycock and those of Jacob Bros. for Richard Jones. Some firms opened mutual accommodation accounts like that between Bull, Banks and Bryson and Richard Read. The extent of the mutual bill dealings between many of the firms examined - the complex of firms which dealt with Jacob Bros. is the best example - suggests that accommodation paper was rife during the first half of 1810.

---

33 The Tradesman, iv, 421, 1 Nov. 1810, letter to the editor from 'J.B.,' who stated that he was not a merchant.

IV

How far does our evidence confirm or modify Tooke's estimates of the average size and usance of bills during the second quarter of the nineteenth century? It will be recalled that he divided bills into three categories, the third of which involved large transactions between merchants, warehousemen and manufacturers. These bills were drawn, on average, for £1,055. 18. 0d. at 4.20 months. The dealings of the leading bankrupts in 1810 facilitate similar conclusions about the use of negotiable instruments in the first decade of the century. Of course, conclusions drawn from such limited evidence may be unrepresentative not only because the samples are small but also because they relate to the acceptances of firms which subsequently failed. In addition, much of the paper was negotiated during the second quarter of 1810 when market conditions were deteriorating rapidly. Nevertheless, the paucity of other information about the use of negotiable instruments during the industrial revolution makes the following analyses, at least, a starting point for further investigation. The discussion examines in turn the available evidence of the employment of bills of exchange, promissory notes and cheques.

It has been argued that the most serious consequences of Brickwood and Co.'s stoppage were produced by the large number of bills which it accepted for clients holding cash balances at the bank. A distinction is apparent between the bills drawn by Bowles and Co. and those by commercial houses. The arrangement of the former appears typical of country banks which, as Burgess stated in 1829, generally drew bills on their London agents at two months.[34] As Table 10.1 shows, Bowles and Co.'s bills for more than £500 were

34 H. Burgess, Petition to the House of Commons . . . respecting Currency and Bankers (1829), p. 35.

uniformly drawn at two months and those for less at one or two months. Ninety-five per cent of all the bills were drawn at two months or less. Bills drawn by commercial houses were generally much larger than those of Bowles and Co. Unfortunately, the files do not provide a clear picture of the type of security which the bank demanded from its drawers. The arrangement with Bracken, Williams and Co., by which the drawers agreed to leave a surplus balance at the bank at all times, is possibly typical. At the time of Brickwood and Co.'s failure, that security consisted of a small mortgage, a cash balance and bills entered short (i.e. bills which were not credited to the account until maturity). The deposit of undue bills frequently caused difficulties when London banks failed. Generally the latter entered such bills short, carrying their value to the customer's account on maturity, in contrast to country banks, which usually entered them as cash.[35] Bankers were under no legal obligation to retain bills until they matured. Indeed, although the banking fraternity generally frowned on the practice,[36] Brickwood and Co. rediscounted many of the bills presented to it at the Bank of England. This was important because, after the bank's failure, the remitters of rediscounted bills could claim only as general creditors of the estate, not for the full amount of the bills. The legal interpretation was that all bills could be rediscounted except in special circumstances: for example, when the banker acted as an agent, receiving commission for holding the client's bills until maturity; where the banker acted as trustee for his customer's bills; where the bills were designed to balance the customer's cash account (by

---

35 J.K. Horsefield, 'British Banking Practices, 1750-1850: Some Legal Sidelights,' Economica, s.2, xix (1952), 316.

36 Pressnell, op. cit., p. 99.

agreement with the bank).[37] Basically, when the correspondent expressly declared that the undue bills were to remain his own property and when, in his transactions, he occasionally permitted the bank to rediscount bills, the bank could not dispose of bills of its own volition and their value was not credited to the customer's account until they were cashed on maturity. If, after the bank failed, the customer was able to pay the bills which it had accepted for him, the short bills were returned. If, however, the customer also failed, as in the case of Bracken, Williams and Co., his assignees were allowed to receive only the surplus proceeds of the short bills, if any, after his bills drawn on the bank were paid. The reason for this was the fact that short bills were deposited specifically as security to the bank that its acceptances would be honoured.[38] In periods of depression, there could be no guarantee that the short bills would produce their face value. Hence, as in the cases of Bracken and Co. and Lowndes and Bateson, the banks refused to return them when they stopped payment.

It seems likely that the acceptances of Brickwood and Co. for individual clients were balanced by the deposit of cash and short bills. The analysis in Table 10.2 of the bank's acceptances which were circulating when it stopped payments demonstrates the mercantile character of its clientele. More than three-quarters of the bills in value were drawn by merchants, most of whom operated in London, and thirteen per cent by London warehousemen. In contrast to those accepted for Bowles and Co. and for manufacturers, most of the bills were for large amounts. Ninety-two per cent were for more than £500 and fifty-eight per cent for more than £1,000, the over-all average amounting to £1,631.

---

37 This account is based on Ex parte Pease (1812) 1 Rose 232.

38 Ex parte Waring (1814) 2 Rose 182, 186.

In addition, the table indicates that almost all Brickwood and Co.'s acceptances were short-dated, the majority being drawn at three months, although those for manufacturers (mainly Lancelot Bracken) were drawn at two months. Examination of the files of other London bankers suggests that the short-dated acceptances of Brickwood and Co. were fairly typical. Table 10.3 indicates that those of Dawes and Co. for Wilson and Williams, Lowndes and Bateson and Moulson and Fawcett were all drawn at three months or less (averaging £1,605). Similarly, all the acceptances of Dorsett, Johnson and Co. of New Bond Street, bankrupt in 1803, were drawn at three months or less, as were those of Mingay and Co. of Smithfield (1810) and Kensington and Co., the Lombard Street bank which failed in 1812.[39]

Although some banks were in the habit of accepting their clients' bills, it is difficult to estimate how far the practice was typical of the London banking fraternity in general. The majority of bills claimed against bankrupts in 1810 were drawn by one commercial house on another. It was suggested earlier that the functions of such houses frequently overlapped. Nevertheless, an aggregative analysis of their bills reveals distinct contrasts between the credit facilities used and demanded by merchants, warehousemen and manufacturers.

The marked feature of the mercantile acceptances analysed in Table 10.4 is the large number drawn by other merchants. There are three possible explanations of this. First, some exporters were in close contact with manufacturers, by-passing the middleman. When selling goods to other exporters, therefore, they acted in the same capacity as warehousemen. Second, many of the bills may represent transferences of colonial goods from one merchant to another for the purposes of re-export. The third

---

39 P.R.O. B3/1268-75 (Dorsett, Johnson and Co.); B3/2820-8 (Kensington and Co.); B3/3223-4 (Mingay and Co.).

explanation is closely related to the difficult trading conditions of 1810. It was noted that the Special Discount Committee of the Bank of England in 1810 was aware of the large volume of paper in circulation drawn by one overseas merchant on another and that the Bank actually discounted such bills (e.g. those between Richard Jones and Jacob Bros.). The bills were designed to allow overseas merchants to withhold stock from the market until its price rose. It is possible that, as prices dropped during the first half of 1810, their volume increased and that many of the bills drawn by merchants in the table were of this variety.

The second outstanding feature of the mercantile acceptances in Table 10.4 is the contrast between the usance of bills drawn by merchants and by the other categories. 26 per cent of bills drawn by merchants were dated at twelve months or more, compared with only 7 per cent of those drawn by both warehousemen and manufacturers. The contrast is possibly a product of the fact that individual trades were accustomed to demanding bills of different tenor. Merchants would naturally use longer credit than the other two categories since the time lag in overseas trade between their initial financial outlay and receipts was frequently long.[40] Manufacturers and, consequently, the warehousemen upon whom they generally drew their bills, on the other hand, favoured shorter-dated bills. It has been suggested that the long credit necessary in overseas trade was the most important reason why manufacturers relinquished their marketing functions.[41] Nevertheless, it is evident that those manufacturers who sold directly to merchants were frequently obliged to receive relatively long-dated bills.

---

40 In the American market, for example, goods were usually sold at more than twelve months. See Buck, op. cit., p. 114.

41 Edwards, op. cit., pp. 178-9.

More than one-quarter of their drawings on merchants were at nine months or more.

It is interesting that, of the 123 bills drawn at twelve months or more in Table 10.4, only eight were negotiated after March 1810. Indeed, only seventeen bills drawn after March were at more than six months. This suggests that, although discounts were not difficult to obtain in the first half of 1810, merchants were not optimistic about future prospects. As noted above, the commercial sector suffered earliest in 1810, and it is possible that, as early as April, the saturation of both English and European markets was deflating mercantile profits. Hence, as in most periods when a tight money market was either operative or anticipated, only bills at short date would circulate freely, since no merchants or banks wished to lock up their capital in long-dated bills at a time when their own debtors might be unable to honour their liabilities. This may explain the peculiar fact that almost all the bills which have definitely been identified as accommodation paper were drawn at under four months.

The second type of commercial acceptances, analysed in Table 10.5, are those of warehousemen. There are two major differences between the acceptances of merchants and warehousemen. First, as might be expected, manufacturers drew a larger proportion of bills on warehousemen. Whereas they drew 77 bills (12 per cent) worth £60,091 (9 per cent) of the bills on merchants, they drew 371 (47 per cent) worth £206,537 (33 per cent) of those on warehousemen. The implication of this is that the warehousemen in the sample were in closer touch with manufacturers than were the merchants. In addition to their purchases from manufacturers, warehousemen seem to have bought from importers goods which they distributed to domestic retailers. Their acceptances for merchants in the table, no doubt, represent such transactions. The third series of acceptances - those drawn by other warehousemen - are probably explained in the same ways as mercantile drawings on other merchants. Again, the Bank of England's Special Discount Committee noted the widespread practice, during difficult periods, of wholesalers accommodating each other. Although it is impossible to calculate the extent of such bills, their obvious efficacy suggests that they became widespread when prices fell sharply in 1810. It is also interesting to note that bills drawn by manufacturers were usually for smaller amounts than those drawn by the other two categories. Bills drawn by merchants and warehousemen average £996 and £1,066 respectively, while those drawn by manufacturers average £557. This contrast, which parallels a similar pattern in bills drawn by manufacturers on merchants, suggests both that warehousemen and merchants bought their goods from a variety of manufacturers in relatively small quantities and that manufacturers required bills of smaller denomination to make their own payments. Thus, 28 per cent of warehousemen's acceptances for manufacturers were for under £100 compared with only 3 per cent and 9 per cent of those for merchants and warehousemen respectively. The second major contrast between the acceptances of merchants and warehousemen is the fact that the latter were drawn, on average, at much shorter date. Thirty per cent of merchants' acceptances were drawn at nine months or more compared with 6.5 per cent of warehousemens'. In neither case is there any obvious correlation between the usance and size of the bills. The contrast, as suggested above, is probably explained by the differing nature of their respective market functions. When paying for goods, whether imported or domestically manufactured, warehousemen seem to have paid with relatively short-dated bills. Certainly, the marked preponderance of short-dated acceptances for manufacturers (76.5 per cent at under four months and 92 per cent at six months or less) indicates, again, their aversion to long credit.

The evidence of bills accepted by brokers and manufacturers is much slighter than that of the other two categories. The dealings of Coles and Co. provide some clues to the nature of brokers' bills. It was noted that Coles bought West India produce from Vos and Essers and other merchants by accepting their bills. These are analysed in Table 10.6. The significant feature in Coles's acceptances is their size, which averaged £2,126. 93 per cent were drawn for more than £1,000 and more than half for over £2,000, suggesting that he bought foreign produce for internal distribution in large quantities. It is interesting that none of the bills drawn at eight or twelve months were negotiated after March 1810. Almost certainly, Vos and Essers, who drew most of them, realised that the usual markets were either closing or becoming saturated and, consequently, they refused bills at long date. Their change in outlook is emphasized by the fact that all the bills at twelve months were drawn in the first quarter of 1810, indicating that they were then optimistic about future prospects. In the light of this evidence it is possible that Coles and Co.'s speculation in Spanish wool was a futile and dramatic attempt to restore solvency.

Bills accepted by manufacturers are relatively infrequent in the records of leading bankruptcies in 1810. Their paucity is, no doubt, exaggerated by the fact that none of the files of manufacturers' commissions have survived. Information can thus be elicited only from the records of other bankrupts. The manufacturing acceptances which have been detected are shown below:

Date	Drawers	Acceptors	Amount (£)	Usance (Months)	Indorsees
(1810)					
26 Jan.	G.Hudson	J.Hodson	852	6	Lloyd, Tabor, Jones (Lothbury, banker)
27 Mar.	Hodson, Quarrell	J. Hodson	1,298	4	Jacob Bros.; Merle & Co. (City, banker)
30 May	"	J. Hodson	2,498	3	V. Stuckey (Sloane St., broker)
28 Feb.	Moulson, Fawcett	B. Aspinall	1,941	6	E., T. Ward; J. Beck (Carlisle, banker)
28 Feb.	"	"	1,265	3	"
24 Dec.	Rowlandson, Bates	Williams, Burford	3,625	12	Moulson Fawcett (Manchester, manufacturer)
10 Jul.	"	Anderton Lightollers	469	6	Sanderson, Dinsdale (Old Broad St., merchant)
(1810)					
10 Jul.	"	"	469	6	"
10 Jul.	"	"	469	6	"
10 Jul.	"	"	469	6	"
1 Sept.	Duckham, Lankester	G. Berry	1,000	5	T. Prescott (Wigan, linen manufacturer)
1 Sept.	"	W. Platt	340	4	Fry & Co. (City, banker)
1 Sept.	"	"	340	2	"
1 Sept.	"	"	320	6	"
4 Sept.	"	G. Berry	1,000	9	"
4 Sept.	"	"	1,000	12	"
4 Sept.	"	"	1,000	15	"

Sources: P.R.O. B3/2677, 4 Dec. 1810; B3/5174, 17 Nov. 1810; B3/1880, 16 Feb. 1816; B3/4881, 22 May 1813; B3/1305, 19 Jan. 1811.

The contrast between the scarcity of bills drawn on manufacturers and the large number which they drew on both merchants and warehousmen is not surprising. The superior negotiability of bills on London houses has been noted as has the fact that most large commercial payments, especially in Lancashire, were made by bills on London. Nevertheless, the bills cited above indicate that manufacturers' acceptances were occasionally used by London concerns and by provincial manufacturers and that they could be discounted at London banks. This applies both to the accommodation bills given by Hodson and Quarrell to Jacob Bros. and to the long-dated paper drawn by Duckham and Lankester after the crisis had broken. The evidence, however, is too narrow to justify any major conclusions about either the size or usance of manufacturers' bills.

So far, we have examined the size and usance of the acceptances of firms which failed in the 1810 crisis. Comparison of these bills and those analysed by Tooke in the middle of the nineteenth century reveals significant differences. The size of the bills used by merchants, warehousemen and manufacturers was smaller in 1810, averaging £870 compared with Tooke's £1,056. This, no doubt, is explained by the increase in the first half of the century of the size and scale of operations of manufacturing and commercial houses. Also, the average usance of Tooke's bills (4.20 months) was smaller than those in our sample, whose average of 4.89 months is probably lower than one might expect in non-crisis years (as noted already).

In addition, the evidence facilitates some tentative conclusions about the velocity of circulation of the bills. It is well-known that, in Lancashire, small bills performed the function of bank notes, frequently passing through many hands before their dates of maturity.[42] Larger bills do not seem to have circulated so widely. Table 10.7 analyses the number of transactions performed by bills drawn respectively on the merchants, warehousemen and banks in our sample. It shows that 43 per cent of bills drawn on merchants and 28 per cent on warehousemen were used simply as security for a debt incurred by one transaction, the drawer anticipating payment of the bill on maturity:

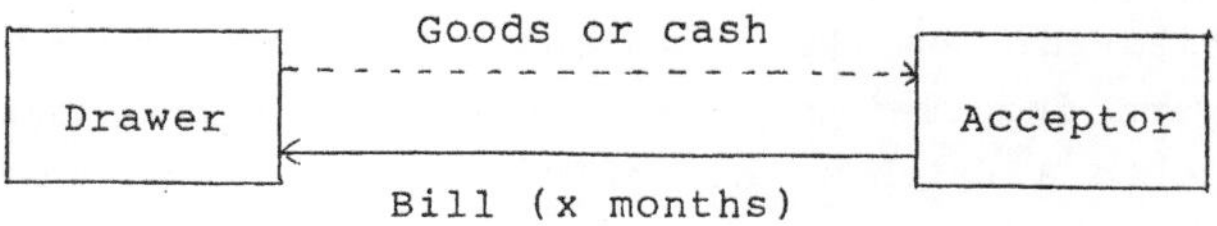

Although the majority of the acceptances of merchants and warehousemen served more than one transaction, only 15 per cent and 21 per cent respectively passed through the hands of three traders and 4 per cent of each through more than four. Those which were used for three transactions were successively transferred by drawers and payees:

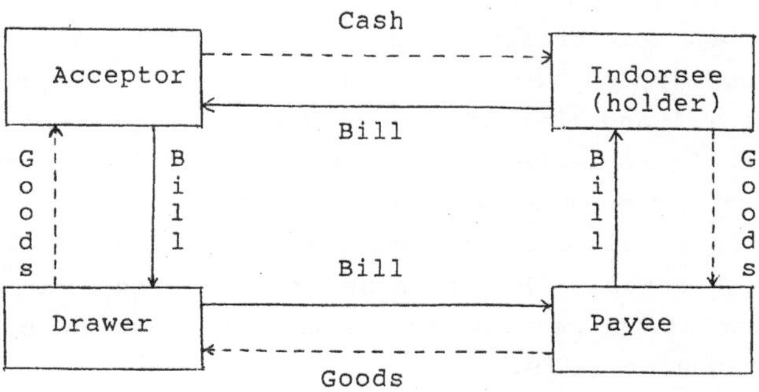

In this model, one bill is used to pay for three transactions before the holder (Indorsee) claims payment from the acceptor on maturity. The majority of bills on

42 See T.S. Ashton, 'The Bill of Exchange and Private Banks in Lancashire, 1790-1830,' in Papers in English Monetary History (ed. T.S. Ashton and R.S. Sayers), (Oxford, 1953), p. 38.

merchants and warehousemen, however, were not indorsed by the payee, the average number of transactions served by merchants' bills amounting to 1.7 and by warehousemens' to 2.0.

In contrast, the average number of transactions of bills accepted by banks was 2.7; only 9 per cent of them were not transferred by their drawers to third parties. This is to be expected since the majority of clients only drew on their deposits in order to pay for transactions with other traders. As the table shows, 53 per cent of bankers' bills were indorsed by the payees to a fourth party and 4 per cent to a fifth. The maximum number of transactions by one bank-acceptance was ten.

It is likely that the velocities which have been described above are a little lower than those of normal bills in the early nineteenth century, because they refer to the bills of firms which failed before their acceptances had matured. However, a comparison of the velocity of the bills with the time for which they had been circulating shows that the picture is not totally unrepresentative. For example, the average of transactions per bill of all mercantile acceptances which had been circulating for nine months or more was 2.1 and that of warehousemen 2.0. In addition, 87 per cent of the bank-acceptances which had been circulating for more than two months had served three or less transactions and none had served more than five. A similar comparison reveals that in none of the categories is there any correlation between the size and average number of transactions of bills.

The general conclusion, therefore, is that commercial bills circulated relatively slowly and that very few served the minimum seven transactions which Newmarch envisaged in the 1840s.[43] The probable reason for this is that the bill

---

43 Cited by R. Cameron, Banking in the Early Stages of Industrialization (Oxford, 1967), p. 51, fn. 58.

was essentially an intractable instrument of payment. Once drawn for a specific amount it could only serve future transactions of similar value. Although, as Ashton points out, this difficulty could be overcome by the practice of crediting the surplus value of a bill to the indorser's account,[44] many creditors of bankrupts in 1810 preferred to draw new bills on their debtors. This is understandable since the financial requirements of different economic sectors contrasted with those of others. The large, long-dated bills which were often used in mercantile transactions, for example, were not always appropriate to the needs of manufacturers, whose drawings were both smaller and shorter-dated. When Anderton and Lightollers wished to pay Ainsworth, Bentley and Co., bleachers in Bolton, 'for work and labour done,' they used short-dated small bills drawn on their warehouseman, John Goodair:

Date (1810)	Drawer	Acceptor	Amount (£)	Usance (Months)	Indorsee
21 April	Anderton & Co.	J. Goodair	300	3	Ainsworth, Bentley.
15 May	"	"	500	3	"
20 May	"	"	200	3	"
26 May	"	"	200	3	"
2 June	"	"	328	3	"

Source: P.R.O. B3/1881, 22 May 1813.

Similarly, Anderton and Co. paid bills on Goodair for the precise value of raw materials supplied to them. Mather, Hampson and Lomax, Manchester merchants, claimed the following bills against Goodair which they had received 'in payment of £1,086. 16. 0d. then due from William Anderton

44 T.S. Ashton, An Eighteenth Century Industrialist. Peter Stubs of Warrington (Manchester, 1939), p. 105.

and Robert Lightollers for wares and merchandizes sold and delivered:'

Date(1810)	Drawer	Acceptor	Amount	Usance (Months)	Indorsee
29 May	Anderton	J. Goodair	£813.14.0d.	6	Hampson, Mather, Lomax
19 June	"	"	273. 2.0d.	6	"

Source: P.R.O. B3/1881, 22nd May 1813.

Many similar examples could be cited of bills drawn for specific purposes. It seems clear that their inflexibility explains the comparatively low velocity of commercial bills. Also, it is likely that their circulation was retarded by the fact that the interest which accrued with age made it worthwhile to retain bills rather than pass them on.

In the circumstances, it is not surprising that some of the bills which have been examined served the same purpose as promissory notes. As Thornton pointed out, a promissory note and an accepted bill were really the same thing[45] and the Bank of England appears to have considered bills which bore only two names (drawer and acceptor) to be promissory notes. The notes claimed against the leading bankrupts in 1810, analysed in Table 10.8, differ little in both size and usance from the commercial bills previously examined. The major contrast between the two lies in the fact that very few of the notes were used for any purpose other than to secure the original debt. Eight of the ninety-two notes performed two transactions, four served three and one served four. The remaining seventy-nine (86 per cent) were not paid to a third party.

Like promissory notes, cheques were not used widely by the 1810 bankrupts. McCulloch maintained that they 'nearly

45 H. Thornton, An Inquiry into the Nature and Effects of Paper Credit in Great Britain (ed. F.A. Hayek), (1939), p. 83.

resemble Bills of Exchange, except that they are uniformly payable to bearer and should be drawn on a regular bank.'[46] The following cheques were claimed against Thomas Laycock, Francis Fisher, Duckham and Lankester and Jacob Bros.:

Date	Drawer	Bank	Amount (£)	Claimant
23 Dec. 1809	T. Laycock	Anderson, Wilson & Co.	500. 0. 0	Leach, Rawson, Saltmarsh & Co. (Corbett Court Warehousemen)
6 Feb. 1810	"	"	800. 0. 0	"
2 Apr. 1810	"	"	1,000. 0. 0	"
5 June 1810	"	"	300. 2. 0	"
17 Apr. 1810	"	"	200. 0. 0	J. Varley (Houndsditch, slopseller
26 Apr. 1810	"	"	100. 0. 0	"
11 May 1810	"	"	222. 0. 0	"
14 June 1810	"	"	79.12. 6	"
14 July 1810	F. Fisher	Masterman & Co.	159.18. 1	A. Hodgson (Wapping, wine merchants)
10 Sept.1810	Duckham, Lankester	Masterman & Co.	300. 0. 0	F. Fearne (Angel Court, insurance broker)
29 June 1810	Jacob Bros.	Newnham, Everitt & Co.	7,000. 0. 0	Cox, Merle & Co. (The City, Banker)

Sources: P.R.O. B3/2929, 13 Nov. 1810, 15 Dec. 1810; B3/1879, 14 July 1810; B3/1305, 28 Nov. 1812; B3/2677, 27 Oct. 1810; B3/1874, 26 Oct. 1810.

---

46 J.R. McCulloch, Dictionary of Commerce and Commercial Navigation (1832), p. 254.

As this shows, some London banks were in the habit of granting chequing facilities and large commercial transactions were occasionally effected by this method. This is corroborated by the files of Mingay and Co., the Smithfield bank and wine merchant, whose unpaid cheques on Smith, Payne and Smith amounted to £9,455. 8. 0d. at the time of their bankruptcy in 1810.[47] The evidence is too slight, however, to suggest that the cheque was yet encroaching on the dominance of the bill as a means of payment. It is evident that, although the concept of deposit banking was well-established and, if Brickwood and Dawes are typical, widely practised, the predominant method of drawing on deposit accounts was still by bill.

V

It must be stressed again that this study has focused upon one particular crisis period and many of the conclusions are tentative. It is incontrovertible, however, that, as early as 1810, the bill of exchange had assumed the central importance in commercial payments which Tooke assigned to it thirty years later when describing his ladder of payments.[48] The crisis of 1810 showed the dangers involved in the bill mechanism for individual traders in particular and for the economy as a whole. On the one hand, the contagious nature of bankruptcy was causally connected to the financial dependence which the bill created. Presumably, the house of cards effect operated just as smoothly during periods of economic stability as in crises. It would be instructive to trace the course of bankruptcy proliferation over four or five years in order to understand its full ramifications upon bankruptcy levels. On the other hand, if such a credit system was left unbridled, as it was during the first decade of the nineteenth century, an

47 P.R.O. B3/3223, 8 Sept. 1810.

48 T. Tooke and W. Newmarch, A History of Prices (1857), vi, 635. Tooke's description was written in 1844.

expanding economy would be liable to extremely severe bouts of overtrading. Indeed, it is likely that they were exacerbated both by the increased facilities provided by the growth of the discount market and by the continued failure of the banking authorities to appreciate the need for monetary management.[49] C. N. Ward-Perkins has shown, for example, that the joint-stock banks were committing blunders in the 1840s similar to those of the private banking partnerships in 1809-10.[50] In this context, it would be interesting to ascertain the effect upon business activity of the reforms, during the 1830s and 1840s, of the laws of partnership and bankruptcy.

It is arguable, however, that without a credit system which was so sensitive to real (rather than monetary) stimuli, economic growth in nineteenth-century England would have been retarded. The facility with which, in 1810, firms were floated and risks taken is symptomatic of the free rein which the credit structure gave to the full exploitation of market opportunities. In the long term, temporary set-backs were insignificant when set beside over-all growth and expansion. Thus, although the 'men of small capital' and adventurers lost heavily by speculative exporting to South America, they performed the useful function of introducing novel goods to an untapped market which, as Robert McKerrell pointed out in 1812, 'has had the effect . . . of altering the customs of the people, and introducing the wear of them.'[51] This line of argument can be pressed too far, but

---

49 For the development of English banking in the nineteenth century, see, for example, Ashton and Sayers, op. cit.; Sir J. Hicks, Critical Essays in Monetary Theory (Oxford, 1967), pp. 155-73.

50 C.N. Ward-Perkins, 'The Commercial Crisis of 1847,' in Essays in Economic History (ed. E.M. Carus-Wilson), (1962), iii, 270.

51 B.P.P. Minutes of Evidence taken before the Committee of the Whole House . . . relating to Orders in Council (1812), III, 525.

it does seem plausible to suggest that the credit mechanism provided an essential stimulus to enterprise and innovation in overseas markets and also, perhaps, in domestic trade and industry.

In view of their large contribution to economic activity during the industrial revolution, the use of negotiable instruments deserves closer attention than historians have accorded to it. The sample examined in this study suggests one or two lines of further inquiry. First, at what stage during trade cycles was accommodation paper likely to flourish? The evidence cited above indicates that the volume of fictitious paper tended to swell as trade became more difficult. Second, to what extent were the principal features of the bills in our sample typical of the early nineteenth century: viz., the low velocity and the contrasting bill usage of different sectors of the economy? Buck has suggested that the growth in profits of overseas trade after 1815 enabled the mercantile sector to use shorter credit.[52] This would explain the contrast between the average usance of bills in our sample and of those analysed by Tooke in the 1840s. It is also conceivable that, as a result of their diminishing usance, the velocity of bills increased. Clearly, this is significant since a large number of high velocity bills would add considerably to the circulating medium and might affect prices. Equally, it is plausible to suggest that the increased circulation of bills diminished the extent to which the 'house of cards' mechanism affected bankruptcy levels during crisis periods. It is beyond the scope of this work to do more than raise these questions. It may be suggested, however, that the files of bankruptcy commissions during subsequent crises provide a source of information to answer them.

---

52 Buck, op. cit., 131-2.

Appendix I The Problem of Bankruptcy Statistics

I

Table A.1 lists three series of statistics relating to the volume of business done by the Bankruptcy Court between 1795 and 1826. It shows that, on average, 1,773 dockets were struck each year, 1,548 commissions were sealed and 1,222 opened. Obviously, many creditors, having struck dockets against their debtors, failed to proceed any further. This practice was no doubt used frequently as a method of threatening the debtor in order to force him either to pay his debt or to enter into a composition. In many such cases, the initial docket was followed by a second or third, eventually leading to a commission, after negotiations had proved unsuccessful.[1] The second series - that of commissions sealed - provides the basis of official statistics issued by the court. Like the statistics of dockets, this is inflated since many of the commissions involved were not opened. Some were abandoned by the petitioning creditors because of technical defects. Others were annulled by the commissioners because the petitioning creditors failed to prove that the prerequisites of bankruptcy had been fulfilled (i.e. the £100 debt, the trading and the act of bankruptcy). The third series - that of commissions opened - has provided the basis of most calculations of bankruptcy statistics in secondary works. Despite the fact that most statisticians have used the London Gazette as their source, it is well-known that there are significant differences in the various series. The main cause of this lies in the repetition in the Gazette of many bankrupts because previous commissions had been either abandoned or superseded. The commonest reason for such

1 For repeated dockets struck against country banks, see L.S. Pressnell, Country Banking in the Industrial Revolution (Oxford, 1956), p. 74.

repetition was the difficulty involved in opening proceedings against partnerships, which were discussed in chapter one. In addition, however, many commissions which had been opened erroneously were superseded and not repeated. Because of insufficient attention to the problem of eliminating repeated and superseded commissions, most bankruptcy series calculated from the Gazette, including those of Silberling listed in Table A.1 (and used in Chapter 5), are probably slightly inflated, thus detracting from their value as precise measurements of bankruptcy levels. Nevertheless, they are a valid indication of general trends and, as Ashton points out, 'a substantial increase may be taken as evidence of a change of economic weather.'[2] Unfortunately, Ashton's own series, which Mitchell and Deane consider to be more reliable than most others,[3] ends in 1800. As the following table shows, however, although Ashton's totals are lower than those of Silberling (by about fifteen p.a.) the general movements of the two in the period 1786-1800 are comparable:

---

2 T.S. Ashton, Economic Fluctuations in England, 1700-1800 (Oxford, 1959), p. 114.

3 B.R. Mitchell and P. Deane, Abstract of British Historical Statistics (Cambridge, 1962), p. 246.

Annual Bankruptcies, 1786-1800

Year	Ashton	Silberling
1786	509	512
1787	487	506
1788	697	754
1789	560	586
1790	574	596
1791	603	615
1792	609	638
1793	1,256	1,377
1794	857	844
1795	731	690
1796	720	749
1797	905	871
1798	767	714
1799	512	546
1800	727	738
Totals	10,514	10,736

Sources: T.S. Ashton, An Economic History of England: The 18th Century (London, 1955), p. 254; N.J. Silberling, 'British Prices and Business cycles, 1779-1850,' Rev. Econ. Stats. (1923), Suppl. 2, 251.

The occasional contrasts in the movements of these two series are probably a product of the fact that Ashton takes 30 September as the end of each year while Silberling uses 31 December.

II

While the Gazette provides a reasonable guide to long-term movements (yearly or quarterly) in the level of bankruptcies, it is inadequate as a source of information about the dates of individual failures and, consequently, is an unreliable guide to short-term statistics (weekly or monthly). This is because of the delays which occurred between each stage of the bankruptcy process: the stoppage, the docket, the seal and the opening of the commission. As was shown in chapter eight, the delay between stoppage and docket could be lengthy. The usual reason for this was the legal necessity for the bankrupt to commit an act of bankruptcy. In some cases, also, after stopping payment, the bankrupt entered into negotiations with his creditors either to gain time or to arrange a composition. In others, creditors, ignorant of the stoppage, failed to visit the debtor's place of business until weeks after he had gone into hiding. It is impossible to gauge the average duration of such delays because of the destruction of most of the commissions files, the only source which records the dates of stoppage. Analysis of fifty bankruptcies between 1809 and 1811 shows that 32 dockets were struck within five days of stoppage, 37 within twenty days, 41 within a month and the remaining nine after more than a month. This suggests that, although the majority of bankruptcies were prosecuted within a week or two of stoppage, the delay in a minority of cases was considerable. Thus, in order to determine the precise dates of individual failures, it is desirable, where possible, to consult the commissions files. The second delay - between the docket and the seal - involved the short period of time required for the Lord Chancellor to expedite legal formalities. In all bankrupcies between April 1810 and July 1811, this took on average five days, although in some cases it took two or three weeks. Of the fifty cases cited above, 44 were sealed within ten days and the remaining six within three weeks. The third delay - between the seal and the opening of the commission - usually lasted three or four days, although again five of the fifty cases took between two and three weeks.

Because of the delays, the Gazette should be treated with caution when calculating short-period statistics. In the absence of precise dates of stoppage of many bankrupts, the most satisfactory picture of short-term movements is obtained by correlating entries in the Docket Books with those in the _Gazette_. This method, which was used in calculating Table 6.4, also enables one to determine more accurately the dates of failure of bankrupts against whom more than one commission was issued, especially those engaged in partnerships. Frequently, as was noted earlier, the final docket, leading to the _Gazette_ entry, followed a series of previous dockets or commissions which were abandoned or superseded on technical grounds (for example, because another docket had been struck against the joint estate rather than against an individual partner). When a series of dockets was struck in rapid succession against partners culminating in a joint commission, it is fairly safe to assume that the first docket approximates more closely to the stoppage than later ones. Even this method is not fool-proof; if all the relevant files had survived, exact dates of failure could be assigned and, in one or two cases, even the original docket bore little relation to the date of failure. Nevertheless, a combination of the Docket Books and the _Gazette_ provides a more accurate way of calculating short-period statistics than the _Gazette_ alone.

Appendix II Deeds of Arrangement

In addition to bankruptcy and insolvency, a number of methods were available during the industrial revolution, as they are today, by which a debtor and his creditors could draw up deeds of arrangement in order to circumvent public proceedings. The basic alternative method was the deed of composition, whereby the debtor agreed to pay his creditor or creditors a negotiated sum in satisfaction of his whole debts. After approval by the creditors' solicitors, the debtor executed the deed. If the deed stipulated that payment should be made by instalment or out of the debtor's future effects, a trustee was appointed, to whom control of the debtor's estate was granted by deed of assignment. A third variant was the deed of inspectorship, which granted continued control of the estate, until it was wound up, to the debtor under the supervision of inspectors chosen by the creditors.

In theory, these arrangements possessed considerable advantages since they allowed debts to be settled without the inefficiency and stigma which attached to bankruptcy proceedings. Also, they were flexible, enabling interested parties to adopt the mode of settlement which was most suited to the peculiar requirements of individual estates. In practice, however, they contained weaknesses which rendered them impracticable as substitutes for bankruptcy before the middle of the nineteenth century. Indeed, Montagu described them in 1823 as 'private bankruptcies with all the mischief and none of the advantage of a commission.'[1] Perhaps their major defect was the debtor's inability to force all his creditors to accede to the arrangement. In many cases, this led to fraud, as intransigent creditors were given preferential treatment or bribed to sign.[2] In

1 B. Montagu, The Law of Composition (1823), pp. 39-40.

2 See B.P.P. Bankruptcy and Insolvency (1840), p. 289, John Pollock; p. 227, Thomas Parker.

most, dissatisfied creditors overturned the arrangement; it was well-known in the 1820s and 1830s that deeds were almost invariably invalidated by creditors who opened commissions of bankruptcy against the debtor.[3] A second defect was expense. Although deeds were sometimes used to avoid the cost of bankruptcy,[4] they were often more expensive both because costs increased according to the number of creditors involved and because solicitors were able to extort fees without restraint.[5] Additional weaknesses included the trustee's inability to inquire into the truth of the debtor's statements and the fact that creditors could only punish fraud concerted between the debtor and the trustee by appealing to Chancery, which imposed further expense.[6] As a result of these practical defects, Fonblanque considered in 1824 that bankruptcy commissions were infinitely preferable to trust deeds.[7]

It is impossible to assess the extent to which deeds were used during the period under discussion because, even when legislation was belatedly passed to facilitate them in 1825, no provision was made either to regulate those which were arranged without the case going to court or to provide for their registration.[8] Compositions seem to have been

---

3 See ibid., p. 358, George Eastlake; p. 361, W.A. Hulton; p. 367, C.A. Helm; p. 370, W. Corbett.

4 Ibid., p. 374, John Fawcett; p. 418, James Wake.

5 Ibid., p. 422, R.G. Bradley; p. 49, Francis Parry.

6 J.S.M. Fonblanque, Observations on . . . the Laws relating to Bankrupts (1824), p. 17.

7 Ibid., p. 16, fn.

8 In 1825, if nine-tenths of creditors consented after the final examination in bankruptcy, a composition was validated and the commission superseded (6 Geo. IV, c. 16). Further legislation, in 1838, facilitated compositions with imprisoned debtors, with the consent

fairly common at the turn of the nineteenth century among insolvents attempting to avoid arrest or to obtain release from gaol. These, however, declined sharply after Redesdale's act which enabled debtors to avoid all their liabilities.[9] Four years later, a solicitor maintained that deeds had not been used extensively in recent years.[10] The witnesses before the commission into bankruptcy and insolvency in 1840 offered a series of contradictory estimates which suggest either that the extent to which arrangements were used varied from area to area or - and more likely - that contemporaries were ignorant of their significance.[11] There is, however, considerable evidence that larger merchants, especially in London, preferred private deeds to bankruptcy, although their calculations were often nullified by one or two creditors who opened bankruptcy proceedings.[12] The most satisfactory conclusion

---

of the majority of creditors (1,2 Vict., c.110); in 1844, an elaborate procedure was established to allow non-traders to use compositions under the supervision of the Bankruptcy Court (see above, chapter two).

9 See B.P.P. Insolvent Debtors (1819), p. 34, James Nicholls.

10 B.P.P. Bankrupt Laws (1817), p. 59, William Stevens.

11 B.P.P. Bankruptcy and Insolvency (1840). James Wake, a commissioner at Exeter, stated that deeds were used extensively (p. 418) while T.E. Drake, a solicitor also from Exeter, said that they were not (p. 456). Many witnesses maintained that, although deeds were widely used, they usually led to bankruptcy proceedings (e.g. p. 361, W.A. Hulton; p. 367, W. Corbett; p. 370, C.A. Helm; p. 475, John Barber; p. 483, W.O. Hare). They were said to be unpopular at Liverpool (p. 386, L.J. Venables) but common in North Lancashire and Westmoreland (p. 422, R.G. Bradley). J.C. Hall, from Nottingham, reckoned that they were used only by non-traders and small bankrupts (p. 392). Others said that they were only used in London (p. 435, G.P. Hester; p. 489, P. Healey).

12 See B.P.P. Bankrupt Laws (1818), p. 90, Montagu; Fonblanque, op. cit., p. 12; B.P.P. Bankruptcy and

is that, while the defects of the debt laws induced many debtors and creditors to seek alternatives, the practical weaknesses of arrangements ensured that most debtors were eventually forced to use the traditional procedures.

It is not surprising, therefore, that agitation for reform of the debt laws was accompanied by demands for greater legal certainty in deeds of arrangement.[13] In practice, traders wished to be able to select the mode of liquidation appropriate to the estate concerned. This was provided by two statutes, in 1849 and 1861, which facilitated private arrangements with or without the intervention of the court and stipulated that all deeds would be registered.[14] McCulloch, who considered that debtors were given far too much scope for fraud and evasion after 1861, gives the number of deeds which were registered in 1864 and 1865:

	1864		1865	
	No. of Deeds	Value of Estates (£)	No. of Deeds	Value of Estates (£)
Deeds of Assignment	2,208	2,138,600	2,733	3,649,500
Deeds of Composition	1,348	1,198,300	2,344	3,166,700
Deeds of Inspectorship	48	465,100	127	2,219,500
Totals	3,604	3,802,000	5,204	9,035,700

Source: J.R. McCulloch, Dictionary of Commerce (London, 1869), p. 741.

Insolvency (1840), p. 227 (Thomas Parker), p. 217 (Germain Lavie).

13 See ibid., p. 94, Samuel Sweet, a solicitor.

14 12,13 Vict., c.106 stipulated that, if six-sevenths of creditors in number and value over £10 agreed, a deed would be valid after three months and a trustee would be appointed to administer it; if nine-tenths in number and value agreed, a composition after adjudication of

The table indicates that assignments and compositions were used extensively but that the minority of inspectorship estates affected very large sums. This tends to confirm the view that substantial traders used the inspectorship method. The mean of the estates in the other two categories is around £1,000, for the inspectorship estates £10,000 to £20,000.

Evidently, the large number of deeds used in the 1860s, when this was said to be the commonest form of settlement, was a consequence of the act of 1861[15] and should not be considered typical of the century as a whole. Before this legislation forced the minority of intransigent creditors to accept the wishes of the majority, most arrangements seem to have been followed by bankruptcy commissions. Nevertheless, some estates in the early nineteenth century were probably settled by deeds, which must unfortunately be considered an unknown variable in discussion of debt during the industrial revolution.

---

bankruptcy would be valid. 24,25 Vict., c.134 stipulated that three-quarters of creditors in number and value could, after adjudication of bankruptcy, resolve to use an arrangement, instead of bankruptcy, which was to be registered.

15 See W. Gibson, A Letter on Reform of Bankruptcy Law (1866), p. 12.

BIBLIOGRAPHY

Manuscript Sources

At the Bank of England

Committee of Treasury, Minute Books, Vol. 8 (15 March 1809 - 1 Aug. 1810); vol. 9 (8. Aug. 1810 - 28 Aug. 1812).

Court of Directors, Minute Books, Fa (12 April 1809 - 4 April 1811); Ga (11 April 1811 - 2 April 1812).

Extracts relating to Discounts (from the minutes of the Court Books on regulations on discounts), ADV/B533 - No. 1.

General Ledger, No. 18 (1 March 1805 - 29 Feb. 1816); No. 19 (1 March 1816 - 29 Feb. 1828).

Special Discount Committee, ADV/586 - No. 1, 22 Dec. 1803 - 12 Feb. 1811.

Weekly Totals (Assets and Liabilities), Book I, 1810-11.

At the British Museum

Minutes of the Proceedings of the Court of Common Council, 1826-1832.

At the Picton Reference Library, Liverpool

Court of Passage, Commitment Books, 1707-13, 1732-64.

At the Public Record Office, London

Bankruptcy Records: Order Books, B1; Commissions Files, B3; Docket Books, B4; Certificate Books, B6.

Chancery Masters Exhibits, C114.

Court of King's Palace: Custody Books, P.C.2.

Fleet Commitment Books, Pris. 1.

King's Bench Commitment Books, Pris. 4.

Official Publications

House of Commons Journals.

Parliamentary Debates.

Select Committees: Minutes and Reports

Report of the Committee of Secrecy on the Outstanding Demands of the Bank of England and on the Restriction of Payments in Cash, Vol. XI, 1797.

Report from the Select Committee appointed to inquire into the State of Ireland, as to its Circulating Paper, its Specie, and Current Coin, and the Exchange between that Part of the United Kingdom and Great Britain, Vol. III, 1803-4.

Report from the Select Committee appointed to inquire into the cause of the High Price of Gold Bullion, and to take into consideration the State of the Circulating Medium, and the Exchange between Great Britain and Foreign Parts, Vol. III, 1810.

Report from the Select Committee appointed to take into Consideration the Present State of Commercial Credit, vol. II, 1810-11.

Minutes of Evidence taken before the Committee of the Whole House, to whom it was referred to consider of the several Petitions which have been presented to the House in this Session of Parliament, relating to the Orders in Council, vol. III, 1812.

Report from the Select Committee appointed to inquire into the State of the Gaol of Newgate, and the Poultry, Giltspur Street, Ludgate and Borough compters, and of any improvement which may be practicable therein, vol. IV, 1813-14.

Report from the Select Committee appointed to inquire into the State of the King's Bench, Fleet and Marshalsea Prisons, together with any improvement that may be practicable, vol. IV, 1814-15.

Report from the Select Committee appointed to inquire into the Effects which have been produced by the Acts 53 Geo. III, c.102 and 54 Geo. III, c.23 for the Relief of Insolvent Debtors in England, vol. IV, 1816.

Report from the Select Committee appointed to Consider of the Bankrupt Laws, vol. V, 1817.

Report from the Select Committee appointed to Consider of the Bankrupt Laws, vol. VI, 1818.

Report from the Select Committee on the Prisons within the City of London and the Borough of Southwark, vol. VIII, 1818.

First and Second Reports from the Committee of Secrecy appointed to Consider of the State of the Bank of England, with reference to the Expediency of the Resumption of Cash Payments at the Period fixed by Law, and into such other matters as are connected therewith, vol. III, 1819.

Report from the Select Committee appointed to take into Consideration the State of the Law respecting the Discharge of Insolvent Debtors, and the Several Acts 53rd., 54th. and 56th. Geo. III relative to the same, and the Effects produced thereby, vol. II, 1819.

Report from the Commissioners appointed to inquire into the State, Conduct and Management of the Prison and Gaol of the Fleet, King's Bench and Marshalsea, Vol. II, 1819.

Report from the Select Committee appointed to inquire into the Mode in which Debts, amounting to less than Fifteen Pounds, are recovered in England and Wales, Vol. IV, 1823.

Minutes of Evidence taken before the Select Committee on the Bill for Preventing Delays in the Proceedings of County Courts and for the more Easy and Speedy Recovery of Small Debts in England and Wales, Vol. X, 1825.

Fourth Report of the Commissioners appointed to inquire into the Practice and Proceedings of the Superior Courts of Common Law, vol. XXV, 1831-2.

Fifth Report of the Commissioners appointed to inquire into the Practice and Proceedings of the Superior Courts of Common Law, vol. XXII, 1833.

Report of the Commissioners for inquiring into Bankruptcy and Insolvency, vol. XVI, 1840.

<u>Accounts and Papers</u>

Volumes III, 1813-14; XI, 1814-15; XVIII, 1816; XVI, 1817; XVI, 1818; XVII, 1819; XIX, 1826-7; XX, 1828; XV, 1831; XLIV, 1835; XLII, 1836; XLIII, 1839; XVII, 1850.

Newspapers and Periodicals

Annual Register, 1810, 1811.

Cowdroy's Manchester Gazette and Weekly Advertiser, 1810.

Exchange Herald. Aston's Manchester Commercial Advertiser, 1810.

Manchester Mercury. Harrop's General Advertiser, 1810.

The Monthly Magazine, 1810, 1811.

Salisbury and Winchester Journal and General Advertiser of Wiltshire, Hampshire, Dorset and Somerset, 1810.

The Times, 1810, 1811.

The Tradesman, 1810, 1811.

Printed Sources

Primary

Sir B.H. Abrahall, Bankruptcy Law Reform (London, 1859).

\- Reform of the Laws relating to Bankruptcy and Insolvency (London, 1861).

J.F. Archbold, The Practice of the Court of King's Bench (2 volumes, London, 1819).

\- The Law and Practice in Bankruptcy (2nd edition, London, 1827).

\- The Practice of the Court of Queen's Bench (6th edition, London, 1838).

\- The Law of Partnership and of Joint Stock Companies (2nd edition, London, 1856).

Bankruptcy and Insolvency. By a Registrar of a District Court of Bankruptcy (Liverpool, 1847).

The Bankrupt's Directory (London, 1708).

Sir J. Bayley, Summary of the Law of Bills of Exchange, Cash Bills and Promissory Notes (5th edition, London, 1830).

J. Bentham, An Introduction to the Principles and Morals of Legislation (2 volumes, 2nd. edition, London, 1823).

- 'Observations on the Bankruptcy Court Bill, 1832,' in The Works of Jeremy Bentham, volume 5, (Edited by J. Bowring), (London, 1843), 565-604.

- 'Of Imprisonment for Debt,' in The Works of Jeremy Bentham, Volume 6, (Edited by J. Bowring), (London, 1843), 176-183.

J.B. Beaumont, The Consequences of the Abolition of Imprisonment for Debt Considered (London, 1836).

Sir W. Blackstone, Commentaries on the Laws of England, Volume 2, (Oxford, 1766).

W. Blake, 'Observations on the Principles which Regulate the Course of Exchange,' in Select Tracts (Edited by Lord Overstone), (London, 1857), 475-563.

Blood for Gold or Death for Forgery (London, 1824).

H. Boase, Letter to Lord King in Defence of the Conduct of the Directors of the Banks of England and Ireland (London, 1804).

J. Britton, Picture of London (27th. edition, London, 1826).

H. Brougham, The Present State of the Law. The Speech of Henry Brougham Esq., M.P., in the House of Commons on Thursday, 7th February 1828 (London, 1828).

- Legal Reform. The Speech Delivered in the House of Peers, Thursday, 2 December 1830, by H. Baron Brougham (London, 1830).

- Speeches of Lord Brougham (London, 1838).

- Letters on Law Reform to the Right Hon. Sir J.R.G. Graham, Bart., M.P. (London, 1843).

- Speech on Law Reform, 19 May 1845 (London, 1845).

- Contributions to the Edinburgh Review by Henry Lord Brougham (Glasgow, 1856), volume 3.

- *The Life and Times of Henry Lord Brougham, by Himself* (London, 1871).

J.W. Buck, *Cases in Bankruptcy* (London, 1820).

H. Burgess, *A Letter to the Right Hon. George Canning to Explain in what Manner the Industry of the People and the Production of this Country are connected with, and influenced by Bills of Exchange, Country Bank Notes and Country Bankers, Bank of England Notes and Branch Banks* (London, 1826).

- *Petition to the House of Commons to Render Manifest the Errors, Injustice and the Dangers of the Measures of Parliament respecting Currency and Bankers* (London, 1829).

Sir J.B. Burges, *Considerations on the Law of Insolvency* (London, 1783).

T.F. Buxton, *An Inquiry whether Crime and Misery are Produced or Prevented by our Present System of Prison Discipline* (London, 1818).

- *Memoirs of Sir Thomas Fowell Buxton* (Edited by his son, C. Buxton), (London, 1848).

G. Chalmers, *An Estimate of the Comparative Strength of Great Britain* (London, 1804).

- *An Historical View of the Domestic Economy of Great Britain and Ireland* (Edinburgh, 1812).

E. Christian, *The Origin, Progress and Present Practice of the Bankrupt Law, both in England and Ireland* (2 volumes, 2nd edition, London, 1818).

- *Practical Instructions for Suing out and Prosecuting a Commission of Bankruptcy* (London, 1820).

The Rev. W.L. Clay, *The Prison Chaplain: A Memoir of the Rev. John Clay, B.D.* (Cambridge, 1861).

The Compting-House Companion: or Laws respecting Bills of Exchange, Promissory Notes, Bank Notes, and Bankers' Checks (London, 1810).

J.S. Copley, *Lords Lyndhurst, Brougham and the Local Courts* (London, 1834).

R.N. Cresswell, *Reports of Cases Heard and Decided in the Court for Relief of Insolvent Debtors* (London, 1830).

C. Crompton, *Rules and Regulations concerning the Court of Passage* (Liverpool, 1844).

A. Cullen, *Principles of the Bankruptcy Law* (London, 1800).

C.S. Cullen, *Reform of the Bankruptcy Court* (London, 1830).

Debtor and Creditors Guide (London, 1813).

R.R. Dees, *The Law and Practice under the Statute 5 and 6 Vict. c.116* (London, 1843).

J. Dornford, *Nine Letters to Right Hon. The Lord Mayor and Aldermen of the City of London on the State of Prisons* (London, 1785).

\- *Seven Letters to the Lords and Commons of Great Britain upon the Present Mode of Arresting and Imprisoning the Bodies of Debtors* (London, 1786).

Sir J.E. Eardley-Wilmot, *Lord Brougham's Acts and Bills, 1811-1857* (London, 1857).

P. Egan, *Life in London* (London, 1821).

J.H. Elliott, *A Remonstrance to the Right Hon. Lord Brougham on the Injustice and Impolicy of the Proposed Abolition of Imprisonment for Debt* (London, 1838).

\- *Credit the Life of Commerce* (London, 1845).

An Exposure of the Injurious Effects of the Present System of Bankruptcy Law. By a Barrister (London, 1841).

The Extraordinary Case of William Penrice. Being a Key to the King's Bench Prison (London, 1768).

Facts for the Times. Notes on Bankruptcy Reform. Reprinted from The Morning Post (London, 1867).

A Faithful Guide through the Insolvent and Bankrupt Courts according to the last Two Acts of Parliament of 1842. By a Solicitor of Twenty Years Experience (London, 1842).

R.G.C. Fane, A Letter Addressed to the Lord Viscount Melbourne (London, 1837).

- Bankruptcy Reform in a Series of Letters addressed to Sir Robert Peel, Bart. (London, 1838).

- Bankruptcy Reform in a Series of Letters Addressed to William Hawes Esq. (London, 1848).

E. Farley, Imprisonment for Debt Unconstitutional and Oppressive (London, 1788).

J.S.M. Fonblanque, Observations on the Bill now before Parliament for Consolidation and Amendment of the Laws relating to Bankrupts (London, 1824).

Fowler. Scraps. Salisbury (Salisbury, 1785).

A Full and Accurate Account of the Trial and Execution of Henry Fauntleroy for Forgery (London, 1824).

A General System of Laws Concerning Bankrupts (2 volumes, London, 1761).

W.S. Gibson, A Letter to the Lord Chancellor on the Amendment of the Law of Bankruptcy (London, 1848).

- A Letter on Reform of Bankruptcy Law Addressed to the Right Hon. Lord Chancellor (London, 1866).

J.W. Gilbart, The History and Principles of Banking (London, 1834).

W. Glover, Lord Brougham's Law Reforms and Courts of Local Jurisdiction (London, 1834).

R. Gordon, A Letter to the Right Hon. Viscount Melbourne, First Lord of the Treasury on the Liberty of the Subject as Affected by the Atrocious System of Imprisonment for Debt (London, 1836).

A. Griffiths, Chronicles of Newgate (2 volumes, London, 1884).

J.J. Gurney, *Notes on a Visit made to some of the Prisons in Scotland and the North of England, in Company with Elizabeth Fry* (London, 1819).

W. Harris, *The Present Distress of the Country and Suitable Remedies* (London, 1816).

B. Hawes, *Abolition of Arrest and Imprisonment for Debt Considered in Six Letters Addressed to a Constituent* (London, 1836).

G. Holford, *Thoughts on the Criminal Prisons of this Country* (London, 1821).

E.D. Holroyd, *Retrograde Legislation in Bankruptcy* (London, 1859).

J. Howard, *The State of the Prisons of England and Wales* (3rd. edition, London, 1784).

W. Huskisson, 'The Question concerning the Depreciation of our Currency Stated and Examined,' in *Select Tracts* (Edited by Lord Overstone), (London, 1857), 567-668.

Imprisonment of Men's Bodies for Debt, as the Practice of England now Stands (London, 1641).

T. Joplin, *An Essay on the General Principles and Practice of Banking* (London, 1822).

- *An Examination of the Report of the Joint Stock Bank Committee* (London, 1837).

Lord King, *Thoughts on the Effects of the Bank Restriction* (London, 1804).

The Law for and against Bankrupts. By a Late Commissioner of Bankrupts (London, 1743).

J.C. Lettsom, *Memoirs of the Life and Writings of the Late John Coackley Lettsom*, volume II (Edited by T.J. Pettigrew), (London, 1817).

A List of Bankrupts with their Dividends and Certificates, January 1 1786 - June 24 1806 (London, 1806).

J.R. McCulloch, *Dictionary of Commerce and Commercial Navigation* (London, 1832).

- Dictionary of Commerce and Commercial Navigation (London, 1869).

T. MacDonald, A Treatise on Civil Imprisonment in England (London, 1791).

D. Macpherson, Annals of Commerce, Manufacturies, Fisheries and Navigation (4 volumes, London, 1805).

Mr. Sergeant Manning, Statement Submitted to the Bankruptcy Committee of the Society for Promoting the Amendment of the Law (London, 1860).

W.R. Minchin, The Present State of the Debtor and Creditor Law (London, 1812).

B. Montagu, Digest of the Bankrupt Laws (4 volumes, London, 1805-7).

- An Enquiry Respecting the Expediency of Limiting the Creditor's Power to Refuse a Bankrupt's Certificate (London, 1809).

- An Enquiry Respecting the Mode of Issuing Commissions of Bankruptcy (London, 1810).

- A Brief Statement of the Proceedings in both Houses of Parliament in the Last and Present Sessions on the Several Bills introduced with a view to the Amendment of the Criminal Law (London, 1811).

- Enquiries Respecting the Administration of Bankrupts' Estates by Assignees (London, 1811).

- Enquiries Respecting the Insolvent Debtors Bill, with the Opinions of Dr. Paley, Mr. Burke and Dr. Johnson (London, 1816).

- Some Observations on Bills submitted to the Legislature (London, 1819).

- A Digest of the New Decisions in Bankruptcy (London, 1820).

- Thoughts on the Abolition of the Punishment of Death in Bankruptcy (London, 1821).

- Digest of the Law of Partnership (2 volumes, 2nd edition, London, 1822).

- Some Observations on the Bill for Improvement of the Bankrupt Laws (London, 1822).

- Summary of the Law of Composition with Creditors (London, 1823).

- Suggestions Respecting the Improvement of the Bankrupt Laws (London, 1824).

- Inquiries Respecting the Courts of Commissioners of Bankrupts and the Lord Chancellor's Court (London, 1825).

- The Evidence in Bankruptcy before the Chancery Commission, with the Report (London, 1826).

-and F. Gregg, Digest of the Bankrupt Laws (London, 1827).

- Some Observations on the Act for Consolidating the Bankrupt Laws (London, 1827).

- Reform (London, 1827).

-and J. Macarthur, Reports of Cases Decided by the Lord Chancellor and Vice-Chancellor (London, 1830).

- The New Bankrupt Court Act, arranged with a Copious Index and Observations (London, 1831).

- Reports of Cases in Bankruptcy (London, 1832).

-and S. Ayrton, The Law and Practice in Bankruptcy (3 volumes, London, 1834-9).

R. Mushet, Enquiry into the Effects Produced on the National Currency and Rates of Exchange by the Bank Restriction Bill (2nd edition, London, 1810).

R.D. Neale, The Prisoner's Guide, or Every Debtor his own Lawyer (London, 1800).

J. Neild, Account of Persons Confined for Debt in England and Wales (London, 1800).

- Account of the Rise, Progress and Present State of the Society for the Discharge and Relief of Persons Imprisoned for Small Debts throughout England and Wales (London, 1802).

The New Rules and Orders made under 5 and 6 Vict. c.122 for the Amendment of the Law of Bankruptcy and under 5 and 6 Vict. c.116 for the Relief of Insolvent Debtors (London, 1842).

A New Tax of £100,000 a year. A Few Observations on the Proposal to Abolish Official Assignees in Bankruptcy (London, 1859).

Observations on the State of the English Prisons. Communicated to the Rev. Henry Zouch by Lord Loughborough (London, 1793).

Official Assignees. Reform in Bankruptcy. Remarks and Suggestions. By an Accountant (London, 1841).

The Piercing Cryes of the Poor and Miserable Prisoners for Debt in all Parts of England (London, 1714).

M. Pitt, The Cry of the Oppressed (London, 1696).

F.G.H. Price, A Handbook of London Bankers (London, 1876).

- A Handbook of London Bankers (enlarged edition, London, 1890).

Proposal for a Slight, but Important, Alteration in Bankruptcy Law for the Benefit of People in Trade and Commerce (London, 1830).

J. Prujean, A Treatise on the Laws of England now in Force for the Recovery of Debt (London, 1791).

J. Rayner, Bankruptcy Law Reform (London, 1859).

Real Life in London; or the Further Rambles and Adventures of Robert Tallyho Esq., and his Cousin the Hon. Thomas Dashall, through the Metropolis. By an Amateur (London, 1822).

Reform of the Bankrupt Court. By a Commissioner of Bankrupts (London, 1829).

A Regular Practice of the Court of King's Bench. By an Old Practitioner (London, 1828).

Remarks on the Bill to Prevent Frauds Committed by Bankrupts with Observations on the Effect it may have on Trade (London, 1706).

Sir S. Romilly, *The Memoirs of the Life of Sir Samuel Romilly* (Edited by his Sons), (3 Volumes, London, 1840).

G. Rose, *Cases in Bankruptcy* (2 Volumes, London, 1821).

G. Ross, *Leading Cases in the Commercial Law of England and Scotland* (London, 1853).

A. Rosser, *Credit Pernicious* (London, 1823).

Runnymede Secundus, *The Prison House Unmasked* (London, 1837).

T. Sands and C. Crompton, *Rules and Regulations Concerning the Court of Passage* (Liverpool, 1844).

Sir. J. Sinclair, *Remarks on Mr. Huskisson's Pamphlet* (3rd, edition, London, 1810).

W. Smart, *Economic Annals of the Nineteenth Century*, Volume I (New York edition, 1964).

A. Smith, *The Wealth of Nations* (London, 1776).

W. Smith, *The Humble Petition of the Prisoners in the Fleet, as it was Presented to His Highness the Lord Protector and his Hon. Council* (London, 1655).

W. Smith, *State of the Gaols in London and Westminster and the Borough of Southwark* (London, 1776).

The Solicitor's Guide and Tradesman's Instructor concerning Bankrupts (London, 1740).

J. Stephen, *Considerations on Imprisonment for Debt* (London, 1770).

J. Story, *Commentaries on the Laws of Bills of Exchange* (London, 1843).

Substance of Two Speeches in the House of Commons by Right Hon. George Canning, 8 and 13 May 1811 (London, 1811).

Substance of Two Speeches of Henry Thornton on the Report of the Bullion Committee, 7 and 14 May 1811 (London, 1811).

H. Thornton, _An Inquiry into the Nature and Effects of Paper Credit in Great Britain_ (Edited by F.A. Hayek), (London, 1939).

A. de Tocqueville, _Democracy in America_ (Edited by P.A. Bradley), (New York, 1945).

T. Tooke and W. Newmarch, _A History of Prices and the State of the Circulation, 1792-1856_ (introduction by T.E. Gregory), (6 volumes, London, 1928).

The Trial of Henry Fauntleroy for Forgery (London, 1824).

The Trial of Henry Fauntleroy for Forgery (Edited by H. Bleackley), (London, 1824).

H. Twiss, _Life of Lord Chancellor Eldon_ (3 volumes, London, 1844).

C. Uniacke, _A Letter to the Lord Chancellor on the Necessity and Practicability of Forming a Code of Laws of England_ (London, 1825).

J. Vesey and J. Beames, _Reports of Cases in Chancery_, 1812-13 (London, 1813).

J. Wade, _The Extraordinary Black Book_ (3rd edition, London, 1832).

T.G. Western, _A Commentary on the Act for Abolishing Arrest on Mesne Process_ (London, 1838).

A. Whiteacre, _Extracts from the New Bankrupt Law, 24 and 25 Vict. c.134_ (London, 1861).

Secondary

B. Abel-Smith and R. Stevens, _Lawyers and the Courts_ (London, 1967).

A. Andréadès, _History of the Bank of England_ (translated by C. Meredith and H.S. Foxwell), (2nd edition, London, 1924).

J.W. Angell, *The Theory of International Prices* (London, 1926).

T.S. Ashton, *An Eighteenth-Century Indsutrialist. Peter Stubs of Warrington* (Manchester, 1939).

- *The Industrial Revolution, 1760-1830* (London, 1948).

- *Iron and Steel in the Industrial Revolution* (Manchester, 1951).

- *An Economic History of England: The 18th Century* (London, 1955).

- *Economic Fluctuations in England, 1700-1800* (Oxford, 1959).

- 'The Bill of Exchange and Private Banks in Lancashire, 1790-1830,' in *Papers in English Monetary History* (Edited by T.S. Ashton and R.S. Sayers), (Oxford, 1953), pp. 37-49.

- 'Some Statistics of the Industrial Revolution in Britain,' in *Essays in Economic History*, Volume III (Edited by E.M. Carus-Wilson), (London, 1962), 237-251.

A. Aspinall, *Lord Brougham and the Whig Party* (Manchester, 1927).

C.M. Atkinson and J.E. Mitchell, *Life and Principles of Sir Samuel Romilly* (London, 1920).

W.O. Aydelotte, 'The Conservative and Radical Interpretations of Early Victorian Social Legislation,' *Victorian Studies*, vol. XI, 1967-8, 225-236.

J.E.D. Binney, *British Public Finance and Administration, 1774-1792* (Oxford, 1958).

M. Blatcher, 'Touching the Writ of Latitat: An Act "of No Great Moment",' in *Elizabethan Government and Society. Essays Presented to Sir John Neale* (Edited by S.T. Bindoff, J. Hurstfield and C.H. Williams), (London, 1961), pp. 188-212.

J. Brooke, *The House of Commons, 1754-1790: Introductory Survey* (Oxford, 1968).

F.K. Brown, *Fathers of the Victorians* (Cambridge, 1961).

N.S. Buck, *The Development of the Organization of Anglo-American Trade, 1800-1850* (Yale U.P., 1925).

M.C. Buer, 'Trade Depression following the Napoleonic Wars,' *Economica*, number 2, 1921, 159-79.

W.L. Burn, *The Age of Equipoise* (2nd edition, London, 1968).

R. Cameron, *Banking in the Early Stages of Industrialization* (Oxford, 1967).

E. Cannan, *The Paper Pound* (London, 1919).

A.M. Carr-Saunders and P.A. Wilson, *The Professions* (Oxford, 1933).

Sir J.H. Clapham, *The Bank of England* (2 Volumes, Cambridge, 1944).

– 'The Private Business of the Bank of England, 1744-1800,' *Economic History Review*, volume XI, 1941, 77-89.

R.H. Condon, 'The Fleet Prison,' *History Today*, Volume XIV (1964), 453-60.

S.R. Cope, 'The Goldsmids and the Development of the London Money Market during the Napoleonic Wars,' *Economica*, new series, Volume IX, 1942, 180-206.

B.A. Corry, *Money, Saving and Investment in English Economics, 1800-1850* (London, 1962).

V. Cromwell, 'Interpretations of Nineteenth-Century Administration: An Analysis,' *Victorian Studies*, Volume IX, 1965-6, 245-54.

F. Crouzet, *L'Economie Britannique et le Blocus Continental (1806-1813)*, (2 volumes, Paris, 1958).

- 'Bilan de l'économie britannique pendant les guerres de la Révolution et de l'Empire,' Revue Historique, number 234, July-September 1965, 71-110.

- 'Wars, Blockade and Economic Change in Europe, 1792-1815,' The Journal of Economic History, Volume XXIV, 1964, 567-88.

A. Cunningham, British Credit in the Last Napoleonic War (London, 1910).

G.W. Daniels, 'The British Cotton Trade during the Revolutionary and Napoleonic Wars,' Transactions of the Manchester Statistical Society, 1915-16, 53-84.

P. Deane, The First Industrial Revolution (Cambridge, 1965).

P. Deane and W.A. Cole, British Economic Growth, 1688-1959 (2nd edition, Cambridge, 1967).

A.V. Dicey, Lectures on the Relation between Law and Public Opinion in England during the Nineteenth Century (London, 1905).

A.B. Dubois, The English Business Company after the Bubble Act, 1720-1800 (New York, 1938).

H.T. Easton, History of a Banking House (London, 1903).

M. Edwards, After Wesley (London, 1935).

M.M. Edwards, The Growth of the British Cotton Trade, 1780-1815 (Manchester, 1967).

Sir A. Feavearyear, The Pound Sterling (London, 1931).

F.W. Fetter, The Development of British Monetary Orthodoxy, 1797-1875 (Harvard, 1965).

- 'The Bullion Report Re-examined,' in Papers in English Monetary History (Edited by T.S. Ashton and R.S. Sayers), (Oxford, 1953), 66-75.

C.H.S. Fifoot, Lord Mansfield (Oxford, 1936).

B.A.M. Finlayson, England in the Eighteen Thirties (London, 1969).

R.S. Fitton, 'Overseas Trade During the Napoleonic Wars, as illustrated by the Records of W.G. and J. Strutt,' Economica, new series, Volume XX, 1953, 53-60.

R.S. Fitton and A.P. Wadsworth, The Strutts and the Arkwrights, 1758-1830 (Manchester, 1958).

A.S. Foord, His Majesty's Opposition (Oxford, 1964).

W. Friedmann, Law in a Changing Society (Pelican Edition, 1964).

W.F. Galpin, The Grain Supply of England during the Napoleonic Period (London, 1925).

G.T. Garratt, Lord Brougham (London, 1935).

N. Gash, Mr. Secretary Peel (London, 1961).

- Reaction and Reconstruction in English Politics, 1832-1852 (Oxford, 1965).

- Sir Robert Peel (London, 1972).

A.D. Gayer, W.W. Rostow and A.J. Schwartz, The Growth and Fluctuation of the British Economy, 1790-1850 (2 volumes, Oxford, 1953).

M.D. George, England in Transition (2nd edition, London, 1953).

- London Life in the Eighteenth Century (2nd edition, London, 1966).

J.A. Gulland, 'The History of the Criminal Law Reforms of the Period of Peel's Home Secretaryship, 1822-1827,' Bulletin of the Institute of Historical Research, Volume VIII, 1930-1, 182-185.

R.M. Gutchen, 'Local Improvements and Centralisation in Nineteenth-Century England,' Historical Journal, volume IV, 1961, 85-96.

E. Halévy, The Growth of Philosophic Radicalism (Pitman edition, Bath, 1952).

- A History of the English People in the Nineteenth Century, Volumes 1-4, (English Translation, Ernest Benn Ltd., 2nd edition, London, 1951).

H.W. Hamilton, Dr. Syntax. A Silhouette of William Combe Esq., 1742-1823 (London, 1969).

A. Harding, A Social History of English Law (Pelican edition, 1966),

J. Hart, 'Nineteenth-Century Social Reform: A Tory Interpretation of History,' Past and Present, Volume XXXI, 1965, 39-61.

R.M. Hartwell, The Causes of the Industrial Revolution in England (London, 1967).

— The Industrial Revolution and Economic Growth (London, 1971).

M. Hastings, The Court of Common Pleas in Fifteenth-Century England (New York, 1947).

R.G. Hawtrey, Currency and Credit (London, 1919).

H. Heaton, 'Benjamin Gott and the Industrial Revolution in Yorkshire,' Economic History Review, Volume III, 1931, 45-66.

— 'Financing the Industrial Revolution,' Bulletin of the Business Historical Society, Volume XI, number 1, February 1937, 1-10.

— 'Non-Importation, 1806-1812,' Journal of Economic History, Volume I, 1941, 178-198.

E.F. Heckscher, The Continental System; An Economic Interpretation (Oxford, 1922).

Sir J. Hicks, Critical Essays in Monetary Theory (Oxford, 1967).

C. Hill, Reformation to Industrial Revolution (2nd edition, London, 1969).

R.S.E. Hinde, The British Penal System, 1773-1950 (London, 1951).

E.J. Hobsbawm, Industry and Empire (2nd. edition, London, 1969).

H. Holborn, A History of Modern Germany, 1648-1840 (London, 1965).

J.M. Holden, The History of Negotiable Instruments in English Law (London, 1955).

Sir W.S. Holdsworth, A History of English Law, Volumes I, V, VIII, XI, XIII (London, 1938).

- 'The Movement for Reforms in the Law (1793-1832),' Law Quarterly Review, Volume LVI, 1940, 33-48, 208-228, 340-353.

- Some Makers of English Law (Cambridge, 1966).

J.H. Hollander, 'The Development of the Theory of Money from A. Smith to Ricardo,' Quarterly Journal of Economics, Volume XXV, May 1911, 429-470.

W.E. Hooper, History of Newgate and the Old Bailey (London, 1935).

J.K. Horsefield, 'Bankers and Bullionists in 1819,' Journal of Political Economy, Volume LVII, 1949, 442-448.

- 'The Cash Ratio in English Banks before 1800,' Journal of Political Economy, Volume LVII, 1949, 70-74.

- 'British Banking Practices, 1750-1850: Some Legal Sidelights,' Economica, new series, Volume XIX, 1952, 308-321.

- 'The Duties of a Banker. I. The Eighteenth-Century View,' in Papers in English Monetary History (Edited by T.S. Ashton and R.S. Sayers), (Oxford, 1953), 1-15.

- 'The Duties of a Banker, II. The Effects of Inconvertibility,' in Papers in English Monetary History (Edited by T.S. Ashton and R.S. Sayers), (Oxford, 1953), 16-36.

- 'The Bank and its Treasure,' in Papers in English Monetary History (Edited by T.S. Ashton and R.S. Sayers), (Oxford, 1953), 50-65.

- 'The Origins of the Bank Charter Act, 1844,' in Papers in English Monetary History (Edited by T.S. Ashton and R.S. Sayers), (Oxford, 1953), 109-125.

B.F. Hoselitz, 'Entrepreneurship and Capital Formation in France and Britain since 1700,' in Readings in the History of Economic Growth (Edited by M.E. Falkus), (Oxford, 1968), 95-134.

M.A. Hudson, 'The Bank of England and its Discounts,' Economic History Review, 2nd series, Volume XVI, 1964, 536-8.

E. Hughes, North Country Life in the Eighteenth Century, Volume I (Oxford, 1952).

J. Hughes, Liverpool Banks and Bankers, 1760-1837 (Liverpool, 1906).

F.E. Hyde, B.B. Parkinson and S. Marriner, 'The Cotton Broker and the Rise of the Liverpool Cotton Market,' Economic History Review, 2nd series, Vol. VIII, 1955-6, 75-83.

A.H. Imlah, Economic Elements in the Pax Britannica (Cambridge, Mass., 1958).

E. Jenks, A Short History of English Law (4th edition, enlarged, London, 1928).

D.M. Joslin, 'London Bankers in Wartime, 1739-1784,' in Studies in the Industrial Revolution (Edited by L.S. Pressnell), (London, 1960), 156-177.

— 'London Private Bankers, 1720-1785,' in Essays in Economic History, Volume II (Edited by E.M. Carus-Wilson), (London, 1962), 340-359.

G.W. Keeton and G. Schwarzenberger, Jeremy Bentham and the Law. A Symposium (London, 1948).

W.T.C. King, A History of the London Discount Market (London, 1936).

D. Landes, The Unbound Prometheus (Cambridge, 1969).

G. Lefebvre, Napoleon from Tilsit to Waterloo, 1807-1815 (fifth edition, translated by J.E. Anderson, London, 1969).

P. Lucas, 'Blackstone and the Reform of the Legal Profession,' English Historical Review, volume LXXVII, 1962, 456-489.

H. Lüthy, La Banque Protestante en France (2 volumes, Paris, 1959).

O. MacDonagh, A Pattern of Government Growth, 1800-1860. The Passenger Acts and their Enforcement (London, 1961).

- 'The Regulation of Emigrant Traffic from the United Kingdom, 1842-1855,' Irish Historical Studies, volume IX, 1954, 162-189.

- 'Emigration and The State, 1833-1855: An Essay in Administrative History,' Transactions of the Royal Historical Society, 5th series, volume V, 1955, 133-159.

- 'The Nineteenth-Century Revolution in Government: A Re-appraisal,' Historical Journal, Volume I, 1958, 52-67.

J. De L. Mann, 'Clothiers and Weavers in Wiltshire during the Eighteenth Century,' in Studies in the Industrial Revolution (Edited by L.S. Pressnell), (London, 1960), 66-96.

F. Markham, 'The Napoleonic Adventure,' in New Cambridge Modern History, Volume IX (1965).

Sir T. Martin, A Life of Lord Lyndhurst (2 volumes, London, 1884).

R.C.O. Matthews, A Study in Trade Cycle History (Cambridge, 1964).

S. Meacham, Henry Thornton of Clapham, 1760-1815 (Cambridge, Mass., 1964).

P. Medd, Romilly (London, 1968).

A. Mitchell, The Whigs in Opposition (Oxford, 1967).

B.R. Mitchell and P. Deane, Abstract of British Historical Statistics (Cambridge, 1962).

C. New, The Life of Henry Brougham to 1830 (Oxford, 1961).

R. North, *The Lives of the Rt. Hon. Francis North, Baron Guilford; The Hon. Sir Dudley North; and the Hon. and Rev. Dr. John North*, Volume I (Edited by A. Jessopp), (London, 1890).

H. Parris, 'The Nineteenth-Century Revolution in Government: A Reappraisal Reappraised,' *The Historical Journal*, Volume III, 1960, 17-37.

T.F.T. Plucknett, *A Concise History of Common Law* (5th edition, London, 1956).

S. Pollard, 'Fixed Capital in the Industrial Revolution,' *Journal of Economic History*, Volume XXXIV, 1964, 299-314.

L.S. Pressnell, *Country Banking in the Industrial Revolution* (Oxford, 1956).

- 'Public Monies and the Development of English Banking,' *Economic History Review*, 2nd series, volume V, 1952-3, 378-399.

R. Prouty, *The Transformation of the Board of Trade, 1830-1855* (London, 1957).

L. Radzinowicz, 'An Early Stage in the Movement for the Reform of the Criminal Law,' *Law Quarterly Review*, Volume LXIII, 1947, 94-111.

W.H. Render, *Through Prison Bars* (London, 1894).

D. Roberts, 'Tory Paternalism and Social Reform in Early Victorian England,' *American Historical Review*, Volume LXIII, 1958, 323-337.

- 'Jeremy Bentham and the Victorian Administrative State,' *Victorian Studies*, Volume II, 1959, 193-210.

C. Robbins, *The Eighteenth Century Commonwealthman* (Harvard, 1959).

L. Robbins, *The Theory of Economic Policy in English Classical Political Economy* (London, 1952).

R. Robson, *The Attorney in Eighteenth-Century England* (London, 1959).

J.H. Rose, 'British West Indian Commerce as a factor in the Napoleonic War,' Cambridge Historical Journal, Volume III, 1929, 34-46.

W.W. Rostow, British Economy in the Nineteenth Century (Oxford, 1948).

G.F.E. Rudé, 'The Gordon Riots: A Study of the Rioters and their Victims,' Transactions of the Royal Historical Society, 5th series, Volume VI, 1955, 93-114.

R.S. Sayers, Lloyds Bank in the History of English Banking (London, 1957).

– 'Ricardo's Views on Monetary Questions,' in Papers in English Monetary History (Edited by T.S. Ashton and R.S. Sayers), (Oxford, 1953), 76-95.

E.B. Schumpeter, 'English Prices and Public Finance, 1600-1822,' Review of Economic Statistics, Volume XX, 1938, 21-37.

H.A. Shannon, 'The Coming of General Limited Liability,' in Essays in Economic History, Volume I (Edited by E.M. Carus-Wilson), (London, 1954), 358-379.

N.J. Silberling, 'The British Financial Experience, 1790-1830,' Review of Economic Statistics, 1919, 282-297, 321-323.

– 'British Prices and Business Cycles, 1779-1850,' Review of Economic Statistics, Volume V, 1923, Supplement 2, 219-262.

– 'Financial and Monetary Policy in Great Britain during the Napoleonic Wars,' Quarterly Journal of Economics, Volume XXXVIII, 1924, 214-233, 397-439.

R. Smith, 'Manchester as a Centre for the Manufacture and Merchanting of Cotton Goods,' University of Birmingham Historical Journal, Volume IV, 1953-4, 47-65.

N.A.H. Stracey, English Accounting, 1800-1954 (London, 1954).

L. Sutherland, 'The Law Merchant in England in the Seventeenth and Eighteenth Centuries,' Transactions of the Royal Historical Society, 4th series, volume XVII, 1934, 149-176.

E.R. Taylor, Methodism and Politics, 1791-1851 (Cambridge, 1935).

E.P. Thompson, The Making of the English Working Class (2nd. edition, London, 1968).

W.J. Thorne, Banking (Oxford, 1948).

M. Thornton, 'The Crisis of 1825. Letters from a Young Lady,' in Papers in English Monetary History (Edited by T.S. Ashton and R.S. Sayers), (Oxford, 1953), 96-108.

Sir G.O. Trevelyan, The Life and Letters of Lord Macaulay (London, 1893).

G.S.L. Tucker, Progress and Profits in British Economic Thought, 1650-1850 (Cambridge, 1960).

A.S. Turberville, The House of Lords in the Age of Reform (London, 1958).

G. Unwin, Samuel Oldknow and the Arkwrights (Manchester, 1924).

J. Viner, Studies in the Theory of International Trade (New York, 1937).

W.J. Warner, The Wesleyan Movement in the Industrial Revolution (London, 1930).

E. Welbourne, 'Bankruptcy before the Era of Victorian Reform,' Cambridge Historical Journal, Volume IV, 1932, 51-62.

R.B. Westerfield, Middlemen in English Business (New Haven, Conn., 1915).

C. Wilson, 'The Entrepreneur in the Industrial Revolution,' History, Volume XLII, 1957, 101-117.

R.G. Wilson, Gentlemen Merchants (Manchester, 1971).

W.H.D. Winder, 'The Courts of Request,' Law Quarterly Review, Volume LII, 1936, 369-394.

H.A. Wyndham, *A Family History, 1688-1837* (Oxford, 1950).

B.S. Yamey, H.C. Edey and H.W. Thomson, *Accounting in England and Scotland, 1543-1800* (London, 1963).

A. J. Youngson, 'The Acceleration of Economic Progress in Great Britain, 1750-1800,' in *Readings in the History of Economic Growth* (Edited by M.E. Falkus), (Oxford, 1968), 63-94.

STATISTICAL SUPPLEMENT

CONTENTS

Tables		Page

Charts

Figures Major Bill Debtors and Creditors of:

Table 1.1 Number of Commissions Files stored at the Public Record Office, 1797 - 1826.

Year	No. of Files	Year	No. of Files
1797	8	1812	106
1798	11	1813	97
1799	10	1814	80
1800	25	1815	114
1801	17	1816	122
1802	27	1817	74
1803	36	1818	56
1804	27	1819	96
1805	16	1820	92
1806	26	1821	125
1807	30	1822	87
1808	18	1823	104
1809	36	1824	122
1810	87	1825	166
1811	131	1826	338

TABLE 1.2. Assets and Charges in 180 Bankrupt Estates, divided into Nine Groups of Twenty, 1832-9.

CATEGORIES AND CHARGES	ASSETS £ 130–199		£ 200–279		£ 280-349		£ 350–449		£ 450–599		£ 600–799		£ 800–1,199		£ 1,200-2,999		£ 3,000-29,999		TOTALS	
	£	%	£	%	£	%	£	%	£	%	£	%	£	%	£	%	£	%	£	%
Amount collected	3,349		4,795		6,118		8,057		10,603		14,171		19,964		38,537		190,341		295,935	
Amount dividend	1,001	30	1,959	41	3,079	50	4,337	54	6,724	63.5	9,692	68	14,485	72	31,812	82	171,737	90	244,826	83
Difference	2,348	70	2,836	59	3,039	50	3,720	46	3,879	36.5	4,479	32	5,479	28	6,725	18	18,604	10	51,109	17
Law charges	793	23	970	20.5	1,192	19	1,407	17.5	1,506	14	1,646	11.5	2,089	11	2,113	5	5,086	2.5	16,802	5.5
Messenger	369	11	417	9	349	6	543	6.75	488	4.5	490	3.5	530	3	688	1	856	0.5	4,730	1.5
Official assignee	246	7.5	358	7.5	455	7.5	541	6.75	635	6	876	6	1,135	6	1,668	4	7,527	4	13,441	4.5
Auctioneer	244	7.5	418	8	379	6.5	503	6	527	5	656	4.5	853	4	1,244	3	3,064	1.5	7,888	2.75
Court fees*	600	21	600	14	600	11	600	9	600	7	600	6.5	600	4	600	5	600	1.5	5,400	2.75
Incidental expenses	96		73		64		126		123		211		272		412		1,471		2,848	
TOTALS	2,348	70	2,836	59	3,039	50	3,720	46	3,879	36.5	4,479	32	5,479	28	6,725	18	18,604	10	51,109	17

* Fiat and choice of assignees

Source: based on data in B.P.P. Report of the Commissioners for inquiring into Bankruptcy and Insolvency (1840), XVI, 508, Commissioner Merivale.

TABLE 2.1. ANALYSIS OF THE DEBTS OF FIVE HUNDRED IMPRISONED DEBTORS, 1814–15.

CATEGORIES OF DEBTOR		£ 0-49	£ 50-99	£ 100-199	£ 200-499	£ 500-999	£ 1,000-1,999	£ Over 2,000	TOTALS
Artisans	(a)	103	25	9	6	–	1	–	144
	(b)	13	21	34	55	17	3	1	
Shopkeepers	(a)	76	30	13	9	–	–	–	128
	(b)	5	12	26	45	24	10	6	
Professions	(a)	19	5	2	3	–	–	–	29
	(b)	1	3	6	11	4	4	–	
Gents/Women	(a)	14	6	5	2	–	–	–	27
	(b)	3	2	6	8	4	1	3	
Innkeepers	(a)	13	4	4	–	–	–	–	21
	(b)	–	4	4	6	6	–	1	
Labourers	(a)	15	1	2	–	–	–	–	18
	(b)	7	4	6	1	–	–	–	
Mariners	(a)	9	3	2	2	–	–	–	16
	(b)	3	3	3	4	3	–	–	
Farmers	(a)	4	3	3	3	–	–	1	14
	(b)	2	–	1	3	6	–	2	
Traders	(a)	1	–	3	2	1	–	–	7
	(b)	–	–	1	1	–	1	4	
Others	(a)	56	20	10	7	1	1	1	96
	(b)	7	13	18	36	15	4	3	
TOTALS	(a)	310(62%)	97(19%)	53(11%)	34(7%)	2	2	2	500
	(b)	41(8%)	62(12%)	105(21%)	170(34%)	79(16%)	23(5%)	20(4%)	

Note: (a) Number of cases in which the plaintiffs claimed the sums shown, e.g. 103 artisans were gaoled by creditors claiming under £50.

(b) Number of cases in which the debtor's total liabilities amounted to the sums shown, e.g. debts owed by each of 13 artisans to all their creditors amounted to under £50.

The following definitions are used 'Artisans' includes carpenters, shoemakers and other craftsmen; 'Shopkeepers' includes butchers, grocers and other retail traders; 'Professions' includes accountants, clerics and schoolmasters; 'Gents/women' refers to 'esquires', 'gentlemen', spinsters, widows and 'yeomen.' 'Traders' refers to 5 merchants, a broker and a warehouseman; 'Others' refers to debtors whose occupations are not recorded.

Source: data based on B.P.P. Accounts and Papers (1814-15), XI, 419-587.

TABLE 2.2. BANKRUPTS, IMPRISONED DEBTORS AND CRIMINAL COMMITTALS, 1750–1826.

Year	Bankrupts	Debtors committed to King's Bench Prison	Year	Bankrupts	Debtors committed to King's Bench Prison	Debtors Imprisoned in England & Wales	Criminal Committals in England & Wales
1750	211	225	1789	586	615		
1751	172	189	1790	596	593		
1752	170	204	1791	615	588		
1753	197	231	1792	638	587		
1754	243	235	1793	1,377	632		
1755	231	185	1794	844	627		
1756	236	193	1795	690	609		
1757	250	212	1796	749	594		
1758	278	285	1797	871	550		
1759	280	268	1798	714	527	3,814	
1760	216	346	1799	546	562	3,944	
1761	178	358	1800	738	535	4,268	
1762	188	212	1801	881	627	4,527	
1763	214	290	1802	833	667	4,417	
1764	284	308	1803	899	713	4,114	
1765	223	324	1804	896	778	4,420	
1766	288	415	1805	867	786	4,803	4.605
1767	334	512	1806	992	799	5,174	4,346
1768	303	442	1807	1,076	835	5,264	4,446
1769	309	362	1808	1,098	894	5,333	4,735
1770	393	406	1809	1,098	893	5,432	5,330
1771	345	460	1810	1,799	1,079	5,858	5,146
1772	484	459	1811	2.112	1,202	6,134	5,337
1773	556	414	1812	1,813	1,101	6,115	6,576
1774	338	501	1813	1,583	1,338	6,806	7,164
1775	332	553	1814	1,258	1,300	6.374	6,390
1776	388	797	1815	1,759	1,429	7,080	7,818
1777	489	581	1816	2,145	1,525	8,379	9,091
1778	662	746	1817	1,573	1,647	9,030	13,932
1779	538	810	1818	1,012	1,651	8,238	13,567
1780	445	1,654	1819	1,582	1,866		14,254
1781	444	2,203	1820	1,385	1,780		13,710
1782	557	623	1821	1,268	1,701		13,115
1783	535	728	1822	1,132	1,802		12,241
1784	544	636	1823	988	1.519		12,263
1785	485	551	1824	999	1,486		13,698
1786	512	573	1825	1,141	1,608		14,437
1787	506	603	1826	2,590	1,893		16,147
1788	754	648					

Note: Statistics of debtors imprisoned in England and Wales, 1798–1818, are incomplete.

Sources: for bankruptcies, T.S. Ashton, An Economic History of England: The 18th Century (1955), p.254; N.J. Silberling, 'British Prices and Business Cycles, 1779–1850', Rev. Econ. Stats. (1923), Suppl. 2, 251.

for committals to King's Bench prison, 1750–98, King's Bench Commitment Books (P.R.O. Pris.4, nos.2–17); 1798–1826, B.P.P. Accounts and Papers (1819), XVII, 163;.

(1826–7), XIX, 344-5.

for committals for debt in England and Wales, 1798-1818, B.P.P. Accounts and Papers (1819), XVII, 145-83.

for criminal committals, B.P.P. Accounts and Papers (1818), XVI, 190; (1850), XVII, 470.

TABLE 2.3. GAOLERS' RETURNS SHOWING THE INCIDENCE OF LONG-TERM IMPRISONMENT FOR DEBT IN EXECUTION, 1792.

CATEGORIES	Size of debts owed £ Under 20	£ 20 – 49	£ 50 – 99	£ Over 100
Length of time for which debtors were imprisoned	'Many' – 8 yrs. 'Some' – 9 yrs. One – 10 yrs. One – 45 yrs.	'Some' – 8 yrs. 'Some' – 9 yrs. 'Some' – 10 yrs. One – 24 yrs.	'Some' – 7 yrs. One – 9 yrs. One – 10 yrs.	'Many' – 9 yrs. 'Some' – 10 yrs. 'Others' – 11 yrs.
Number of debtors who died in some prisons, 1780-92	9 after 2 yrs. 4 after 3 yrs. 1 after 5 yrs. 1 after 45 yrs.	16 after 2 yrs. 10 after 3 yrs. 1 after 11 yrs.	9 after 2 yrs. 5 after 3 yrs. 1 after 9 yrs.	22 after 2 yrs. 9 after 3 yrs. 2 after 7 yrs. 1 after 10 yrs. 1 after 15 yrs.

Note: The prisons to which this refers are not recorded.

Source: House of Commons Journals, **XLVII (1792), 647.**

TABLE 2.4. NUMBER OF PRISONERS WHO USED THE INSOLVENT DEBTORS COURT, 1813–30.

YEAR	TOWN	COUNTRY	TOTAL
1813	61	—	61
1814	984	909	1,893
1815	1,483	1,403	2,886
1816	1,470	1,793	3,263
1817	1,705	1,843	3,548
1818	1,727	1,757	3,484
1819	1,770	1,582	3,352
1820	1,751	1,789	3,540
1821	2,586	2,673	5,259
1822	2,241	2,820	5,061
1823	2,033	2,300	4,333
1824	2,007	2,064	4,071
1825	2,089	1,636	3,725
1826	2,553	2,155	4,708
1827	2,019	2,215	4,234
1828	2,040	1,699	3,739
1829	2,225	1,842	4,067
1830	2,245	2,134	4,379
TOTALS	32,989	32,614	65,603

Source: B.P.P. Accounts and Papers (1826-7), XIX, 57; (1831), XV, 89.

TABLE 6.1. OVERSEAS TRADE OF GREAT BRITAIN, 1805-16. Official Values (£000)

Year	Northern Europe		Southern Europe		Asia		Africa		British North America		United States		British West Indies		Foreign West Indies and South America	
	Imports	Exports	Imports	Exports	Imports	Exports	Imports	Exports	Imports	Exports	Imports	Exports	Imports	Exports	Imports	Exports
1805	7,137	13,026	2,872	2,440	6,073	1,669	107	991	294	865	1,767	7,147	6,720	3,832	736	319
1806	5,805	10,533	2,392	2,678	3,755	1,937	116	1,433	330	951	2,000	8,613	8,815	4,734	1,227	1,796
1807	5,154	9,412	2,819	3,278	3,402	1,884	122	798	450	1,061	2,848	7,921	7,980	4,579	1,341	1,326
1808	2,120	4,734	2,091	6,547	3,858	1,933	143	533	827	1,125	836	3,992	8,778	5,929	2,838	4,830
1809	5,660	13,666	3,935	10,055	3,366	1,648	185	706	678	1,748	2,205	5,188	7,703	5,975	5,090	6,382
1810	7,480	11,221	4,996	8,385	4,710	1,717	257	484	885	1,845	2,614	7,813	8,258	4,790	6,961	5,970
1811	2,652	2,358	1,685	12,606	4,106	1,665	189	317	802	1,910	2,309	1,432	8,452	4,123	3,831	3,047
1812	3,213	5,460	2,952	15,528	5,602	1,779	172	444	720	1,419	1,294	4,136	7,487	4,767	2,471	4,115
1813	–	–	–	–	–	–	–	–	–	–	–	–	–	–	–	–
1814	6,399	22,922	3,443	12,348	6,304	1,698	269	422	323	4,093	23	7	8,497	6,315	6,220	4,302
1815	4,986	19,860	3,244	9,071	8,042	2,093	325	393	369	3,099	2,370	11,937	8,527	6,916	3,371	3,786
1816	2,784	18,493	2,068	9,000	8,313	2,205	240	380	493	2,208	2,386	7,800	7,547	4,608	1,974	3,284

Source: B.R. Mitchell and P. Deane, Abstract of British Historical Statistics (Cambridge, 1962), p.311. The records for 1813 were destroyed by fire.

TABLE 6.2. BRITISH EXPORTS TO EUROPE, 1806-11. Official Values (£000,000).

Year	Sweden	Germany	Prussia	Spain and Canaries	Gibraltar, Malta, Ionian Isles	Norway, Denmark	Rússia
1806	0.2	5.6	0.5	0.1	0.8	1.4	1.7
1807	0.7	0.4	0.2	0.1	1.6	4.9	1.7
1808	2.4	1.5	0.1	0.9	4.3	0.0	0.4
1809	3.5	6.0	0.6	2.4	5.8	0.3	0.9
1810	4.9	2.2	2.6	1.4	4.0	0.2	0.9
1811	0.5	0.1	0.1	1.2	5.4	0.7	0.7

Source: A.D. Gayer, W.W. Rostow and A.J. Schwartz, The Growth and Fluctuation of the British Economy, 1790-1850 (Oxford, 1953), i, 89.

Table 6.3. SOME ECONOMIC INDICATORS, 1809-11.

	1809 (quarters)				1810 (quarters)				1811 (quarters)			
	1	2	3	4	1	2	3	4	1	2	3	4
Imported Commodity prices (1821-5 = 100)	173.9	158.8	144.8	155.9	162.6	160.0	149.3	143.5	137.8	135.2	128.1	131.4
Very ordinary West India coffee (£ per cwt.)	3-15	4-3	3-14	3-17	4-4	3-3	3-1	2-17	2-2	1-10	1-9	1-5
Fine West India coffee (£ per cwt.)	6-5	6-10	6-1	6-3	6-13	5-19	5-5	4-17	4-4	3-4	3-3	2-19
Jamaica Brown Sugar (£ per cwt.)	3-16	3-8	3-8	3-16	3-17	3-15	3-16	3-11	3-9	3-3	3-4	3-8
Fine Jamaica Sugar (£ per cwt.)	4-5	3-14	3-18	4-4	4-4	4-3	4-4	3-19	3-19	3-18	3-14	4-0
Cotton wool, Bahia (s. per lb.)	2-8	1-10	1-11	2-1	2-2	1-11	1-10	1-9	1-8	1-7	1-3	1-4
Riga hemp (£ per ton)	126	116	98	82	75	70	66	74	75	75	74	92
Irish bacon (£ per cwt.)	3-11	3-14	4-1	4-2	3-14	3-13	3-11	3-11	3-12	3-14	3-8	2-12
Price of 3% Consols (first month each quarter)	66 1/8	68	68 7/16	68 11/16	69 3/8	69 3/16	69 3/4	65 1/4	66 3/16	64 7/16	62	63 1/2
Hamburg Exchange (sterling rate in schillings and grotes)	31-2	30	29	28-9	28-7	31	30-7	29-4	25-2	23-7	25-9	25
Av. comm. paper under discount at Bank of England (£000,000)	14.4	14.8	15.6	16.5	19.1	19.8	20.8	18.3	15.8	13.7	12.4	12.9
Bankruptcies (quarterly totals)	279	281	228	310	344	351	424	680	645	511	467	489

Sources: for imported commodity prices and consols, A.D. Gayer, W.W. Rostow and A.J. Schwartz, The Growth and Fluctuation of the British Economy, 1790-1850 (Oxford, 1953), i, 94, 97.

for individual commodity prices (quarterly averages) and Hamburg exchange rates, The Tradesman, 1809-11.

for average commercial paper under discount at the Bank of England, and bankruptcies, N.J. Silberling, 'British Prices and Business Cycles, 1790-1850', Rev.Econ.Stats (1923), Suppl. 2, 251, 256.

TABLE 6.4. ANALYSIS OF BANKRUPTS, April 1810 – July 1811.

	Location/occupation	1810 April	May	June	July	Aug.	Sept.	Oct.	Nov.	Dec.	1811 Jan.	Feb.	March	April	May	June	July	TOTAL	%age of Bankruptcies	Bankrupts per thousand people
London	Merchants	11	12	12	19	12	9	18	22	16	17	11	10	12	13	10	11	215	(8)	
London	Entrepreneurs	3	5	2	7	3	4	7	7	7	8	10	4	0	5	3	4	79		
London	Brokers	2	3	2	1	0	1	3	3	1	3	0	2	2	2	5	7	37		
London	Miscell.	39	50	45	39	37	40	49	88	53	70	50	47	62	49	37	39	794		
London	Total	55	70	61	66	52	54	77	120	77	98	71	63	76	69	55	61	1,125	43	1.0
Lancashire – Manchester	Merchants	2	0	0	1	4	2	4	4	2	2	1	3	1	1	0	3	30		
Lancashire – Manchester	Entrepreneurs	0	0	0	0	1	0	1	3	0	2	0	0	0	0	0	2	9	(5)	(1.5)
Lancashire – Manchester	Textile mfrs.	0	1	3	1	1	2	7	3	1	8	5	3	2	0	2	0	39		
Lancashire – Manchester	Miscell.	1	1	3	3	3	2	5	1	8	8	3	1	6	3	4	4	56		
Lancashire – L'pool	Merchants	0	4	2	1	1	2	11	7	8	15	8	9	5	11	5	2	91	(6)	(1.6)
Lancashire – L'pool	Miscell.	3	5	3	3	7	3	6	6	6	4	7	5	2	6	4	4	74		
Lancashire – Els'whr.	Textile mfrs.	1	0	2	3	4	1	3	8	13	6	6	3	3	5	4	4	66		
Lancashire – Els'whr.	Miscell.	2	5	2	0	3	1	4	3	5	6	10	8	4	5	4	5	67		
Lancashire	Total	9	16	15	12	24	13	41	35	43	51	40	32	23	31	23	24	432	16	0.5
West Country	Devon	2	2	9	4	9	3	4	12	9	7	5	7	3	5	2	3	86		
West Country	Somerset	3	3	4	4	1	2	3	7	5	5	4	3	3	1	3	1	52		
West Country	Hants.	2	0	5	5	2	2	6	3	3	4	2	4	2	0	2	4	46		
West Country	Wilts.	3	3	2	6	2	2	5	4	3	4	4	3	2	2	1	0	46		
West Country	Elsewhere	1	6	6	4	7	11	13	23	15	13	9	15	16	18	13	2	172		
West Country	Total	11	14	26	23	21	20	31	49	35	33	24	32	26	26	21	10	402	15	0.2
	Yorkshire	9	8	10	27	4	5	12	12	7	12	13	7	6	10	7	10	159	6	0.15
	Bristol	1	2	2	5	3	6	8	10	3	10	6	5	5	1	4	3	74	2.5	1.0
	Birmingham	1	2	1	2	1	1	3	4	3	2	2	7	5	3	1	4	42	1.5	0.5
	Elsewhere	17	20	25	20	17	19	29	43	29	32	31	28	26	43	35	26	440	16	0.1
	TOTAL	103	132	140	155	122	118	201	273	197	238	187	174	167	183	146	138	2,674	100	

The following descriptions are adopted: 'Merchants' - This was a vague term at the start of the nineteenth century. In the Bankruptcy Court it referred generally to importers and exporters.

'Entrepreneurs' refers to warehousemen and wholesale dealers.

'Textile mfrs.' refers to all occupations associated with the manufacturing process.

For the 'Miscellaneous' category, see Table 6.5.

The West Country category 'Elsewhere' includes Cornwall, Dorset, Gloucs., Worcs. and South Wales.

Sources: Bankruptcy Court, Docket Books (P.R.O.B4/29, 30); London Gazette, 1810, 1811; B.R. Mitchell and P. Deane, Abstract of British Historical Statistics (Cambridge, 1962), pp.20, 24-6 (for population statistics, 1811).

TABLE 6.5. Analysis of Miscellaneous London Bankrupts, April 1810-July 1811.

Type of Trader	1810 April	May	June	July	Aug.	Sept.	Oct.	Nov.	Dec.	1811 Jan.	Feb.	March	April	May	June	July	Total	%age
Shopkeepers	12	20	15	14	16	12	18	32	17	23	16	19	17	16	15	12	274	34.5
Artisans	7	13	12	7	6	13	15	33	19	26	21	14	24	17	15	13	255	32
Clothiers	3	4	6	4	6	5	8	7	8	7	4	6	13	9	–	–	90	11
Victuallers	6	5	3	7	3	3	3	6	3	4	4	4	2	4	2	4	63	8
Builders	3	1	1	2	2	2	1	2	3	3	2	2	2	1	–	3	30	4
Innkeepers	3	–	1	–	1	1	1	1	–	1	1	–	1	1	1	–	13	1.5
Scriveners	1	5	2	–	1	–	–	–	–	1	–	1	–	1	–	1	13	1.5
Brewers	1	1	–	–	–	–	1	1	–	1	–	1	–	–	–	1	7	1
Bankers	–	–	1	1	1	–	–	–	–	–	–	–	–	–	–	1	4	0.5
Others	3	1	4	4	1	4	2	6	3	4	2	–	3	–	4	4	45	6
Total	39	50	45	39	37	40	49	88	53	70	50	47	62	49	37	39	794	100

The following definitions are adopted:

'Shopkeepers' includes bakers, butchers, book-sellers, grocers and other retail firms.

'Artisans' includes bricklayers, carpenters, carvers, coach-makers, furniture-makers, joiners, masons, potters, printers, silversmiths, tanners, upholsterers, etc.

'Clothiers' includes drapers, hosiers, mercers, milliners, etc.

Sources: Bankruptcy Court, Docket Books (P.R.O. B4/29,30); London Gazette, 1810, 1811.

TABLE 6.6. Bank of England Discounts and Note Circulation, June–Dec.1810.

Dates (starting Mondays)		Volume of bills and notes discounted (£000,000)	Date		Volume of bills and notes under discount (£000.000)	Volume of Bank notes in circulation (£000.000)
June	4–10	2.86	June	6	18.61	20.67
	11–17	2.22		13	18.37	21.34
	18–24	2.61		20	18.56	21.15
	25– 1	3.83		27	19.48	21.46
July	2– 8	4.03	July	4	21.46	25.25
	9–15	1.98		11	21.10	21.46
	16–22	3.33		18	20.66	22.82
	23–29	2.62		24	20.33	24.72
	30– 5	2.59				
			Aug.	1	20.02	25.20
Aug.	6–12	2.64		8	19.69	25.04
	13–19	2.47		15	19.10	24.56
	20–26	2.79		22	19.16	23.97
	27– 2	3.09		29	18.97	24.21
Sept.	3– 9	2.32	Sept.	5	19.04	24.09
	10–16	2.21		12	18.49	23.80
	17–23	2.29		19	18.12	23.55
	24–30	2.79		26	18.10	24.00
Oct.	1– 7	4.26	Oct.	3	18.84	25.98
	8–14	3.14		10	20.13	28.53
	15–21	1.80		17	19.66	25.67
	22–28	1.73		24	18.82	24.92
	29– 4	2.27		31	17.99	24.78
Nov.	5–11	1.80	Nov.	7	16.93	24.25
	12–18	1.84		14	16.27	25.15
	19–25	2.17		21	15.84	23.36
	26– 2	2.93		28	15.12	23.05
Dec.	3– 9	2.75	Dec.	5	16.10	22.90
	10–16	2.59		12	16.07	22.23
	17–23	2.75		19	16.43	23.68
				24	16.90	24.57

Sources: Volume of bills and notes discounted, calculated from Bank of England, General Ledger, No.18, ff.181, 187. Volume of bills and notes under discount and Bank notes in circulation, Bank of England, Weekly Totals, No.1, Assets and Liabilities.

TABLE 8.1. MAJOR CLAIMANTS AGAINST BRICKWOOD and Co., BANKERS, LOMBARD STREET (stopped payments, 6 July, 1810)

Bankers London	Reason for claim	Amount claimed (£)
Marsh	I	70,000
Bank of England	I	48,418
Postlethwaite	I	23,876
Hammersley	I	13,000
A.Anderson	I	12,700
Newnham	I	6,000
Fry	I	1,400
Lloyd	I	1,000
J.S.Barber	I	1,000
		177,394
Elsewhere		
Bowles (New Sarum)	B	114,670
Hurst (Warrington)	I	20,784
Heywood (Liv.)	I	5,850
Whitefield (Lewes)	I	5,000
Rowton (Chester)	I	3,632
Sparkes (Exeter)	I	3,000
Prideaux (Devon)	I	2,990
Tate (Croydon)	B	2,055
Miller (Leicester)	I	2,000
S.Edwards (Lincs)	I	1,500
Troughton (Coventry)	I	1,500
Piper (Surrey)	I	1,000
		163,981
Total		341,375

Merchants London	Reason for claim	Amount claimed (£)
D.Oliviera	I	18,363
F. de Tastet	I	11,573
F. Millett	I	8,550
J.Cockerill	I	8,000
S.Cohen	I	5,519
J.Mackenzie	I	5,000
S.Williams	I	3,963
E.Bourne	I	3,848
C.Grill	I	3,500
W.Adam	I	3,000
W.Hallett	I	3,000
P.Blackburn	I	2,598
A. de Paiva	I	2,519
H.Solly	I	2,500
J.Todhunter	I	2,420
E. Curling	B	2,311
J. Paget	B	2,002
G. Meyer	I	2,000
J.Bell	I	1,900
L.Paleski	I	1,900
W. Pratt	I	1,722
G. Paton	I	1,540
J. Forbes	I	1,538
R.Lee	I	1,500
J.Bowden	I	1,500
T.Elmslie	I	1,497
Smith.McGeorge	I	1,200
H.G.Helbus	I	1,100
A. Gumage	I	1,000
		107,063
Elsewhere		
W.Monteeth (Glasgow)	DI	30,231
J.Sill,W.Watson (Liv.)	I	5,000
W.Harrison (Man.)	I	2,500
		37,731
Total		144,794

Traders London	Reason for claim	Amount claimed (£)
N.C.Collison	B	5,652
J. Hunter	I	4.642
W. Bennett	G	3,013
M.Eldridge	G	2,716
W.Allder	I	2,570
T.J. Moore	I	2,514
J.S.Moline	I	2,488
J.Stephenson	G	2,325
C.Edelman	B	2,026
G.Vipond	B	1,675
D.Montague	I	1,500
J.Scotthup	I	1,500
J.M.Shakespeare	G	1,348
W.Gosling, J.Eve	B	1,022
R.Houlden	B	1,004
M. Clarke	I	1,000
		36,995
Elsewhere		
J.Parkinson (Man.)	I	1,642
M.Sanders (Birmingham)	I	1,592
G.Bayly (Rotherhithe)	B	1,350
J.Marriott (Oxford)	G	1,050
		5,634
Total		42,629

Warehousemen London	Reason for claim	Amount claimed (£)
R.Fort	D	44,638
J.Brockbank	I	2,371
J.Bowman, J.B.Spencer	I	2,000
J.Goodair	I	1,991
E. Ambrose	B	1,027
T.Langston	I	1,000
J. Peel	I	1,000
R. Burra	I	1.000
		55,027
Brokers (London)		
K.C.Mackenzie	I	6,500
R.Bruce	D	6.100
W.J.Jones (Stockbr.)	I	2,388
C.Brooke	I	2,000
J.Reynolds	B	1,250
Sir J.Zowlin	I	1,250
W.Thomas	I	1.056
		20,544
Gentlemen		
J.Whitfield (London)	I	3,000
J.Broderick (Plymouth)	I	2,403
G.Herbert (Plymouth)	I	1,500
H.Tucker (Bermuda)	B	1,251
		8,154
Others		
British Herring Fishing Co.	B	4,575
S.Goodbihere (goldsmith)	I	1,906
C.Bishop (proctor)	B	1,083
J.Phillips, J.Homan (auctioneer)	B	1,030
		8,594
Total		92,319

Total (£621,117)

DIVIDENDS

1 Feb., 1812	1–10d.
1 Aug., 1812	1– 1d.
8 May, 1813	8d.
21 Dec., 1813	4d.
22 Aug., 1814	10d.
15 June, 1824	6d.
22 Aug., 1826	5d.
18 March, 1828	2½d.
13 Jan., 1858	0.2/11d.
?	1.5/8d.
?	0.13/48d.
	6–0.305/528d.

KEY

B – balance of account

D – drawer of bankrupt's bills

G – goods sold and delivered

I – indorsee of bankrupt's bills

— – firms which failed during the crisis of 1810-11 are underlined

TABLE 8.2. Analysis of Bills drawn by Samuel Cooke.

Bills accepted by	Value (and number) of bills paid to or discounted by: Banks £		Brokers £		J.F.Harrison £		Merchants, Wholesalers etc. £		Total £	
Brickwood & Co.	59,700	(29)	10,745	(5)	34,519	(14)	44,433	(22)	149,397	(70)
Harrison & Co.	42,480	(26)	7,264	(3)	–		16,638	(13)	66,382	(42)
Harrison & Gorst	21,738	(9)	35,351	(15)	–		41,556	(16)	98,645	(40)
Total	123,918	(64)	53,360	(23)	34,519	(14)	102,627	(51)	314,424	(152)
Percentage	39		17		11		33		100	

Sources: P.R.O. B3/252-4; B3/2150-1.

TABLE 8.3. MAJOR CLAIMANTS AGAINST HARRISON and Co., MERCHANTS, TOWER STREET (stopped payments, 6 July 1810)

Bankers	Reason for claim	Amount claimed (£)
London		
Marsh	I	114,427
Newnham	I	113,885
Postlethwaite	I	25,376
Freen	I	21,200
A.Anderson	I	14,221
Bank of England	I	10,642
Kensington	I	5,451
Masterman	I	5,000
Barnett	I	4,627
G.Simpson	I	3,700
Martin	I	2,500
N.Graham	I	2,480
J.S.Barber	I	1,000
		324.509
Elsewhere		
Marshall (Newcastle)	I	15,718
Boyd (Newcastle)	I	9,137
Townsend (Honiton)	I	5,000
Heath (Andover)	I	5,000
Sharp (Southampton)	I	4,500
Prideaux (Devon)	B	2,990
Hardcastle (Pontefract)	I	2,500
Scott (Grantham)	B	2,000
Langhorn (Berwick)	B	2,000
S.Edwards (Lincs)	I	1,500
Sparkes (Exeter)	I	1,000
		51,345
Total (£515,394)		375,854

Merchants	Reason for claim	Amount claimed (£)
London		
D.Oliviera	I	14,088
B.Donaldson	I	6,000
J.Mackenzie	I	5,000
J.Cockerill	I	5,000
C.Fry	I	4,993
J.Higgin	I	4,357
S.Williams	I	3,963
W.Adam	I	3,000
C.Ogleby	I	3.000
T.Moxon	I	3,000
W.Stanley	G	2,827
H.Parker	I	2,519
J.Robertson	I	2,500
J.Hodgson	I	2,113
J.C.Splitgerber	I	1.875
J.Watson	D	1,168
E.Bourne	I	1,000
		66.403
Elsewhere		
J.Hall (Antigua)	B	2,253
J.Tamer (West Cowes)	B	1,123
		3,376
Total		69.779

Traders	Reason for claim	Amount claimed (£)
London		
W.Gray	B	4,694
J.Scotthup	I	4,019
W.Allder	I	2,570
T.Hill	I	2,512
Smith, Wood, Gregory	I	2,479
R.James	I	1,523
J. Hardie	I	1,000
		18,797
Newcastle-on-Tyne		
T.Head (timber mt.)	G	2,613
J.Collins (timber mt.)	I	2,511
T.Cookson (iron founder)	G	2,237
G.Hodgson (iron founder)	G	2,053
R.Greenwell (timber mt.)	G	1,469
J.Glynn (iron founder)	G	1,442
		12,325
Elsewhere		
J.Haigh (Edinburgh distiller)	I	2,900
G.Hudson (Durham woolmonger)	G	1,262
		4,162
Total		35,284

Warehousemen	Reason for claim	Amount claimed (£)
London		
J.Webber	I	5,000
T.Langston	I	3,000
		8,000
Brokers (London)		
J.May	I	10,000
J.C.Herries (Ins)	Pr.	6,977
K.C.Mackenzie	I	2.000
		18.977
Gentlemen		
R.Creed (London)	I	5,000
Others		
W.Lucas (underwriter)	I	2,500
Total		34.477

DIVIDEND

10 July, 1813 3–4d.

KEY

B – balance of account

D – drawer of bankrupt's bills

G – goods sold and delivered

I – indorsee of bankrupt's bills

Pr – insurance premiums

– – firms which failed during the crisis of 1810-11 are under-lined.

TABLE 8.4. MAJOR CLAIMANTS AGAINST J. GOODAIR, WAREHOUSEMAN, QUEEN STREET (Docketed 27 October, 1810)

Bankers	Reason for claim	Amount claimed (£)	Merchants	Reason for claim	Amount claimed (£)	Traders	Reason for claim	Amount claimed (£)	Warehousemen	Reason for claim	Amount claimed (£)
London			London			London			London		
Bosanquet	I	8,735	F. de Tastet	B	29,277	B. Heseltine	I	2,000	R.Harris	M	3,000
			J.Sanderson	I	12,025	<u>E. & T.Ward</u>	I	1,986	<u>S.Rowlandson</u>	I	2,033
Elsewhere			W.Pratt	I	3,193			3,986			5.033
			G.Heinzelman	I	3,127	Elsewhere			Gentleman		
Pedder (Preston)	Bd.I	31,743	R.Mckerrell	M	2,682	P.Ainsworth (Bolton)	D	1,859	N.Middlecoat (Cornwall)	M	2.695
			J.Harkness	I	1,838						
Sharp (Southampton)	I	29,335	Smith, McGeorge, Watson	I	1,596						
Beck (Carlisle)	I	11,633	R.Grant	I	1,300						
		72,711			55,038						
			Elsewhere								
			R.Aitken (Glasgow)	I	7,375						
			W.Monteeth (Glasgow)	I	1,204						
			J.Alexander (Glasgow)	I	1,204						
			R.Hampson (Man).	I	1,073						
					10,856						
Total (£160,913)		81,446			65,894			5,845			7,728

DIVIDENDS

22 May, 1813	2– 0d.
24 Jan., 1818	8d.
24 July, 1824	11d.
9 Nov., 1832	1– 7d.
	5– 2d.

KEY

B – balance of account

Bd.– bond

I – indorsee of bankrupt's bills

M – money lent and advanced

– – firms which failed during the crisis of 1810-11 are under-lined.

TABLE 8.5. MAJOR CLAIMANTS AGAINST ROWLANDSON, ISAAC, BRIEN and Co., WAREHOUSEMEN, CHEAPSIDE (stopped payments, 14 Aug., 1810)

Bankers	Reason for claim	Amount claimed (£)
London		
Newnham	I	60,472
Masterman	I	37,041
Freen	I	17,752
Smith, Payne, Smith	I	13,994
Bank of England	I	10,694
Kensington	I	8,248
Lloyd	I	7,398
Burgess	I	5,180
J.S.Barber	I	2,582
		163,361
Elsewhere		
Sharp (Southampton)	I	23,853
Milford (Exeter)	GI	13,958
Crewdson (Kendal)	I	8,647
Pedder (Preston)	I	3,750
Bellairs (Lincs)	I	2,668
G.Watson (Glasgow)	I	1,344
		54,220
Total (£508,218)		217,581

Merchants	Reason for claim	Amount claimed (£)
London		
J.Shaw	GI	36,116
E.Sage	DG	17,830
L.Alexander	DG	16,450
J.B.Richards	G	6,513
J.MacKenzie	DI	5,355
J.Parker	DG	5,354
N.M.Rothschild	DG	4,157
H.Waddington	I	4,060
C.Ogleby	DG	3,590
A.Mells	DG	2,880
T.Dutton	G	2,341
H.L.Hoffham	B	2,747
I.Selig	BI	2,182
J.E.Hyman	DG	1,822
W.Morley	G	1,817
J.Wilkinson	DG	1,719
J. & M.Smith	G	1,704
B.G.Jeffrey	GI	1,558
J.Styan	I	1,402
G.Heinzelman	I	1,399
P.Schidtmeyer	B	1,224
W.Bedford	D	1,204
B.Linthorne	M	1,199
A. de Paiva	I	1,150
		125,773
Elsewhere		
J.Hargreaves (Man)	I	3,088
J.Blair (Man.)	G	2,868
A.Clegg (Man.)	M	2,616
T.Barland (Perth)	DI	1,786
D.Beatson (Perth)	DG	1,513
E.Cragg (Westmorland)	D	1,301
		13,172
Total		138,945

Traders	Reason for claim	Amount claimed (£)
London		
E.Jones	DI	4,156
T.Bates	D	3,635
C.W.Hick	G	2,200
R.James	I	1,814
W.Agnew	I	1,276
		13,081
Elsewhere		
Moulson, Fawcett (Man.)	DI	37,238
J.Young (Perth)	DG	14,944
W.Weston (Man.)	DG	4,550
G.Lang (Glasgow)	DG	1,856
		58,588
Total		71,669

Warehousemen	Reason for claim	Amount claimed (£)
London		
T.Langston	DG	10,894
C.C. Deacon	DGI	7,338
A.Sangster	DG	6.580
Lee, Martineau	DG	3,890
J. Earle	DM	3,600
Bowdler, Gilgrest	DM	3,519
C.Rogers	I	3.059
J.Sheldon	DI	3,005
S.Cater	BI	2,825
A.Rowlandson	I	2,717
T.Nightingale	D	2,563
W.Lloyd	DG	2,090
E.Roberts	DG	1,760
J.Bury	DG	1,653
J.Tiplady	G	1,582
W.Stirling	DG	1,472
J.Bulmer	DG	1,290
R.Locke	DG	1,110
		60,947
(Elsewhere)		
E.Turner (Man).	DG	3,497
Brokers (London)		
T.Fellows	I	5,000
J.Kirkman (Ins).	I	1,901
W.J.Jones (Stockbr.)	I	1,100
J.May	I	1,045
		9,046
(Elsewhere)		
J.Hardman (Liv.)	I	2,437
Gentleman		
I.Joseph	I	1,596
Other		
S.Goodbihere (goldsmith)	MI	2,500
Total		80,023

DIVIDENDS

25 July, 1812	4–0d.
10 March, 1813	9d.
1 Dec., 1813	2½d.
28 Oct., 1815	3d.
24 Oct., 1818	2½d.
20 June, 1820	1d.
5 Nov., 1825	1d.
14 Nov., 1828	0S/6d.
	5–7.5/6d.

KEY

B – balance of account

D – drawer of bankrupt's bills

G – goods sold and delivered

I – indorsee of bankrupt's bills

M – money lent and advanced

– – firms which failed during the crisis of 1810-11 are under-lined.

TABLE 8.6. MAJOR CLAIMANTS AGAINST JACOB Bros., MERCHANTS, NEWGATE STREET (stopped payments, 18 July, 1810)

Bankers	Reason for claim	Amount claimed (£)
London		
Bank of England	I	28,572
Merle	I	17,364
Newnham	I	16,902
Lloyd	I	11,667
Masterman	I	11,250
Haddock	I	4,735
J.S.Barber	I	4,021
A.Anderson	I	3,791
Burgess	I	3,000
Bosanquet	I	2,800
Down	I	2,018
Freen	I	1,894
Smith, Payne, Smith	I	1,510
		109,524
Elsewhere		
Pedder (Preston)	I	13,000
Rishworth (Halifax)	I	3,348
Gidley (Somerset)	I	1,224
		17,572

Merchants	Reason for claim	Amount claimed (£)
London		
F.de Tastet	I	20,891
J.Gilliatt	D	14,784
A.Mells	D	10,035
R.H.Martin	M	6,108
R.Brown	DI	5,776
G.Paton	I	5,017
W.Routh	DI	5,007
P.M.Samuel	D	4,204
J.Peele	I	3,900
J.Jacks	DI	3,383
S.S.Robinson	I	3,020
J.Ranking	D	2,770
E.Leathley	D	2,355
J.Robertson	I	2.315
J.C.Chryssell	I	2,285
W.Savill	D	2,215
J.Foulerton	I	2,000
J.Mather	In.	2,000
M.Joy	M	1,830
J.Cooper	I	1,723
T.Davy	Bd.	1,600
T.Noyes	I	1,500
J.Braddick	I	1,251
J.Thornton	D	1,202
R.Mountford	D	1,083
		108,254
Elsewhere		
C.Hebblethwaite (Leeds)	M	3,023
B.Wilson (Man.)	G	2,986
A.Turner (Leeds)	D	2,926
A.Rhodes (Leeds)	G	2,274
J.Gibson (Great St.Helens)	D	2,182
S.Reinhold (Man)	B	1,751
S.Greig (Man.)	MG	1,125
H.Greaves (Man.)	I	1,000
		17,267

Traders	Reason for claim	Amount claimed (£)
London		
J.B.Plowman	B	5,000
W.Christie	I	3,528
J.Gibbs	D	3,140
G.Bacchus	I	3,029
C.Johnson	D	1,427
E.G.Barnard	D	1,261
J.Pritt	G	1,233
J.Fielding	M	1,205
R.Mangles	G	1,110
A.Pellatt	G	1,091
T.Wilson	G	1,055
W.Sharp	G	1,033
		24,112
Elsewhere		
J.Perry (Essex)	D	1,906
T.A.Shuter (Horsley Down)	G	1,703
S.Galton (B'ham)	D	1,482
T.Fisher (Dorchester)	D	1,250
		6,341

Warehousemen	Reason for claim	Amount claimed (£)
London		
J.Procter	D	5,755
J.Bowman, J.B. Spencer	D	3,776
J.Lawrence	D	3,380
T.Milton	MG	2,752
T.Britten	D	1.871
A.Rowlandson	I	1,510
W.Simpson	I	1,286
		20,330
Brokers (London)		
V.Stuckey	DI	18,971
R.Winstanley	I	2.500
R.Cowie (Ins.)	Pr.	2,190
T.Edwards	I	1,730
J.W.Buckle	G	1,126
F.Meredith (Ins.)	Pr.	1,020
		27,537
Gentlemen (London)		
R.Marston	D	3,100
C.Foster	B	3,000
J.Leatt	D	2,845
F.Anderson	D	2,000
		10,945
Others		
C.S.Foster (Hampstead, mariner)	M	4,862
S.Goodbihere (goldsmith)	DM	4,350
J.Gunston (secretary)	I	1,315
		10.527

Total (£352,409)	Bankers	Merchants	Traders	Warehousemen, Brokers, Gentlemen, Others
	127,096	125,521	30,453	69,339

DIVIDENDS

25 Jan.,	1812	3–4d.
23 Oct.,	1813	1–2d.
27 June,	1834	3d.
		4–9d.

KEY

B – balance of account

Bd – bond

D – drawer of bankrupt's bills

G – goods sold and delivered

I – indorsee of bankrupt's bills

In. – indenture

M – money had and received

Pr. – insurance premiums

— – firms which failed during the crisis of 1810-11 are under-lined

TABLE 8.7. MAJOR CLAIMANTS AGAINST WINSTANLEY, HUDSON and Co., WAREHOUSEMEN, MANCHESTER
(stopped payments, 5 Nov. 1810)

Bankers London	Reason for claim	Amount claimed (£)	Merchants London	Reason for claim	Amount claimed (£)	Traders London	Reason for claim	Amount claimed (£)	Warehousemen London	Reason for claim	Amount claimed (£)
Lloyd	I	18,127	F. de Tastet	I	6,303	G. Heinzelman	I	4,978	R.Harris	I	2,620
Bank of England	I	11,734	C.C.Hall	I	3,192				E.Walton	I	1,879
Bosanquet	I	7,204	T.Davy	I	2,315	Elsewhere			W.Jones	I	1,210
Masterman	I	4,825	J.Scott	I	1,450						5,709
Newnham	I	2,000			13,260	<u>Foden, Slatter</u> (Chester)	D	4,978	Others		
		43,890				P.Cleworth (Chowbent, Lancs)	D	2,041	R.Winstanley Sr. (Auctioneer)	D	10,323
Elsewhere			Elsewhere			T.Ridgway (Norwich)	I	1,355			
Duncan (Halifax)	I	1,702	H.Pope (Man.)	I	1,446			8,374			
Worswick (Lancaster)	I	1,169									
Briggs (Halifax)	I	1,000									
		3,871									
Total (£91,851)		47,761			14,706			13,352			16,032

DIVIDENDS

19 Feb., 1814	2–0d.
22nd Dec., 1826	3–5½d.
9 Jan., 1832	0.17/32d.
10 May, 1837	0.3/16d.
	5–6.7/32d.

KEY

D – drawer of the bankrupt's bills

I – indorsee of the bankrupt's bills

– – firms which failed during the crisis of 1810-11 are underlined.

TABLE 8.8. MAJOR CLAIMANTS AGAINST BULL, BANKS, BRYSON and Co., WHOLESALE LINEN DRAPERS, CHEAPSIDE, (stopped payments 17 July, 1810)

Bankers London	Reason for claim	Amount claimed (£)	Merchants London	Reason for claim	Amount claimed (£)	Traders London	Reason for claim	Amount claimed (£)	Warehousemen London	Reason for claim	Amount claimed (£)
Bank of England	I	24,642	F. de Tastet	I	1,986	B.Heseltine	DI	2,523	J.Wheelwright	DI	3,573
Masterman	I	9,104	T.Stansfield	I	1,950	J.Wright	D	1,217	W.Shiking	I	2,163
Cobb	I	6,075	T.Sangster	DI	1,269			3,740	J.Sheldon	D	1,962
Newnham	I	5,049	H.Waddington	I	1,215				J.Bury	I	1,920
Burgess	I	4,243	C. Wright	D	1,183	Elsewhere			J.Lawrence	D	1.607
Lloyd	I	2,737			7,603				T.Baker	I	1,476
Kensington	I	2,109				T.Jackson (Man)	DI	5,552			
Down	I	1,805	Elsewhere			J.Litt (Man)	G	1,116			12,701
Smith, Payne, Smith	I	1,764	J.Davidson (Glasgow)	I	4,975			6,668	Others		
Freen	I	1,729	G.Hole (Man)	D	1,566				R.Lloyd (ship insurance broker)	I	1,243
Birchall	I	1,586	H.Greaves (Man)	I	1,210				R.Winstanley Sr. (auctioneer)	I	1,000
		60,843			7,751						2,243
Elsewhere											
Bellairs (Lincs)	I	4,343									
Roscoe (Liv.)	I	2,960									
Scott (Grantham)	I	1,843									
Crewdson (Kendal)	I	1,390									
Total (£112,085)		71,379			15,354			10,408			14,944

27 Aug.,	1811	2–6d.
15 Dec.,	1811	1–4d.
18 March	1831	4¼d.
21 Feb.,	1843	0.61/64d.
		4–3.13/64d.

D – drawer of bankrupt's bills

G – goods sold and delivered

I – indorsee of bankrupt's bills

– – firms which failed during the crisis of 1810-11 are underlined.

TABLE 8.9. MAJOR CLAIMANTS AGAINST J. LEIGH, MERCHANT, LIVERPOOL (stopped payments, 10 August, 1811)

Bankers London	Reason for claim	Amount claimed (£)	Merchants London	Reason for claim	Amount claimed (£)	Traders London	Reason for claim	Amount claimed (£)	Warehousemen London	Reason for claim	Amount claimed (£)
Fry	I	22,414	J.Lornt	I	1,500	A.Reid	I	1,000	T.Brown	I	2,890
Brickwood	I	13,000	J.B. de Silly	I	1,000				R. Fort	I	1,700
A.Anderson	I	4,331			2,500						4,590
		39,745	Elsewhere						Brokers		
Elsewhere			J.Sill, W.Watson (LIV.)	I	17,000				D.Rainier (Lon.)	I	1,663
Hurst (Warrington)	I	37,941	R.Taylor (Liv.)	I	4,500				J.Marsden (Liv.)	I	1,590
Heywood (Liv.)	I	18,334	W.Leigh (Liv.)	I	2,937						3,253
Bullin (Liv.)	I	3,198	W.Molyneux (Liv.)	I	1,037				Gentleman		
Dale (Liv.)	I	2,000	T.Woodward (Liv.)	I	1,030				M.Byron (Birkenhead)	M	1,265
		61,473	T.Alison (Liv.)	I	1,000						
					27,504						
Total (£141,330)		101,218			30,004			1,000			9,108

DIVIDEND

13 Jan., 1851 –3½d.

KEY

I – indorsee of bankrupt's bills

M – money lent and advanced

– – firms which failed during the crisis of 1810-11 are under-lined

TABLE 9.1. MAJOR CLAIMANTS AGAINST DAWES, NOBLE and Co., BANKERS, PALL MALL (stopped payments 30th July 1810)

Bankers	Reason for claim	Amount claimed (£)
London		
Barclay	I	8,449
Bank of England	I	3,218
Down	I	2,030
Cazalet	I	1,492
Waters	I	1,000
Barnett	I	1,000
		17,189
Elsewhere		
Hughes(Chester)	I	12,848
Heywood (Liv.)	I	9,600
Dale (Liv.)	I	7,020
Gurney (Norwich)	I	1,583
Boulton (Durham)	I	1,321
		32,372
Total (£454,749)		49,561

Merchants	Reason for claim	Amount claimed (£)
London		
W.Mitchell	I	9,435
T.Shepherd	I	7,126
J.Murray	I	3,200
J.Martindale	I	3,161
J.Anderson	I	1,973
R.Joffray	I	1,810
A.de Paiva	I	1,437
T.Gudgeon	I	1,250
W.Harwood	I	1,228
J.Akenhead	I	1,000
		31,620
Elsewhere		
T.Allen (Huddersfield)	I	3,413
J.Touchet (Man.)	I	2,976
J.Machell (Liv.)	G	2,319
W.Armitage (Yorks)	B	1,899
C.Humberton (Liv.)	B	1,840
J.Parkinson (Man.)	I	1,804
E.R.Elsden (Lyme Regis)	B	1,353
W.Caper (Birmingham)	I	1,000
		16,604
Traders (London)		
B.Vulliamy	B	6,709
W.Smith	B	2,387
J.Crake	B	1,489
H.M.Wagner	B	1,308
D.Cooper	B	1,195
J.Monday	B	1,073
C.Magnay	B	1,000
		15,161
(Elsewhere)		
J.Dunning (Devon)	B	3,163
Brokers		
S.Gurney	I	20,000
D.Rainier	I	2,368
		22,368
Other		
S.Goodbihere (goldsmith)	I	2,500
		91,416

Non-traders (nobles,'gentlemen','esquires', women) (London unless stated)	Reason for claim	Amount claimed (£)
J.Hutchison	B	47,737
E.Hughes (Flint clerk)	B	20,894
Lord Denorben	B	20,894
J.Wrigglesworth (Hants)	B	16,776
J.Balfour	B	16,483
Sir F.Standish	B	9,306
Sir J.Gallini	B	7,764
Anne Johnes (Hertford)	B	7,663
N.Clayton (Newcastle)	B	7,000
Elizabeth Johnes (Hertford)	B	6,245
J.Budworth (Somerset)	B	5,522
A.MacDonald	B	5,430
S.P.Cockerill	B	5,286
Sir G.Glynn (Dorset)	B	4,833
E.Morris (Herts)	B	4,808
Countess of Pomfret	B	4,751
Lolita Ironside (Cheltenham)	B	4,544
R.Houlton (Bath)	B	4,357
R.Fuller (Bath)	B	4,357
J.F.Scott	B	4,357
S.Johnes (Hertford,clerk)	B	4,249
Lady Stanhope	B	3,974
J.Crawley (Luton)	B	3,732
Sir N.Hart	B	3,581
J.Edwards (Flint)	B	3,561
Sir J.Whitshed	B	3,031
J.Garnett	B	3,000
Dame A.D. Somiane	B	2,972
J.Clarke (Barnstaple)	B	2,910
T.Williams (Berks)	B	2,710
Sir W.Smyth (Essex)	B	2,679
W.Close (Yorks)	B	2,677
W.Whithead	B	2,661
Maria Robinson (Wilts)	B	2,560
J.Butler	B	2,560
C.Lyley (Carshalton)	B	2,487
S.Davies	B	2,482

Non-traders (continued)	Reason for claim	Amount claimed (£)
D.P.Downing (Flint)	B	2,424
Sir J.Chichester (Devon)	B	2,283
Lord Viscount Bulkeley(Sussex)	B	2.165
Mona Milne	B	1,982
J.Probert (Salop)	B	1,956
N.Kirkland	B	1,927
Mary Jane Ormsby Gore	B	1,906
J.Hyde	B	1,805
Baroness of Penrhyn	B	1,775
Elizabeth White (Glouces)	B	1,773
Countess Coyningham(Bucks)	B	1,749
Letitia Ironside (Cheltenham)	B	1,697
C.Hunt	B	1,676
J.Dyneley	B	1,645
Marchioness of Clanricarde (Bath)	B	1,500
Elizabeth Knight (Salop)	B	1,493
H.Howarth	B	1,479
R.Blair	B	1,473
R.Barclay Jr.	B	1,472
Sir J.Palmer (Leics)	B	1,426
Mary Burton	B	1,321
Sir H.Mann (Margate)	B	1,303
Bishop of Worcester	B	1,273
Jane Brice (Bath)	B	1,280
D.Gregory	B	1.272
Sir H.Palmer (Leics)	B	1,253
Sir J.Wyndham	B	1,171
J.Weyland	B	1,112
Elizabeth Baugh (Ludlow)	B	1,091
Sir J.Bond	B	1,077
Sarah Spragg (Bath)	B	1,073
F.Winsor	B	1,043
E.Rolfe (Norfolk)	B	1,041
J.Trevelyan (Northumberland)	B	1,023
T.Bowman (clerk)	B	1,000
		313.772
		313,772

DIVIDENDS

11 May, 1811	4–0d.
7 April, 1812	1–4d.
4 Dec., 1813	1–0d.
11 Feb., 1817	1–0d.
5 May, 1818	1–2d.
25 July, 1820	1–6d.
21 Dec., 1831	1–0d.
22 Apr., 1839	6d.
3 Nov., 1863	4d.
?	3.17/32d.
	12–1.17/32d.

KEY

B – balance of account

G – goods sold and delivered

I – indorsee of bankrupt's bills

TABLE 10.1. Analysis of Bills drawn by Bowles and Co. on BRICKWOOD and Co.

Size of Bills (£)	No. of bills drawn at the following dates (months):				Total	Value (£)
	1	2	3	12		
Under 100	22	44	1	3	70	3,644
100–499	5	13	1	–	19	6,924
500–999	–	8	–	–	8	7,300
1,000–1,999	–	–	–	–	–	–
2,000 and over	–	7	–	–	7	18,608
Total	27	72	2	3	104	
Value (£)	2,327	33,463	536	150		36,476

Source: P.R.O. B3/252–4.

TABLE 10.2. ANALYSIS OF BILLS DRAWN BY COMMERCIAL FIRMS ON BRICKWOOD and CO.

CATEGORIES OF DRAWER AND SIZE OF BILLS (£)	No. of bills drawn at the following dates (months): 2	3	9	Total	Value of bills £
Merchants					
Under 100	3	1	–	4	170
100-499	2	4	–	6	1,412
500-999	10	43	–	53	50,347
1,000-1,999	3	49	1	53	87,791
2,000 and over	3	62	–	65	182,478
Total (%)	21 (11.5)	159 (88)	1 (0.5)	181 (100)	(av. 1,780)
Value (£)	24,273	296,283	1,642		322,198
Warehousemen					
500-999	1	2	–	3	2,800
1,000-1,999	–	15	–	15	24,282
2,000 and over	–	10	–	10	26,203
Total (%)	1 (4)	27 (96)	–	28 (100)	(av. 1,903)
Value (£)	800	52,485	–		53,285
Manufacturers					
100-499	7	–	–	7	3,500
500-999	29	3	–	32	23,700
1,000-1,999	–	3	–	3	4,418
2,000 and over	–	1	–	1	2,500
Total (%)	36 (84)	7 (16)	–	43 (100)	(av. 793)
Value (£)	24,200	9,918	–		34,118
Others					
100-499	1	–	–	1	356
1,000-1,999	–	2	–	2	3,750
2,000 and over	–	1	–	1	3,750
Total (%)	1 (25)	3 (75)	–	4 (100)	(av. 1,964)
Value (£)	356	7,500			7,856
Over-all total (%)	59 (23)	196 (76.5)	1 (0.5)	256 (100)	(av. 1,631)
Over-all value (£)	49,629	366,186	1,642		417,457

Source: P.R.O. B3/252-4.

TABLE 10.3. ANALYSIS OF BILLS DRAWN ON DAWES, NOBLE and Co.

CATEGORIES OF DRAWER AND SIZE OF BILLS (£)	No. of bills drawn at the following dates (months): 2	3	Total	Value (£)
Merchants				
2,000 and over	–	10	10	28,000
Value		28,000	10	28,000
Manufacturers				
500–999	–	3	3	2,138
1,000–1,999	1	9	10	14,251
Total	1	12	13	(av.1,261)
Value (£)	1,241	15,148		16,389
Others				
Under 500	1	3	4	1,939
500–999	–	4	4	3,511
1,000–1,999	1	31	32	45,998
2,000 and over	–	8	8	18,138
Total	2	46	48	(av.1,449)
Value (£)	2,473	67,113		69,586
Overall total (%)	3 (4)	68 (96)	71 (100)	(av.1,605)
Overall value	3,714	110,261		113,975

Source: P.R.O. B3/1295-1301.

TABLE 10.4. ANALYSIS OF BILLS ACCEPTED BY EIGHT MERCHANTS

CATEGORIES OF DRAWER AND SIZE OF BILLS(£)	No. of bills accepted at the following dates (months): 1	2	3	4	5	6	7	8	9	10	11	12	Over 12	Total	Value (£)
Merchants															
Under 100	1	1	–	–	–	–	–	–	–	–	–	6	–	8	581
100-499	4	23	39	10	1	5	7	2	7	1	–	17	4	120	41,960
500-999	1	12	36	13	1	11	2	–	8	1	–	27	6	118	91,181
1,000-1,999	–	21	29	13	1	8	1	5	3	2	–	20	14	117	166,240
2,000 and over	1	1	5	3	–	5	–	1	–	–	–	5	2	23	64,967
Total (%)	7(2)	58(15)	109(28)	39(10)	3(1)	29(7)	10(3)	8(2)	18(5)	4(1)	–	75(19)	26(7)	386(100)	(av.944)
Value (£)	5,042	49,449	103,320	41,037	2,486	36,832	7,032	9,392	12,505	4,320	–	64,852	28,662		364,929
Warehousemen	–														
Under 100	–	–	–	–	–	–	–	–	–	–	–	–	–	–	–
100-499	–	8	14	3	–	2	1	1	6	5	–	2	–	42	14,349
500-999	–	6	19	8	–	1	–	–	2	–	–	2	–	38	28,810
1,000-1,999	–	5	8	3	–	4	–	2	2	1	–	–	–	25	34,549
2,000 and over	–	1	3	–	–	2	–	–	–	–	–	4	–	10	28,119
Total (%)	–	20(17)	44(38)	14(12)	–	9(8)	1(1)	3(3)	10(9)	6(5)	–	8(7)	–	115(100)	(av.924)
Value (£)	–	16,899	35,850	12,992	–	14,748	107	2,532	6,147	2,561	–	13,991	–		105,827
Manufacturers															
Under 100	–	2	–	–	–	–	–	–	2	–	–	2	–	6	546
100-499	–	5	13	3	–	3	–	–	5	2	1	3	–	35	10,982
500–999	–	2	5	4	–	1	–	–	5	–	–	–	–	17	14,625
1,000-1,999	–	1	3	5	–	3	–	–	–	–	–	1	–	13	19,236
2,000 and over	–	1	–	–	–	5	–	–	–	–	–	–	–	6	14,702
Total (%)	–	11(14)	21(27)	12(16)	–	12(16)	–	–	12(16)	2(3)	1(1)	6(7)	–	77(100)	(av.780)
Value (£)	–	6,801	14,200	12,793	–	18,692	–	–	4,885	669	441	1,610	–		60,091
Others															
Under 100	2	–	–	–	–	–	–	1	–	–	–	–	–	3	144
100-499	–	7	5	4	1	2	1	–	–	–	–	4	–	24	7,085
500-999	–	3	5	2	–	–	–	–	–	–	–	–	–	10	6,943
1,000-1,999	1	4	5	3	–	–	–	–	11	–	–	–	–	24	43,609
2,000 and over	–	–	1	–	–	–	–	1	–	–	–	1	3	6	30,000
Total (%)	3(4)	14(21)	16(24)	9(13)	1(2)	2(3)	1(2)	2(3)	11(16)	–	–	5(7)	3(5)	67(100)	(av.1150)
Value (£)	1,316	19,882	14,568	7,467	105	954	347	6,027	18,300	–	–	3,815	15,000		87,781
Overall total (%)	10(1.5)	103(16)	190(29)	74(11)	4(0.5)	52(8)	12(2)	13(2)	51(8)	12(2)	1	94(15)	29(5)	645(100)	(av.959)
Overall value (£)	6,358	93,031	167,938	74,289	2,591	71,226	7,486	17,951	41,837	7,550	441	84,268	43,662		618,628

Note: The eight merchants were: Q. and J. Dick; Greaves, Sharp and Fisher; Jacob Bros.; R. Jones; Parkin and Scobell; Vos and Essers; Wilson and Williams; and W.Wilson.

Sources: P.R.O. B3/1302-4, 1874-8, 2677-80, 3889-91, 5106-7, 5175-9.

TABLE 10.5. ANALYSIS OF BILLS ACCEPTED BY SIX WAREHOUSEMEN

CATEGORIES OF DRAWER AND SIZE OF BILLS(£)	No. of bills accepted at the following dates (months): 1	2	3	4	5	6	7	8	9	10	11	12	Over 12	Total	Value (£)
Merchants															
Under 100	–	2	3	1	1	–	–	–	–	–	–	–	–	7	313
100-499	–	27	26	5	1	3	–	2	1	–	–	–	–	65	18,980
500-999	1	10	27	5	–	6	–	4	8	–	–	–	3	64	49,769
1,000-1,999	–	8	14	3	–	7	–	2	5	–	–	3	–	42	52,916
2,000 and over	–	4	6	1	1	9	1	1	6	2	–	1	–	32	87,266
Total (%)	1(0.5)	51(24)	76(36)	15(7)	3(1.5)	25(12)	1(0.5)	9(4)	20(10)	2(1)	–	4(2)	3(1.5)	210(100)	(av.996)
Value (£)	750	37,726	64,377	11,133	5,070	35,951	3,000	8,780	30,886	4,157	–	5,773	1,641		209,244
Warehousemen															
Under 100	–	6	9	–	2	1	–	–	–	–	–	–	–	18	1,736
100-499	–	27	21	5	2	5	2	1	5	–	–	1	–	69	21,692
500-999	–	13	10	8	1	4	1	2	–	–	–	1	–	40	31,340
1,000-1,999	–	7	5	7	1	11	–	3	2	2	–	1	–	39	76,792
2,000 and over	–	–	4	7	1	8	2	2	–	1	–	1	1	27	74,327
Total (%)	–	53(27)	49(25)	27(14)	7(4)	29(15)	5(3)	8(4)	7(3.5)	3(2)	–	4(2)	1(0.5)	193(100)	(av.1,066)
Value (£)	–	30,774	51,341	40,563	2,236	47,695	6,404	10,380	4,216	2,174	–	6,110	3,994		205,887
Manufacturers															
Under 100	1	67	34	2	–	–	–	–	–	–	–	–	1	105	5,166
100-499	–	33	81	7	1	12	1	9	1	–	–	–	–	145	50,333
500-999	–	6	44	8	–	11	–	4	3	–	–	–	–	76	66,314
1,000-1,999	–	6	7	7	–	8	–	3	3	3	–	–	–	37	63,284
2,000 and over	–	4	1	–	–	2	–	–	–	1	–	–	–	8	21,440
Total (%)	1(0.5)	116(31)	167(45)	24(6)	1(0.5)	33(9)	1(0.5)	16(4)	7(2)	4(1)	–	–	1(0.5)	371(100)	(av.557)
Value (£)	40	43,148	76,142	20,524	265	38,772	499	11,828	7,367	7,916	–	–	36		206,537
Others															
Under 100	1	1	1	–	–	–	–	–	–	–	–	2	–	5	163
100-499	–	5	4	1	–	–	–	–	–	–	–	–	–	10	3,372
500-999	–	1	–	–	–	–	–	–	–	–	–	–	–	1	688
Total (%)	1(6)	7(44)	5(31)	1(6)	–	–	–	–	–	–	–	2(13)	–	16(100)	(av.264)
Value (£)	21	3,590	1,065	500	–	–	–	–	–	–	–	47	–		4,223
Overall total (%)	3(0.5)	227(29)	297(38)	67(8)	11(2)	87(11)	7(1)	33(4)	34(4)	9(1)	–	10(1)	5(0.5)	790(100)	(av.792)
Overall value (£)	811	115,238	192,925	72,720	7,571	122,418	9,903	30,998	42,469	14,247	–	11,930	5,671		625,891

Note: The six warehousemen were: Bull, Banks and Bryson; Duckham and Lankester; J.Goodair; T.Laycock; Rowlandson, Isaac and Brien; and Winstanley and Hudson.

Sources: P.R.O. B3/269-70, 1305-6; 1880-1; 2928-9; 4181-2; 5174.

TABLE 10.6. ANALYSIS OF BILLS ACCEPTED BY THOMAS COLES and Sons.

SIZE OF BILLS	No. of bills accepted at the following dates (months):						Total	Value (£)
	1	2	3	4	8	12		
Merchants								
Under 100	–	–	–	–	–	–	–	–
100-499	1	–	–	–	–	1	2	536
500-999	–	1	–	1	–	–	2	2,786
1,000-1,999	–	2	14	6	–	2	24	32,532
2,000 and over	–	1	9	14	1	5	30	87,441
Total (%)	1(1.5)	4(7)	23(40)	21(36)	1(1.5)	8(14)	58(100)	(av.2,126)
Value (£)	400	8,183	43,227	51,449	5,000	15,036		123,295

Sources: P.R.O. B3/252-4, 5106-7.

TABLE 10.7. CIRCULATION OF BILLS ACCEPTED BY BANKS, MERCHANTS AND WAREHOUSEMEN

No. of transactions performed by bills	Percentage of the bills accepted by: Banks	Merchants	Warehousemen
1	9	43	28
2	38	42	51
3	39	11	17
4	10	3	3
More than 4	4	1	1
Average no. of transactions per bill	2.7	1.7	2.0

TABLE 10.8. ANALYSIS OF PROMISSORY NOTES PAID BY FIFTEEN FIRMS

Size of note (£)	Promissory notes paid at the following dates (months): On demand	1	2	3	4	6	8	12	Over 12	Total
Under 100	3	–	–	–	16	–	–	–	–	19
100-499	6	2	3	–	5	–	1	4	7	28
500-999	8	–	–	4	1	2	3	3	6	27
1,000-1,999	1	1	1	2	–	2	–	–	2	9
2,000 and over	1	1	–	3	3	–	–	–	1	9
Total	19	4	4	9	25	4	4	7	16	92
Value (£)	19,777	5,388	1,795	16,540	11,837	5,957	2,186	3,002	11,748	78,230

Note: The fifteen firms were: J.Brickwood Jr.; Bull, Banks and Bryson; T.Coles; Dawes, Noble and Co.; J.T.Deal; Duckham and Lankester; F.Fisher; Hardy, Ottley and Co.; Jacob Bros.; T.Laycock; Parkin and Scobell; Rowlandson, Isaac and Brien; T.Starkey; Vos and Essers; and Wilson, Williams and Co.

Sources: P.R.O.B3/252, 269-70, 1294-6, 1874, 1879-81, 2677, 2680, 2928, 3889, 4181-2, 5106, 5178, 7305.

TABLE A.1. ANALYSIS OF CASES IN BANKRUPTCY, 1795–1826.

YEAR	DOCKETS STRUCK	COMMISSIONS SEALED	COMMISSIONS OPENED
1795	1,050	879	690
1796	1,211	954	749
1797	1,368	1,115	871
1798	1,112	911	714
1799	912	717	546
1800	1,168	951	738
1801	1,487	1,199	881
1802	1,241	1,090	833
1803	1,428	1,214	899
1804	1,297	1,117	896
1805	1,352	1,129	867
1806	1,475	1,268	992
1807	1,555	1,362	1,076
1808	1,588	1,433	1,098
1809	1,521	1,382	1,098
1810	2,616	2,314	1,799
1811	2,841	2,500	2,112
1812	2,446	2,228	1,813
1813	2,131	1,953	1,583
1814	1,780	1,612	1,258
1815	2,489	2,284	1,759
1816	2,905	2,731	2,145
1817	2,055	1,927	1,578
1818	1,335	1,245	1,012
1819	2,178	2,056	1,582
1820	1,790	1,695	1,385
1821	1,683	1,587	1,268
1822	1,546	1,419	1,132
1823	1,361	1,250	988
1824	1,336	1,240	999
1825	1,650	1,475	1,141
1826	3,564	3,307	2,590
Totals	55,471	49,544	39,092
Av. per annum	1,733	1,548	1,222

Sources: Dockets calculated from Bankruptcy Court, Docket Books (P.R.O.B4)
for commissions sealed, B.P.P. Accounts and Papers (1822), xxi, 101; (1833), xxxi, 187.
for commissions opened, N.J. Silberling, 'British Prices and Business Cycles, 1779-1850, Rev.Econ.Stats. (1923), suppl.2, 251.

CHART 5.1. Bankruptcies and Official Values of Overseas Trade (in £000,000), 1795-1826.

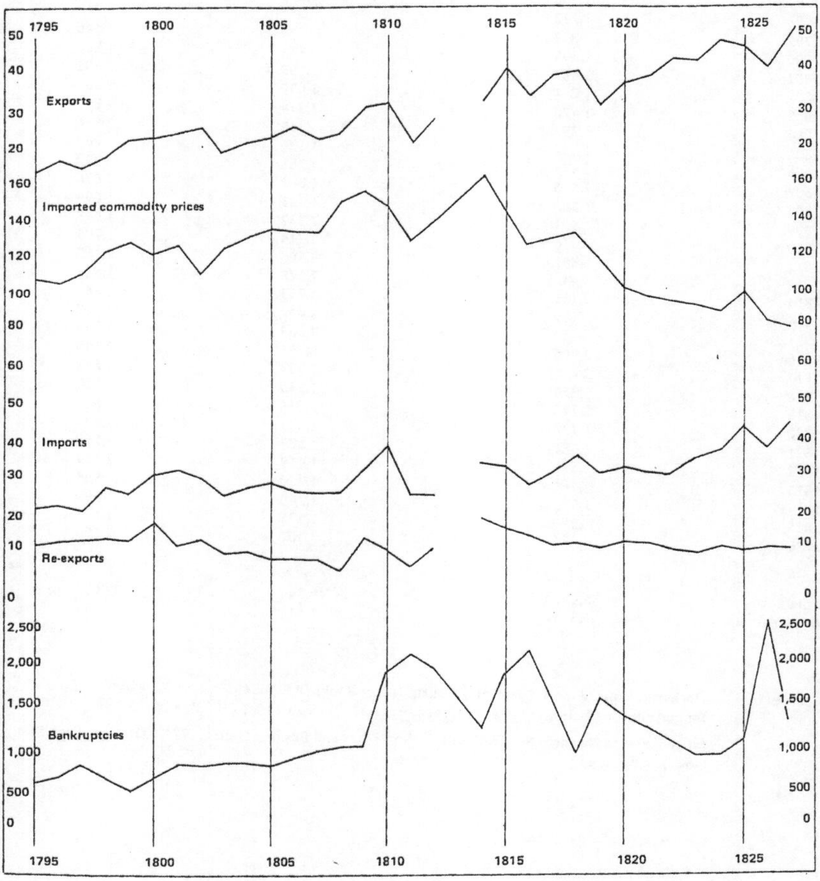

Note: The imported commodity price index is that of A.D. Gayer, W.W. Rostow and A.J.Schwartz

Source: B.R. Mitchell and P. Deane, Abstract of British Historical Statistics (Cambridge, 1962), pp.281-2, 470.

CHART 5.2. Bankruptcies and Official Values of Four Imports (in £000,000) 1795-1826.

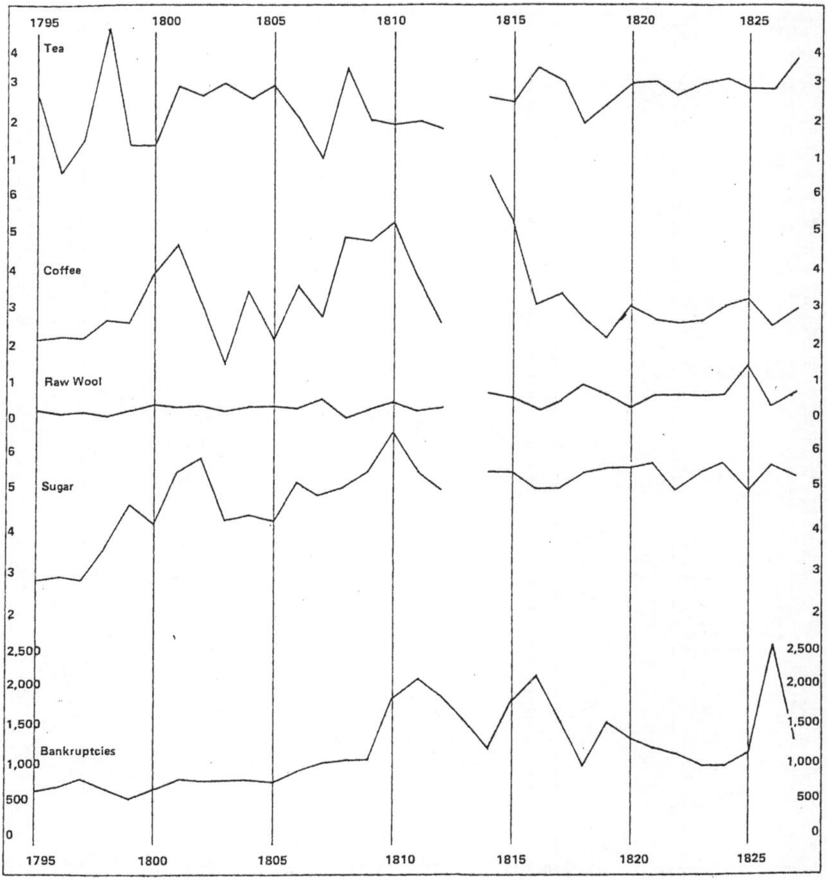

Source: B.R.Mitchell and P. Deane, Abstract of British Historical Statistics (Cambridge, 1962), p.289.

CHART 5.3. Bankruptcies and Official Values of Cotton Imports, Cotton and Wool Exports (in £000,000), 1795-1826.

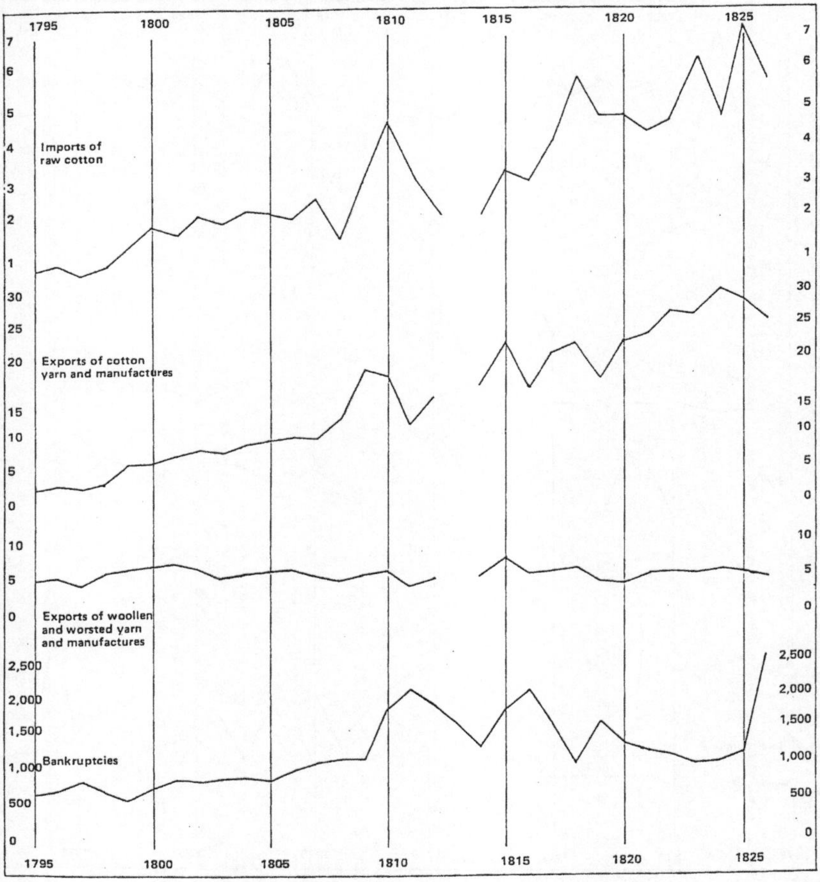

Source: B.R. Mitchell and P. Deane, Abstract of British Historical Statistics (Cambridge, 1962), pp.289, 295.

CHART 5.4. Bankruptcies and Wheat Prices (ann.av., s. per quarter),. 1795-1826.

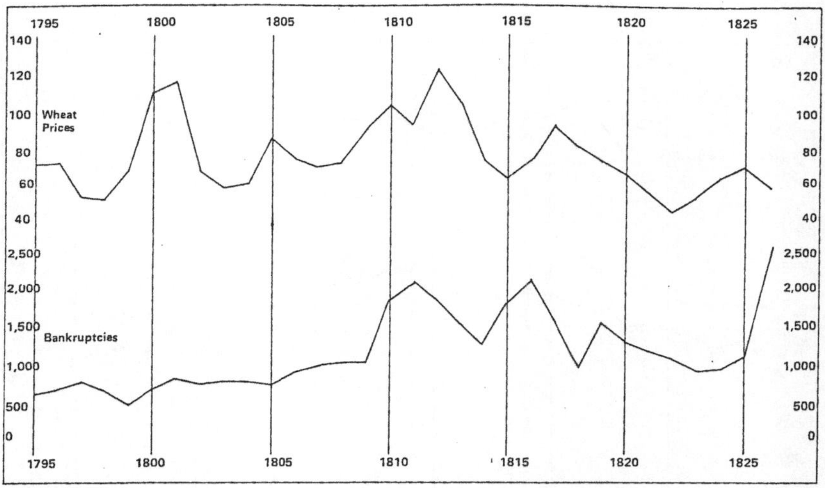

Source: W.W. Rostow, British Economy of the Nineteenth Century (Oxford, 1948), pp.124-5.

CHART 5.5. Bankruptcies, the Yield on Consols (annual average) and Bank of England Discounts (in £000,000), 1795-1826.

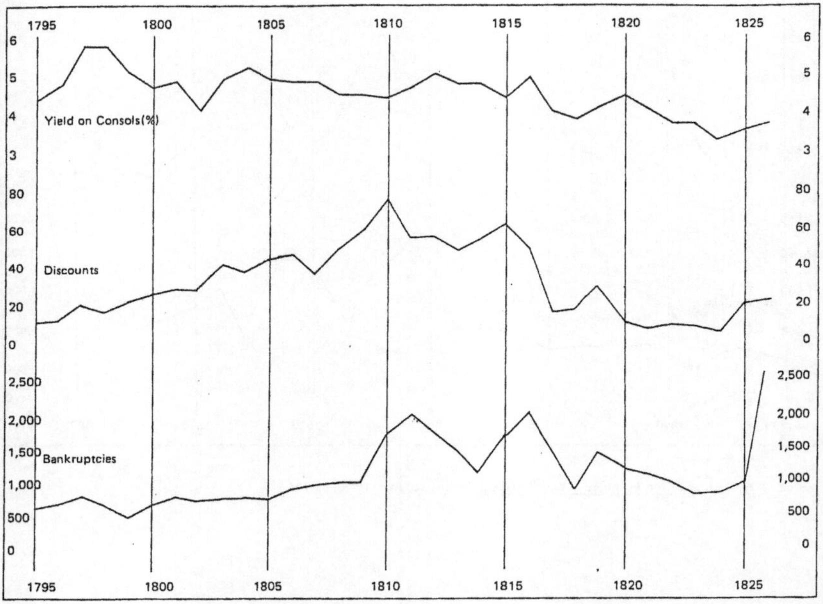

Sources: for the yield on consols, T.S.Ashton, 'Some Statistics of the Industrial Revolution', in Essays in Economic History (ed.E.M.Carus-Wilson), (1962), iii, 247.
for Bank of England discounts, N.J. Silberling, 'British Prices and Business Cycles, 1779-1850, 'Rev.Econ.Stats. (1923) Suppl.2, 256.

CHART 6.1. ANALYSIS OF BANKRUPTS, April 1810–July 1811.

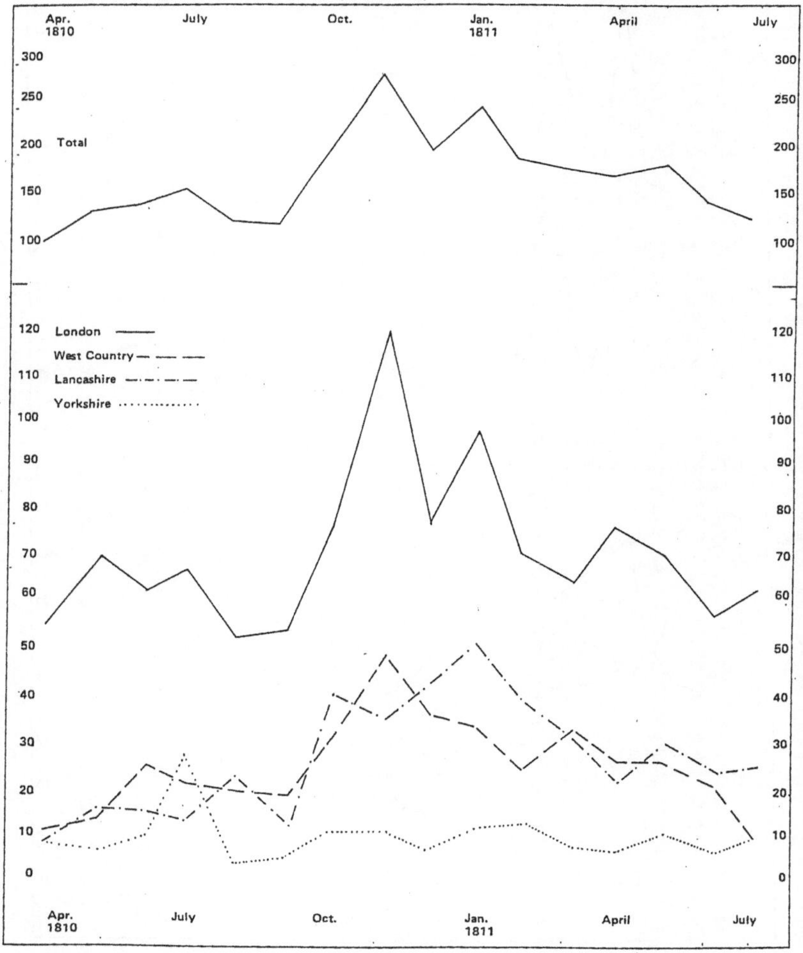

Source: for data, see Table 6.4.

CHART 6.2. Bank of England Discounts and Note Circulation, June-Dec. 1810 (in£000,000)

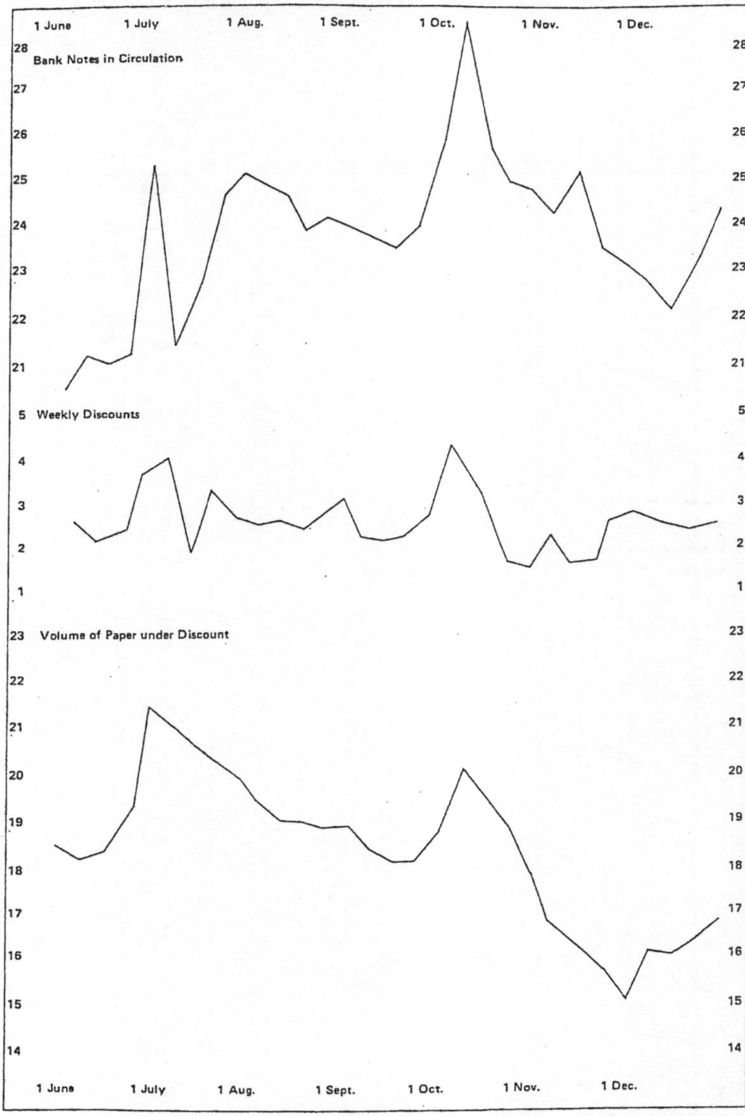

Source: for data, see Table 6.6.

FIG. 8·1 MAJOR BILL DEBTORS AND CREDITORS OF T.COLES AND SONS, BROKERS, MINCING LANE.

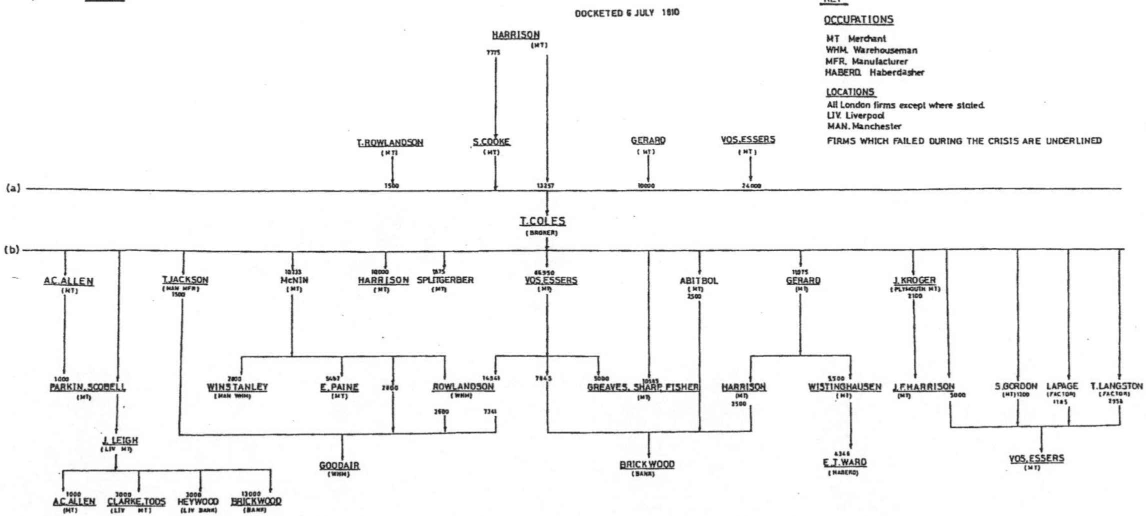

FIG. 8.2 MAJOR BILL DEBTORS AND CREDITORS OF BRICKWOOD AND CO., BANKERS LOMBARD STREET

STOPPED PAYMENT, 6 JULY 1810

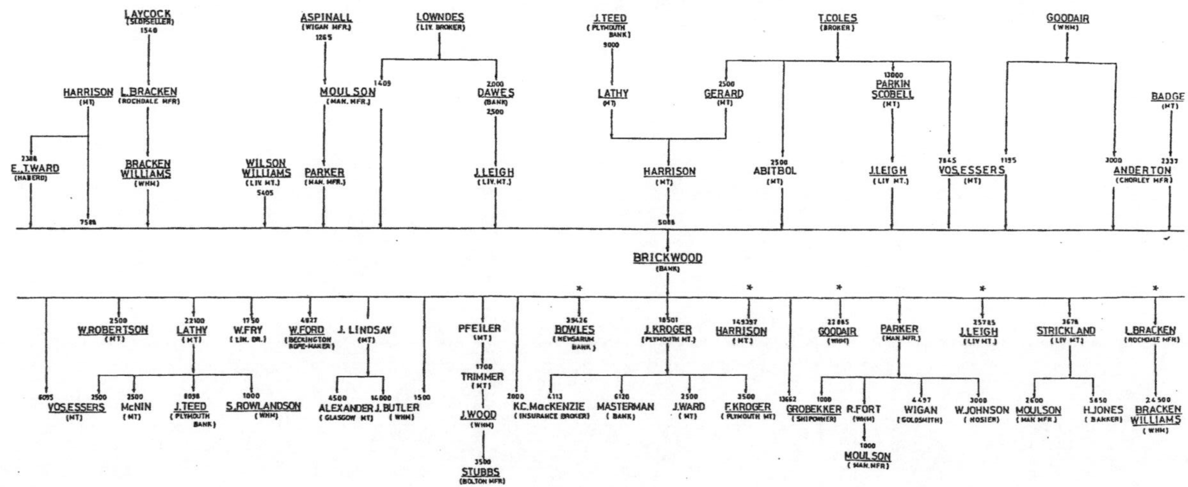

FIG.8·3 MAJOR BILL DEBTORS AND CREDITORS OF HARRISON AND CO., MERCHANTS AND SHIPOWNERS, TOWER STREET

STOPPED PAYMENTS 6 JULY 1810

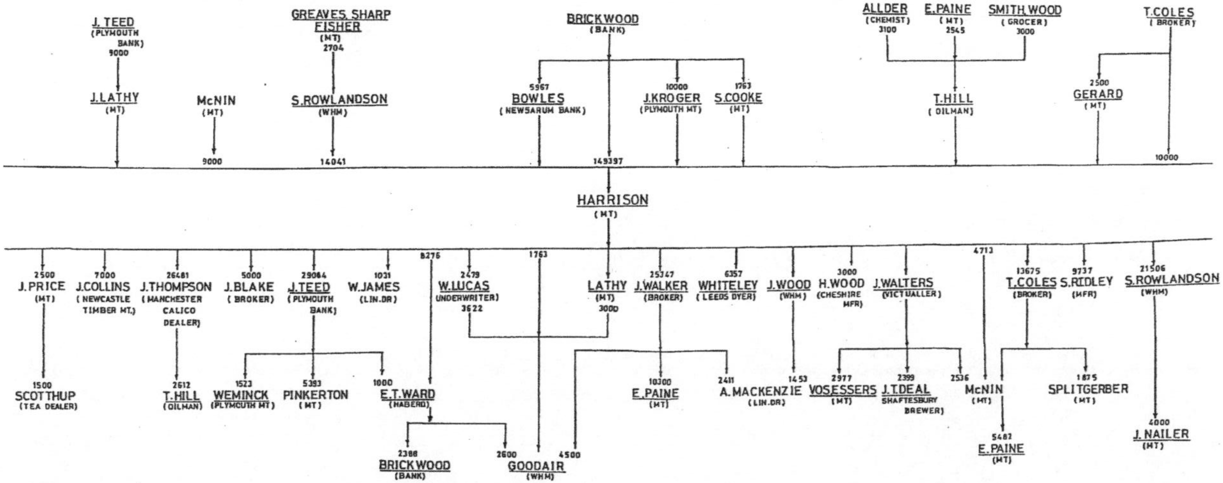

FIG.8·4 MAJOR DEBTORS AND CREDITORS OF J.GOODAIR, WAREHOUSEMAN QUEEN STREET

DOCKETED, 27 OCTOBER 1810

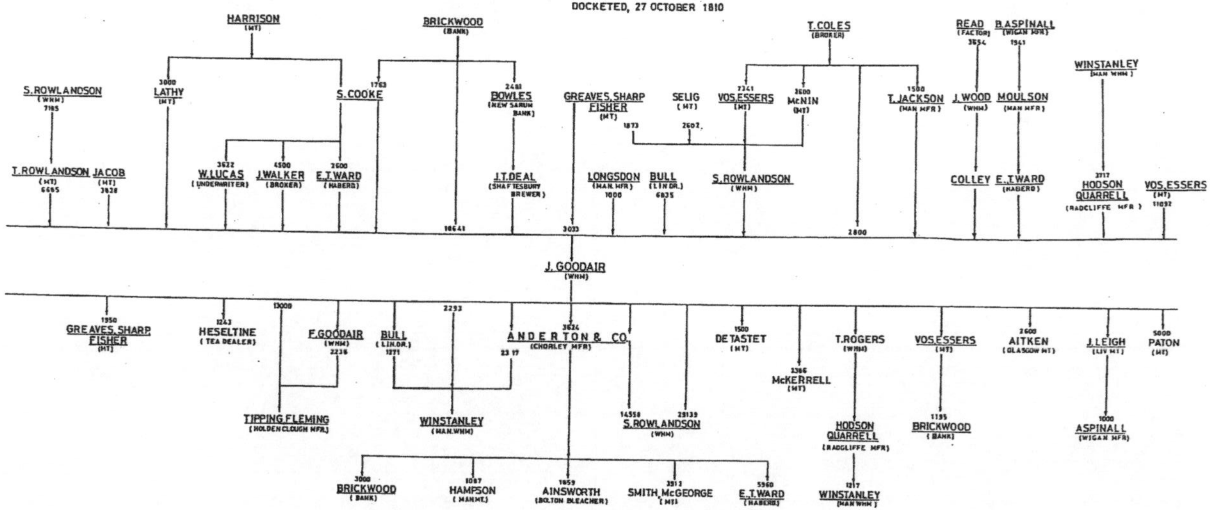

FIG. 8·5 MAJOR BILL DEBTORS AND CREDITORS OF ROWLANDSON, ISAAC AND BRIEN, WAREHOUSEMEN CHEAPSIDE

STOPPED PAYMENT, 14 AUGUST 1810

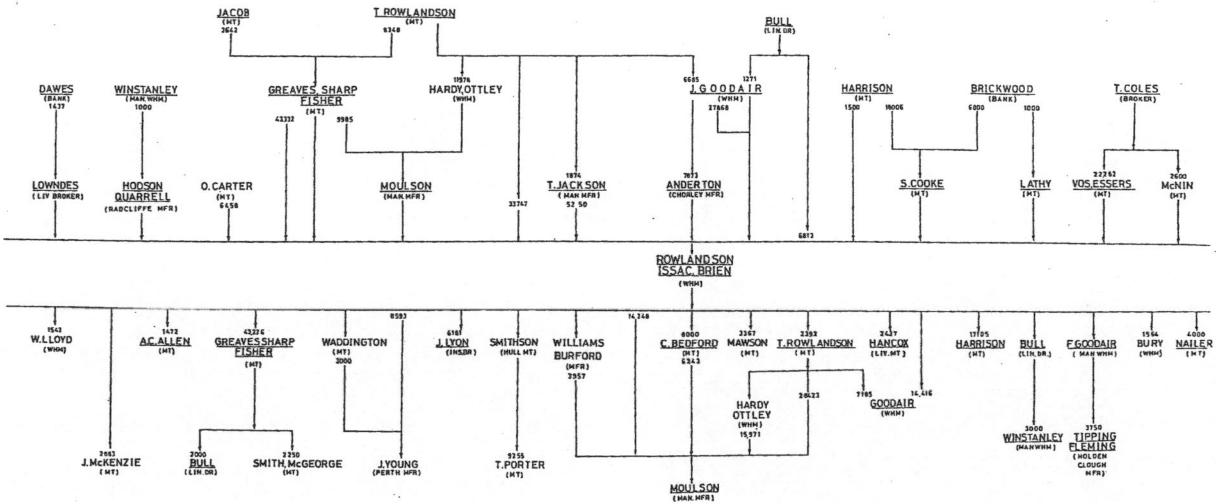

FIG. 8·6 MAJOR BILL DEBTORS AND CREDITORS OF JACOB BROS., MERCHANTS, NEWGATE STREET

STOPPED PAYMENT 18 JULY 1810

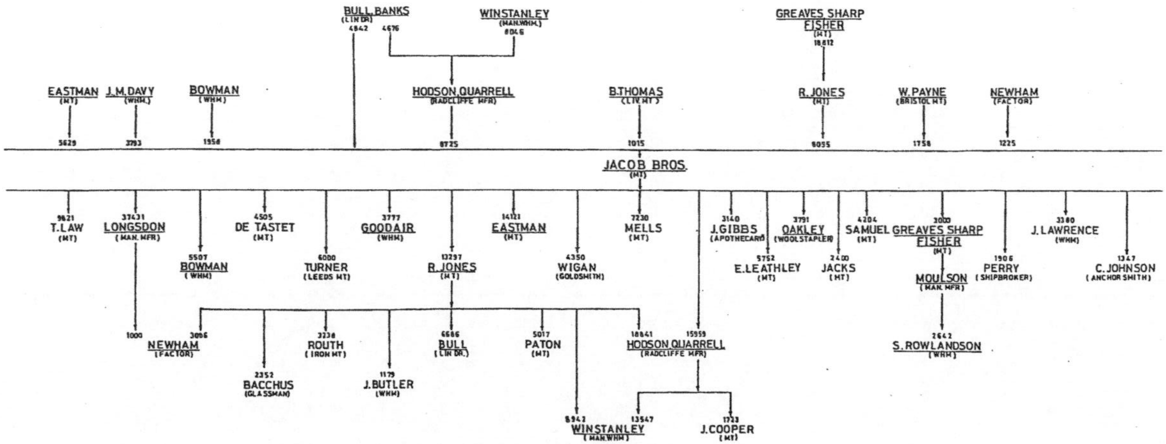

FIG 8·7 MAJOR BILL DEBTORS AND CREDITORS OF J. LEIGH, MERCHANT, LIVERPOOL.

STOPPED PAYMENT 10 AUGUST 1811

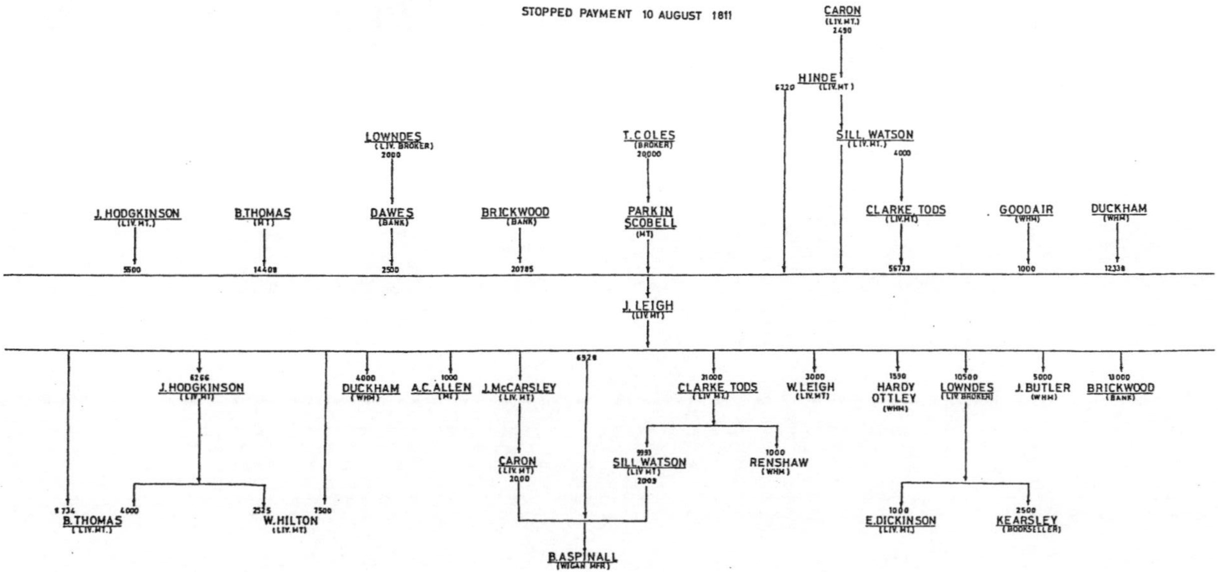

LIST OF FIRMS MENTIONED IN PART TWO

Dates in round brackets refer to dockets which were followed by commissions. Dates in square brackets refer to dockets which were not followed by opened commissions. Unbracketed dates refer to stoppages of payments. Proceedings were not started against undated firms.

Name of Firm	Address	Occupation	Date of Stoppage or Docket
Abitbol, M.	Minories	Merchant	
Ackers, T.	London	Merchant	
Adam, W., Robertson, A.	Old Broad St.	Merchant	
Agnew, W.	Hebbury Grove	Shipowner	
Aguilar, I.	Liverpool	Merchant	(10 Jan. 1811)
Ainsworth, D., Catterall, P.	Preston	Cotton spinners	
Ainsworth, P., Bentley, D.	Bolton	Bleacher	
Aitken, R., Findlay, K., Smith, A., Hodson, J.	Glasgow	Merchant	
Akenhead, J.	London	Merchant	
Aldebert, I., Beecher, C.C., Hargreaves, J.	St. Paul's Churchyard	Merchant	(12 Oct. 1811)
Alexander, J., Leskie, D.R.	Glasgow	Merchant	
Alexander, L.	Old Jewry	Merchant	
Alison, T.	Liverpool	Merchant	
Allder, W.	Seward St.	Chemist	(28 Dec. 1810)
Allen, A.C.	Ironmonger Lane	Merchant	(1 Dec. 1810)
Ambrose, E.	Cheapside	Warehouseman	
Anderson, A., Wilson, A.G.	Philpot Lane	Banker	
Anderson, F.	Hammersmith	Esquire	
Anderson, J.A.	Throgmorton Street	Merchant	
Anderton, W., Lightollers, R.	Chorley	Cotton spinner	(29 Oct. 1810)
Armitage, W.	Yorkshire	Merchant	
Ashton, T.	Manchester	Merchant	
Aspinall, B.	Wigan	Manufacturer	(20 Dec. 1810)

Name of Firm	Address	Occupation	Date of Stoppage or Docket
Bacchus, G., Ogden, J.	Upper Thames St.	Glassman	
Badger, J.J.	Old Jewry	Merchant	(10 Jan. 1811)
Baker, T.	The Poultry	Warehouseman	
Barber, J.S., Fraser, S., Perring, J., Shaw, B.	Cornhill	Banker, broker	
Barber, W.R.	Cheapside	Warehouseman	(4 Feb. 1811)
Barland, T.	Perth	Merchant	
Barnard, E.G.	Deptford	Ship-builder	
Barnett, G.,H.,J., Hoare, S.S.	Lombard St.	Banker	
Barnsley, J.	Manchester	Cotton merchant	(13 Aug. 1810)
Bates, T., Burford, D.,E., Williams, J.	The Poultry	Calico printer	
Bayly, G.	Bermondsey	Sailmaker	
Beatson, D.	Perth	Merchant	
Beck, J., Warwick, R., Mounsley, R., Graham, J.	Carlisle	Banker	
Bedford, C.	Manchester	Merchant	(18 Aug. 1810)
Bedford, W., Deacon, J.	Lad Lane	Merchant	
Bell, J., J.C.C., Grant, R.	Angel Court	Merchant	
Bellairs, A.W.	Stamford, Lincs.	Banker	
Bennett, W.	Hackney	Cabinet-maker	
Berry, G.	Barnsley	Linen manufacturer	(17 Nov. 1810)
Bigge, T.H., Boyd, W.	Newcastle-on-Tyne	Banker	
Birchall, R.	London	Banker	
Bishop, C., Nicholl, J.	Doctors' Commons	Proctor	
Blackburn, P.	Bloomsbury Square	Merchant	
Blair, J., Gratrix, S.	Manchester	Merchant	
Blake, J.	Nicholas Lane	Broker	
Bosanquet, S., Beechcroft, R.	Lombard St.	Banker	
Bourne, E., Monkhouse, J.	Lombard St.	Merchant	
Bowden, J.	Tokenhouse Yard	Merchant	

Name of Firm	Address	Occupation	Date of Stoppage or Docket
Bowdler, W., Gilchrest, B	Cheapside	Warehouseman	(8 Feb. 1811)
Bowett, W., Nickson, J.	Coventry	Cotton manufacturer	
Bowles, W., Ogden, T., Wyndham, G.	New Sarum	Banker	7 July 1810
Bowman, J., Spencer, J.B.	Bucklesbury	Warehouseman	(5 Oct. 1811)
Boyd, W., Bigge, T.H.	Newcastle-on-Tyne	Banker	
Bracken, R.L., Williams, T.	Rochdale, Lothbury	Flannel manufacturer Warehouseman	(24 July 1810)
Braddick, J.	Tower Hill	Merchant	
Brickwood, J., Rainier, J., Morgan, W., Starkey, J.	Lombard St.	Banker	6 July 1810
Briggs, R., Rawson, W.,J., Rhodes, J.	Halifax	Banker	
Britton, T., Olive, J.	Suffolk Lane	Factor	
Brockbank, J., Royds, J.	Bucklesbury	Factor	
Broderick, J.	Plymouth	Esquire	
Brooke, C., Russell, R.	Basinghall St.	Factor	
Brown, T.,R.,B., Rogers, C.	Cheapside	Warehouseman	
Brown, R.,J.	Cheapside	Merchant	
Bruce, R., Warren, T.	Throgmorton St.	Broker	
Buckle, J.W.	Mark Lane	Broker	
Bull, J., Banks, W., Bryson, G.	Cheapside	Wholesale linen draper	17 July 1810
Bullin, C.,R., Leyland, T.	Liverpool	Banker	
Bulmer, J., Healds, J.	Watling St.	Warehouseman	
Burgess, W.H.	Birchin Lane	Banker	
Burra, R.	Watling St.	Warehouseman	
Burrough, M.	New Sarum	Banker, Man's mercer	
Bury, J.,J., Miller, C.	Cheapside	Warehouseman	
Butler, J., Dodgson, T., Wood, J.	Cheapside	Warehouseman	[4 Jan. 1811]
Byrom, M.	Birkenhead	Esquire	

Name of Firm	Address	Occupation	Date of Stoppage or Docket
Caper, W.W.	Birmingham	Merchant	
Caron, A., Distell, P.	Liverpool	Merchant	(21 Mar. 1811)
Carter, O.	Camomile St.	Merchant	(17 Dec. 1810)
Cater, S., Marshall, J.	St. Paul's Churchyard	Warehouseman	(17 Dec. 1810)
Christie, J.,W.	Wapping	Biscuit-baker	
Chryssell, J.C.	Southwark	Merchant	
Clarke, H., Tods, J.	Liverpool	Merchant	(21 May 1811)
Clarke, M., Cuthbert, J.	Savage Gardens	Wine merchants	
Clegg, A.	Manchester	Cotton merchant	
Clement, T., Andrews, T.W.	Basinghall St.	Factor	(24 June 1810)
Clementson, J., Borrodaile, T.	Basinghall St.	Merchant	
Cleworth, P., Newton, G.,S.	Chowbent, Lancs.	Manufacturer	
Clugston, A., McCall, G., Boyd, G.	Watling St.	Merchant	
Cobb, T.,G., Brown, T.	Lombard St.	Banker	
Cockerill, J., Paxton, W., Traill, H.	Pall Mall	East India Agent	
Cohen, S.,L.	Angel Court	Merchant	
Coles, T.	Mincing Lane	Broker	(6 July 1810)
Collins, J.	Newcastle-on-Tyne	Timber merchant	
Collison, N.C.	Gracechurch St.	Linen draper	
Cookson, T.	Newcastle-on-Tyne	Ironfounder	
Cooper, J.	Queen St.	Merchant	
Cowie, R.	Bartholomew Lane	Insurance broker	
Crewdson, W.D., Maude, Wilson	Kendal	Banker	
Crooke, J.,J.	Bolton	Cotton manufacturer	[21 Dec. 1810]
Curling, E., Goodwin, E.	Birchin Lane	Merchant	
Dale, G.E., Moss, J., Rogers, E.	Liverpool	Banker	
Davidson, J.	Glasgow	Merchant	
Davy, J.,M.	Bread St.	Warehouseman	(5 Dec. 1810)

Name of Firm	Address	Occupation	Date of Stoppage or Docket
Davy, T., Roberts, J.	Gould Square	Merchant	
Dawes, J., Noble, W., Croft, R.H., Barwick, R.	Pall Mall	Banker	30 July 1810
Deacon, C.C., M., W.W., Ellis, J.	Milk St.	Warehouseman	
Deal, J.T.	Shaftesbury	Brewer	12 July 1810
Dick, Q.,J.	Finsbury Square	Merchant	(20 Nov. 1810)
Dickinson, E.	Liverpool	Merchant	(25 Oct. 1810)
Ditchfield, J.	Manchester	Cotton manufacturer	(2 Oct. 1810)
Donaldson, B., Thompson, A.	Warwick Square	Merchant	
Down, E.,R., Thornton, H., Free, P.	Bartholomew Lane	Banker	
Dubois, G.	London Wall	Merchant	
Duckham, J., Lankester, R.	Bread St.	Warehouseman	4 Jan. 1811
Duncan, A., Wainhouse, N., E.,R.	Halifax	Banker	
Dunning, J.	Devon	Baker	
Dutton, T., Williamson, J.	Watling St.	Merchant	
Earle, J., Lyon, J.	Watling St.	Warehouseman	
Earnshaw, R.	Manchester	Cotton merchant	(17 Oct. 1810)
Eastman, T.	Clement's Lane	Merchant	(6 Nov. 1810)
Edelman, C.	Queen St.	Sugar refiner	
Edwards, S., W.B., Hill, J., Harper, W.	Stamford, Lincs.	Banker	
Edwards, T.	Tower St.	Broker	
Eldridge, M.	Tottenham	Grocer	
Elsden, E.R.	Lyme Regis	Merchant	
Elmslie, T.	Brunswick Square	Merchant	

Name of Firm	Address	Occupation	Date of Stoppage or Docket
Fellows, T.	Aldersgate	Broker	
Fielding, J.,H., Margerison, E.	Friday St.	Manufacturer	
Fisher, J.	Angel Court	Insurance broker	
Fisher, T.	Dorchester	Grocer	
Foden, J., Slatter	Chester	Linen draper	(14 Nov. 1810)
Forbes, J.	Fitzroy Square	Merchant	
Ford, W.	Beckington	Rope-maker	(2 Nov. 1810)
Forde, W.	Edinburgh	Merchant	
Fort, R., Hargreaves, T., Dugdale, A.	Abchurch Lane	Warehouseman	
Foster, C.	Middlesex	Esquire	
Foster, C.S.	Hampstead	Mariner	
Foulerton, J.	Fenchurch St.	Merchant	
Freen, T.P.C., Bryce, C., Sampson, G.	Bartholomew Lane	Banker	
Fry, C.	London	Merchant	
Fry, J.	St. Mildred's Court	Banker	
Fry, W.	Leicester Square	Linen draper	[5 Dec. 1810]
Galton, S.	Birmingham	Gun-maker	
Gaskill, J.,J.	Minories	Woollen draper	(13 Nov. 1810)
Gatliff, W.	Leeds	Calico manufacturer	[22 Sept.1810]
Gerard, J.G.	Basinghall St.	Merchant	18 May 1811
Gibbs, J.	Paternoster Row	Apothecary	
Gibson, J., Fuller, J., Stratton, S.	Great St. Helens	Merchant	
Gidley, B.	Somerset	Banker	
Gilliatt, J.	London	Merchant	
Glynn, J.	Newcastle-on-Tyne	Iron-founder	
Goodair, J.	Queen St.	Warehouseman	(27 Oct. 1810)
Goodbihere, S., Wigan, E., Bult, J.	Cheapside	Goldsmith	
Gordon, A.S., Emmott, W., Sinclair, J.	Fish Street Hill	Merchant	
Gosling, S.,J.,A.	Mark Lane	Merchant	(17 Nov. 1810)

Name of Firm	Address	Occupation	Date of Stoppage or Docket
Gosling, W., Eve, J.	Leadenhall St.	Ironmonger	
Graham, N., Newman, J., Ramsbottom, J.,J.,R.	Lombard St.	Banker	
Grant, R.	Angel Court	Merchant	
Gray, W.	Water Lane	Wine merchant	
Greaves, C.	Stratford, Essex	Calico printer	
Greaves, H.	Manchester	Merchant	
Greaves, J.P., Sharp, H., Fisher, F.	King's Arms Yard	Merchant	(15 Oct. 1810)
Greaves, P.	Chorley	Cotton manufacturer	
Greenwell, R.R.	Newcastle-on-Tyne	Timber merchant	
Greig, S.	Manchester	Merchant	
Grill, C.	Mincing Lane	Merchant	
Grobekker, W.A.	Great St. Helens	Shipowner	(18 Jan. 1811)
Gumage, A., Saple, F.	Coleman St.	Merchant	
Gurney, S., Richardson, T., Overend, J.	Lombard St.	Bill-broker	
Gunston, J.	Thames St.	Secretary to the Gov. of the Co. of Copper Mines in England	
Haddock, J., Whitehead, J., Howard, M.	Caterton St.	Banker	
Haigh, D., Maskell, J.	Aldermanbury	Warehouseman	
Haigh, J.	Edinburgh	Distiller	
Hall, C.C.	Southwark	Merchant	
Hall, J.	Antigua	Merchant	
Hallett, W., Hardy, J., May, H.	Cheapside	Merchant	
Hammersley, T.,H., Brooksbank, H.	Pall Mall	Banker	
Hamper, J.	Southwark	Hosier	(13 Mar. 1811)
Hampson, R., Mather, J., Lomax, J.	Manchester	Merchant	
Hancox, J., Cooper, T.	Liverpool	Merchant	(19 Oct. 1810)
Hardcastle, C.	Pontefract	Banker	

Name of Firm	Address	Occupation	Date of Stoppage or Docket
Hardie, J.	Queen St.	Wholesale druggist	
Hardy, Ottley	Cheapside	Warehouseman	
Hargreaves, J.	Manchester	Merchant	
Harkness, J.	City Road	Merchant	
Harris, R.,R., Wilkinson, J.	Size Lane	Wholesale linen draper	
Harrison, W.,W., J.F., Gorst, W., Cooke, S.	Tower St.	Merchant, shipowner	6 July 1810
Harrison, W.	Manchester	Merchant	
Haywood, J., Jones, J.	Wood St.	Linen draper	(10 Sept.1810)
Head, T.	Newcastle-on-Tyne	Timber merchant	
Heald, J., Dickinson, J.	Cloak Lane	Merchant	24 Oct. 1810
Heath, C.	Andover	Banker	
Hebblethwaite, C.	Leeds	Merchant	
Heinzelman, G., Rickarby, R.	Cheapside	Merchant	
Helbus, H.G., James, R., Buth, C.	London St.,	Merchant	
Herries, J.C.	Hoxton, Midd.	Insurance broker	
Heseltine, B.	Nicholas Lane	Wholesale tea dealer	
Heywood, A., Thompson, S., Jones, H.	Liverpool	Banker	
Hick, C.W.	Cheapside	Hatter	
Higgin, J., Whiteley, G.	Fenchurch St.	Merchant	
Hill, T., Wood, H.	Thames St.	Oilman	(13 Dec. 1810)
Hilton, W.	Liverpool	Merchant	
Hinde, S., T.	Liverpool	Merchant	(5 Jan. 1811)
Hodgkinson, J.	Liverpool	Merchant	10 Aug. 1811
Hodgson, G.	Newcastle-on-Tyne	Iron-founder	
Hodgson, J.	Size Lane	Merchant	
Hodson, J., Quarrell, C.	Radcliffe	Calico printer	(19 Oct. 1810)
Hoffman, H.L., Jeelin, J.J.	Rotherhithe	Merchant	
Hole, G., Wilkinson, J., Gartside, J.	Manchester	Merchant	

Name of Firm	Address	Occupation	Date of Stoppage or Docket
Holland, S.	Liverpool	Merchant	(26 Oct. 1810)
Hoppe, J.	Minories	Merchant	
Houlden, R.	Southwark	Linen draper	15 Nov. 1810
Hudson, G.	Durham	Woolmonger	
Humberton, C.	Liverpool	Merchant	
Hunters, Rainey	Size Lane	Merchant	(9 July 1811)
Hunter, M.,J.	St. Martin's Lane	Mercer	
Hurst, W., Parr, J., Lyon, J.	Warrington	Banker	
Hyman, J.E.	Caterton St.	Merchant	
Jacks, J.	White Lion Court	Merchant	
Jackson, T.	Manchester	Calico printer	(28 Feb. 1811)
Jacob, J.,W.	Newgate St.	Merchant	18 July 1810
James, R.	Bishopsgate St.	Linen draper	
James, W.	Holborn	Linen draper	
Jeffrey, B.G.,T.	Throgmorton St.	Merchant	
Jennings, R., Sage, E.	Cheapside	Merchant	
Johnson, C.	Wapping	Anchorsmith	
Johnson, W.	Cheapside	Hosier	
Jones, E.	Piccadilly	Linen draper	
Jones, H.	Mansion House St.	Banker	
Jones, R.	St. Mary's Axe	Merchant	19 July 1810
Jones, W., Bennett, T.	Watling St.	Warehouseman	
Jones, W.J., Woolley, J.	Change Alley	Stock-broker	
Joseph, I.	Bedford Square	Esquire	
Joy, M.	Richmond, Surrey	Merchant	
Jukes, E., Mors, J., Langley, J.	Gosport	Banker	(12 July 1810)

Name of Firm	Address	Occupation	Date of Stoppage or Docket
Kearsley, G.	Fleet St.	Bookseller	(8 Nov. 1810)
Kemp, Bailey	Cheapside	Wholesale linen draper	
Kensington, E., Pooley, J., Styan, H.K., Adams, D.	Lombard St.	Banker	
Kirkman, J.	London	Insurance broker	
Kroger, J.	Plymouth	Merchant	7 Jan. 1811
Lang, G., MacFie, J.	Glasgow	Calico printer	
Langhorn, J.	Berwick-on-Tweed	Banker	
Langston, T., Timmins, T.	Watling St.	Warehouseman	
Lapage G.	Milk St.	Cloth factor	
Law, T.	London	Merchant	
Lawrence, J., Holland, C.	Ludgate St.	Warehouseman	
Lawson, J.R.	The Poultry	Warehousman	
Laycock, T.	Minories	Slopseller	11 July 1810
Leathley, E.	Hackney	Merchant	
Leatt, J.	Hammersmith	Esquire	
Lee, J., Martineau, S., Wilkinson, J.	Temple Bar	Warehouseman	(25 Feb. 1811)
Lee, R., Payne, D.	Old Bond St.	Merchant	(19 Jan. 1811)
Leigh, J.	Liverpool	Merchant	10 Aug. 1811
Lindsay, J.,G.	Lawrence Pountney Hill	Merchant	
Linthorne, B., Jolliffe, J.H.	Walbrook	Merchant	
Litt, J., Ratcliffe, T., Smith, R.	Manchester	Calico printer	
Living, H., Downes, J.	Goodman's Field	Merchant	(10 Nov. 1810)
Lloyd, L., Fox, W., Jones, W., Tabor, J.	Lothbury	Banker	
Lloyd, W.	Cheapside	Warehouseman	
Locke, R.	Bow Church Yard	Warehouseman	
Longsdon, M.,P.	Manchester	Fustian manufacturer	(18 Aug. 1810)

Name of Firm	Address	Occupation	Date of Stoppage or Docket
Lornt, J.	Mincing Lane	Merchant	
Lowndes, T., Bateson, R.	Liverpool	Broker	(11 Jan. 1811)
Lucas, W.	Clapton	Underwriter	(17 Oct. 1810)
Lyon, J., Van Dyck, F.A.	Leadenhall St.	Insurance broker	(4 May 1811)
Magnay, C.	London	Stationer	
Mangles, R.	Wapping	Ship chandler	
Marriott, J.,W.M.	Witney	Blanket-weaver	
Marsden, J.	Liverpool	Cotton broker	(1 Mar. 1811)
Marsh, W., Sibbald, J., Fauntleroy, H.	Berner's St.	Banker	
Marshall, H.	Newcastle-on-Tyne	Banker	
Marston, R.	Holborn	Esquire	
Martin, J.,J., Stone, G.	Lombard St.	Banker	
Martin, R.H.	America Square	Merchant	
Masterman, J., Peters, H., Maude, J.	White Hart Court	Banker	
Mather, J.	Mincing Lane	Merchant	
Mawson, J.	Manchester	Merchant	
	Watling St.	Warehouseman	
May, J.	Abchurch Lane	Broker	
Maydew, J., Scott, W.	Austin Friars	Merchant	
McCarsley, J.	Liverpool	Merchant	[14 Nov. 1810]
MacFie, J.	Glasgow	Calico printer	
McKenzie, A.	Manchester	Linen draper	[30 Oct. 1810]
Mackenzie, J.J.	King's Arms Yard	Merchant	
McKenzie, K.C.	Finch Lane	Insurance broker	
McKerrell, R.	Lombard St.	Merchant	
McNair, A.	Abchurch Lane	Merchant	25 Sept. 1810
McNin, M.	Haydon Square	Merchant	[11 July 1810]
Mells, A., Pead, B., Lancaster, T.J.	Old Jewry	Merchant	
Meredith, F.	Lloyds Coffee House	Insurance broker	

Name of Firm	Address	Occupation	Date of Stoppage or Docket
Merle, W., Dorrian, T., Meyers, D.	The City	Banker	
Meyer, G.	Bishopsgate St.	Merchant	
Middlecoat, N.	Cornwall	Esquire	
Milford, J., Nation, W.,	King's Arms Yard	Merchant	
Hutchings J.	Exeter	Banker	
Miller, T., Mansfield, J.	Leicester	Banker	
Millett, F., Evans, J.J.	New Broad St.	Merchant	
Milton, T., Wood, J.,J.	Cheapside	Warehouseman	
Moline, J.S.	Leadenhall St.	Leather factor	
Molyneux, W.,E.	Liverpool	Merchant	
Monday, J.	London	Bricklayer	
Montague, D.	Smithfield	Soapmaker	
Monteeth, W., Bogle, H.M.,A.	Glasgow	Merchant	
Moore, T.J.	Newcastle St.	Currier	
Morley, W.	Cheapside	Merchant	
Moulson, R.P., Fawcett, P.	Manchester	Manufacturer	(29 Oct. 1810)
Mountford, R.	Birchin Lane	Merchant	
Moxon, T.	Throgmorton St.	Merchant	
Murdoch, T.	Broad St. Place	Merchant	
Nailer, J.	St. Mary's Axe	Merchant	23 Feb. 1811
Naylor, W.	Wigan	Dyer	(22 Sept.1810)
Newham, D., Oliphant, J., McCall, G.	Mitre Court	Factor	(18 Jan. 1811)
Newnham, N., Everett, W., Tapps, J.	Mansion House	Banker	
Nightingale, T.	Milk St.	Warehouseman	
Noyes, T.	London	Merchant	
Oakley, W., Overend, W.	Southwark	Wool-stapler	26 May 1810
Ogleby, C.	Bishopsgate St.	Merchant	
Oliviera, D.	Upper Seymour St.	Merchant	
Orrell, J.	Manchester	Manufacturer	(20 Sept.1810)

Name of Firm	Address	Occupation	Date of Stoppage or Docket
Paget, J., Slater, T.	Tower St.	Merchant	
Paine, E.	Dowgate Hill	Merchant	2 Jan. 1811
de Paiva, A., Parker, H.	Pancras Lane	Merchant	
Paleski, L.	Lime St. Square	Merchant	
Parker, J.	Queen St.	Merchant	
Parker, R.	Manchester	Calico printer	(24 Sept.1810)
Parkin, T., Scobell, T.	Broad St.	Merchant	(18 Sept.1810)
Parkinson, J.	Manchester	Cotton dealer	
Paton, G.	Pancras Lane	Merchant	
Payne, W.	Bristol	Merchant	(10 Sept.1810)
Peel, J.	Lawrence Lane	Warehouseman	
Peele, J.,J.	Cheapside	Merchant	
Pellatt, A.	St. Paul's Churchyard	Glass manufacturer	
Perry, J.	Blackwall, Essex	Ship-broker	
Pfeiler, J.,W.	Throgmorton St.	Merchant	
Phillips, J., Homan, J.	Fenchurch St.	Auctioneer	
Phillips, J., Atkinson, T.	Gracechurch St.	Linen draper	
Pinkerton, T.	Abchurch Lane	Merchant	
Piper, I.	Surrey	Banker	
Platt, W.,R.	Bolton	Manufacturer	(19 Nov. 1810)
Plowman, J.B.	Chandos St.	Silk mercer	
Pope, H., Edwards, S.,W., Wright, J.	Manchester	Merchant	
Porter, T.	Union Court	Merchant	(23 July 1810)
Postlethwaite, T., Sansom, H.,P.	Lombard St.	Banker	
Pratt, W., Clagett, H.	America Square	Merchant	
Price, J.	Copthall Buildings	Merchant	
Prideaux, W., Square, J., Kingston, J.	Kingsbridge, Devon	Banker	
Pritt, J.	London	Hosier	
Procter, J., Brownlow, W.	Fleet St.	Warehouseman	

Name of Firm	Address	Occupation	Date of Stoppage or Docket
Rainier, D. Ballard, H., Morgan, J.	Cornhill	Broker	
Ranking, J.,G., Railton, I.	Cheapside	Merchant	
Read, R.	Lothbury	Factor	24 July 1810
Reid, A., Meux, T.	Liquor Pond St.	Brewer	
Reinhold, S.	Manchester	Merchant	
Renshaw, E.	Shadwell	Warehouseman	
Reynolds, J.	Idol Lane	Broker	
Rhodes, A.	Leeds	Merchant	
Richards, S., J.C., Peters, H.	Aldermanbury	Merchant	
Richards, S.,R.	Drury Lane	Man's mercer	
Ridgway, T.,J.	Norwich	Bleacher	
Ridley, S.	Newgate St.	Lace manufacturer	
Rishworth, T., Townsend, G.	Wakefield	Banker	
Roberts, E.	Old Change	Warehouseman	
Robertson, J.	Threadneedle St.	Merchant	
Robertson, W.	Great St. Helens	Merchant	(3 Oct. 1810)
Robinson, S.S.	New Broad St.	Merchant	
Rogers, C.,T.,R., Brown, B.	Cheapside	Warehouseman	
Rogers, T.	Walbrook	Warehouseman	
Roscoe, W.S.	Liverpool	Banker	
Rothschild, N.M.	New Court	Merchant	
Routh, W., Crawshay, W.R., Moser, R.	Thames St.	Iron merchant	
Rowlandson, A., Burra, R.	Watling St.	Warehouseman	
Rowlandson, S., Isaac, E., Brien, W.	Cheapside	Warehouseman	14 Aug. 1810
Rowlandson, T., Bates, J.	Cheapside	Merchant	(16 Aug. 1810)
Rowton, W., Morhall, T.	Chester, Shrewsbury	Banker	(19 Oct. 1810)
Sage, E., Jennings, R.	Cheapside	Merchant	
Samuel, P.M.,S.	Minories	Merchant	
Sanders, M.	Birmingham	Button-maker	

Name of Firm	Address	Occupation	Date of Stoppage or Docket
Sanderson, J., Dinsdale, R.J.	Old Broad St.	Merchant	
Sangster, T., Timms, J.F.	Watling St.	Merchant	
Sangster, A., Atkinson, G., Taylor, D.	Milk St.	Warehouseman	
Savill, W.	Minories	Merchant	
Schmidtmeyer, P.	Little St. Mary's Axe	Merchant	
Scott, J., Manner, J.	Grantham	Banker	
Scotthup, J., Shuttleworth, R.	Queen St.	Tea dealer	
Seaton, J.,R., Foster, J.	Pontefract	Banker	(12 Oct. 1810)
Selig, I.	Moorfields	Merchant	
Shakespeare, J.M., A.	Stepney Causeway	Rope-maker	
Sharp, D.,T., Thomas, J	Southampton	Banker	
Sharp, W.	Threadneedle St.	Dealer	
Shaw, E., Hitchcock, J.G.	Bath	Banker	(18 July 1810)
Shaw, J., Fletcher, J., Smith, A.	Ironmonger Lane	Merchant	
Sheldon, J., Cass, F.	Milk St.	Warehouseman	
Shepherd, A.	Huddersfield	Cloth-dresser	(27 May 1811)
Shiking, W.	Bow Church Yard	Warehouseman	
Shuter, T.A.	Horsley Down	Cooper	
Sill, J., Watson, W.	Liverpool	Merchant	(31 Oct. 1810)
de Silly, J.B.	The Poultry	Merchant	
Simpson, G.	Bartholomew Lane	Banker	
Simpson, W.	Foster Lane	Warehouseman	
Smith, G.,A., Payne.	Mansion House St.	Banker	
Smith, J., McGeorge, J., Watson, T.	Watling St.	Merchant	
Smith, J., Wood, Z., Gregory, R.	Old Fish St.	Grocer	[15 Dec. 1810]
Smith, J.,M.	Cheapside	Merchant	

Name of Firm	Address	Occupation	Date of Stoppage or Docket
Smithson, Barker	Kingston-on-Hull	Merchant	
Solly, H.	Cannon St.	Merchant	
Sparkes, J., Williams, J., Cross, R.	Exeter	Banker	
Splitgerber, J.C.	Newcastle Court College	Merchant	
Staines, J., Carpenter, C.	Ironmonger Lane	Merchant	
Stanley, W.,G., R.S., Hawks, S.	Billiter Square	Merchant	
Stansfield, T.	London	Merchant	
Stephenson, J.	Gracechurch St.	Ironmonger	
Stirling, W., Coates, M.	Bow Church Yard	Warehouseman	
Storey, R.	Gracechurch St.	Merchant	
Strickland, L., Brickwood, J.N.	Liverpool	Merchant	(1 Nov. 1810)
Stroud, J.	Swansea	Banker	(17 Aug. 1810)
Stubbs, A., Wood, J.	Bolton	Cotton manufacturer	(9 Nov. 1810)
Stuckey, V., S.,G.	Sloane St., Langport, Somerset	Broker Banker	
Sturges, J., Gould, W., Tucker, J.	Bath	Banker	[16 July 1810]
Styan, J. Bishop, J.	Scot's Yard	Merchant	
Tamer, J.	West Cowes	Merchant	
de Tastet, F., Lacoste, J., Sartoris, L.	Bishopsgate St.	Merchant	
Tate, T.	Croydon	Banker	
Taylor, R., Callow, P.M.	Liverpool	Merchant	
Teed, J.	Plymouth	Banker	
Thomas, B.	Liverpool	Merchant	(6 July 1811)
Thomas, W., Gell, T.	Lombard St.	Broker	
Thompson, J., Lister, T.	Manchester	Calico dealer	
Thornton, J., R.,S., Bayley, D.	Coleman St.	Merchant	

Name of Firm	Address	Occupation	Date of Stoppage or Docket
Tiplady, J., Cowtail, C., Harrison, T.	Lad Lane	Warehouseman	
Tipping, R., Fleming, G.	Holden Clough	Calico printer	(1 Aug. 1810)
Todhunter, J.	Billiter Square	Merchant	
Touchet, J.	Manchester	Merchant	
Townsend, J., Smith, R., Brooke, E.	Honiton	Banker	
Trimmer, E.	Botolph Lane	Merchant	
Troughton, J., J.B., Newcombe, C.	Coventry	Banker	
Turner, A.	Leeds	Merchant	
Turner, E.,W.	Manchester	Warehouseman	
Varley, J.	Houndsditch	Slopseller	(31 Oct. 1810)
Vipond, G.	Ludgate Hill	Linen draper	
Vos., H., Essers, J.C.	Crutched Friars	Merchant	(10 July 1810)
Waddington, H.,J.	New Bridge St.	Merchant	
Wagner, H.M.	London	Hatter	
Wainhouse, J.	Salford	Twist dealer	(7 July 1810)
Walker, J.	Castle St.	Broker	(3 Oct. 1810)
Walters, J.	Webb Square	Victualler	(22 Nov. 1810)
Walton, E.,J., Pears, J.	Cheapside	Warehouseman	
Ward, E.,T.	Cheapside	Haberdasher	(13 July 1810)
Ward, J.,W.	Caterton St.	Merchant	
Waters, W.	Lombard St.	Banker	
Watson, G.,R.	Glasgow	Banker	
Watson, J.	Watling St.	Merchant	(26 Apr. 1811)
Webber, J.	Milk St.	Warehouseman	
Weminck, J.G.	Plymouth	Merchant	(17 Dec. 1810)
Weston, W., Taylor, W., Calvert, T.	Manchester	Cotton manufacturer	
Whateley, W.	Lawrence Pountney Hill	Merchant	(27 Apr. 1811)
Wheelwright, J.	Budge Row	Warehouseman	
Whitefield, L., Molyneux, J.	Lewes	Banker	
Whiteley, W.,J.	Leeds	Dyer	
Wilkinson, J., Cooper, W.	Lad Lane	Merchant	

Name of Firm	Address	Occupation	Date of Stoppage or Docket
Williams, J., Burford, D.E., Bates, T.	The Poultry	Calico printer	
Williams, S.	Finsbury Square	Merchant	(22 Apr. 1811)
Wilson, B.	Manchester	Merchant	
Wilson, M., Williams, J.F.H.	Liverpool	Merchant	1 Aug. 1810
Wilson, R., Ogleby, J.	Bow Church Yard	Merchant	
Wilson, T.	Wapping	Ship-chandler	
Winstanley, R., Hudson, G.	Manchester	Warehouseman	5 Nov. 1810
Wistinghausen, F.W.	Lawrence Pountney Hill	Merchant	(17 Dec. 1811)
Wood, H.	Cheshire	Cotton spinner	
Wood, J.	Cheapside	Warehouseman	(9 Nov. 1810)
Woodward, T.	Liverpool	Merchant	
Worswick, R., A.	Lancaster	Banker	
Wright, C.	Old Jewry	Merchant	
Wright, J.	Cheapside	Calico printer	
Young, J., Ross, J.R., Richardson, J.	Perth	Manufacturer	
Zowlin, Sir J.	Royal Exchange	Broker	